Curriculum and the Teacher

Even though the curriculum can be tightly specified and controlled by strong accountability mechanisms, it is teachers who decisively shape the educational experiences of children and young people at school.

Bringing together seminal papers from the *Cambridge Journal of Education* around the theme of curriculum and the teacher, this book explores the changing conceptions of curriculum and teaching and the changing role of the teacher in curriculum development and delivery.

This book is organised around three major themes:

- Taking its lead from Lawrence Stenhouse, Part I looks at 'defining the curriculum problem' from a variety of perspectives and includes papers from some of the most influential curriculum theorists over the last thirty years.
- Part II explores the framing of new orders of educational experience. It has papers from leading educational thinkers who have contributed to debates about how to make education more inclusive, humane, liberating, creative and educational.
- Part III is focused on teachers and teaching. It offers a selection of papers from significant scholars in the field reflecting on the experience of teaching and how it is personally as well as socially constructed and theorised.

The papers are drawn from important and eventful periods of educational history spanning the curriculum reform movement of the 1960s and 1970s to the present age of surveillance, accountability and control. A specially written Introduction contextualises the papers.

Part of the Routledge Education Heritage series, *Curriculum and the Teacher* presents landmark texts from the *Cambridge Journal of Education*, offering a wealth of material for students and researchers in education.

Nigel Norris is Professor of Education at the Centre for Applied Research in Education, University of East Anglia, Norwich. He is a member of the Editorial Board of the *Cambridge Journal of Education*.

Education heritage series

Other titles in the series:

From Adult Education to the Learning Society
21 years from the *International Journal of Lifelong Education*
Peter Jarvis

A Feminist Critique of Education
Christian Skelton and Becky Francis

Overcoming Disabling Barriers
18 years of disability and society
Len Barton

Tracing Education Policy
Selections from the *Oxford Review of Education*
David Phillips and Geoffrey Walford

Making Curriculum Strange
Essays from the *Journal of Curriculum Studies*
Ian Westbury and Geoff Milburn

Education, Globalisation and New Times
Stephen J. Ball, Ivor F. Goodson and Meg Maguire

Forty Years of Comparative Education
Changing contexts, issues and identities
Michael Crossley, Patricia Broadfoot and Michele Schweisfurth

Education and Society
25 years of the *British Journal of Education*
Len Barton

Curriculum and the Teacher

35 years of the *Cambridge Journal of Education*

Edited by Nigel Norris

Routledge
Taylor & Francis Group

LONDON AND NEW YORK

First published 2008
by Routledge
2 Park Square, Milton Park, Abingdon, Oxon OX14 4RN

Simultaneously published in the USA and Canada
by Routledge
270 Madison Ave, New York, NY 10016

Routledge is an imprint of the Taylor & Francis Group, an informa business

Typeset in Goudy by Wearset Ltd, Boldon, Tyne and Wear
Printed and bound in Great Britain by TJI Digital, Padstow, Cornwall

British Library Cataloguing in Publication Data
A catalogue record for this book is available from the British Library

Library of Congress Cataloging in Publication Data
A catalog record for this book has been requested

ISBN10: 0-415-45533-2 (hbk)
ISBN10: 0-203-93085-1 (ebk)

ISBN13: 978-0-415-45533-6 (hbk)
ISBN13: 978-0-203-93085-4 (ebk)

Contents

Preface and acknowledgements

In making the selection for this collection from the *Cambridge Journal of Education* I tried to follow three selection criteria. First, papers should be of enduring interest and relevance to national and international audiences. Second, papers should reflect the development, character and strengths of the journal over the years. Third, to provide some measure of coherence to the book, I thought the papers should cluster around specific themes. There are, of course, other thematic collections that could be published from the volumes of the *Cambridge Journal of Education* and other stories that could be told about education. The theme that emerged while I was sifting and sorting through the back issues was *curriculum and the teacher*. Editors past and present helped to direct my attention to particular papers that warranted inclusion in what rapidly became an overcrowded long-list from which I made the final cut. I am especially grateful to Les Tickle, Mary Jane Drummond, David Bridges, John Elliott, Terry Haydn and Anne Chippindale. I am also immensely grateful to my wife, Jill Robinson, for her support and advice. Most probably I have missed important papers that merited a place and inevitably there are a large number of papers that could have been included but didn't make it for one reason or another – the fault is all mine. I have very much enjoyed assembling this collection and doing the background research for the introductory chapter. In conclusion I would like to thank my fellow editors from the Journal for giving me the chance to bring together this collection and learn so much from doing so.

Nigel Norris
Centre for Applied Research in Education
University of East Anglia
June 2007

Introduction

Curriculum and the teacher

Nigel Norris

Beginnings and preoccupations

In what follows I have tried to give a flavour of the times and the social and intellectual context in which the papers presented in this collection were written. In doing so I have drawn on the papers themselves, other papers from the Journal and other contemporary texts and historical commentaries. There are many educational topics and controversies that have fuelled the *Cambridge Journal of Education* over the past thirty-five years, but three related and recurring themes seem to have predominated: the curriculum, the teacher and change. In the first article to be published in the Journal Alex Evans noted that 'we live in an age in which change, not stability is the norm'.[1] Unsurprisingly this was a theme that was to reverberate across the volumes of the Journal since its inception.

The original ambition of the Journal was

> to become the medium for a serious and developing discussion on questions of general educational interest, on problems more specifically to do with the professional education of teachers, and on issues arising out of the concerns of those working in this field in the Cambridge area.[2]

As it transpired two groups were influential in shaping the early years of the Journal. The first was a group of philosophers of education, working at the Cambridge Institute of Education and Homerton College who were influenced by Richard Peters at the Institute of Education, London University. They included David Bridges, who was the editor,[3] Hugh Sockett, Charles Bailey, Peter Scrimshaw, John Elliott and Richard Pring. The second group were the Humanities Curriculum Project (HCP) team, who were originally based at Phillippa Fawcett College, London, but had moved to the University of East Anglia in 1970 to form the Centre for Applied Research in Education (CARE). This group comprised Lawrence Stenhouse who was the director of HCP and CARE, Barry MacDonald, Jean Rudduck and also John Elliott, who was a member of both groups. Although it has had special issues focused on particular topics and themes, the Journal has retained its generalist character, making it a rich repository of educational history and record of continuity and change.

In his 1978 Wood Memorial Lecture at Hughes Hall, Cambridge, Sir Toby

Weaver, formerly Deputy Secretary at the Department of Education and Science, divided the previous forty years of educational history into four identifiable stages: the age of stagnation and disruption lasting roughly from 1936 to 1946; the age of make do and mend, lasting from 1946 to 1956; the age of expansion, from 1956 to 1972; followed by the age of uncertainty.[4] The first issue of the *Cambridge Journal of Education* was published in the Lent term of 1971. It was a child of the age of expansion, significantly shaped by those times.

By 1971 curriculum reform was sufficiently well established to be called a movement. The pressure for curriculum reform stemmed from renewed concerns about curriculum obsolescence, especially in those subjects that were thought to be crucial to the scientific and technological development needed to sustain economic growth and national security. There were also concerns about the relevance of the curriculum for all children, especially those who would have to stay on at school until the age of sixteen.[5] Another spur to change was a growing awareness that schooling largely reproduced the social order, coupled with a growing conviction that education could be a potent force against poverty and cycles of deprivation. There was too something forward looking, optimistic, experimental and exciting about the times that gave licence and impetus to break with educational tradition. Modernisation was a powerful political rhetoric.

In *The Future of Socialism* (1956) Crosland had written about the divisive, unjust, unequal and wasteful nature of schooling in Britain, arguing that it denied even limited equal opportunities.[6] Crosland took up office at the Department of Education and Science (DES) in January 1965, at a time when education was seen as a political backwater or worse a graveyard. Christopher Price, his Parliamentary Private Secretary, recalled how Crosland arrived at the job by accident.[7] A reshuffle caused by Patrick Gordon Walker's failure to win the Leyton by-election and get back into Parliament led to a vacancy in Education. The post was first offered to Roy Jenkins, but he turned it down.[8] The waste that Crosland had written about was well documented in a 1954 report from the Central Advisory Council for Education on *Early Leaving*.[9] It was also a subject of attention in the growing field of the sociology of education. In their analysis of secondary schools and the supply of labour, Jean Floud and Chelly Halsey, for example, described the complex interactions between family background and educational opportunities and outcomes. They argued that selection at 11+ and segregation into separate schools was educationally and vocationally undesirable.[10] Crosland was a supporter of comprehensive education and a vehement opponent of grammar schools.[11] Halsey became one of his personal advisors.

In primary education progressive theory and practice found endorsement in the publication of *Children and their Primary Schools*. This was the last report from the Central Advisory Council for Education[12] which was reconstituted in October 1963 and chaired by Bridget Plowden. She reported to Tony Crosland in November 1966, the report being published in January 1967. Brian Simon noted that the report 'received a warm welcome right across the board – in the newspapers, the educational press and on television'.[13] Maurice Kogan, who was Secretary to the Plowden Committee, says the report assumed that:

education best began by generating pupil motivation within an informal but firm relationship established by the teachers and by eschewing a teacher dominated curriculum. This view was well nourished by the practitioner evidence reaching the Committee but also fell in well with the developmental theories contained in the second chapter of the Report.[14]

The Plowden Report became a major point of reference in primary education and set the tenor for thinking about the education and care of young children. Interestingly, given the contemporary emphasis on integrated services for children and young people, Plowden considered the health and social services provision for children and recommended closer co-operation between family doctors, school and public health services and hospitals as well as closer collaboration between social workers and health professionals. Among other things the Plowden Report proposed a national policy of positive discrimination favouring schools in neighbourhoods where children were most 'severely handicapped by home conditions'. It recommended that the Department of Education formally designate those schools and areas in most need as 'educational priority areas' and that research should be started to discover which of the developments in these areas had the most constructive effects.[15] Commenting on the Plowden Report, Halsey wrote that it seemed at the time to be 'a welcome push in the direction of solving the central problem of educational inequality through its concern with the mainstream of state-provided schools for the vast majority'.[16] He recalled that Crosland was sceptically enthusiastic about the idea of action research in Educational Priority Areas.[17]

In secondary education two organisations were especially influential in shaping curriculum reform: the Nuffield Foundation and the Schools Council for Curriculum and Examinations. It was the Nuffield Foundation's Science Teaching Project that created the template for curriculum change. The project was set up in 1962 and was to be designed 'for teachers by teachers'.[18] According to Mary Waring the model for curriculum development was akin to action research,

> The new approach, defined and exemplified in draft materials by the central team, would be tested in schools, following careful briefing of teachers to ensure understanding of the ethos. Feedback from trials could then be used to modify, replace and generally improve the materials before publication. Trials would also make possible the use of materials in a variety of classrooms with teachers of varying degrees of experience and expertise, and so provide further information as to the overall feasibility of the materials as a set of resources 'on offer' to teachers. They would also mean that a large number of teachers other than team members would be involved from a very early stage.[19]

The Schools Council was established in October 1964, in the heyday of the 'swinging sixties'. It was the brain-child of Derek Morrell and recommended by the Lockwood report. It was closed in 1984 by Sir Keith Joseph,[20] heralding a step closer to the central control of education suggested by the Orwellian year of the Council's demise.[21]

In a report on its first year's work the Council acknowledged the lead that had been given to curriculum development by the Nuffield Foundation in science, mathematics and foreign languages.[22] The Council's *Working Paper No. 2* published in 1965 outlined the beginning of a five year programme of research, enquiry and development in anticipation of the raising of the school leaving age to sixteen.[23] *Working Paper No. 11* published in 1967 in collaboration with the Nuffield Foundation focused on society and the young school leaver and considered a humanities programme in preparation for raising the school leaving age. *Working Paper No. 11* was the result of an inquiry commissioned by the Nuffield Foundation and directed by Michael Schofield, a sociologist who had recently completed a survey on the sexual behaviour of young people. Schofield's inquiry began in the autumn of 1965 and explored the achievements and needs of schools in teaching humanities and social studies. In his report Schofield suggested that local development groups should be established to discuss and try out ideas for improving teaching in the humanities. He also argued that a central team, of the kind made familiar by the Nuffield projects, would be vital to support local development groups, not least by preparing and disseminating teaching and learning materials.[24] *Working Papers No. 2* and *No. 11* provided the background and justification for setting up the Humanities Curriculum Project. *Working Paper No. 2* defined the problem of the humanities as giving all young people some access to a complex cultural inheritance, some hold on their personal life and on relationships with the various communities to which they belonged and some extension of their understanding of, and sensitivity towards, other people. The aim was to forward understanding, discrimination and judgement in the human field (para. 60).

Defining the curriculum problem

From his appointment as Director of the Humanities Curriculum Project[25] to his tragically premature death in 1982, Lawrence Stenhouse was one of the most influential and at times controversial curriculum theorists. There were five features that made the Humanities Curriculum Project especially significant and influential. First the HCP team produced an innovative definition of the humanities curriculum and the educational issues it posed for the teacher. They defined humanities as the study of important human issues and the aim of the humanities in the secondary school as the development of understanding of human acts, of social situations, and of the problems of values which arise from them. The curriculum problem in the humanities was how the teacher should handle controversial value issues in the classroom. Second, the project developed an approach to teaching and learning humanities that was based on discussion and the consideration of evidence. To support discussion-based learning the project team produced eight packs of exemplary multi-media materials. Third, the project conceptualised the role of the humanities teacher in a way that was unusually principled and immediately shocking and contentious. They said that in handling controversial issues in the classroom the teacher's role should be premised on neutrality. The teacher was chair of the discussion and had responsibility for quality and learning standards. The teacher was in authority, but was not an authority in the controversial matters under consideration. Fourth, Stenhouse's strategy for curriculum development saw the project team as a research group and the participating teachers as researchers in their own classrooms, putting the ideas of the project to the test of practice. A notable outcome of the Humanities Curriculum Project was the growth of the teacher-researcher and classroom action research movements. Finally, the project had a full-time independent evaluation team led by Barry MacDonald that pioneered the use of case study and developed one of the first examples of what is now known as mixed-method approaches to evaluation.

What marked out Stenhouse's contribution to the field of curriculum was his understanding of the implications of the relationship between education and autonomy and his distinctive conceptualisation of the relationship between curriculum and practice. In a paper on values and curriculum, Stenhouse argued for an approach to 'education for innovation in values' that neither chained the future to the past by conservatism nor chained it to the present by indoctrination, but instead was guided by free inquiry and discussion.[26] He thought that education enhances freedom by inducting people into the knowledge of culture as a thinking system.[27] 'The most important characteristic of the knowledge mode', wrote Stenhouse, 'is that one can think with it'.[28] It was his evaluative standard for the success of education that was strikingly unusual. Stenhouse thought that education as induction into knowledge was successful to the extent that it made 'the behavioural outcomes of the students unpredictable'.[29] This idea was in sharp contrast to the prevailing beliefs about curriculum and evaluation which emphasised the importance of behavioural objectives and measuring the extent to which they had been achieved by the students. In contrast to the objectives model, Stenhouse advocated a 'process model' for curriculum design and development based on establishing principles for selecting content, developing an appropriate teaching strategy and evaluating student and teacher progress. Stenhouse defined curriculum as 'the means by which the experience of attempting to put an educational proposal into practice is made publicly available'.[30] Curriculum development was, for Stenhouse, quintessentially an experiment and curricula were hypotheses to be tested by teachers in classrooms.[31]

One preoccupation of curriculum theorists in the late 1960s and 1970s was the role of objectives and specifically behavioural objectives in curriculum development and planning. Hugh Sockett and Richard Pring mounted compelling philosophical critiques of Bloom's Taxonomy of Educational Objectives and the model of rational (means/end) curriculum planning 'in which the curriculum planner pre-specifies the behaviours he wants the student to learn and then chooses the means (the learning experiences) by which these objectives might be reached'.[32] This approach to curriculum planning owed much to Ralph Tyler and his work on the famous Eight Year Study. Tyler regarded evaluation as an integral part of curriculum and instruction. For Tyler educational objectives gave clear purpose and direction to learning: they were the essential building blocks of the curriculum and provided the means by which it was possible to evaluate success.[33] The dominance of an objectives approach to curriculum and its evaluation occasioned a small invitational conference at Churchill College, Cambridge, funded by the Nuffield Foundation. Convened by Barry MacDonald and Malcolm Parlett, it was the first in a long line of 'Cambridge evaluation conferences' that have been reported in the Journal.[34] The conference brought together evaluators and policy makers from Britain, the USA, Sweden as well as representatives from the OECD to explore alternatives to the traditional 'objectives model' of curriculum evaluation.

In *Curriculum criticism: misconceived theory, ill-conceived practice* Rex Gibson took issue with what he saw as a worrying trend in curriculum studies: 'the view that the curriculum can be regarded as an art object, a literary object' and 'that the concepts and methods of artistic and literary criticism can yield deeper understanding of curriculum processes'. A leading figure in 'curriculum criticism' was Elliot Eisner, an early critic of behavioural objectives and advocate of what he called 'connoisseurship' in curriculum evaluation. Others in the curriculum criticism camp included David Jenkins, William Pinar, Madeleine Grumet and Edward Milner.

In his paper *The idea of a pastoral curriculum* Terence McLaughlin was concerned with the development of autonomy, the development of rationally autonomous individuals as he put it. He unpacked the portmanteau concept of a pastoral curriculum to establish what was meant by the term, the principles for determining its character and content and whether the school should be concerned with the pastoral curriculum. In *Pastoral Care*, Michael Marland – the influential headmaster of Woodberry Down School, London said that the disadvantage of the book's title was that it could be interpreted as dividing school life into two sides, the pastoral and the academic. Marland saw a central purpose of education as helping the individual pupil to find him- or herself and find meaning in their studies and in life.[35] Like Marland, McLaughlin argued that the 'pastoral curriculum' needs to be linked with the rest of the curriculum and he identified this as a major challenge and task of great complexity.

Compulsion in curricular matters is largely taken for granted: children at school should learn things that political authorities think are good for them. For much of the post-1945 period Britain was unusual, at least by European standards, in having a decentralised curriculum. While Secretary to the Curriculum Study Group at the Ministry of Education, Derek Morrell wrote the constitution for the Schools Council. Morrell, who was to become the first joint secretary to the Schools Council in October 1964, reaffirmed the:

> importance of the principle that the schools should have the fullest possible measure of responsibility for their own work, including responsibility for their own curricula and teaching methods, which should be evolved by their own staff to meet the needs of their own pupils.[36]

In the case of elementary schools the Board of Education had effectively deregulated the curriculum in May 1926, although secondary schools were bound by a prescribed curriculum until 1945.[37] The formal autonomy accorded teachers and schools over the curriculum had been enshrined in the 1944 Education Act and was well established by the 1960s. Although there were many limitations (examinations, resources, tradition and wider expectations) on the freedom of schools to devise their own curriculum, just as there were constraints on individual teacher autonomy, nonetheless there was space for teachers to exercise their professional judgement over a wide variety of educational decisions. The debate between Michael Bonnett and John White about a compulsory curriculum occurred eleven years before Kenneth Baker, then Secretary of State for Education, announced his intention to introduce a national curriculum. John White, like the authors and supporters of the national curriculum, argued that a certain curriculum should be insisted on if children are to gain the knowledge and understanding that autonomy depends on. At the core of Bonnett's case against a compulsory curriculum was the argument that compulsion was likely to be antithetical to the promotion of personal autonomy. When the 'Great Education Reform Bill', as it was conceitedly called at the time, gained Royal assent in July 1988, out went the last vestiges of teacher and local autonomy and in came the national curriculum with its associated attainment targets, programmes of study and national testing. And once governments got a taste for interfering in education their appetite for intervention and prescription was difficult to contain. Prompted by Kenneth Baker's Education Act, in *Curriculum Reform and Curriculum Theory: a case of historical amnesia* Ivor Goodson looked at the dismantling of curriculum reform efforts in the 1960s and the re-constitution of traditional subjects as the mainstay of schooling. The 1988 Education Act provided the Secretary of State for Education with extensive powers over many aspects of schooling, including curriculum and assessment. But Morrell's convictions about autonomy of schools over curriculum matters had been under attack since the mid 1970s.

The speech on 18 October 1976 by James Callaghan at Ruskin College has come to signify a tipping point in educational atmosphere and direction. Whereas in the lead up to the 1964 general election Harold Wilson spoke of the scientific age of expansion and the excitement of discarding an Edwardian establishment mentality and building a modern Britain, by 1976 Callaghan, who had succeeded him as Prime Minister, was telling the Labour Party that the nation could not spend its way out of recession, signalling an end to the Keynesian post-war economic consensus. In education Callaghan called for changes in curriculum, assessment, teacher training and the relationship between school and working life.[38] Maurice Kogan once wrote that 'prime ministers don't usually give a damn about education ... and hardly ever intervene in it'.[39] Perhaps it was no coincidence that education became the subject of a 'great debate', precisely at a time of 'stagflation' and enormous pressure on public finances. Some saw Callaghan as stealing the thunder of the right wing and their 'Black Paper' colleagues.[40] Regardless of how opportunistic the decision to intervene in education might have been, it also reflected Callaghan's interest in education and his conviction that signs of public discontent and professional anxiety were warranted.[41] The 'great debate' that Callaghan asked for was a stage-managed affair offering little of the moral deliberation that William Reid later argued was at the core of curriculum planning.[42] Although Callaghan never used the term accountability in his Ruskin speech, he did talk about opening up education to greater public scrutiny and the need for teachers to satisfy the requirements of parents and industry. According to Stuart Maclure the then editor of the *Times Educational Supplement*, the 'threats were veiled but unmistakeable'.[43] The spectre of falling standards was on parade mustering recruits for centralisation and control. A year before the Ruskin speech, a prescient Ernest House drew attention to some of the pernicious effects of accountability in the USA, arguing that educational testing and teacher and school evaluation had considerable potential to standardise and dehumanise schooling.[44]

New orders of experience

What are the conditions needed for children and young people to participate more actively in the construction of their own education? Historically pupils and students have had little say over the content and processes of schooling and their voices are seldom heard in discussions about the purposes of education or its governance and accountability. The autonomy that Michael Bonnett was reaching for in education – not so much 'something to be eventually achieved by pupils' but rather 'something to be respected and maintained in pupils' – is rarely a guiding principle of the school curriculum.[45] Mostly around the globe it is the state authorities who think they know best what it is that children are in need of knowing and doing. This is what Nel Noddings calls 'inferred needs' and in 'trying to meet inferred needs' she argues, 'we often neglect the expressed needs of our students'.[46]

The first three papers in this section draw directly from the Humanities Curriculum Project (HCP). The concept of the neutral teacher was controversial in the 1960s and remains so today. In *Teaching through small group discussion: formality, rules and authority*, Lawrence Stenhouse set out why he believed that teaching through discussion, a central feature of HCP, needs to be governed by explicit rules, conventions and roles. His concern was to find ways to develop the autonomy of students by lessening the attitude of dependence that students can have in the face of the traditional authority of the teacher. John Elliott's paper on the *Concept of the neutral teacher* and Charles Bailey's response to it seek to clarify the idea of neutrality in teaching.

Social stratification and differentiation both within and between schools has been an enduring issue in education. By 1967, as Tessa Blackstone observed, the central role of education in determining life chances was an accepted tenet,[47] and various reports of the Central Advisory Council for Education[48] had reinforced and further disseminated knowledge about the relationship between social class and educational outcomes as well as drawn attention to the disadvantages suffered by many children. The impact of school organisation on the educational attainments of children of different social backgrounds was perhaps less well understood. In his classic study of ability and attainment in the primary school, J.W.B. Douglas found streaming by ability reinforced the process of social selection and that children who came from

> well-kept homes and who are themselves clean, well clothed and shod, stand a greater chance of being put in the upper streams than their measured ability would seem to justify. Once there they are likely to stay and to improve in performance in succeeding years. This is in striking contrast to the deterioration noticed in those children of similar measured ability who were placed in the lower streams.[49]

The effects of streaming were also apparent in secondary schooling where those in low-ability groups were found to do worse, while those in high-ability groups tended to improve their performance. In a study of the effects of ability grouping in British secondary schools, Kerckhoff found that the 'losses by students in low ability groups, combined with the gains by students in high ability groups, make the overall effect of ability grouping very striking'.[50] In his 1976 article, *The social organisation of the classroom and the philosophy of mixed ability teaching*, David Bridges cast a philosopher's eye on the issue and explored the ways in which differences about mixed ability teaching were rooted in different social philosophies and principles.

In 1998 – eight years after Nelson Mandela was released from prison and four years after South Africa's first democratic election took place – Penny Enslin and Shirley Pendlebury from the University of Witwatersrand compiled a special issue of the Journal on transforming education in South Africa. In their introduction to the collection of papers they wrote:

> As we write the introduction to this special issue of the *Cambridge Journal of Education*, South Africans are pondering the dismal 1997 matriculation results. The pass rate improved in only one of the nine provinces. In the North Western Province it dropped from 66 to 50% and in our own Gauteng province, which has the biggest share of the population, barely half the candidates passed. These grim results suggest that many of the characteristics of the old system persist. Despite the hard won struggle against apartheid education, public examination results continue to be influenced by race, poor resources, incompetent teaching, dysfunctional schools and inefficient procedures. Overcoming the past is going to take a long time. In the wake of apartheid, South Africa's most urgent and difficult project is to reconstruct and develop all spheres of public life so as to establish enabling conditions for a flourishing democracy. Under apartheid, education was a site of contestation. Now it is supposed to be a site of transformation, not only for its own sake but also because it is crucial to transforming other spheres. A primary goal of the ANC's policy framework is to transform the institutions of society in the interests of all and so enable social, cultural, economic and political empowerment of all citizens. Many South Africans see educational transformation as the key to transforming society at large. If we cannot transform education, what chance do we have of transforming anything? People's hopes for improved employability, democratic citizenship and a better life are pinned on education. Insistence on transformation rather than reform may be due to a deep suspicion of reform as a strategy. The previous government used reform to contain opposition, maintain the status quo and evade critical issues of inequality and oppression. So much was rotten in the old system that only radical, thorough-going and systemic change could overcome its authoritarian, unequal, wasteful and demoralising practices.

Nazir Carrim's article, *Anti-racism and the 'new' South African educational order*, traces the desegregation of South African schools, and considers the mission of the complete transformation of every aspect of the education system. A system that since 1948 when the Nationalist Government came to power was built on enforced segregation and predicated on racism. Carrim explored problems with 'assimilationalism' and multiculturalism and argued for a critical anti-racism to ensure a 'de-essentialised' sense of people's identities.

In 2001 Lani Florian and Martyn Rouse edited an edition of the Journal on special education. Their own paper, 'Inclusive practice in English secondary schools: lessons learned' explored how teachers respond to the tension between 'equity' and 'excellence' as defined by policy makers and school effectiveness researchers. The edition arose from a programme of comparative research that began in 1994 and explored 'how different national and local jurisdictions have approached the reform of special education policies, practices and provision in the context of larger educational reforms'.[51] Florian and Rouse wrote that special education 'has become a proxy for wider concerns about education and social policy'.[52] Key debates have revolved around issues of inclusion and exclusion and the preservation of separate systems of special education versus creation of a fully inclusive general education system. There is an apparent tension between the goals of inclusive education and the perception that having a high proportion of pupils with special educational needs in a school lowers standards.[53] New market-based forms of public management in education have put enormous pressure on schools to meet and preferably exceed pupil performance targets and do well in published league tables. It is against this backdrop that schools and teachers have to find ways of developing inclusive practice. The economic rationale that underpins these market-based reforms reinforces the existing stratification of schools and learners. It is socially conservative and divisive.

Environmental education has been a recurrent theme for the Journal since the 1990s.[54] In 1999 Michael Bonnett and John Elliott edited a special issue of the Journal on environmental education, sustainability and the transformation of schooling. In the editorial they of course stressed the great importance of the relationship between humankind the environment, but they went on to argue that environmental education properly conceived may require a radical transformation of the nature of teaching and schooling. The special issue grew out of an environmental education initiative (ENSI) sponsored by the OECD. The Environment and Schools Initiative was launched in 1986. According to Peter Posch the idea emerged from a Conference of Ministers of Education of OECD Member countries held in Paris in 1984, when Minister Herbert Moritz of Austria underlined that environmental education was one of the most important priorities for the future development of education.[55] Following this the OECD Centre for Educational Research and Innovation decided to include environmental education in its Innovation and Exchange Programme and invited member countries to participate. The initiative involved a commitment to develop dynamic qualities in students through their involvement with environmental problems and solutions, inter-disciplinary learning and research, and reflective action to improve environmental conditions. Peter Posch was a leading figure in the Initiative and with John Elliott and Kathleen Lane was responsible for articulating its educational values and principles. In *The ecologisation of schools and its implications for educational policy*,

Posch describes a project exemplifying the principles established in the Environment and Schools Initiative.

Shirley Brice Heath is renowned for her work on language and literacy exemplified by her ethnography of two communities in the Piedmont Carolinas of the Southern USA.[56] Her paper formed part of a millennium special issue of the Journal edited by Morag Styles and John Beck that looked to the curriculum of the future. In *Seeing our way into learning*, Brice Heath argues for a much broader conception of literacy and a radical shift towards visual arts as well as print literacies and oral communication. She sees that a central curricular issue is how schools can provide ample authentic practice opportunities for students who have highly varied approaches to learning and knowledge representation.

For many years Jean Rudduck's research focused on issues to do with promoting more participative forms of learning and engagement with school, the space for pupil voice and the difference it can make to school improvement.[57] Her collaboration with Julia Flutter began around 1994 with a longitudinal study of pupils' perspectives on schooling. Their paper *Pupil participation and pupil perspective: 'carving a new order of experience'* explores what teachers and schools can learn from their students if they could only find ways of listening. Listening to young people is a signal theme in *Identifying and responding to needs in education*, by Nel Noddings.[58] Her work stands in sharp contrast to the metrics of accountability that dominate education. She reminds us that many children come to school with overwhelming needs (homelessness, poverty, poor health, sick or missing parents, emotional damage) that must be addressed in some way if they are to benefit from education. She argues that significant time in school should be given over to the development of care and trust and 'the search for connections among interests and aims, the identification of learning objectives (that may vary from student to student), and free gifts of intellectual material that students may pick up and use to satisfy their own needs'.[59] In *A curriculum for the future*, Gunter Kress contrasts education for periods of relative stability with education for periods of instability and rapid social and economic change. The old organisational, temporal, social and knowledge 'frames' that encompass and structure education, he believes, are loosening their grip and alternative frameworks for education are beginning to emerge – for example new forms of representation and communication are redefining the meaning and scope of literacy. Kress sees curriculum as a design for the future and design as a central category of the school curriculum. He argues that 'putting design at the centre of the curriculum and of its purposes is to redefine the goal of education as the making of individual dispositions oriented towards innovation, creativity, transformation and change'.[60]

Teachers and teaching

The experience of teaching, often in contrast to the experience of being taught, can be a remarkably solitary and professionally lonely experience. That teaching is emotionally demanding work is mostly absent from much of the academic and official literature on education. In a special volume of the Journal devoted to teaching and the emotions Mary Jane Drummond and Marilyn Osborn were invited to prepare review essays of books that had made a valuable contribution to our knowledge of emotions in teaching. The books they chose were:

- Willard Waller (1932) *The Sociology of Teaching*, New York: Wiley;
- Arthur T. Jersild (1955) *When Teachers Face Themselves*, New York: Teachers College Press;
- John Gabriel (1957) *An Analysis of the Emotional Problems of the Teacher in the Classroom*, London: Angus & Robertson;
- Philip Jackson (1968) *Life in Classrooms*, New York: Holt, Rinehart and Winston;
- Dan Lortie (1975) *Schoolteacher: a sociological study*, Chicago: University of Chicago Press;
- Isca Salzberger-Wittenberg, Gianna Henry & Elsie Osborne (1983) *The Emotional Experience of Learning and Teaching*, London: Routledge & Kegan Paul;
- Jennifer Nias (1989) *Primary Teachers Talking: a study of teaching and work*, London: Routledge.

Willard Waller was a sociologist with a wide range of interests which included studies of the family, divorce and readjustment, First World War veterans and teaching. His sociology of teaching was similarly wide ranging. He was associate professor of sociology at Bernard College, Columbia University.[61] *The Sociology of Teaching* was first published 1932 three years in to the Great Depression. In the preface Waller explained the purpose of the book in the following way:

> What this book tells is what every teacher knows, that the world of school is a social world. Those human beings who live together in the school, though deeply severed in one sense, nevertheless spin a tangled web of relationships; that web and the people in it make up the social world of the school. It is not a wide world, but, for those who know it, it is a world compact with meaning. It is a unique world. It is the purpose of this book to explore it.[62]

Waller trained to be a teacher and worked in a high school, Morgan Park Military Academy, teaching French and Latin for six years. It was this experience that informed his sociological analysis of teaching,[63] and for Waller 'teaching makes the teacher'.[64]

John Gabriel says that the seeds of his study were sown when he read E.K. Wickman's *Children's Behavior and Teachers' Attitudes* (New York: Commonwealth Fund, 1928). Wickman's monograph was a report of a study on the reactions of teachers to behavioural problems in the classroom. Gabriel's research was conducted between 1948 and 1950 during a period of continued austerity, rationing and reconstruction. It was based on two surveys of teachers in England, the first comprising 162 responses and the second 736 responses.[65] By 'emotional problems', Gabriel meant problems which give rise to 'negative feelings of worry or strain, annoyance or concern'.[66] Among other things Gabriel concluded that the implications of his surveys seem to 'confirm Wickman's original findings, and we may say, as did Wickman, that this concern arises, in part, from their desire to carry out their academic teaching duties and to maintain a position of authority within the school and classroom, and, in part, from their severe attitudes towards violations of the social and moral codes of the community'.[67]

Arthur Jersild was Professor of Education at Teachers College Columbia. The research for *When Teachers Face Themselves* was done under the auspices of the Horace Mann–Lincoln Institute of School Experimentation. The research involved:

> a survey of reactions to the idea of self understanding as a basic aim of educa-tion; a series of personal conferences; a survey of personal problems as revealed by written responses to an inventory; and ratings and evaluations of lectures and discussions dealing with various aspects of self-understanding.[68]

The themes of the book, anxiety, loneliness, the search for meaning, sex, hostil-ity and compassion, don't seem unique to teaching but certainly seem an import-ant part of education. The research for Philip Jackson's *Life in Classrooms* was, by contrast, based not on surveys but on detailed long-term observation and inter-views. Jackson says his aim was to 'arouse the reader's interest and possibly awaken his concern over aspects of school life that seem to be receiving less attention than they deserve'.[69] The book had it origins in Jackson's dissatisfac-tion with psychometric research and a one-year Fellowship at the Center for Advanced Study in the Behavioral Sciences at Palo Alto, California in 1962, during which time he observed a small number of elementary school classrooms, 'moving up close to the realities of school life' as he put it. When he returned to Chicago in 1963 he embarked on two further years of systematic observation of four classrooms in the Lower School of the University of Chicago Laboratory School. For Jackson the distinctive flavour of classroom life is characterised by crowds, praise and power which form a 'hidden curriculum' which students and teachers must master if they are to cope with school. In addition to classroom observation Jackson interviewed fifty teachers about classroom life.[70] Jackson concludes his chapter on the teachers' views by considering what he calls the 'fundamental ambiguity in the teacher's role'. He describes the teacher 'as working for the school and against it', because he has a dual allegiance to the institutional order and to the well-being of the students. It is the 'double concern and the teacher's way of dealing with it', says Jackson, that imbues teaching 'with a special quality'.[71]

Dan Lortie's *Schoolteacher: a sociological study*, is concerned with the nature and content of the ethos of teaching. The research which resulted in the book was based on 'historical review, national and local surveys, findings from observational studies and a content analysis of intensive interviews'. Ninety-four interviews were completed with 'elementary and senior high school teachers from upper income communities, junior high school teachers from middle range and elementary and senior high school teachers from lower income settings'.[72] Most of interviews were conducted in 1963. Lortie noted 'that relationships with other adults do not stand at the heart of the teacher's psychological world' which is shaped more by 'deeper commitments to students'[73] and found that the significant components in the ethos of the American classroom teacher were 'conservatism, individualism and presentism'.[74]

The Emotional Experience of Learning and Teaching was based on work that the authors did with teachers on a course called 'Aspects of Counselling' at the Tavistock Clinic, London. Isca Salzberger-Wittenberg and her colleagues worked within the psychoanalytic tradition and were influenced by Wilfred Bion and Melanie Klein. Jennifer Nias was Tutor in Curriculum Studies at the Cambridge Institute of Education. Her book *Primary Teachers Talking* was based on the personal accounts of teachers who trained in one-year Post Graduate Certificate in Education (PGCE) courses for work in infant, junior and middle schools.[75] Between 1975 and 1977 she interviewed ninety-nine teachers, thirty men and sixty-nine women. Nias had been the course tutor to many of them. Twenty-two of the sample also kept diaries for one day a week for one term. The first set of interviews were followed up ten years later with a further fifty interviews in 1985.[76] *Primary Teachers Talking* was published at the end of a period in which primary teachers had a large degree of formal autonomy in matters of curriculum and pedagogy which had framed the professional identity of many teachers.

Teaching and the Self by Jennifer Nias is drawn from the same body of work as *Primary Teachers Talking*. In this paper Nias argues that in primary school teaching it is the teacher as a person that has been most important rather than the teacher as a subject specialist. For the primary school teacher it is the self that is the crucial element in the way they construe the nature of their job. Continuing the theme of the emotions in teaching, in her study of teachers' participation in large-scale reform Judith Warren Little observed that emotions lie very near the surface of schools caught up in systemic change. Her paper explored the sources of long-term optimism and fatalism in teachers' encounters with reform movements. Ernest House once said that the burden of innovation was shouldered by the teacher.[77] Warren draws our attention to the possible impact of educational change on learners, noting that reform draws emotional energy away from teacher–student relationships and instead invests it in the relationships with colleagues needed to make reform work.

In recent years there has been a growing interest in and rediscovery of the power of narrative to illuminate the world of education. Narrative offers a way of understanding education from the perspectives of its participants. Teachers' stories and stories about teachers as well as students' stories and stories about students[78] are ways of personalising education, making it more humane. Three papers in this collection focus on the importance of narrative for understanding education. Madeleine Grumet writes about finding authentic feminist voices for educational studies: voices that have three parts; situation, narrative and interpretation; voices that are collaborative but not drowned out by coercive consensus. Since her book with William Pinar, *Toward a Poor Curriculum*, and her later influential book *Bitter Milk: Women and Teaching* (University of Massachusetts Press 1988), Grumet has been writing about women's voices and challenging the hegemonic discourse of educational politics, management and administration. Mary Louise Holly, whose work on the professional development of university teachers has been much acclaimed, writes about journal writing as a powerful means for teachers to explore and reflect on practice. She says 'writing works because it enables us to come to know ourselves through the multiple voices our experiences take'.[79] Following on from this, Jean Clandinin and Michael Connelly explore the role of narrative in teacher development and curriculum, drawing on Dewey's distinction between the laboratory and apprenticeship in teacher education and using a case study of a teacher in her first year of teaching to illustrate their thinking.

The aim of improving teaching has at various times been thought to be susceptible to technocratic solutions, systematisation and standardisation. For those who see teaching as largely or solely a technical accomplishment, honing the technology of teaching is a way of improving the efficiency and effectiveness of education. In the nineteenth and early twentieth century there were advocates of a science of education based on psychological principles, mental testing and scientific management and administration. Some in the curriculum reform movement of the 1950s and 1960s saw 'teacher proof' curricula as offering a way to reform the practice of education. More recently the proponents of evidence-based practice, for example, have commended the virtues of good experimental designs and systematic reviews as a basis for informing policy and shaping practice. The basic idea is that the careful accumulation of knowledge about education and its application to policy and practice is necessary to inform political or professional judgement and ensure a reasoned basis for educational decision-making. Few would probably quibble with such a view. But what this does, can and should mean in practice is far from settled business. Questions about the relationship of research or theory to practice are also bound up with issues of professional identity and status. Research and teaching could be seen as different realms of professional action, with different rationales, taking place in different contexts and different emotional space. For many years action research has been advanced as a methodology for systematic improvement by relating research to the problems of action. Action research has featured strongly in issues of the Journal since the mid 1970s.[80] Kurt Lewin is often thought of as the person who articulated action research as a systematic approach to achieving greater organisational effectiveness through democratic participation.[81] Since the 1960s there has been a revival of interest in action research and a growing variety of theory, practice and fields of application. In Britain in the 1970s and 1980s educational action research was perhaps best represented by the work of John Elliott in his early leadership of the Classroom Action Research Network and the many teachers and teacher educators who got involved in action research through the Cambridge Institute of Education. *Becoming Critical: knowing through Action Research*, by Wilfred Carr and Stephen Kemmis[82] (1983) was seen by many as a key text in the evolution and dissemination of action research. Carr and Kemmis related action research to critical theory, in particular to the work of Habermas, and to the project of emancipation. Their book was reviewed by Rex Gibson in an acerbic essay entitled *Critical Times for Action Research*, where he likened the action research movement to the Salvation Army.[83] Others saw it as inspirational.[84]

One way of describing the social relations of research and teaching is that theory is produced by researchers to be taught or applied by teachers. In *Educational theory and the professional learning of teachers* and elsewhere[85] John Elliott offers a vision of the relationships between theory and practice, research and teaching, that is about the development of practical wisdom. For Elliott the practice of teachers should be informed by their own research and it is the critical reflective theorising of teachers that holds the most promise to improve classroom practice. Teaching is thus disciplined by the teacher as a researcher. This is a line of thought that takes us back to the work of Lawrence Stenhouse and to the idea of research as the basis of teaching.[86] What brings alive the autonomy of the teacher is the capacity to critically reflect on practice and to develop it through ones own research. Christine O'Hanlon's paper *Alienation within the profession – special needs or watered down teachers? Insights into the tension between the ideal and the real through action research*, provides an example of a programme of professional development for special educational needs teachers based on action research. The context for the professional development programme was the introduction in Northern Ireland of legislation paralleling the 1981 Education Act in England and Wales. This Act gave effect to recommendations of the Warnock Committee on provision for children with special educational needs.[87]

In the foreword to *Excellence and Enjoyment: a strategy for primary schools*, Charles Clarke, Secretary of State for Education and Skills at the time, said that what makes a good primary education 'is the fusion of excellence and enjoyment', and he went on to blend high standards in literacy and numeracy with enjoyment, which he described as the birthright of every child.[88] Excellence is, of course a euphemism for high test scores. The reference to enjoyment calls to mind a time when the motivations and interests of the child were seen as a key to successful learning. It is testament to the utilitarian view of schooling that any government feels it has to issue a policy statement about 'enjoyment' in education. Perhaps it signalled growing concerns about the narrowing of the primary curriculum and the damage to children's well-being from the relentless pressure to perform well on tests. The final paper in this edited collection is Robin Alexander's *Still no pedagogy? Principle, pragmatism and compliance in primary education*. It is a scathing critique of primary education policy, in particular *Excellence and Enjoyment*. The title of Alexander's paper refers back to a paper by Brian Simon: *Why no pedagogy in England?*[89] Among other things Simon was critical of the child-centred theories of Friedrich Froebel and his followers and what he called the 'pedagogic romanticism' of the Plowden Report. Simon argued:

> that to start from the standpoint of individual differences is to start from the wrong position. To develop effective pedagogic means involves starting from the opposite standpoint, from what children have in common as members of the human species; to establish the general principles of teaching and, in the light of these, to determine what modifications of practice are necessary to meet specific individual needs.[90]

Alexander defines pedagogy as 'the act of teaching together with its attendant discourse', and says that 'curriculum is just one of its domains, albeit an important one.'[91] He offers an account of pedagogy that encompasses a wide range of educational practice and discourse; including an understanding of children, learning, teaching, curriculum, schools and policy as well as an understanding of the broader cultural and historical context of education. His criticism of the Primary Strategy is sharp and to the point. He writes that it 'is badly written, poorly argued and deeply patronising in its assumptions that teachers will be seduced by Ladybird language, pretty pictures, offers of freedom and enjoyment, and populist appeals to their common sense'.[92]

Postscript

I began this introduction with a depiction of the periods of post-war educational history by Sir Toby Weaver. He concluded his 1978 Wood Memorial Lecture with some remarks about the threats to the spirit of partnership and trust that he thought characterised the education system of the time.

> This spirit, and with it the freedom of action and sense of fellowship it confers on the partners, is under severe test. How far it can survive the impact of exacerbated political partisanship, central and local; the clumsy application of corporate management; the centripetal pressures towards uniformity; the growing replacement of reason and persuasion by force as an acceptable method of resolving differences; the corrosion of what were thought to be professional imperatives by the acids of militancy; the frustrations of financial retrenchment: all this hangs in the balance.[93]

Within a few years of the Journal becoming established recession and retrenchment changed the climate for education irrevocably. The age of uncertainty as Weaver called it gradually gave way to the age of accountability and control. From the vantage point of 2007 it would be hard not to conclude that the spirit of partnership and trust that Weaver thought so important to education has been severely undermined. What is striking, however, is not the continued importance of the relationship between the economy and education, but the widespread application of market ideology and micro-economic thinking to schools and educational institutions more generally. It is this that has had such a deleterious effect on thinking about the purpose and process of education and its role in promoting well-being and sustainable futures. Over the years the *Cambridge Journal of Education* has provided space for advocates of richer, more humane, responsive and socially responsible forms of education. Its original purpose was to be a medium for serious and developing discussion on matters of general educational interest. I hope the papers presented here capture that aspiration.

Notes

1 Alex Evans had been Secretary of the Association of Teachers in Colleges and Departments of Education. His article was entitled 'Colleges of Education – the next phase' *Cambridge Journal of Education*, 1 (1): 4–15.
2 The Journal was originally envisaged as a regional journal with contributors and readers from the Cambridge Institute of Education and its partner colleges through its role as the Area Training Organisation, the Cambridge Department of Education and other bodies in the East Anglia area.

3 In addition to David Bridges, the Journal had an Editorial Panel consisting of John Child (Chair) and Hugh Sockett from the Cambridge Institute of Education, G.D. Booker, Balls Park College; R.P. McKechnie, Saffron Walden College; and Raymond O'Malley, University of Cambridge, Department of Education.

4 See Sir Toby Weaver (1979) 'Education: retrospect and prospect: an administrator's testimony' *Cambridge Journal of Education*, 9 (1): 2–17.

5 The plan was to raise the school leaving age in 1970–71; however the leaving age was not raised to sixteen until September 1972.

6 Crosland, A. (2006) *The Future of Socialism*, London: Constable & Robinson (first published in 1956 by Jonathan Cape).

7 Price, C. (1999) 'Education Secretary', in D. Leonard (ed.) *Crosland and New Labour*, London: Macmillan.

8 Pimlott, B. (1992) *Harold Wilson*, London: HarperCollins.

9 Under the chairmanship of S. Gurney-Dixon, the Central Advisory Council for Education (England) looked at the factors which influenced the age at which boys and girls left secondary schools. Their report, entitled *Early Leaving*, was published in 1954.

10 Floud, J. and Halsey, A.H. (1956) 'English Secondary Schools and the Supply of Labour', *The Yearbook of Education 1956*, London: Evans Brothers.

11 He told his wife Susan that he wanted to destroy every grammar school in England, Wales and Northern Ireland.

12 Central Advisory Councils for Education, one for England and one for Wales, were established by the 1944 Education Act. For an account of the Councils see Kogan, M. and Packwood, T. (1974) *Advisory Councils and Committees in Education*, London: Routledge & Kegan Paul.

13 Simon, B. (1991) *Education and the Social Order*, London: Lawrence & Wishart, p. 363.

14 Kogan, M. (1987) 'The Plowden Report Twenty Years On' *Oxford Review of Education*, 13 (1): 13–20.

15 Central Advisory Council for Education (1967) *Children and their Primary Schools*, London: HMSO.

16 Halsey, A. H. and Sylva, K. (1987) 'Plowden: history and prospect', *Oxford Review of Education*, 13 (1): 3–11.

17 Ibid.

18 Waring, M. (1979) *Social Pressures and Curriculum Innovation – A study of the Nuffield Foundation Science Teaching Project*, London: Methuen, p. 2.

19 Ibid., p. 91.

20 Sir Keith Joseph was Secretary of State for Education and Science in Margaret Thatcher's administration from 1981 to 1986.

21 When Sir David Eccles set up the Curriculum Studies Group he did so partly to increase the role of the Ministry of Education in the process of schooling. This seemingly mild intervention by the Ministry was seen in some quarters as the thin end of a centralist or worse totalitarian wedge. See Jennings, A. (1985) 'Out of the Secret Garden', in Plaskow, M. (ed.) *Life and Death of the Schools Council*, London: Falmer Press, pp. 15–39.

22 Schools Council (1965) *Change and Response – The first year's work: October 1964–September 1965*, London: HMSO.

23 After 1922 the school leaving age was fourteen. A leaving age of fifteen was written in to the 1944 Education Act. Its implementation, delayed until April 1947, had to be pushed through Attlee's post-war Cabinet by Ellen Wilkinson, Minister of Education, in the face of significant opposition from the Treasury – see Beckett, F. (2000) *Clem Attlee*, London: Politico. Following recommendations from both Crowther and Newsom, in 1964 Sir Edward Boyle, Minister of Education, announced the raising of the leaving age to sixteen from 1970: implementation was delayed until September 1972.

24 Schools Council (1967) *Working Paper No. 11 – Society and the Young School Leaver*, London: HMSO.

25 The Humanities Curriculum Project was set up in September 1967. It was sponsored by the Schools Council and the Nuffield Foundation. The main project team consisted of

Lawrence Stenhouse (Director), Gillian Box (1967–70), Ann Cook, (1967–68), John Elliott (1967–72), Patricia Haikin (1968–70), Jim Hillier (1968–69), John Hipkin (1968–72), Andrew McTaggart (1969–70), Maurice Plaskow (1967–70), Jean Rudduck (1968–72), Diana Vignali (1968–69). In addition the HCP evaluation team included: Barry MacDonald (Director), Stephen Humble (from 1969) and Gajendra Verma (from 1970).

26 Stenhouse, L. 'Values Curriculum' Humanities Curriculum Project, 3 October 1967: HCP Archive CARE, University of East Anglia, Norwich.

27 See Stenhouse, L. (1975) *An Introduction to Curriculum Research and Development*, London: Heinemann.

28 Ibid., p. 82.

29 Ibid.

30 Ibid., p. 5.

31 Some years later, reviewing the lessons to be learnt from a century of public school reform in the USA, David Tyack and Larry Cuban were to make a similar point about policies. They suggested that the educational goals and plans of policy makers might profitably be construed as hypotheses. Tyack, D. and Cuban, L. (1995) *Tinkering Toward Utopia*, Cambridge, Mass: Harvard University Press.

32 Pring, R. (1971) 'Bloom's Taxonomy: A Philosophical Critique (2)', *Cambridge Journal of Education*, 1 (2): 83–91.

33 See Madaus, G. and Sufflebeam, D. (eds) (1989) *Educational Evaluation: Classic Works of Ralph W. Tyler*, London: Kluwer.

34 Adelman, C., Jenkins, D. and Kemmis, S. (1976) 'Re-thinking Case Study: notes from the second Cambridge Conference', *Cambridge Journal of Education*, 6 (3); Jenkins, D., Simons, H. and Walker, R. (1981) 'Thou Art my Goodness: naturalistic inquiry in educational evaluation', *Cambridge Journal of Education*, 11 (3); Bridges, D., Elliott, J. and Klass, C. (1986) 'Performance Appraisal as Naturalistic Inquiry: a report from the fourth Cambridge conference', *Cambridge Journal of Education* 16 (3); Stronach, I. and Torrance, H. (1995) 'The Future of Evaluation: a retrospective', *Cambridge Journal of Education*, 25 (3).

35 Marland, M. (1974) *Pastoral Care*, London: Heinemann.

36 Jennings, A. (1985) 'Out of the Secret Garden', in Plaskow, M. (ed.) *Life and Death of the Schools Council*, London: Falmer Press p. 20.

37 The removal of any reference to subjects (with exception of Practical Instruction) in the 1926 Code from the Board of Education meant that the teaching of particular subjects was not a condition of grant. See White, J. (1975) 'The End of the Compulsory Curriculum' University of London, Institute of Education; *The Curriculum – The Doris Lee Lectures 1975*, London: University of London, Institute of Education.

38 See Simon, B. (1991) *Educational and the Social Order*, London: Lawrence & Wishart, especially chapter nine.

39 Kogan, M. (1980) 'Policies for the School Curriculum in their Political Context', *Cambridge Journal of Education*, 10 (3): 122–133.

40 Simon, B. (1991) *Educational and the Social Order*, London: Lawrence & Wishart, p. 451.

41 See Judge, H. (1984) 'A Generation of Schooling', Oxford: Oxford University Press, especially Chapter 11. Callaghan's biographer Kenneth Morgan indicates that education was a long-standing concern to Callaghan. See: *Callaghan A Life* (Oxford: Oxford University Press, 1997). Callaghan's commitment to and interest in education is also commented on by Roy Hattersley in his memoirs. He says that when the 1967 devaluation of the pound forced Callaghan to resign from the Treasury, 'his first choice of alternative ministry was the Department of Education and Science'. See: *Fifty Years On – A Prejudiced History of Britain Since the War*, (London: Little, Brown, 1997, p. 241).

42 Reid, W.A. (1983) 'Curriculum Design and Moral Judgement', *Cambridge Journal of Education*, 13 (1): 3–7.

43 Maclure, S. (1978) 'Background to the Accountability Debate', in Becher, T. and Maclure, S. (eds) *Accountability in Education*, Windsor, Berks: NFER Publishing Co.

44 House, E. (1975) 'Accountability in the USA', *Cambridge Journal of Education*, 5 (2): 71–78.

45 Bonnett, M. (1976) 'Authenticity, Autonomy and Compulsory Curriculum', *Cambridge Journal of Education*, 6 (3): 107–121.

46 Noddings, N. (2005) 'Identifying and Responding to Needs in Education', *Cambridge Journal of Education*, 35 (2): 147–159.

47 Blackstone, T. (1967) 'The Plowden Report', *British Journal of Sociology*, 18: 291–302.

48 *Early Leaving*, Report of the Central Advisory Council for Education (England), London: HMSO; *Fifteen to Eighteen*, Report of the Central Advisory Council for Education (England) – The Crowther Report – HMSO, 1959; *Half our Future*, Report of the Central Advisory Council for Education (England) – The Newsom Report – HMSO, 1963; *Children and their Primary Schools*, Report of the Central Advisory Council for Education (England) – The Plowden Report – HMSO, 1967.

49 Douglas, J.W.B. (1964) *The Home and the School*, London: Macgibbon & Kee, p. 118.

50 Kerckhoff, A.C. (1986) 'Effects of Ability Grouping in British Secondary Schools', American Sociological Review, 51 (6): 842–858.

51 Florian, L. & Rouse, M. (2001) 'Editorial', *Cambridge Journal of Education*, 31 (3): 285.

52 Ibid.

53 Florian, L., Rouse, M., Black-Hawkins, K. and Jull, S. (2004) 'What Can National Data Sets Tell us about Inclusion and Pupil Achievement?', *British Journal of Special Education*, 31 (3): 115–121.

54 See Gayford, C. (1991) 'Environmental Education – a Question of Emphasis in the School Curriculum', *Cambridge Journal of Education* 21 (1): 73–78; Bonnett, M. (1998) 'Environmental Education and Primary School Children's Attitudes towards Nature and Environment', *Cambridge Journal of Education* 28 (2): 159–175.

55 See Posch, P. (1991) 'Environment and Schools Initiative: background and basic premises of the project', CERI, *Environment, Schools and Active Learning*, Paris: OECD.

56 Brice Heath, S. (1983) *Ways with Words – Language, life, and work in communities and classrooms*, Cambridge: Cambridge University Press.

57 Her work on these issues goes back to the Humanities Curriculum Project and her subsequent research on pupil perspectives and the role of pupils in innovation.

58 Nel Noddings has been a long time advocate of more caring forms of education built on trust and an ethic of care. Also see, for example: Noddings, N. (2002) *Starting at Home: caring and social policy*, Berkeley, CA: University of California Press; Noddings, N. (2003) *Caring – a Feminine Approach to Ethics and Moral Education*, Berkeley, CA: University of California Press (second edition, first published 1984); Noddings, N. (1992) *The Challenge to Care in Schools: an alternative approach to education*, New York: Teachers College Press.

59 Noddings, N. (2005) 'Identifying and Responding to Needs in Education', *Cambridge Journal of Education*, 35 (2): 147–159.

60 Kress, G. (2000) 'A Curriculum for the Future', *Cambridge Journal of Education*, 30 (1): 141.

61 Willard Waller did his undergraduate studies at the University of Illinois, an MA at Chicago and a PhD at the University of Pennsylvania. With Talcott Parsons he was elected to the Sociological Research Association in 1938. He was president of the Eastern Sociological Society in 1940, a significant achievement and mark of recognition. He died of a heart attack aged forty-six. See Joseph Folsom's obituary 'Willard Waller, 1899–1945' *Marriage and Family Living*, 7 (4); Goode, W.J., Furstenberg, F.F. and Mitchell, L.R. (eds) (1970) *Willard W. Waller*, Chicago: University of Chicago Press.

62 Waller, W. (1932) *The Sociology of Teaching*, New York: Wiley.

63 Goode, W.J., Furstenberg, F.F. and Mitchell, L.R. (eds) (1970), op. cit. 57.

64 Waller, W. (1932) op. cit. p. 375.

65 Gabriel, J. (1957) *An Analysis of the Emotional Problems of the Teacher in the Classroom*, London: Angus & Robertson.

66 Ibid., p. 2.

67 Ibid., pp. 120–121.

68 Jersild, A. (1955) *When Teachers Face Themselves*, New York, Columbia University: Teachers College Press, p. 14.

69 Jackson, P. (1990) *Life in Classrooms*, New York: Teachers College Columbia (reissued with a new introduction, first published 1968), p. xxi.

70 The teachers were selected with the help of administrators and supervisors who were asked to identify a group of outstanding teachers. The sample was mostly drawn from suburban communities surrounding Chicago. The tape-recorded interviews focused on how the teachers knew they were doing a good job in the classroom, the relationship between work and the institutional framework of schooling and the personal satisfactions of teaching. See Jackson, P. (1990) chapter 4.

71 Ibid., p. 154.

72 See 'Appendix A Sample Description', in Lortie, D. (1975) *Schoolteacher: a sociological study*, Chicago: University of Chicago Press.

73 Lortie, D. (1975) *Schoolteacher: a sociological study*, Chicago: University of Chicago Press p. 187.

74 Ibid., p. 212.

75 Interestingly the book is dedicated 'to the unnamed driver of the Corporation refuse-collection van' who helped Nias 'rake through a quarter of a ton of urban garbage to rescue the first set of interviews which had been inadvertently consigned to the university dustbins by over-zealous cleaners'.

76 See Nias, J. (1989) *Primary Teachers Talking – A Study of Teaching as Work*, London: Routledge, p. 5.

77 House, E.R. (1974) *The Politics of Educational Innovation*, Berkeley, CA: McCutchan.

78 "Teachers' stories and stories about teachers" is a phrase that Michael Connelly and Jean Clandinin use. See Connelly, M. and Clandinin, D.J. (1990) 'Stories of Experience and Narrative Inquiry', *Educational Researcher*, 19 (5): 2–14.

79 Holly, M.J. (1989) 'Reflective Writing and the Spirit of Inquiry', *Cambridge Journal of Education*, 19 (1): 78.

80 See for example: Cooper, D. and Ebbutt D. (1974) 'Participation in Action Research as an In-service Experience', *Cambridge Journal of Education*, 4 (2): 65–71; Brooks, E. (1984) 'Action Research in the Classroom: A case study and a case record', *Cambridge Journal of Education*, 14 (2): 18–25; Keiny, S. (1985) 'Action Research in the School', *Cambridge Journal of Education*, 15 (3): 148–145; Walker, M. (1988) 'Thoughts on the Potential of Action Research in South African Schools', *Cambridge Journal of Education*, 18 (2): 147–154; Somekh, B. (1991) 'Pupil Autonomy with Microcomputers: rhetoric or reality? An Action Research Study', *Cambridge Journal of Education*, 21 (1): 47–64; Lomax, P. and Parker, Z. (1995) 'Accounting for Ourselves: the problematic of representing action research', *Cambridge Journal of Education*, 25 (2): 301–314.

81 Adelman, C. (1993) 'Kurt Lewin and the Origins of Action Research', *Educational Action Research*, 1 (1): 7–24. For a contrasting account of the origins of action research see Bain, R. (1951) 'Action Research and Group Dynamics', *Social Forces*, 30 (1): 1–10.

82 Carr, W. and Kemmis, S. (1986) *Becoming Critical: knowing through Action Research*, London: Falmer Press.

83 Gibson, R. (1983) 'Critical Times for Action Research', *Cambridge Journal of Education*, 15 (1): 59–64. A reply by Stephen Kemmis was published in 16 (1): 50–52.

84 For example, Tichen, A. and Manley, K. (2006) 'Spiralling Towards Transformational Action Research: philosophical and practical journeys', *Educational Action Research*, 14 (3): 333–356.

85 For example: Elliott, J. (2005) 'Becoming Critical: the failure to connect', *Educational Action Research*, 13 (3): 359–373.

86 'Research as a Basis for Teaching' was the title of Lawrence Stenhouse's inaugural lecture. It was published in Stenhouse, L. (1983) *Authority, Education and Emancipation*, London: Heinemann.

87 In 1973, Margaret Thatcher, Secretary for Education, set up a Committee of Enquiry,

chaired by Mary Warnock, to consider the needs of handicapped children and young people. The Committee reported in 1978, affirming that the aims of education were the same for all children and endorsing the principle of integrating students with disabilities into ordinary schools. See: *Report of the Committee of Enquiry into the Education of Handicapped Children and Young People*, London: HMSO – The Warnock Report.

88 Department for Education and Skills (2003) *Excellence and Enjoyment: a strategy for primary schools*, London: DfES, Reference Number DfES0377/2003.

89 Simon, B. (1981) 'Why no Pedagogy in England?', in B. Simon and W. Taylor (eds) *Education in the Eighties*, London: Batsford Academic, pp. 124–145.

90 Ibid., p. 141.

91 Alexander, R. (2004) 'Still no Pedagogy? Principle, pragmatism and compliance in primary education', *Cambridge Journal of Education*, 34 (1): 11.

92 Ibid., p. 28.

93 Weaver, T. (1979) 'Education: retrospect and prospect: an administrator's testimony', *Cambridge Journal of Education*, 9 (1): 16.

Part I

Defining the curriculum problem

1   Defining the curriculum problem

Lawrence Stenhouse[*][†]

On my desk before me is a book of 350 pages. It is called *Mønsterplan for Grunnskolen*.[1] I bought it in a bookshop in Oslo. It is the curriculum of the Norwegian comprehensive school. Beside it is an Open University coursebook, *Thinking about the Curriculum*. On page 91 I read:

> What we shall do here is to offer a definition which can serve temporarily both as a starting point for our discussion and as a comfort for those who like to have precise statements as a guideline for their thinking. However, as you will find, we qualify this definition constantly as we develop our ideas in the units that follow. It is no "catch-all" definition by any means, and should never be regarded as such. Here it is:
>
>> A curriculum is the offering of socially valued knowledge, skills and attitudes made available to students through a variety of arrangements during the time they are at school, college or university.[2]

Is the *mønsterplan* a curriculum? Or is the curriculum what happens in Norwegian schools?

If the latter, I shall never know it. I cannot get five years' leave of absence to attempt to describe all the diverse things that happen in Norwegian schools. And five years is not enough.

I asked a Norwegian curriculum research worker if the *mønsterplan* was followed in the schools. He said that it was widely followed, but that many older teachers resisted it and did not follow it, particularly in methods. There was, however, little reformist departure from it. Only tradition seemed strong enough to resist it. Tradition in a sense kept alive the old curriculum of the unreformed school.

How far does the curriculum tie the teacher down? (I asked). If I observe him in the classroom, how much of what I see is determined by the *mønsterplan*?

I was told that the teacher always had the *mønsterplan* in mind, but that it left him a fair degree of individual freedom. It defined a minimum coverage of subject matter and the outline of a method.

It sounded like a child's colouring book, I thought.

I find the definitions of curriculum I have come across unsatisfactory, because the problems of curriculum I have encountered in practice as a curriculum research worker slip through them. Perhaps, then, it would be better to attempt to define "the curriculum problem".

The curriculum problem most simply and directly stated is that of relating ideas to realities, the curriculum in the mind or on paper to the curriculum in the classroom.

The curriculum problem lies in the relationship of the *mønsterplan* to the practice of the Norwegian school.

Notionally the essence of curriculum might be located in the relation of my own ideas as a teacher to the reality of my classroom: "the true blueprint is in the minds and hearts of the teachers".[3] But the plural here is important. Except for empirical micro-studies of the classroom, the private curriculum of the individual teacher is not of central interest. What is of practical importance in curriculum work is the public curriculum or curricula, that is, curricula that can be held to be in some sense and to some extent publicly accessible to "the minds and hearts" of many teachers.

Thus, a curriculum may be said to be an attempt to define the common ground shared by those teachers who follow it. Although it may sometimes be useful to think of it as the offering to pupils, we must always bear in mind that any similarity between the offering in one classroom and another, in one school and another, must begin in the like-mindedness of teachers.

Most commonly this like-mindedness is a matter of tradition. Induction into the profession includes induction into the curriculum. The formulation of the curriculum tradition may be partly a matter of paper syllabuses, even government reports or Handbooks of Suggestions to Teachers, but it is largely an oral process. And it is often largely oblique, the indirect communication of assumptions and premises through discourse which rests on them rather than states them.

This curriculum tradition is potent. Some mastery of it is required of the new teacher before he be accepted as a "professional"; so the teacher learns to define himself by it. In so far as it is not formally stated, analysed and defended, the traditional curriculum is not easily subjected to criticism. In so far as it is institutionalised in the school system, the school, textbooks and the classroom, the traditional curriculum, however critical I may be of it, is not easy to escape. And as the observation of my Norwegian acquaintance suggests, the traditional curriculum is a force strong enough to resist all the pressures of a centralised educational system where, as is the case in Norway, policies are based on a remarkable degree of social consensus.

Philosophers are likely to be impatient of the traditional curriculum because it is so badly formulated, and its position is so strong that its adherents can afford to neglect justification of their position. Social reformers who, unable to create a new society through political action, hope to do so through the schools are also impatient of the traditional curriculum. It holds the old order in place.

But it is not necessary to question the school either philosophically or socially to want to change the curriculum. Even in its own terms the traditional curriculum is unsuccessful. The greater part of any population is not in the traditional sense either educated or accomplished.

This is not because teachers and educational administrators are uncommonly stupid or lazy or inefficient. It is just that schools are, like factories or shops or football teams, ordinary and imperfect human institutions. We sometimes appear to forget that this much will always be inevitable. Perhaps the school's commitment to educational ideals and high principles fosters optimism.

Curriculum change is necessary and, if it is of real significance, difficult. It is bound to be partial and piecemeal even in centralised systems where educational edicts by no means always command those to whom they are addressed. It always has to fight the comfort of tradition. "Habits are comfortable, easy and anxiety-free".[4] For a teacher, taking up a new curriculum is as difficult as going on to a rigorous diet.

In short, it is difficult to relate new ideas to realities.

The problem is to produce a specification to which teachers can work in the classroom, and thus to provide the basis for a new tradition. That specification needs to catch the implication of ideas for practice.

A curriculum is a specification which can be worked to in practice.

A new curriculum will never be secure until it accumulates around it a tradition. The strain of a uniformly self-conscious and thoughtful approach to curriculum is in the long run intolerable. No doubt self-critical analysis is always desirable, but not analysis of everything. New curricula, too, however much the idealist may regret it, must develop comfortable, easy and anxiety-free habits – though not be captured by them.

A new curriculum expresses ideas in terms of practice and disciplines practice by ideas. It is, I would maintain, the best way of dealing in educational ideas. In curriculum the educationist's feet are kept on the earth by the continual need to submit his proposals to the critical scrutiny of teachers working with them in practice. And because they are related to practice, ideas become the possession of the teacher.

The ideas of a curriculum must be understood, and understood in their relation to practice. The practice of a curriculum must be subject to review in the light of understanding of ideas, but much of it must be learnable as skills and habits. All action cannot be reflective and deliberate.

If curriculum change depends on the writing of specifications of ideas in terms of practice, how are we to do this? There appear to be some working in the curriculum field who believe we can do this by taking thought. I believe that we can only do so by observing classrooms. If a curriculum specification is to inform practice, it must be founded on practice.

The central problem of curriculum is in curriculum change and consists in the task of relating ideas to practice by producing – in whatever form – a specification which shall express an idea or set of ideas in terms of practice with sufficient detail and complexity for the ideas to be submitted *to* the criticism of practice and modified by practice with due regard to coherence and consistency as well as piecemeal "effectiveness".

Such specifications can only be written from the study of classrooms.

It follows that a new curriculum must be implemented in practice before it is defined. A group of people, usually including curriculum workers and teachers, must work together and in dialogue on defined problems and tasks until they begin to develop a new tradition which is a response to those problems and tasks. This tradition must then be translated into a specification which transmits the experience captured by the experimental teachers to their colleagues at large.

Exploration must precede survey, survey must precede charting.

This is the basic justification for curriculum experiment.

Notes and references

* Lawrence Stenhouse is Director of the Centre for Applied Research in Education, University of East Anglia.

† Originally published in: *Cambridge Journal of Education* 5: 2, 104–108.

1 *Mønsterplan for Grunnskolen*. Midlertidig utgave. Oslo: Aschehoug, 1971.

2 Bell, Robert, *Thinking about the Curriculum*. "The Curriculum: Context, Design and Development. Unit 1." Bletchley: The Open University Press, 1971.

3 Spears, Harold, *The High School for Today*. New York: American Book Company, 1950, p. 27 quoted in Short, Edmund C and Marconnit, George D., *Contemporary Thought on Public School Curriculum*. Dubuque, Iowa: Wm. C. Brown, 1968.

4 Rubin, Louis, *A Study of Teacher Retraining*. Santa Barbara: University of California, Centre for Co-ordinated Education quoted in MacDonald, B. and Rudduck, Jean, "Curriculum Research and development projects: barriers to success". *British Journal of Educational Psychology*, 41, 2, June 1971, pp. 148–154.

2 Bloom's taxonomy

A philosophical critique (1)

Hugh Sockett[*][†]

The Curriculum Reform Movement in this country has not so far developed any distinctive theoretical foundations in what American scholars call the field of Curriculum. No doubt historians of Education will be able to provide a coherent explanation of this, not unrelated perhaps to the fact that the prime mover in English Curriculum Reform, the Schools Council, has seen its central task to be the production of materials for use in schools: financial considerations have allowed some Project Directors no more than a quick glance at their theoretical foundations. The practical results of this policy will have to be evaluated in due course. However, the fact is that Curriculum Developers and Planners in this country have inevitably looked to American Curriculum Theory to provide a rationale or a theoretical foundation for their problems of curriculum construction and evaluation.

The Taxonomy of Educational Objectives[1] is one of the major works in the field of Curriculum, to be ranked alongside a slimmer but equally influential work, Preparing Instructional Objectives, by R. F. Mager. In this country the influence of the Taxonomy grows apace. The North West Regional Curriculum Development Group,[2] perhaps the most systematic attempt on a large scale to tackle the problems of raising the school leaving age, sees it as a 'model for pupil growth'. Wiseman and Pidgeon in their missionary monograph Curriculum Evaluation[3] see it, with Scriven's amendments, as a crucial contribution to planning and evaluation. In articles on Craft Education,[4] and Further Education[5] and again in a recent book on Environmental Studies,[6] the Taxonomy is used as theoretical under-pinning.

If empirical validation of the Taxonomy has so far been relatively scarce, philosophical criticism has been positively scanty.[7] It seems appropriate therefore to devote some attention to the philosophical issues the Taxonomy raises, particularly as they occur in the first volume: the Cognitive Domain. If the proffered criticisms are valid, Projects which depend on the Taxonomy must be theoretically suspect. The overriding criticism is that the Taxonomy operates with a naive theory of knowledge which cannot be ignored however classificatory and neutral its intentions: this will be developed in this paper and in a subsequent article by Richard Pring.

I

The context in which the Taxonomy is to be viewed is of considerable importance, and it would require more than a short paper to set this out in more than crude and simple terms. The following account must therefore be seen with this qualification in mind.

Rational Curriculum Planning, it is held, is both desirable and possible. An 'ideal' model of the Rational Curriculum Plan can be extrapolated from the various Curriculum models published. Such a model distinguishes between:

1   *Ends*, i.e.   a   Values
                    b   General Educational Aims (derived from (a)) and
                    c   Specific Objectives (derived from (b))

2   *Means*, i.e.   Units of instruction, learning experiences, etc., containing statements of both content and method.

The objectives are seen as statements of behavioural goals. Since Education is seen as changing behaviour, the precise way in which behaviour is to be changed has to be carefully delineated. One thus plans a learning experience to bring about a behavioural goal: one selects a means to achieve an end.

The variations on this 'ideal' model are considerable. A most important variable is the precise position of content within it. Ralph Tyler, the acknowledged source in the Taxonomy for the model in accordance with which the Taxonomy is worked out, argues that 'a statement of objectives clear enough to be used as guiding the selection of learning experiences and in planning instruction will indicate *both* the kind of behaviour to be developed in the student *and* the area of content or of life in which the behaviour is to be applied'.[8] Goodlad,[9] although he sees the model from a different perspective, labels these elements within statements of objectives, the 'behavioural' and the 'substantive' elements. This would of course put some statements of content within statements of objectives. Wheeler and others, however, appear to regard content as firmly embedded within statements of means, i.e. learning experiences and instructional units.

The major assumption underlying this model is what Lindblom[10] has called a 'rational-comprehensive' model of decision making. Two of the main characteristics of this model are: a) the clarification of values, and b) the means–ends analysis.

a   Values and objectives are clarified separately from, usually as a prerequisite to, the empirical analysis of alternative policies (i.e. curriculum strategies).
b   The test of a good learning experience (instructional unit or whatever) given this rigid separation of means and ends, is how far the means are appropriate to the desired ends.

This 'ideal' model seems to impose a Behaviourist view of learning on the curriculum. Learning is responding to a stimulus: the response is the behavioural outcome or objective. The teacher, in this case, can be said to be bringing about certain changes in behaviour, ends which he desires, by the use of certain means.

In the Taxonomy the precise view of learning is unclear, for the content does appear to be part of a complete statement of objectives, though as a matter of fact Bloom and his associates are not concerned with this substantial element. However, even to posit – for whatever purposes – this separation of behaviour and content leads to considerable difficulties.

It is not the object of this article to argue that detailed analysis of what teachers want children to learn is undesirable, nor is it being argued that the means–ends model is necessarily useless in considerations of Curriculum Planning. Indeed it may in some contexts be positively helpful provided one is clear that the relationship is not just de facto: there may be, indeed there are, certain logically necessary conditions to the achievement of any given end and to work these out in logical terms may be a useful aid to curriculum planning.

The context in which the Taxonomy is to be viewed, then, is that of an 'ideal' model of the Curriculum in which ends are rigidly distinguished from means and a distinction is made between the behavioural and substantive elements of any particular instructional objective.

II

What is it that Bloom *et al.* are classifying and what are the organising principles of their classification in the cognitive domain? 'What we are classifying is the *intended behaviour* of students – the ways in which individuals are to act, think and feel as a result of participating in some unit of instruction'.[11] 'Educational objectives stated in behavioural form have their counterparts in the behaviour of individuals. Such behaviour can be observed and described, and these descriptive statements can be classified'.[12] The emphasis on the behaviour-content dichotomy is maintained: 'We determined which part of the objective stated the behaviour intended and which stated the content or object of the behaviour. We then attempted to find divisions or groups into which the behaviours could be placed…'[13]

Now the declared purpose of the Taxonomy is to introduce greater precision into the specification of objectives. It is possible however to classify a range of objectives into differently related groups without making each class of objectives any more precise. Let us assume that to say of someone that he has an objective x is to say (a) that he desires x, and (b) that x can be specified in some detail. Let us say further that he has a range of objectives x, xi, x2, etc., which could perhaps be related together in terms of some general aim. Now one *could* classify the different statements of objectives which make up his general aim on a continuum based on the number of words in each sentence in which he makes his statements of objectives. On this classification, when new objectives appeared, the criteria for classification into short, middling or long sentences would be fairly clear and we could classify them accordingly. This would have nothing to do with what he was actually trying to *achieve*. If one is to be specific about a classification of objectives, it must at least be possible (if the classification is to be of any use) easily to recognise instances – in this case instances of whether the sentence in which the objective is expressed is short, middling or long according to the criteria.

Now Bloom *et al.* take such educational objectives as intended behaviours to be such behaviours as 'remembering, reasoning, concept-formation, problem-solving, creative thinking'.[14] What precisely is an instance of 'remembering'? (Note that, on these terms, the behaviour 'remembering' is not to be confused with 'remembering p' for 'p' is the substantive element). It is not apparent that we have any criteria at all for noticing instances of observable, describable behaviours called 'remembering'. We are told simply that it is a psychological process. The difficulty is two-fold. First everything we do, as opposed to things that happen to us, could be seen as an instance of remembering. At this level I remember how to walk when I jump out of bed in the morning, I remember my wife's birthday and I remember the complex details of a traffic accident when asked to recount them from the witness box. Second 'remembering' is unintelligible just as a psychological *process* (even if we lay aside its counterpart – forgetting) for we remember *something*, cases of remembering are cases of being *right* about what was or is the case. We cannot posit remembering in any sense *apart* from content. If remembering is thought of as content-free we have an empty concept which could not be even part of an educational objective. Bloom *et al.* do not give us any criteria for noticing instances of remembering as such: because there aren't any.

The same is true of the other 'behaviours'. Take concept-formation. Are there criteria for this as a behaviour devoid of the content that would be supplied by any particular concept that is being formed? It is possible to suggest criteria for testing a person's understanding of a particular concept, and to formulate some general rules for 'having a concept', but what is it to exhibit this behaviour content-free as if forming a concept were like batting an eyelid? Now it may be objected that this is to misunderstand Bloom, for put like this, it is so manifestly incoherent. It may be said that if this is seen as a classification on certain principles, and if this is seen within a context of evaluating a student's performance and planning his learning experience, so the usefulness of the classification of 'intended behaviours' will become apparent. But it is interesting to note Bloom's qualification on this point: 'we have not succeeded in finding a method of classification which would permit complete and sharp distinctions among behaviours': that is, the criteria for calling any piece of behaviour a case of remembering as opposed to reasoning are unclear. The reasons given for this difficulty by Bloom *et al.* are that (a) 'two boys may appear to be doing the same thing; but if we analyse the situation, we find that they are not': and (b) 'that the more complex behaviours include the simpler behaviours': i.e. that instances of reasoning will include instances of remembering and not vice versa.

This latter qualification is unacceptable. If the classification is of specific objectives, and this is thought to be in principle possible, albeit in a taxonomic form, there must be criteria at the simple level and criteria for distinguishing radically different behaviours at the more complex levels. If there are not behavioural criteria for distinguishing different pieces of behaviour (e.g. remembering), (although this might still count as a classification of behaviour) it lacks any value as a classification of educational objectives since it lacks the specificity it was conceived to promote. The first qualification is thought to be soluble in principle given a sufficient analysis of the 'experiential background of the pupils'. Information of this kind however cannot help to demarcate specific criteria for different behaviours. Explicit reference has to be made to the content (in this case, learning algebra) for the problem to be coherent. Thus

a   the notion of a content-free behaviour is unintelligible, and
b   the claim to provide a classification of objectives as intended behaviours runs
    into difficulties. It cannot be specific, because there is nothing to be specific
    about.

Locked in the assertion of 'behavioural' and 'substantive' elements within educational objectives, Bloom *et al.* are obliged either to abandon specificity or look at
particular (i.e. not content-free) situations.

III

The reasons for some of these difficulties are to be found in the statements made
on the organising principles of the classification: 'The taxonomy should be an educational – logical – psychological classification system' but the educational considerations are of first importance in that boundaries between categories should be
closely related to the 'distinctions that teachers make in planning curricula or
learning situations'.[15] Teachers, we are told, do not make the kinds of distinctions
a psychologist would make, but the psychological distinctions, where they conflict
with the distinctions made by teachers, are 'favourably considered' for inclusion, as
are relevant and important psychological distinctions *not* made by teachers. In
practice this means that the psychological considerations are overriding. The taxonomy is also based on logical considerations in that terms are defined as precisely
as possible and used consistently.
    There are therefore three principles at work in the construction of the Taxon-
omy:

a   the educational principle is that boundaries between categories are closely
    related to the distinctions teachers actually make.
b   the psychological principle is that where distinctions are made by teachers
    which conflict with established psychological theories or evidence, the latter
    should override the former, and where 'important' psychological distinctions
    are neglected, they should be incorporated.
c   the logical principle is that terms should be denned precisely and used consis-
    tently.

Presumably the authors were presented with a battery of statements of educational objectives: the only way in which they characterised them as *educational* was
that they emanated from teachers: the educational principle is thus simply descriptive and secondary to psychological principles. Even here, however, where
teachers' statements did not lend themselves to specificity, in Bloom *et al.*'s view,
they were ignored, as in the quoted case of getting children to 'understand
Society'. Of course, if the criteria for classification had been between general and
specific objectives, rather than the vague non-criteria we are offered, such an educational objective would have found a place.
    The most important point however is that Philosophy is conceived in the Tax-
onomy as vaguely to do with values: since the Taxonomists claim to be neutral in

their classification, they consider that they need not concern themselves with philosophical issues. The logical principle is limited to internal consistency between what are intended as precisely used definitions. Now it is one thing to produce a coherent, i.e. *internally consistent*, classification or taxonomy: it remains a further question whether there is any correspondence between those definitions and divisions that might be made by philosophers working in theory of knowledge or indeed in our everyday discourse.

For instance, chess is internally consistent: the complex network of rules fit together and definitions (naming pieces, etc.) are regularly applied. It would make no difference to the game if, for stranger reasons than might occur to arch-republicans, the Queen were called 'Knowledge', the King 'Belief', the Bishops 'Truths' and Pawns 'Facts'. Some damage would however be done to our conceptions of Knowledge, Belief, Truth and Fact if we began talking about truth moving diagonally, or my checkmating your Belief with my Knowledge and a couple of Facts. For such a classification as Bloom's to have any bite on what we do and how we think about educational problems, we would need to be sure that the way in which the terms operate within this internally consistent system do in fact relate to the way in which we use these words, or, if some dramatic new use of these concepts is being suggested, we would require to know just how cogent the novelty is.

The major difficulties which this problem poses for the Taxonomy cannot be dealt with in any detail here. Two examples, one general and one specific, may suffice. The division of the Cognitive Domain into Knowledge *and* Intellectual Skills and Abilities, while a possible means of classification, assumes that such a separation makes some kind of sense: but in the range of things we are said to 'know' in the first part there are necessarily embedded all manner of 'intellectual skills and abilities'. 'To define technical terms by giving their attributes, properties or relations' (an example of knowledge of Terminology (i. n)) presupposes and contains the ability to understand concepts related to each other in distinct way, and to understand a concept is to know how to use it. A specific example of the breathtaking naivety of the Bloom epistemology appears in i. 12 (Knowledge of Specific Facts) classed as 'Knowledge of Dates, Events, Persons, Places',[16] as if they were all on the same logical (or even psychological) plane; knowing (or even remembering) a person is very different from knowing of a particular event. The criteria we would use for claiming to know a person or an event are complex and quite different.

The Taxonomy therefore has to be seen as a taxonomy of cognitive processes – if one could be sure what they are. Whether it then has any use as a taxonomy of educational objectives is a further question. Certainly taking statements from teachers, imposing an incoherent set of criteria of classification and then supposing that what results constitutes a taxonomy of *educational objectives* is more than suspect. If these classifications are of instances of cognitive processes, to rank them in a simple-complex hierarchy either means that as a matter of fact people find reasoning more difficult than remembering – which may or may not be true – or that there are logical complexities in reasoning not present in remembering, which has not been shown. For to discuss this problem coherently there has to be a classification of content, and that the taxonomists do not undertake.

In summary therefore, the Taxonomy rests on the possible distinction between behavioural and substantive elements in statements of educational objectives. This conception is incoherent, but is to be seen within the particular context of the 'ideal' model outlined as the Rational Curriculum Plan, with its means–ends analysis. Second, in persisting with this division the attempt to specify, i.e. delineate criteria for different behaviours, runs into difficulties, not merely because it cannot be done without specifying a content, but simply because there are none. Third, the organising principles boil down to a psychological principle: Philosophy is emasculated via logic to mean internal consistency, and Education is merely a label. The result is that philosophical work in the Theory of Knowledge which has a prima facie claim for inclusion is ignored. Whether a taxonomy of cognitive processes itself would be useful within psychology is one problem: whether this has any relevance at all to the classification of educational objectives, stated in behavioural terms or not, is a further question.

Notes

* Hugh Sockett is Research Fellow at the Cambridge Institute of Education.
† Originally published in: *Cambridge Journal of Education* 1: 1, 16–25.
1 Bloom, Benjamin S. *et al. Taxonomy of Educational Objectives*. Longman, London 1966.
2 Following the publication of their pamphlet 'Forward From Newson: A Call to Action' in November 1966, this Project, supported by 13 LEA's and the University of Manchester School of Education, has published detailed statements of 'General Objectives' and 'Specific Objectives' through different subject panels: see particularly 'General Objectives' pp. 35–48.
3 Wiseman, S. and Pidgeon, D. *Curriculum Evaluation: NFER 1970*. pp. 67–70.
4 Sumner, R. *The Objectives of Craft Education. The Vocational Aspect of Education* (Summer 1968) Vol. XX, No. 46, pp. 137–149.
5 Bennett, Y. R. *The Range of Goals and Objectives in Industrial Training and Further Education. The Vocational Aspect of Education* (Autumn 1969) Vol. XXI, No. 50, pp. 113–118.
6 Watts, D. G. *Environmental Studies*, Routledge and Kegan Paul 1969 pp. 77–78.
7 But see Gribble, J. H. 'Pandora's Box: The Affective Domain of Educational Objectives' in *Journal of Curriculum Studies*; Vol. II, No. 1, May 1970: and Morshead, R. W. 'Review of Taxonomy of Educational Objectives', Vol. II in *Studies in Philosophy and Education* IV. 1. (Spring 1965) 164–170: and Kerr, J. F. *Changing the Curriculum*, University of London Press 1968: esp. article by P. H. Hirst.
8 Tyler, R. W. *Basic Principles of Curriculum and Instruction*. University of Chicago Press 1949 p. 48.
9 Goodlad, John E. and Richter, Maurice N. *The Development of a Conceptual System of Dealing with Problems of Curriculum and Instruction, Report of an Inquiry supported by the Cooperative Research Programme of the Office of Education, U.S. Department of Health, Education and Welfare*. Mimeographed copy: University of California, Los Angeles.
10 Lindblom, C. E. 'The Science of Muddling-Through'. Public Administration Review 1959, reprinted in Gore, W. J. and Dyson, J. W. *The Making of Decisions*, Free Press of Glencoe 1964.
11 Vol. I op. cit., p. 12: Note means-ends terminology.
12 Op. cit., p. 5.
13 Op. cit., p. 15.
14 Op. cit., pp. 15/16.
15 Op. cit., pp. 13/14 and Chapter 2.
16 Op. cit., p. 201.

3 Bloom's taxonomy

A philosophical critique (2)

*Richard Pring**[*][†]

I

In the first issue of the Journal, Hugh Sockett argued that the Taxonomy adopts a means/end model of curriculum planning, in which the curriculum planner pre-specifies the behaviours he wants the student to learn and then chooses the means (the learning experiences) by which these objectives might be reached. Criticism of this model for *all* curriculum designs would be twofold. First, it might not be possible to reduce educational objectives to a pre-specified output in terms of certain very specific behaviours. Second, it would seem that the isolation of 'behaviours' (for example, 'remembering') from the learning experiences through which they are to be learnt is not possible where the ends and the means are logically, not contingently, related – *remembering that* William the Conqueror landed in 1066 is a quite different sort of behaviour from that of *remembering how* to ride a bicycle, and the differences in behaviour can only be identified within the particular context. These criticisms are alike in that they both arise from the failure of the Taxonomy to establish a sound epistemological basis for the divisions and subdivisions of cognitive and affective objectives. That there is such a failure, and that this has important implications for the classification, is the subject of my contribution to the criticism of the Taxonomy.

Bloom is concerned with the formulation and classification of educational objectives so that teachers can discuss, communicate, and evaluate what they are doing. It follows from this that questions must arise about what is to count as educational objectives (how one is to set about describing them) and on what principles they are to be classified so that they become manageable teaching units. Because education is centrally concerned with cognitive development in its different modes, such questions about the description and classification of *educational* objectives will necessarily raise epistemological questions about the nature of knowledge, understanding, and so on.

With reference to the first sort of question (namely, that concerned with what are to count as objectives) Bloom would wish to omit from any list of objectives any statement of aims which is so general that it cannot give practical guidance to what to do 'here and now' (for example, 'understanding society'); objectives must be much more specific than that. On the other hand it is not clear how specific any goal has to be before it would count as an objective – whether it has to be as specific and unambiguous as some overt behaviour. The more, however, the description of objectives approximates to a description of overt behaviour, the greater the need to examine the difficulties in translating propositions about the mind into those that describe what can be observed. Such an examination would be essentially philosophical. That what can be described empirically is necessarily a test or criterion for some mental achievement (whether it be knowledge or understanding or so on) is not doubted; that it can be *identified* with such achievements needs to be argued. And until such issues are dealt with explicitly, it is not clear what precisely is meant by 'the intended behaviour of students' which is to be classified.

With reference to the second sort of question (namely, on what principle are these behaviours to be classified), Bloom argues that they are to be classified on educational, logical, and psychological grounds – namely, on the basis of how in fact teachers do classify what they are doing, on the basis of consistency within such a statement of the teacher classification, and in the order of simplicity before complexity. However, such a threefold basis for classifying objectives is inadequate. There is no analysis of what is *meant* by the particular objectives listed. We are told that the list is obtained from teacher statements about what they are doing. But to collect a lot of statements about what teachers see to be their objectives and to think that this is in some way a *comprehensive* collection is not just an empirical matter; decisions about what is to be included in any list of objectives and what the precise relation is between two or more statements of objectives depend upon some analysis of the peculiar things that one is collecting. In the Taxonomy these are concerned with the development of mind, knowledge, understanding, awareness, feeling, attitudes and so on, and thus any list of objectives has necessarily built into it a certain view of knowledge and meaning. If it is a wrong or an incoherent view, then the classification of objectives will itself be either misleading or incoherent. The threefold basis on which the classification is made however makes no attempt to examine whether the implicit theory of knowledge is correct or even hangs together. Bloom just doesn't examine this sort of question. But since they are cognitive and affective objectives that are being classified, this is the most important question to be asking. If it is knowledge you are going to meddle with then you can't ignore what knowledge is – and that is very complicated.

The description and classification of objectives does in this respect go quite wrong in two important places – important because it affects and distorts everything that follows. First, the entire taxonomy depends upon the distinction between the cognitive and the affective domains of objectives. Second, within the cognitive domain, one is asked to distinguish between knowledge and intellectual abilities which themselves are differentiated into comprehension, application, analysis, synthesis, and evaluation. This latter distinction determines the entire hierarchy and organisation of objectives. If the distinction is a nonsense then the entire organisation of objectives will be a nonsense too. And those who lean upon this classification for organising their own curriculum within different subjects will either be creating quite impossible units of instruction (because what is a logical nonsense must be a practical impossibility) or be attaching wrong labels to describe what they are in fact doing. This may not matter too much – educational theory might be described as a systematic mislabelling of what teachers are doing – but it

certainly ensures the very opposite from what Bloom set out to do, namely, facilitating communication – and it may even misguide teachers into doing something
that they ought not to be doing. My more detailed criticism therefore is twofold:
first, it is levelled at the cognitive/affective distinction; second, it is levelled at the
knowledge/intellectual abilities distinction.

II

It may seem trivial to describe in greater detail the distinction between cognitive
and affective but possibly, in being so described, the distinction itself may seem
more obscure, and less serviceable, than common sense would immediately
suggest. The distinction rests upon the belief that the cognitive capacities – the
ability to know and to think and to understand – can be conceptually isolated
from the feeling side of mental life and *analysed* without reference to it
(although, of course, the Taxonomy sees the need to bring the two together after
the analysis). It would follow from this, if it were true, that the cognitive objectives could be isolated from the affective and, as such, form distinctive goals in
directing what the teacher plans and does. But on the other hand, if the analysis
is false – if the cognitive capacities cannot be considered in isolation from the
feeling side of mental life – then any statement of cognitive objectives must
contain also reference to the relevant feelings. And here the argument is quite
simple. It does not make sense to have knowledge as one's objective – the differentiated way in which we come to understand both ourselves and our environment – without the caring about those standards of truth and correctness which
are built into what it *means* to know and to understand and to appreciate. To
think scientifically entails a concern – a feeling, if you like – for the standards of
scientific truth. This partly is what would distinguish knowledge and understanding from mere sophistry and rhetoric, and it has doubtless been part of many
readers' experience how often so called education is reduced to this. If knowledge
and understanding and evaluation – or the various capacities to achieve these –
are to be one's objectives, then inseparable from any such statement of these
objectives will be the stated concern or caring for achieving these objectives and
standards which constitute what it is to know, to understand, and to evaluate.
Even Kant's moral man who acted not according to feeling but in conformity to
the universal law of morality could get going only if he had a feeling of respect
for the law. But such a feeling cannot be isolated as a little thing on its own – to
be a different sort of objective in the affective classification of objectives. It is to
be understood only in its logical connection with the moral objectives which he
spelt out.

Turning to the affective side and looking at that in isolation from the cognitive,
we have an even stronger case in criticising the dichotomy that underlies Bloom's
taxonomy. It is a quite misconceived notion of feelings, valuings, attitudes and all
else that falls under the umbrella of 'the affective' if these are to be understood
without reference to the particular knowledge, understanding, and evaluations by
which they are identified and to which therefore they are logically connected. It is
a logical point to say that the identity of any emotion lies in the sort of judgment

being made and the sort of object to which intentional reference is directed. Thus it does not make sense to talk of 'anger', or 'jealousy' or 'envy' or 'pity' unless there is an object or a person with whom one is angry, or of whom one is jealous or envious, or whom one does pity. Moreover to be angry or jealous or envious or pitying presupposes some prior judgment of the situation – namely, that someone has done something he ought not to have done, or has something which he lacks and to which he thinks he has a right, or has something to which he has no right but would like, or is in a state which is in some way sad. Feelings and their further refinement incorporate a range of judgments both empirical and evaluative, and thus any affective objectives must embody also the appropriate cognitive capacities. It simply does not make sense to talk of attitudes or feelings or sensitivity or valuings without reference to the sort of understandings by which these are identified; and thus to distinguish two domains of objectives – the cognitive and the affective – as though these can be identified as such and as though they separately describe different ranges of objectives, is to set us off on the wrong track from the very beginning. It is of course possible to attempt to organise a curriculum on such misconceptions, but the consequence would be a distortion of valid educational objectives.

Let me illustrate briefly how this might be. In the area of moral education the distinction between the cognitive and the affective would argue for a rational working out of, first, the need for principles, second, those principles which are central to any moral life whatsoever (such as concern for justice, respect for persons, equal consideration of different points of view), and, thirdly, the skills for applying such high level principles to developing practical rules of conduct and the capacity to make correct decisions. It would be a distinct and quite separate task to inculcate the appropriate attitudes and feelings for thinking in these terms (i.e. for engaging in this type of intellectual exercise), for thinking in terms of justice and impartiality, and for abiding by the decision made (intellectually) in the light of these general principles. It is not indeed clear what sort of processes would be involved in inculcating the right feelings at the right places. But the major criticism is that, in any case, the whole enterprise would seem to be misconceived. For this simply is not how the practical mind works, nor indeed is this account based upon any acceptable analysis of the moral judgments made or of the moral attitudes adopted. Any such analysis would reveal the poverty of a moral education that was based upon such a fundamental division of objectives. Aristotle saw the development of virtue to be the central task of moral education. But no analysis of courage or magnanimity etc. could isolate for separate consideration the evaluation of the situation from the appropriate feelings. The cognitive divisions in the moral area of discourse only make sense in the practical context of action and decision-making where one is already motivated to doing something, and the identity of certain feelings necessarily refers to the particular way one has come to distinguish principles, evaluate persons, classify objects, and so on.

III

The second major criticism of Bloom's taxonomy is in the distinction he makes between knowledge and intellectual abilities, namely, comprehension, application, analysis, synthesis, and evaluation. It is not immediately clear what 'knowledge' could be where it is distinguished from comprehension or indeed from application. To say that one *knows* that something is the case, namely, that Henry VIII had six wives or that gases expand when heated, means that one understands not only the concepts employed but also under what sort of conditions these statements might be considered true or false. That is, knowledge entails both comprehension and application – it is not possible to aim at knowledge and *then* at the understanding of this knowledge and *then* at applying it. To know that something is the case entails understanding what it means to say that something is the case and this in turn entails being able to apply this knowledge to particular situations.

This seems such an obvious point that one is forced in justice to examine the precise way in which Bloom is using these terms here. Has he developed a technical use of these terms such that appeal to what they normally mean is just irrelevant? This might be the case. If it is, then one requires two things – first, that the technical use should be clearly defined and, second, that such a use will be preserved consistently throughout the taxonomy. However, upon examination, it is not possible to find a closely defined technical use of these terms which is consistently applied. Either Bloom does try to limit his use of these terms in which case it is not consistently applied or he does not limit his use of these terms, in which case he trades on their ordinary usage and thereby introduces all the complicated epistemology that lies beneath that usage. Even if a technical usage of these terms was introduced and applied consistently, it would not be a suitable framework for the range of possible educational objectives unless the new map of cognition did justice to the many features that are present in our normal cognitive vocabulary. But such a mammoth task is nowhere attempted by Bloom.

I wish to illustrate this very general point by reference to his account of knowledge. He identifies knowledge with remembering or recall. But these terms are by no means precise. Remembering could at one extreme be simply a case of producing a particular response to a particular stimulus on the basis of past experience, and indeed rote learning has much in common with such a model of mental processes. This however must quite clearly be distinguished from remembering where past information is used in a reorganised way for a new type of situation. Remembering in this latter sense presupposes both understanding and application. The former sense of remembering carries with it no reference to understanding or application, and to that extent hardly warrants the description 'knowledge', or 'remembering'. Moreover, it is difficult to see what place such limited objectives could have in an educational programme. The more that remembering is considered without reference to understanding and to application, the less it describes any other process than that of responding to a particular stimulus in a regular way with a pre-programmed set of gestures or sounds. It is possible of course to train someone to respond to a particular stimulus with certain sounds such as 'Henry VIII had six wives', but unless this was more than just a response – unless it was an intelligent application to a particular situation of past information – then the utterance of such sounds would hardly constitute a worthwhile educational objective. Underlying Bloom's analysis of knowledge seems to be the model of a computer controlled filing cabinet. If you press the right button, the right file will pop out – although what is on the file will have to be read by someone else, for the file is but 'knowledge' and cannot either understand or apply.

The general point that I am making here – namely, that, through lack of any epistemological analysis of cognitive processes, the taxonomy makes false distinctions and thereby provides a nonsensical classification – can be illustrated again and again through the book. Take, for example, 'knowledge of specifics', which is to include the hard core of facts and terminology in each field – the elements *to be used* by the specialists. To isolate the facts from the theoretical framework within which these are to be identified *as facts* is to make of them a set of noises, which *might* be repeated upon a given signal but which are removed from the possibility of intelligent grasp or comprehension. Such 'logical atomism' misses the important point that for something to be recognised as a fact requires some comprehension of the concepts employed and thus of the conceptual framework within which the concepts operate. Similarly with regard to the knowledge of terminology, it does not make sense to talk of the knowledge of terms or of symbols in isolation from the *working* knowledge of these terms or symbols, that is, from a comprehension of them and thus an ability to apply them. To dissect the 'cognitive' in this way is, through lack of analysis, to miss the essential unity in the development of thinking. And this is dangerous because it encourages a design of the curriculum in which the output is a set of unconnected skills but not an educated person. This dissection depends upon the logical possibility of providing distinct categories into which behaviours might be slotted. But just as 'knowledge' cannot be distinguished from 'comprehension' or 'application' and so on, so further up the hierarchy of the classification it is impossible to maintain these as distinct classes of behaviour. 'Knowledge of reliable sources of information' must require some comprehension of, say, what it is for these sources to be reliable, and this would require more than a simply 'learning off' someone else's judgment as to their reliability. The behaviour, 'ability to apply principles to new situations', is part of what it means to comprehend those principles – these are not distinct behaviours. Similarly, within the major categories, behaviours are distinguished which cannot logically be separated from other so called behaviours. In so far as 'translation' is part of comprehension, it cannot be distinguished as an identifiable behaviour from 'interpretation'.

IV

To summarise the criticism that I have made: Bloom is concerned with the classification of teaching objectives. In so far as teaching objectives are centrally concerned with the development of mind – with thinking, knowing, understanding, feeling and so on – then the basis of the taxonomy must be some analysis of what it *means* to know, to understand, and so on. Bloom however fails to conduct such an analysis, and he therefore makes distinctions which provide an 'a priori' framework for planning the curriculum that is mistaken. The consequent classification, therefore, either misleads or is quite inadequate for its task. The two fundamental distinctions which distort the whole enterprise are the one he makes between the cognitive and the affective, and the one he makes between knowledge and intellectual abilities. In either case the taxonomy depends upon a dissection of mental processes into behaviours which can be isolated and identified as such. In so far as this dissection is not possible without a total misrepresentation of what is going on (in so far as it makes distinctions which are not logically acceptable) it cannot be the basis for describing educational objectives. The importance of this criticism extends beyond the Taxonomy itself. It embraces all those schemes which adopt the rational curriculum plan described by Hugh Sockett, in which the curriculum planner identifies his behavioural objectives and then chooses those learning experiences which enable him to achieve those objectives. Given this model, then some scheme, such as the Taxonomy presents, must be undertaken in order for these objectives to be described. The failure therefore of the Taxonomy for epistemological reasons to provide an adequate description casts doubt upon the very relevance of such a model to *educational* processes.

Notes

*   Richard Pring is Research Associate at the Cambridge Institute of Education.
†   Originally published in: *Cambridge Journal of Education* 1: 2, 83–91.

4 Re-thinking evaluation

Notes from the Cambridge Conference

Barry MacDonald* and Malcolm Parlett[†‡]

In December 1972 the authors convened a small working conference of people concerned with educational evaluation.[1] The meeting took place at Churchill College, Cambridge, and was financed by the Nuffield Foundation. Its aim was to explore 'non-traditional' modes of evaluation and to set out guidelines for future developments in this field. Participants were chosen for their known reserve about established evaluation practice, or because they had suggested or experimented with new approaches.[2] The conference arose out of preliminary talks between the authors and the officials of the Nuffield Foundation, the Department of Education and Science, and the Centre for Educational Research and Innovation in Paris. These talks had reflected, on the part of these agencies, a general concern that the rapid increase of evaluation activities was not being accompanied by an equivalent surge of new thinking about either evaluation methods or their usefulness for decision-making.

First, a word about the traditional style of evaluation whose continued predominance the conference set out to challenge. Five years ago, at the inaugural meeting of evaluators of Schools Council curriculum projects, the chairman opened the proceedings with the remark: 'Can I assume that we're all familiar with Bloom's Taxonomy of Educational Objectives?' Nobody laughed. The assumption was reasonable, the issue crucial to the matters in hand. Most of those present, novices in the field, shared the chairman's implied view that the task of the evaluator was to determine the congruence of pupil performance and project objectives, i.e. to assess the extent to which pupils exposed to a new curriculum achieved its intended learning outcomes. They were further agreed that the assessment procedures incorporated should be de-personalised and preferably psychometric in form. What could be more central to such a task than the Bloom/Krathwohl formulations of curriculum objectives in terms of measurable learned behaviour!

This model of evaluation stemmed from a long established and securely rooted tradition of educational measurement on both sides of the Atlantic. It had been a dominant influence in American education since its prototype was launched by Ralph Tyler in the early 1930s.[3] In the sixties, with the influx of massive federal finance for curriculum improvement, the model came into its own. Federal policy-makers demanded of educational innovators that they both pre-specified the intended performance gains and provided subsequent proof of 'pay-off'. Despite mounting criticisms of the engineering-type assumptions of such 'pre-ordinate' evaluation,[4] and the tentative emergence of alternative approaches,[5] the model was still serviceable enough to be exported to us, and to command the initial allegiance of the first wave of professional evaluators in Britain. It was endorsed by our doyens of educational research, and found consistent with the influential pre-occupations of prominent curriculum philosophers. But it didn't work. Most of these evaluators, having experienced the conceptual and practical inadequacies of the model, are still licking their wounds. They found, for instance, that not all the curriculum developers shared the model's assumptions about the essential need to clarify goals in advance. Even with defined objectives the problems of measurement were far from tractable – even less so in practice than they were in theory. They discovered, too, that the task of evaluation seemed to call for a greater variety of research skills and to raise more complicated issues, than those involved in educational measurement.[6]

In America, in the last few years, disillusion at the apparent failure of the curriculum reform movement has sharpened criticism of its assumptions and techniques, and those of evaluation; and has evoked a greater willingness to face the daunting complexity of educational realities. The optimistic rationalism which shaped and sustained the movement has been muted, its inherent assumption of value-consensus exposed as an hallucination. In a paper written for the conference one of the American participants, Robert Stake, pin-pointed some of the weaknesses of the evaluation mode which characterised the movement:

> It is likely to be underfunded, understaffed, and initiated too late. But even under optimum conditions it often will fail. A collection of specific objectives will understate educational purposes. Different people have different purposes. Side effects – good ones and bad – get ignored. Program background, conditions, transactions are likely to be poorly described. Standardised tests seldom match objectives, criterion referenced tests oversimplify and fail to measure transfer, and custom-built tests are poorly validated. And people cannot read many of the reports or do not find them useful.

This brief historical overview describes some of the background dissatisfaction that prompted the conference. The question uppermost was where do we go from here? One way ahead was indicated in 1969 by Tom Hastings in his presidential remarks to the American National Council for Measurement in Education, when he made a plea for psychometrists to join forces with historians, economists, sociologists, and anthropologists in a concerted attack on the problems of educational evaluation.[7] In a way the Cambridge conference was an attempt to open up evaluation thinking in this direction, seeing what could be learned from other research standpoints, and assessing the implications, difficulties, and potentialities of new evaluation styles. As convenors of the conference, we were particularly concerned to address what we judged to be one crucial problem for new evaluation designs – namely, the fact that educational decision-makers are forced by the complexity of required decisions to review a much wider range of evidence than has usually been gathered in evaluation research. In Ernest House's phrase, the decision-maker's 'vocabulary of action' is not matched by the current lexicons of evaluators.[8]

The second day of the conference was devoted to intensive review of three evaluation reports produced by participants.[9] In each study the evaluator had rejected the 'agricultural-botany' assumptions of the classical model in favour of an approach rooted more in sociology and social anthropology. The three reports – though far from uniform in style and aims – nevertheless had major features in common. For instance, each evaluation (i) featured naturalistic, process-oriented field studies of educational experiments which attempted to portray the innovation in the context of a recognisable social reality; (ii) documented a full range of phenomena, perspectives, and judgements that might have relevance for different audiences and diverse interest groups; (iii) utilised observational and interview techniques extensively, and gave less than usual prominence to measurement procedures; (iv) followed a flexible rather than pre-determined research plan, thus enabling the investigation to be responsive to unpredictable and atypical phenomena and to sudden changes of direction in the form of the experiment, as well as to the planned and to the typical.

There was general agreement that such studies – more extensive, naturalistic, and adaptable than evaluation designs in the past – represented the best and possibly only way of bridging the gap between evaluation research and the more practical and down-to-earth concerns of practitioners and local and government officials. Against this background of consensus, however, were many points of discussion and dispute. Clearly it is impossible to summarise all of these here. But three recurrent themes of discussion deserve mention.

The first theme centred on methodology. For those in educational research who revere the canons of tradition, the 'anthropological' style of evaluation raises the twin spectres of subjectivism and a fatal lack of discipline. Conference participants pointed out, first, that the intrusion of the researcher's own values is equally a problem in traditional-type evaluations, though often effectively concealed amid numerical analyses; second, that to permit methodological considerations to determine what is significant and relevant research to do, is rather like confining a search to the area under the lamp post because that's where the light is; and, third, that other disciplines (e.g. history and anthropology) have standards of what constitutes valid and reliable evidence that are generally considered reasonable given the nature of their subject-matter, and which might well be appropriate to adopt in the evaluation field. Over other methodological issues there was clearly less agreement: for instance about how soon and how much should an evaluation researcher focus his enquiries; and about whether objective testing, as a mode of inquiry, is compatible with the maintenance of the good personal relations necessary for informal observation and interviewing.

A second group of issues related not so much to detailed tactics as to broader research strategy. For example, in setting up a study, should the evaluator have a 'contract' with his sponsors, or not? In favour was the argument that establishing the scope and basic form of the study in advance, lessened the possibility of subsequent misunderstandings. The view against the contract was that 'it stagnates, it ritualises, it forces things, just like pre-ordinate designs and experimental method'. Another extremely tricky question was whether an evaluator should intervene if he sees a programme going 'wildly off the rails'. Morally, he perhaps should – even if he is summative 'rather than formative' – but if he does so, an opportunity may be lost for seeing how the innovation or scheme stands up to particular types of acute strain. There were questions, too, of how evaluation studies should be reported. Should they constitute a 'display', in 'raw' form, of the range of different opinions, results from questionnaires, and so on? Or, alternatively, should the report distil, summarise, organise, and interpret the data for its different audiences? The argument for the former approach was that readers should be given the opportunity to judge the scheme reported for themselves; and that structuring the report could inevitably influence the reader in one way or another. It is the reader's task to 'evaluate', in the literal sense of the concept, and the evaluator's task to provide the reader with information which he may wish to take into account in forming his judgement. The arguments against this, and in favour of a more interpretive treatment, were that 'straight narrative reporting' is probably a misnomer anyway; that without distillation the report is likely to be long or indigestible for readers; and that a focussed, more analytic treatment is necessary in order to contribute to a deeper understanding of the phenomena reported.

This issue related to the third area of discussion, namely the role of the evaluator vis-à-vis the decision-maker. Should the evaluator be 'subservient' or 'dominant'? Should he be merely providing information along lines requested, or should he be an independent, challenging, and critical figure, who introduces new notions from his expert position with which to confront decision-makers? There was a range of opinion, from those who argued that the evaluator should 'contain his arrogance', reflect 'society's values', and fit his studies closely to the needs of policy-makers; to those who thought there was an obligation to 'educate decision-makers', if not to a particular point of view, at least into a more sophisticated way of examining educational issues.

These represent a handful of the topics discussed during the four-day conference, which also included – as an exercise – devising evaluation designs for an impending British curriculum project; and review of possible future plans for developing non-traditional evaluation in Britain.

At the end of the conference, the participants decided that it might be useful to make available an agreed summary of their conclusions, drawing attention to significant issues which still divided them. The statement, or manifesto, which is still in a draft form, reads as follows:

> On December 20, 1972 at Churchill College, Cambridge, the following conference participants[10] concluded a discussion of the aims and procedures of evaluating educational practices and agreed
>
> I   That past efforts to evaluate these practices have, on the whole, not adequately served the needs of those who require evidence of the effects of such practices, because of:
>
> a   an under-attention to educational processes including those of the learning milieu;
>
> b   an over-attention to psychometrically measurable changes in student behaviour (that to an extent represent the outcomes of the practice, but which are a misleading over-simplification of the complex changes that occur in students); and

c the existence of an educational research climate that rewards accuracy of measurement and generality of theory but overlooks both mismatch between school problems and research issues and tolerates ineffective communication between researchers and those outside the research community.

II They also agreed that future efforts to evaluate these practices be designed so as to be:

a responsive to the needs and perspectives of differing audiences;
b illuminative of the complex organisational, teaching and learning processes at issue;
c relevant to public and professional decisions forthcoming; and
d reported in language which is accessible to their audiences.

III More specifically they recommended that, increasingly,

a observational data, carefully validated, be used (sometimes in substitute for data from questioning and testing);
b the evaluation be designed so as to be flexible enough to allow for response to unanticipated events (progressive focusing rather than pre-ordinate design); and that
c the value positions of the evaluator, whether highlighted or constrained by the design, be made evident to the sponsors and audiences of the evaluation.

IV Though without consensus on the issues themselves, it was agreed, that considered attention by those who design evaluation studies should be given to such issues as the following:

a the sometimes conflicting roles of the same evaluator as expert, scientist, guide, and teacher of decision-makers on the one hand, and as technical specialist, employee, and servant of decision-makers on the other;
b the degree to which the evaluator, his sponsors, and his subjects should specify in advance the limits of enquiry, the circulation of findings, and such matters as may become controversial later;
c the advantages and disadvantages of intervening in educational practices for the purpose of gathering data or of controlling the variability of certain features in order to increase the generalisability of the findings;
d the complexity of educational decisions which, as a matter of rule, have political, social and economic implications; and the responsibility that the evaluator may or may not have for exploring these implications;
e the degree to which the evaluator should interpret his observations rather than leave them for different audiences to interpret.

It was acknowledged that different evaluation designs will serve different purposes and that even for a single educational programme many different designs could be used.

Notes

*   Barry MacDonald is Head of the Evaluation Unit at the Centre for Applied Research in Education, University of East Anglia.
†   Malcolm Parlett is at the Centre for Research in the Educational Sciences at the University of Edinburgh.
‡   Originally published in: *Cambridge Journal of Education* 3: 2, 74–82.

References

1   The conference participants were as follows:
    Mike Atkins, University of Illinois; John Banks, Department of Education and Science; Tony Becher, Nuffield Foundation; Alan Gibson, Department of Education and Science; David Hamilton, University of Glasgow; David Jenkins, Open University; Barry MacDonald, University of East Anglia; Tim McMullen, Centre for Research and Innovation in Education, OECD; Malcolm Parlett, University of Edinburgh; Louis Smith, Washington University of St Louis; Robert Stake, University of Illinois; David Tawney, University of Keele; Kim Taylor, Centre for Research and Innovation in Education, OECD; Erik Wallin, Pedagogiska Institutionen, Goteborg.
2   See, for instance,
    MacDonald, B., 'Briefing Decision Makers: an evaluation of the Humanities Curriculum Project', *Schools Council, Bulletin of Evaluation Studies* (in press).
    Parlett, M. and Hamilton, D., 'Evaluation as Illumination: a new approach to the study of Innovatory Programs', *Occasional Paper 9, Centre for Researching the Educational Sciences*, University of Edinburgh, 1972.
    Smith, L. M. and Geoffrey, W., *The Complexities of an Urban Classroom*, Holt, Rinehart and Winston, 1968.
    Stake, R., 'The Countenance of Educational Evaluation', *Teachers College Record, Vol.* 68, 1967, pp. 523–540.
    Taylor, L. C, *Resources for Learning*, Penguin Books, 1971.
3   Tyler, R. W., *Constructing Achievement Tests*, Ohio State University, 1934.
4   See, particularly,
    Atkin, J. Myron, 'Some Evaluation Problems in a Course Content Improvement Project', *Journal of Research in Science Teaching, Vol. I*, pp. 129–132, 1963.
    Eisner, Elliot, W., 'Educational Objectives: Help or Hindrance', *The School Review*, *LXXV* (Autumn 1967), pp. 250–260.
5   Stake, R., op. cit.
    Stufflebeam, Daniel L., *'Evaluation as Enlightenment for Decision Making'*, an address delivered at the Working Conference on Assessment Theory, sponsored by ASCD Sarasota, Fla., January 1968.
6   Experience was mixed. For an overview of the work of Schools Council evaluators see *Bulletin of Evaluation Studies*, Schools Council, 1973. (In press). This includes an account of a successful operationalisation of the objectives model by the evaluator of the Science 5–13 Project, Win Harlen.
7   Hastings, J. Thomas, 'The Kith and Kin of Educational Measurers', *Journal of Educational Measurement*, Vol. 6, No. 3, Autumn 1969.
8   House, Ernest R., *'The Conscience of Educational Evaluation'*, paper originally presented to the Ninth Annual Conference of the California Association for the Gifted. February 1972, Col. 73, No. 3.
9   Stake, R. and Gjerde, C., 'An Evaluation of TCITY: the Twin City Institute for Talented Youth', CIRCE, University of Illinois at Urbana-Champaign, 1971.
    MacDonald, B., A draft section from forthcoming report on the Schools Council Humanities Curriculum Project.
    Parlett, M. R., 'A study of two experimental undergraduate programs at the Massachusetts Institute of Technology' (Unpublished Report), 1971.
10 It was intended that the statement, after further drafting, should be signed by all participants (except those representing the Department of Education and Science).

5 Curriculum criticism

Misconceived theory, ill-advised practice

Rex Gibson[*†]

There is a delusion abroad; a fantasy that has already misled some researchers in education and which seems likely to beguile even more who are attracted by 'illuminative' methods. This chimera is known as 'curriculum criticism'.[1] It flourishes in the United States and is already gaining currency in British curriculum studies. Some of its leading proponents are Mann, Willis, Eisner and Jenkins.[2] Although it has a history of a dozen years or so, it is so new that a recent comprehensive review of educational research methods fails to give it mention.[3] I believe its theory and practice to be deeply flawed and urge that great caution is required lest a whole generation of teachers studying curriculum are encouraged to set off in pursuit of this mirage.

What is 'curriculum criticism'? Fundamentally it comprises two basic assumptions: first, that the curriculum can be regarded as an art object, a literary object; and second, that the concepts and methods of artistic and literary criticism can yield deeper understanding of curriculum processes. Let the advocates speak for themselves. First, the curriculum as an art object; Mann, whose views have been seminal, begins

> I will ask what is involved in talking about curriculum as if it were a literary object ... I will use as an exemplum to be guided but not bound by – Mark Schorer's lucid treatment of the story ... (he) focuses ... firmly on the literary object itself ... I would like to propose that a curriculum can be regarded in the same manner.[4]

And within two pages Mann is unequivocally calling a curriculum 'a work of art.'[5] Willis supports him in seeing the curriculum as a 'work', and asserting that a curriculum 'shares the same functions of any work of art'.[6]

The second assumption ('use the methods of literary criticism') has two versions: the first urges that certain concepts can be taken over from literary criticism and applied to education: 'work' 'author' 'world' 'audience'[7] or 'metaphor' 'point of view' 'plot' and 'theme'.[8] However, the second version is much more radical; in Eisner's words:

> the *methods used must be artistically critical*. The educational critic must be able to create, render, portray and disclose in such a way that the reader will be able to empathetically participate in the events described ... (he) *exploits the*

potential of language to further human understanding. The language she or he uses is expressive so that the kinds of understanding the reader can secure is one that reaches into the deeper levels of meaning children secure from school experience. To convey such meaning, *the artistic use of language is a necessity*.[9] (my italics)

What is being demanded here is not simply that the critic can be a critic, he must be an artist too. As we shall see, it is very difficult for the average human being to resist such a flattering and seductive invitation.

Now, what I shall show is that the first assumption is simply wrong: the curriculum is *not* an art object and it is exceedingly unhelpful to conceptualise it as such; and the second assumption is delusory, disclosing more the literary shortcomings of the curriculum critics than providing curriculum illumination. Thus, taken together the two assumptions have resulted in a rash of narcissistic, self-indulgent 'research' or 'evaluation' documents.

Before embarking on the critique, it is necessary to note briefly two claims of curriculum criticism; claims that, in any approach, invariably signify rhetoric rather than ideas. The first is that a 'new language' is needed. Thus Mann advocates a move 'Toward a New Language'[10] and Willis wishes to develop 'a new language of curriculum criticism'.[11] Certainly, some relief from the older 'scientific' approach is required but any call for a 'new language' is simply bombast.

The second warning signal is the over-inflated claim of criticism's vital contribution to moral growth. Willis, for example, argues that the focal points, methodology and values within curriculum criticism will somehow have the result that:

> members of the audience become discerning and autonomous moral agents within the process of change. They make possible a similar kind of change for the curriculum worker himself, for in his role as maker of artistic choices he is also heightening his own moral vision.[12]

Such lack of modesty requires the cold-water treatment of David Daiches (1980) on similarly grandiose claims for literary criticism: 'The ability to read great writers with penetrating discrimination does not necessarily make one a better person or enable one to make morally better choices in real life.'[13]

What's wrong with curriculum criticism?

Curriculum criticism has three major defects: its assumption that a curriculum is a work of art or can be treated as one; its assumptions about literary criticism; and, resulting from these two, its practice. Let us examine each in turn.

A curriculum is not a work of art

The advocates of curriculum criticism are confident that a curriculum can be seen as a work of art:

Curriculum criticism ... enable(s) the curriculum worker ... to see differences – especially ethical differences – between teaching predetermined subject matter and engaging in a professional discipline involved in teaching curricula considered as works of art.[14]

But when the reasons are given for treating curricula as works of art they seem pretty strange, coming, as they do, from writers who claim particular sensitivity to language. For example, just *why* does Mann assert that a curriculum may be regarded as an art object? Because, it would appear, that curriculum, like fiction, is about *selection*, about *choice*. Thus, an artist selects 'from a universe of possibilities', and 'the selection made, considered against the infinite background of selections passed over constitutes an assertion of meaning'.[15]

So, for Mann, what art appears to comprise of is that it involves selection, and has meaning. So, too, he argues, does the curriculum: choice and meaning are central. But, so, too, the sceptic would retort, does all human activity: political, religious, economic, leisure pursuits: all involve choice and meaning. So, too, does this paper you are now reading, with these words, these ideas, rather than others. This, too, on Mann's criteria, is a work of art! It is evident that Mann and his followers use words and construct definitions in a very loose, all-embracing fashion.

What is lacking is an understanding that *all* life has meaning, because it is embedded in social practices. Mann makes much of the assertion that 'raw life is formless, chaotic and without meaning until man-the-artist creates meaning by bounding it'.[16] This is simply nonsense. Existentialism itself cannot break free of meaning: Sartre's *La Nausee* is strictly bounded, defined, meaning-*full*, not merely contingent. Every aspect of human life has meaning because man puts it there – indeed can't help putting it there – and he doesn't have to claim the pretentious title of 'man-the-artist' to do so. When Mann claims that 'To listen to a chaotic, infinite universe and then answer with form, finitely, is to order chaos and to assert meaning. Such answering is the hallmark of man-the-artist: his answers are his works of art'[17] we recognise rhetoric and flattery: it is paying every human being in the world the compliment of the title 'artist'. But it simply evacuates the word 'artist' of all precision; it becomes merely a synonym for 'man'.

A further misunderstanding of curriculum critics relates to the nature of artistic activity. Mann claims that 'Mallarme stood in terror before the blank page: while it was blank it was infinite possibility, but to write a word upon it was to limit the possible meanings of the page.'[18]

Mann appears to regard this statement as a literal fact. It's not and cannot be. It belongs to a fictional world where infinite possibilities exist. Further, it belongs to an untenable view of artist as transcendental genius. But all men, including those who are artists, are bounded, confined, subject to history and convention. Mallarme was restricted in what he might write by his society and its history, his own personal biography, the customs, manners, values and standards of his generation, and, crucially, by his thinking of himself as 'poet'. There *is* large freedom there, but it is not infinite. And what is true of Mallarme is even more true of 'curriculum workers' (whatever that curious expression of the curriculum critics might mean). They are circumscribed by history, by material conditions, by convention – by man's meaning-seeking capacities themselves. Choice and selection is always limited, and such limitation must be acknowledged. 'Infinite possibility' is a misleading dream even in art.

In addition to looseness of language and overestimation of artistic freedom, there are many other reasons for disputing the claim that the curriculum can be regarded as an art object. Let us take literature as an example. A novel or a poem is, in a sense, 'fixed': its 'writtendownness' is, in a sense, all we have. Its interpretations and valuations will change over the years, but its words remain as the artist first set them down. Now not only does the 'writtendownness' of a curriculum change over time, but its crucial dimension is *action*: pupils and teachers in classrooms *doing* mathematics or history or morality. Curriculum is a moving, changing, continuous process involving the interaction of many people; a play, novel or poem is realised by actors, spectators, readers, but all except the most arrogant participant recognise that the major, the fundamental contribution is provided by the words on the page, by the original artist. A work of art is just that: 'a work'; a curriculum is 'work'. To put it bluntly: any fool can write 'history' or 'mathematics' on a sheet of paper and call it a curriculum. Only an artist of genius can write *Hamlet*. The 'givenness' of *Hamlet* is of a quite different order from any curriculum 'givenness'. Its particularity makes it distinct from the generalities of curriculum characteristics or criteria. *Hamlet* is irreplaceable, no commentary is ever a substitute for it; it is the thing itself to be interpreted, analysed; but a curriculum is most vitally the *actions* of teachers and pupils, not the given text of a written curriculum. Not only does the writing of a work of literature require quite different qualities from those of writing of a curriculum, but, crucially, the participation or collaboration involved by others in the realisation of works of art or curricula are of quite different orders. Pupils and teachers are not called upon to write their own Hamlet. They work *at* it in present, joint activity.

Then, too, a work of literature is consciously a fiction; curriculum activity is not. One obvious sense in which this is true is that schooling involves actual children, and teachers, and thus important consequences, moral and cognitive, flow directly from their interaction. A work of art affords greater distancing, more opportunities for imaginative rather than actual participation. Another strong sense of this difference is argued by Frank Kermode[19] who shows clearly that literature is ordered in a way that reality is not. In brief, a work of literature has an *ending*; in contrast everyday life inevitably goes on. In three hours or 300 pages the play or novel is completed. Such neatness has no parallel in classrooms, in everyday life. There is no curriculum equivalent of 'Go, bid the soldiers shoot.'

A work of art represents an act of sustained, imaginative expression and heightened consciousness; a curriculum simply cannot be thought of in this way. The practice that is curriculum includes the mundane as well as the imaginative: boredom and engagement, sheer slog and moments of inspiration. A work of art, however produced, excludes those dogged, workaday, habitual elements. In mundane contrast a curriculum covers more ground, more time, more of the sheerly ordinary in human experience. There is a great difference in the intensity embodied in a work of literature from that in a curriculum. *Middlemarch* may be about the everyday affairs of a midland town, but its significances are differently, more consistently and intently charged than the diffuse activities of life itself.

A further crucial difference, which curriculum critics are all too prone to overlook, is that the aims and activities of teachers and artists are rarely similar. The aim of the teacher is to 'educate' – however that word is interpreted – very few artists see 'education' as the main purpose of their activity, indeed, it is often vigorously denied. Unlike teachers, artists do not think primarily of particular children, at a particular age, to be affected in particular ways: cognitively, emotionally, morally, physically, socially. In spite of all the problems that attach to the recovery of the author's intention, we can be sure that such intentions are crucially different from those of teachers.

There are many other objections that could be raised to treating the curriculum as an art object, particularly the place of theory in relation to each, and the nature of the relationship of each to the reality with which it deals.

Literary criticism and curriculum criticism

Although literary criticism may well have much to offer our understanding of curriculum, the promise of the self-styled curriculum critics is, as yet, unredeemed. Their large claims are often simply embarrassing in their pomposity: 'In doing so (adopting the aesthetic perspective), the curriculum worker may gain professional autonomy, become a discerning moral agent, and foster mental health.'[20] At least the 'may' takes some of the edge off the pretentiousness. But the inflation hints at the defects in the literary curriculum criticism analogy. First, Mann's original formulation seems, on close reading, to have little to do with literary criticism as such. In his very appropriate concern to focus on the processes rather than the products of education, in his attempt to provide an alternative to technological-rational approaches to curriculum, Mann advocates literary criticism as a model, but in fact is doing little more than arguing an ethical stance. He starts from the position: 'As with literary criticism, the function of the curricular critique is to disclose its meanings, to illuminate its answers.'[21] Leaving aside the highly arguable 'answers', and the fact that many contemporary critics would deny their function as the disclosure of meaning, this is stating no more than the claims of social science or history. The elasticity of language is again evident. And this lack of precision continues: 'Meaning, then, abides in the design of selections ... the critic discloses meaning by explaining designs.'[22] What is specifically *literary* about this? The argument goes on: 'to account for the choices in a work of art is precisely to discover what the choices mean'.[23]

Here, huge assumptions about intentionality are made, and we have nothing that is specifically literary. And it is now that Mann moves away from literary criticism (not that he seems ever to have engaged with it) into a form of ethical theory. Polyani's alluring 'personal knowledge' is to become the basis of the curriculum critic's theory and practice. It is the critic's 'personal knowledge' that will guide his choice of what to study, will prevent subjectivity and will help him to discover significant designs and meanings. And of what, we can ask, does the curriculum critic's 'personal knowledge' consist? Mann grounds it in 'Knowledge about ethical reality'.[24] Thus: 'Personally held and universally intended knowledge about good and evil or right and wrong stands as a valuable guide to the processes of curriculum critique.'[25] There is something very strange here. First, it would appear to suggest that the best curriculum critic is likely to be a priest or a moral philosopher; second, it implicitly plays down knowledge of subject matter about curriculum; and third it has the characteristic hubris of curriculum critics in implying that a critic's 'knowledge about ethical reality' is somehow superior to a layman's or is more likely to issue in better choices. David Daiches' strictures on this last point have already been noted. Mann's proposals have far less to do with literary criticism than with a claim to superior ethical knowledge. His concern for the identification of designs does not constitute any advance on social science or historical methods and his rhetorical, enthusiastic, hurrah-type language ('new propositions', 'new understanding', 'heuristic leap', 'disclosure models lead without end to the unfolding of the world') collapses into banality ('a model is useful if it does disclose meaning and useless if it does not').

The second reason for dissatisfaction with the current state of curriculum criticism lies in its apparent lack of awareness about the fragmented state of literary criticism in the 1970s and 1980s.[26] As much as education or sociology, literary criticism is characterised by competing schools, theories, fashions. Marxism, structuralism, new criticism, hermeneutics, deconstruction, formalism, archetypalism, receptionism, transactionism ... the educational researcher greets the near-endless list with a wry smile of recognition. But generally curriculum critics seem unaware of the range of what counts as literary criticism. They seem tied to a narrow 'disclosure of meaning' model. For such ignorance we must be thankful. What a curriculum critic with an acquaintance with Derrida or Lacan would produce is a frightening prospect. (It will, however, come.) At the present moment curriculum criticism both advocates and practises the unproblematic taking over and application of literary concepts (work, author, world, audience, metaphor plot, theme) to curriculum. What would be welcome is far more caution with regard to the very different world to which literary concepts are applied.[27] To treat the teacher as 'author' or the student as 'audience' is more likely to obscure than illuminate.

As has been made clear above, the root of such unsubtle transfers is the erroneous assumption that the curriculum is an art-object. The error is compounded when the curriculum critic assumes it is his task to produce his own work of art. Although literary criticism may aid our understanding of curriculum, it is a task calling for far more delicacy of treatment than has so far been evidenced.

Third, curriculum critics show little awareness of the problem of the relationships between language and what it claims to describe. This central problem, not only for literary criticism but for social science, indeed, for all disciplines, is unacknowledged. It is most evident in the writings of curriculum critics in relation to what might be called the theory of the artist. Thus, as between Aristotle's *mimesis*, the imitation of an action, and the romantic concept of art as *expression*, curriculum critics have seemed to plump for the latter. But this is to infer from their practice: the matter is simply never discussed, and the vital but uneasy relationship of language to reality remains a blank.

It is perhaps unfair to level charges of neglect of the diversity of literary approaches at such a comparatively new movement as curriculum criticism. However, if its promises are to stand any chance of being redeemed it will simply have to acknowledge the sheer variety of literary criticism. To mention only two: Marxist criticism (itself very diverse) provides a valuable antidote to simple-minded idealism and expressionism and the reduction of explanation to naive individual psychology; it provides a constant reminder that individual actions are embedded in a social structure. And second, greater attention to questions of content and form would not only supply useful conceptual tools for examining curriculum patterns, it would, like Marxism, very quickly reveal the genuine differences that exist between schooling and literature.

A final problem of the critical analogy inheres in the relationship between a work of art and a critic. Apart from such rare instances as Johnson or Eliot it is one of inequality: the enterprise, the imaginative and expressive abilities of the artist far exceed those of the critic. However, for the curriculum critic the terms of the relationship are surely equal. But the development of curriculum criticism has been one of distortion. Those whose aspire to be critics have been encouraged to see themselves *as* artists, to produce their own 'literature', their own 'works of art'. In short, they have been deluded into believing that 'the artistic use of language is a necessity'.[28] To the sad results of this mirage we now must turn.

The practice of curriculum criticism

Some criticism, because of its restraint, is convincing;[29] much, because it strains after 'the artistic use of language' is painful to read and carries little credibility. A quite classic example is Jenkins,[30] but before examining his study, a few examples from American writers show the defects of the method.

1 A self-centred, narcissistic tone

The egocentricity that the approach encourages makes the critic the real subject of the research, rather than the teacher or the pupils. After observing a difficult lesson Greer comments: 'I was drained after the tension of the interchanges I had just witnessed. Miss M. too, was weary.'[31] Miss M., poor devil, is only the teacher who has been involved in the 'interchanges' witnessed. Grumet chooses a revealing image that places the tortured critic firmly at the centre of the research:

> I felt sorry for myself, victimised as I had felt during the discussion, seated in the centre of a circle of students, trying to hear them and to hold off the images of the stoning scene from *Zorba the Greek* that kept coming to mind. I am compelled to relate my response to this evening, not to make you cringe (assuming that you empathise) but to acknowledge the curriculum and my students' response to it as my situation and to assume responsibility for what I may make of it.[32]

Well, the reader does cringe, but not because of empathy. This case study is set very significantly in a two page opening from Sartre's *La Nausee*, and a final three pages in which almost every sentence is self-referential. Perhaps the 'existential aesthetic' that underpins the study is some explanation, but the whole essay smacks of the narcissism of the curriculum critic's response with a vengeance.

Pinar's study consists of extracts from his diary, giving his responses to reading Sartre. Here, 'I' is the prime word throughout and he concludes: 'personal knowledge ... is not principally knowledge about ethical reality as Mann maintains. It *is* about ethical reality, but on a deeper level it is about life history and direction, about biographic issues and movement.'[33]

However, the reader feels uncomfortably that the 'life history', 'direction', 'movement' referred to are purely personal, solipsistic. Much criticism reads more like therapy, like *personal* disclosure. The self-absorption excludes any sense of the social structures within which individuals act.

2 Omniscience

The self-centredness of the curriculum critic can produce all-knowing judgements, frequently delivered in the authentic voice of Mr. Pooter or A.J. Wentworth B.A.:

> As I looked round rather pointedly at the mess, Miss M. seemed to become more aware of it. At her rather embarrassed comment, 'And after my careful preparation too', I couldn't help laughing at the helplessness teachers so often feel in the face of the high spirits that had just spilled out into the courtyard.[34]

There is often a certainty that suits ill with the openness and provisionality of judgement so often recommended: 'I had offered *currere* and some had returned the gift unopened.'[35] Again, the image of 'the gift' is significant. Moreover, it is seen as foolproof: 'Some had tried to use it but had not used the instructions and were understandably annoyed when the thing broke down.'[36]

3 Grandiloquent style

Milner digs a pit for himself: 'The analogy invoked here is that curriculum is like art and should be critiqued accordingly.'[37] And promptly leaps into it: 'The Dionysian communalism of frenzy later passed to the abstract individualization of Apollonian remoteness.'[38] 'Time flowed through his being as it did for Rousseau or for Augustine.'[39]

> He arranged both form and content for his curriculum for the day so as to initiate the Judeo-Christian action. Not the pathetic modern action of conformity, nor the tragic action of autonomy, but the redemptive action of openness.[40]

If this reminds one most of Donald Wolfit, Pinar's 'criticism' echoes a pseudo-scientific Polonius: 'This method which guarantees nothing (it is only a tool you may or may not use effectively) is the regressive-progressive-analytic-synthetic.'[41]

4 Dubious images: a self conscious searching for effect

In the straining after vividness, in an attempt to turn everyday life into high drama, the effort shows: 'As she looked up and saw me there was a fleeting moment when she had the startled expression of an animal interrupted when drinking.'[42] 'Dink's teeth sharpened into spearpoints when he grinned.'[43] Eisner,[44] coiner of the unfortunate phrase 'educational connoisseurship', presents three examples of educational criticism. The first two, in their opening sentences reveal the forced searching for the evocative image: 'The classroom is almost a caricature of the society. The curriculum is served up like Big Macs. Reading, math, language, even physical and affective education are all pre-cooked, prepackaged, artificially flavored.'[45]

> The splendid houses perched majestically upon the hills peek out from between the lush growth of trees and well-tended foliage that dress them. Many seem to snicker at the laws of gravity as they balance themselves so casually upon the slanted land.[46]

Eisner must bear much of the responsibility for such artifice, for he has encouraged his many students at Stanford University to believe that 'Criticism itself is an art form.'[47]

5 The status of critical judgements

Eisner's assertion coupled with a view of art as expression can result in the abandonment of any notion of objectivity. The status of critical judgement is undermined as the slide into mere subjectivity develops. In a revealing comment Grumet writes:

> 'One student demanded to know why I had not come to see him perform in a play ... that had figured prominently in his early journal entries. I tried to show him that I was not there to share his experience as a close friend or a parent might, to confirm or contradict it with my interpretation but to listen to his interpretation. Had I seen his play, *all he would have received was my version, no more or less valid than* his own.'[48] (my italics)

Now if a drama teacher's views are no more or less valid than anyone else's it raises the awkward question as to why should her views on curriculum be worth reading. The uneasy equation of criticism with merely personal response is an issue barely addressed by the curriculum critics.

Let us now examine a British case study, claimed to be 'rich with detail and incident' 'rather telling' with 'elaborately drawn characterisation' where 'disclosure of meaning flows directly from the observations of the narrator'[49] From such remarks it would appear to carry the seal of approval of the critical school. David Jenkin's study is of a one week residential course he attended at London Business School[50] in which he describes and analyses his experiences of curriculum, tutors, fellow students.

What are the failings of Jenkins' case study? First, its use of language. There is an inability to confine an image within any appropriate bounds. The laboured effort to produce 'literature' produces only poor journalism. Warning is given in Jenkins' own description of his study: an attempt to hold a narrative line side by side with an analysis, which is itself elaborately metaphorical, of the hidden curriculum, for example in seeing the competing pedagogies within the single course as a kind of re-run of Elijah versus the prophets of Baal.[51]

Such overdramatisation and grand analogies are invariably the mark of poor criticism. It assumes that the invocation of great names, transcendental themes, super-human stories, will cause the mantle of literature to fall on weak writing. There are many examples: 'the wooden horse inside Andrew's Trojan citadel'[52]; 'he deals, like the Gospels, not in anecdotes but in parables'[53]; 'Philip's altar for calling down the divine fire was undoubtedly the simulation exercise'[54]; 'It was through this breach in nature that ruin entered'[55]; 'The MSc Course thus becomes the New Hampshire primary in Philip's bid for the White House'[56]; 'the danger of epistemological overkill, the scorched-earth policy that undermines the manager's view that he has at least a commonsense understanding of what using words is all about'[57]; 'Once the rites of passage were over, with all attendant impurities and danger, work began in earnest.'[58]

Along with such overdrawn images, mechanically strung together in an attempt to heighten the dramatic effect, to evidence the writer's erudition and grasp of great themes, goes a self-conscious style: a flashiness and quick, one-line put-downs. Flip and inaccurate metaphors are sprinkled around in the straining after vividness. The effect is however simply one of ostentatious display: 'the facade is a set piece of stage decor for the CBS street theatre'[59]; 'It's problem isn't the excellence of the centre, but the centrality of the excellence'[60]; 'A kind of intellectual Kenwood Autochop turning the whole world to mince before your very eyes'[61]; 'almost inviting students to treat him as a body-on-the-barbed wire'[62]; 'Philip's box 4 ... is like a bank, which will lend you money if you prove you don't need it'[63]; 'Someone who could mastermind police tactics in the London Spaghetti Restaurant siege but who could not be expected to haggle over the provision of chemical toilets'[64]; 'Andrew's early warning system for this possibility is so sensitive that alarms ring at the first migrating Russian goose'[65]; 'To borrow Roy Lichenstein's key concept. WHAM!'[66]

Each image is overdrawn, over-dramatic, self-consciously inserted. The result is to create disbelief; the reader simply is not convinced by the portrayal because he quickly becomes sated with mere flamboyance. The glittering surface does not conceal the poverty of the piece. In the characterisations of the course tutors all the pretentiousness of the style is evident: 'Philip is an earthbound spirit, a hoverer, the earnest young man at the cocktail party'[67]; 'young, watchful, nerve-wracked and angular as a hairpin, but quite exceptionally bright'[68] (Angular as a hairpin!); 'Sylvia Maynard ... long haired, theatrical, and rather beautiful in a whimsical kind of way.'[69]

Nothing comes to mind more than Pope's 'with every word a reputation dies.' And in the convoluted struggle of portrayal, random pieces of information are offered with pseudo-significance: 'His father is an inventive cartoonist.'[70] The reader can only wonder about his mother.

What this misuse of language conveys most vividly is the second defect of curriculum criticism: its self-referentiality. The curriculum takes second place to the critic. 'Look at me' is what comes through most strongly. Not only is the case study self-consciously constructed as 'a work' of 'literature' (which it certainly is not), it is all too obviously about the writer rather than the course. Its value is in showing how crucial are the views and perceptions of the case study writer, but in this instance shows how much in question is their validity for the mannered writing evidences an uncomfortable narcissism. Jenkins is always centre stage, other people find him interesting, mysterious, unclassifiable:

> On Wednesday evening in the bar Kevin (a charismatic character with real-life claims to fame as the Malcolm Allison of Gaelic football) got close to breaking my cover … 'It's funny' he said 'but your philosophy of industrial relations hasn't come through yet. You're the only course member that I can't place'[71]

Note that the 'charismatic' Kevin is an interesting character too, but he is puzzled by, and interested in, the enigmatic Jenkins. And Jenkins 'knows' people, 'important' people:

> Roger Graef: 'Knowing Roger, I had a dreadful fear that he would inadvertently blow my cover'[72]
>   Philip Boxer (Course tutor) 'I had made the mistake of relaxing too much too much … talking to Phil Boxer as if I knew him well (which of course I did…)'[73]

The case study writer has a God-like omniscience. Jenkins shares his secret knowledge of the inadequacies of the course's construction with a friend. 'I wonder who Walter is filling in for? queried an inside contact of mine.'[74]

Note that 'inside contact'. Clearly, both Jenkins and his friend 'know' Prof. Walter Reid has taken on a lecture brief beyond his competence. This image of omniscience has been noted in the American criticism above, but it is most marked in Jenkins. He always knows what is happening, why it is happening: 'Andrew (course director) entered at this point (I waved him across but did not explain what was happening for fear of breaking cover)'[75]; 'Where, I wondered, was the really wild card going to come from, the concept capable of giving a new purchase on problems.'[76]

His evaluations read like Olympian judgements, with a barb in every line, damning with faint praise: 'Philip is young … but quite exceptionally bright'[77]; 'Andrew, who seems a natural teacher … is gifted at exposition and explanation (a skill surprising rare in teachers at any level) but clearly sees the knowledge component of the course as dormant knowledge to be handed on'[78]; 'Although it's not a line I'd care to argue myself, it does have a certain zany appeal'[79]; 'Andrew's … analysis was scintillating, fair, and (I felt) potentially useful'[80]; '(they) are excellent teachers within *their chosen modes*, although –.'[81]

And the put down, the condescending sneer, is ever present: '"Dear Rhoda," I write, sending a postcard to my Mum in Cardiff, "What a mental life do these people have."'[82]

All the defects of the curriculum criticism are present: the abuse of language in the search for a grandiloquent style, omniscience, narcissism, self-centredness. Criticism becomes display. Even the deception practised to gain access to the course is turned to account. Jenkins 'was pretending to be a negotiator from the Association of University Teachers.'[83] He was in fact no such thing and through-out the study he speaks (in typical language) of his concern not to 'blow my cover.' Over and over he uses the same expression and when at the end of the course 'cover was blown', although he admits to 'some embarrassment' he keeps himself, consistent to the last, centre stage in the final sentences of his case study. The course director, objectively and understandably found Jenkins' deceit 'a shock and a disappointment'. Jenkins did not attend the final session of the course but he ends by quoting from the course director's letter – 'Participant observation requires immense discipline and the ability to sustain this. I feel you just ran out of both, just when it looked as if you might be achieving a minor triumph.'[84]

The curriculum critic, not the curriculum remains the firm focus of attention. The attempt to redress the dehumanisation of positivist approaches to education has overbalanced into egoistical subjectivity.

Conclusion

Do the strictures of the preceding analysis mean that the methods and concepts of literary criticism cannot be applied to curriculum? Is it the merely seductive will o' the wisp I have presented in this paper? My own conclusion is not quite as pes-simistic as might be inferred for I believe that the method might yield some illumi-nation of school and classroom processes. But it will only do so if far more thought and caution are exercised than is presently evident. Many of the issues requiring attention have been identified above, but finally – and all too briefly – I list, as rec-ommendations, some items that need urgent consideration if curriculum criticism is to become a worthwhile practice.

1   The assumption that the curriculum is a work of art, or can be treated as one, must be abandoned.
2   The limits of the analogy: literary criticism = curriculum criticism, must be more fully appreciated. In particular, prospective critics must respect the dif-ferent natures, practices, and functions of art and education.
3   The language of curriculum criticism must guard against high sounding but empty expression. In particular, Eisner's assertion that 'the artistic use of lan-guage is a necessity' should be seen for what it is: flattering but dangerously seductive; an ill-advised invitation that is more likely to produce purple patches of pseudo-literature rather than authentic portrayals.
4   If curriculum criticism is to draw on literary criticism, the sheer variety of the latter must be understood. In particular, close attention to (the varieties of) Marxist criticism would yield a valuable corrective to the notion of criticism as personal response and is more likely to ensure a due balance between psy-chological and structural factors.

5   Curriculum critics should resist the temptation to elevate all classroom processes into high drama. The analogy of the classroom as theatre is an attractive but flawed and seductive image. Reality includes the mundane as well as the exotic.

6   The validity of curriculum criticism requires far more grounding than it has yet received. Such an enterprise involves rigorous examination of the relationship between language and what it describes. If some objective criteria of judgement cannot be established, there is no reason why criticism should be taken seriously.

7   Curriculum critics should guard against narcissism and self-indulgence. Too many studies read like an exercise in personal therapy: the result both of too narrow a view of what constitutes literary criticism, and of Mann's exhortation to ground criticism in personal knowledge.

8   Curriculum criticism (indeed all research) should be more modest in its claims. Such modesty can be developed by reading more examples of literary criticism and literature, by regarding the word 'new' with scepticism, and by the recognition that all critics and artists work within, and are constrained and aided by, convention and history. Albert Einstein was once asked what one should do with an original idea. He replied after some thought 'I don't know. I only ever had one.'[85]

Notes

*   Rex Gibson is Tutor in Sociology of Education at the Cambridge Institute of Education.
†   Originally published in: *Cambridge Journal of Education* 11: 3, 190–210.

References

1   Eisner, Eliot (1978) 'Humanistic Trends and the Curriculum Field' *Journal of Curriculum Studies*, 10, 3: 197–204.
2   Willis, George, ed. (1978) *Qualitative Evaluation: Concepts and Cases in Curriculum Criticism*. McCutchan Publishing Corporation (see his own paper 'Curriculum Criticism and Literary Criticism' pp. 93–111)
    Mann, John S. (1978) 'Curriculum Criticism' in Willis ibid., pp. 74–90.
    Eisner, Eliot W. (1979) *The Educational Imagination: On the Design and Evaluation of School Programs*. Macmillan.
    Jenkins, David (1979) 'Business as Unusual: The "Skills of Bargaining" Course at LBS' inWillis ibid., pp. 345–369.
3   Cohen, Louis and Manion, Lawrence (1980) *Research Methods in Education*. Croom Helm.
4   Mann ibid., p. 75.
5   Mann ibid., p. 77.
6   Willis ibid., p. 109.
7   Willis ibid., p. 100ff.
8   Kelly, Edward, F. (1978) 'Curriculum Evaluation and Literary Criticism: Comments on the Analogy' in Willis ibid., pp. 116ff.
9   Eisner (1978) ibid., p. 199.
10 Mann ibid., p. 88.
11 Willis ibid., p. 110.
12 Willis ibid., p. 108.

13 Daiches, David (1980) 'The Critical Voice in the Wilderness' *Times Higher Education Supplement*, 19.9.80 p. 13.
14 Willis ibid., p. 109.
15 Mann ibid., p. 75.
16 Mann ibid., p. 76.
17 Mann ibid., p. 76.
18 Mann ibid., p. 76.
19 Kermode, Frank (1967) *The Sense of an Ending*. OUP.
20 Willis ibid., p. 92.
21 Mann ibid., p. 77.
22 Mann ibid., p. 77.
23 Mann ibid., p. 78.
24 Mann ibid., p. 80.
25 Mann ibid., p. 80.
26 See for example: Watson, George (1978) *Modern Literary Thought*, Carl Winter. Bloom, Harold *et al.* (1979) *Deconstruction and Criticism*, RKP. Eagleton, Terry (1978) *Criticism and Ideology*, Verso. Williams, Raymond (1977) *Marxism and Literature*, OUP.
27 Kelly ibid., is a notable exception here. A commendably cautious tone characterises his paper.
28 Eisner (1978) ibid., p. 199.
29 McCutchan, Gail (1979) 'A Conflict of Interests: An Educational Criticism of Mr. Williams Fourth Grade Class' in Eisner, Eliot (1979) ibid., pp. 245–260.
30 Jenkins ibid.,
31 Greer, W. Dwaine (1978) 'A Model for the Art of Teaching and a Critique of Teaching' in Willis ibid., pp. 163–185 (this reference pp. 181/2)
32 Grumet, Madeleine (1978) 'Songs and Situations: The Figure/Grand Relation in a Case Study of *Currere*' in Willis ibid., pp. 276–315 (this reference pp. 311/12).
33 Pinar, William, F. (1978) '*Currere*: A Case Study' in Willis ibid., pp. 318–342 (this reference p. 340)
34 Greer ibid., p. 178–179.
35 Grumet ibid., p. 312.
36 Grumet ibid., p. 312.
37 Milner, Edward, W. (1978) 'The Amphibious Musician' in Willis ibid., pp. 252–273 (this reference p. 266).
38 Milner ibid., p. 257.
39 Milner ibid., p. 259.
40 Milner ibid., p. 256.
41 Pinar ibid., p. 323.
42 Greer ibid., p. 175.
43 Milner ibid., p. 253.
44 Eisner, Eliot (1979) ibid.
45 Donmoyer, Robert (1979) 'School and Society Revisited: An Educational Criticism of Miss Hill's Fourth Grade Classroom' in Eisner (1979) ibid., pp. 229–240 (this reference p. 229).
46 Barone, Thomas (1979) 'Of Scott and Lisa and Other Friends' in Eisner (1979) ibid., pp. 240–245 (this reference p. 240).
47 Eisner, Eliot (1979) ibid., p. xiii.
48 Grumet ibid., p. 311.
49 Willis ibid., pp. 243–244.
50 Jenkins ibid.
51 Jenkins, David and O'Toole, Bridget (1978) 'Curriculum Evaluation, Literary Criticism and the Paracurriculum' in Willis ibid., pp. 524–554 (this reference p. 540).
52 Jenkins op. cit. p. 349.
53 Jenkins ibid., 352.
54 Jenkins ibid., pp. 355–356.

55 Jenkins ibid., p. 358.
56 Jenkins ibid., p. 367.
57 Jenkins ibid., p. 368.
58 Jenkins ibid., p. 351.
59 Jenkins ibid., p. 345.
60 Jenkins ibid., p. 346.
61 Jenkins ibid., pp. 353–354.
62 Jenkins ibid., p. 354.
63 Jenkins ibid., p. 354.
64 Jenkins ibid., p. 368.
65 Jenkins ibid., p. 369.
66 Jenkins ibid., p. 369.
67 Jenkins ibid., p. 355.
68 Jenkins ibid., p. 346.
69 Jenkins ibid., p. 350.
70 Jenkins ibid., p. 346.
71 Jenkins ibid., p. 369.
72 Jenkins ibid., p. 357.
73 Jenkins ibid., p. 369.
74 Jenkins ibid., p. 348.
75 Jenkins ibid., p. 360.
76 Jenkins ibid., p. 359.
77 Jenkins ibid., p. 346.
78 Jenkins ibid., pp. 351–352.
79 Jenkins ibid., p. 352.
80 Jenkins ibid., p. 353.
81 Jenkins ibid., p. 369.
82 Jenkins ibid., p. 361.
83 Jenkins ibid., p. 350.
84 Jenkins ibid., p. 369.
85 Watson, George (1978) *The Discipline of English*. Macmillan p. 106.

6 Authenticity, autonomy and compulsory curriculum

*Michael Bonnett**

This paper has a limited purpose. It does not pretend to present a rigorously argued position. Rather it represents, in part, an attempt to indicate in brief outline a way in which some ideas developed in what could broadly be termed "the existentialist tradition" might be brought to bear on a topic of current interest in educational theorising. This will take the form of a sketch of a critique of a currently fashionable view on the topic to be considered. But, to reiterate, what follows is a sketch, only.

In several places in the recent literature of philosophy of education and curriculum theory it is sought to draw a practical connection between the following of one or other sort of compulsory curriculum and the development of personal autonomy. In this chapter I wish to outline an argument for the following position:

1   Those proposals for compulsory curricula which have been suggested by their authors to be justifiable, in part at least, in terms of promoting personal autonomy are not so justifiable, because:
2   The notion of a compulsory curriculum, *in so far as it results in specification of content independently of an individual learner's motivations at a particular time*, is likely to be antipathetic to the promotion of that end.

In generalised terms, the view to be criticised is the one which, developing the idea that autonomy at least involves making informed choices, draws the seemingly plausible conclusion that the end of developing personal autonomy is best served by the compulsory initiation of pupils into public forms of knowledge which provide frameworks for informed choice. While emphases differ, I believe that it is correct to attribute this view to such writers as R. S. Peters, P. H. Hirst, R. F. Dearden, J. P. White and D. Lawton.[1] By way of illustration, I intend to consider in a little more detail the work of White. I will confine myself to his recent book *Towards a Compulsory Curriculum* in which his views are particularly clearly expressed.

The basic idea in White's book is that ultimately a person must determine where his own good lies for himself, for there is no satisfactory account to be given of a notion of *objective* intrinsic worth. Intrinsic worth can only be satisfactorily denned *subjectively*: as that which someone desires for its own sake on reflection. I cannot, and need not, go into the arguments which White adduces to support his view here; though certainly the idea of something's being intrinsically valuable in an objective sense is problematic.[2] What is important in the present context, however, is the move from this premise to certain prescriptions for curriculum design. On White's view it becomes an important aim of education, and a justifiable interference of their present liberty, to bring pupils to approach an ideal state of being able to choose for themselves what they are to do with their lives. By "ideal state" is meant being in a position of having rationally reflected upon all the realistic possibilities open to an individual, so that he can conceive of a way of life which will actually maximise opportunities for having those experiences which, after due reflection, are considered by that individual to constitute his own good. (Certain strictures on this principle arising from moral grounds are dealt with by White – and indeed form an important part of his overall thesis – but it is not necessary to complicate the argument in this way for my limited purpose.)

Naturally, White emphasises the ideal nature of the state of a person who has an adequate knowledge and understanding of all the options relevant to choosing a way of life for himself; nonetheless, as an ideal it sets down several substantive guidelines for educational practice in schools. One of the chief of these is that all pupils should be compelled to engage in at least those activities which it can be shown require actual *participation* in order for understanding of them to occur. Thus, it is claimed, one could gain some understanding of, say, mountain climbing as an activity by watching a film of others so engaged, but watching a mathematician or scientist at work could, by itself, in no way lead to an understanding of these activities. To gain understanding in areas such as these requires that one actually *does* some maths or science. In no other way could one acquire those concepts, ways of thinking and structuring experience, which give those activities their distinctive meaning and value, fundamentally making them what they are. White's claim would be, presumably, not that one could learn nothing at all from a film, say, of a scientist at work discussing hypotheses, conducting experiments, making accurate records of observations, etc., but that one would gain no understanding of scientific thinking from the *inside*, that is the nature of the problems as they confront the scientist, for they are constituted by his peculiar perspective on the world, involving a restructuring of the everyday world. The extent to which one could understand *this*, one would *ipso facto* already be engaging in scientific thinking and this, it seems safe to assume, is not a capacity to be gained purely as a result of watching a film of a scientist at work. Rather its acquisition requires a more or less lengthy period of initiation into grappling firsthand with scientific problems – applying relevant concepts and coming to see their interrelationships in the context of a scientific investigation.

Activities which require engagement for understanding to occur White terms "category I" activities, and they include: using one's mother tongue (preeminently), engaging in pure mathematics, engaging in the exact physical sciences, appreciating works of art, philosophising. In order that all children know about the whole range of activities they might want to choose for their own sake, we are, according to White, justified in compelling them to attend at least to category I activities until they have acquired an understanding of them in the sense indicated above. However, these are not the only activities which White argues should form part of a compulsory curriculum. There are those studies such as history which are necessary for a person to conceive of a range of ideal ways of life; others such as economics, political science, self-knowledge (e.g. an understanding of the unconscious), careers information, he will need in order to make realistic plans for future action. The result is a compulsory curriculum of quite formidable breadth and depth.

Autonomy, authenticity and information

The thesis in this section is that White is operating with a faulty notion of autonomy: he distorts the notion by placing undue emphasis on one of its constituent moments – that of being informed (or misinformed) – at the expense of a more centrally constituent moment – that of authenticity.

Autonomy is frequently explicated in terms of a man making choices according to a code of principles which are his own. Dearden, for example, suggests the following three necessary conditions for a person to be autonomous:[3]

1   that to explain important areas of a person's action, it is necessary to refer to his own choices, deliberations, decisions;
2   that the person has a reflective and critical attitude towards the criteria upon which he bases his judgments;
3   that his thought and action are consistent with his reflections.

Now what, immediately, needs to be said here is that "own" in the first condition surely cannot merely signify that one *has* certain thoughts, etc., for in this sense any thoughts which occur to one would be one's "own". For the condition to be effective a certain pregnant sense of "own" must be in operation. If relevant to the idea of autonomy, it must be a sense of "own" which indicates that somehow one's choices, deliberations, decisions, etc., are not purely the result of such possible external influences as subliminal or hypnotic suggestion, another's charisma, brainwashing, drugs, overwhelming pressure of social norms, stereotypes, or other's expectations, etc., *but that one's thoughts are in some sense self-originated.* Similarly, this same pregnant sense of "own" must be incorporated into the second condition, for again, one can adopt a reflective and critical attitude to one's judgments on the basis of some set of further criteria which one holds to be appropriate only through the influence of factors of the above mentioned kind. I will return to the significance of this point shortly.

To refer back to White's position, I would like to make the further point that there is nothing inherently strange in the idea of someone's acting autonomously either when his options are very limited in reality, or when his options are very limited in belief. That is to say, freedom and autonomy are not coextensive here. For example, the decision as to whether or not to die for one's regiment is one which could be quite autonomous despite (a) the fact that one's options were clearly limited; (b) if in reality one made a decision on the basis of false beliefs about the prevailing military situation. Autonomy has nothing to do with the range of options available (with the exception, of course, of the limiting case of there being no alternatives), and certainly it can in no way guarantee action which is appropriate to an objective situation. Autonomy requires only that one rationally chooses for oneself between the options as they are believed to be. That is to say that in this respect autonomy involves rationality, but not necessarily knowledge. The information requirement here is only that there be a choice in the sense that the alternatives that exist for a subject are at least accompanied by distinguishing beliefs concerning them which the subject perceives to be adequate to his purposes. There is a rationality requirement in the sense that the decision is ultimately grounded in the subject's lived experience through a conception of means to ends, which has at some stage been critically reflected upon in the light of his existing meaning system. And there is the further requirement, what one might term an "authenticity" requirement, that the ends must be the subject's own in some pregnant sense. To this sense I will now return, for the way in which this problem of "ownership" is resolved is central to the critique to be suggested of White's compulsory curriculum as a means of furthering personal autonomy. The consideration of this problem will involve a brief account of the development of a notion of authenticity, followed by an attempt to resolve in outline what will be taken to be one of its central problems – the nature of a 'self basic to authenticity'.

Authenticity

There exists a considerable body of literature in the existentialist tradition which is concerned to give an account of both the nature and the importance of the sense of "own" with which it is suggested we should now be concerned. In what follows I wish to indicate the possible contribution of some particular insights which have been developed by J.-P. Sartre and M. Merleau-Ponty. In doing so, I do not wish to be understood to be necessarily developing a view of authenticity with which either of these thinkers would ultimately agree. My intention here is strictly limited to an attempt to sketch a notion of authenticity which may illuminate the present problem.

In *Being and Nothingness*, Sartre gives a view of man and his relationship to the world which is particularly significant. He does this by means of a distinction between the "in-itself" and the "for-itself", which roughly corresponds to a distinction between non-self-aware and self-aware entities. The "in-itself" is thinglike ("massif"), it does not exist for itself and therefore is not capable of self-determination, for there is no space between it and the world. It is wholly bound in with the causal world. By contrast, the "for-itself" is an object for itself, and it is thus capable of being aware of its relationship to the world. This is possible, Sartre asserts, only through a negation of being such that there exists a space ("nothingness") which insulates the "for-itself" from the pervasive immediacy of the world, making possible the idea of choice. For Sartre, man constitutes the class of the "for-itself" and man is thus characterised by his potential for free choice. Man is freedom incarnate, though often, through ignorance or fear, he does not recognise his essential freedom, trading it for the security born of social (or other) conformity. He deceives himself into thinking that he is "thinglike", determined by, for example, his social roles, his habits and personality traits, laws and principles. In this way he seeks to escape the responsibility for making real choices, thus avoiding the sense of anxiety which is held to be attendant upon the realisation of this. Formally man is free, he *could* always have chosen to do other than he did. To live in a way which does not acknowledge this essential fact is to live in the way of "*bad faith*", to live *inauthentically*.

Now this account seems to me to have some merit, bringing into prominence, as it does, a self-evident but important truth about the nature of man. This is the fact that for man there is always the possibility of choice. This is true only formally speaking, for a situation may not be *experienced* as offering choice to an individual. He may act unreflectively out of habit or under pressure at gunpoint, but he could (ontologically) always choose to do otherwise, and it has been the mission of some existentialist philosophers to make us realise this. For to appreciate its formal truth may facilitate its truth in practice.

However, as Merleau-Ponty has pointed out, as it stands this analysis of the human situation is misleading.[4] It suggests that human freedom is absolute on the subjective side. It suggests that because one can, in thought, stand back from the on-going world, from one's past, from one's present situation, and from one's projects for the future, there is nothing that need condition one's choices. It would appear that the only limits on freedom are those that it sets itself in the form of its various initiatives – a rock face is only unclimbable (in the sense of being a barrier to freedom) for someone whose projects involve climbing it – and the projects which one has one could always choose differently. One's past aspirations, intentions, projects, way of life, need in no way determine one's present and future projects. One could always choose to do something else. Now the objection here is that if freedom were *everywhere* in man's decisions it would also be *nowhere*. Choice would amount to chaos. As Merleau-Ponty puts it, freedom must be buttressed by being. It is an important truth that one's choices are never *causally determined*, but it is an equally important truth that they are *motivated*.

He makes this point in the following way. Freedom should not be equated with conscious voluntary deliberation leading to a decision, for what count as motives and reasons in this process and their weighting must *already* have been decided. A motive can only have force (i.e. *be* a motive) by virtue of some prior "secret" decision to which it either conforms or runs counter. In voluntary deliberation we are, as it were, just going over the possibilities in an attempt to make explicit a decision which was already implicit, for how else could there be a weighing up? Factors are not consciously endowed with their weighting, i.e. *made* factors, they enter the area of conscious deliberation already as such, their precise relative worth to be discovered. The final decision, then, is not, and could not be, *absolutely* free. Free choice is never wide open on the subjective side any more than it is on the objective side. If it were, deliberation would be anarchy. Previous acts of freedom involve some sort of future commitment, for this is just what it is to decide to take up a project. The past must condition (but not determine) the future. Freedom could not be purely gratuitous, it must be related to what a person truly *is*. In short, it must be *his* freedom. For Merleau-Ponty, freedom consists in willing what we are, in taking up the situation in which we find ourselves – pursuing projects, creating a field of action. Thus freedom requires a universal commitment to the world which enables one to interrupt one project *in order to pursue another* ("we never remain suspended in nothingness"). It is not in spite of my motives that I am free, but by means of them. Only by being what I am have I the chance to communicate with the world, and the chance to move forward.

Now this account of personal freedom is particularly significant in the present context, incorporating, as it does, a notion of authenticity in which a self is given prominence, and linking this up to the possibility of entering into meaningful relationship with the world. However, in conditioning choice – in reinterpreting the way of "bad faith" as not simply a denial that there is always a choice, but rather as a denial of one's true decisions which are conditioned by what one *is*, as it were, one's "true" self – the need arises for a closer specification of this latter notion.

Authenticity and the "constitutive self"[5]

What constitutes the self is a problem that has long exercised the minds of philosophers, but it may be that many of the difficulties associated with the general problem can be circumvented if we keep before us our particular purposes in asking this question in the present context. We are interested in the relationship between the expression of self in framing and carrying out its projects, and the way in which a person can enter into meaningful relationship with the world. The suggestion is that the former is the means as to the latter. Passive receptivity to sensory input could not be a mode of significant awareness, for a principle for interpreting and relating such input is lacking. It is being suggested that it is *action* which is a person's primary point of contact with a significant world, for it is primordially through the medium of *practice* that otherwise isolated items of input (or, equally, amorphous input) are distinguished and brought into significant relationship. Through our particular attempts to act we are "brought up against the world", feel its "resistance", and it is this which constitutes our personal understanding of it. We find it, for example, either accommodating or repulsing, friendly or hostile to such and such a degree and in such and such a manner with respect to our particular actions, and also, maybe, our actions in general. Similarly, once we have some first-hand acquaintanceship with the world through concrete action, we may acquire some theoretical understanding of it through attempting to anticipate the consequences of connected but new possibilities for action. In sum, when we act, or seriously contemplate an action, the world takes on certain properties for us; we encounter objects in our path whose precise significance for us is determined by the quality of resistance they offer.

Now an action can only be characterised from the point of view conception of what he is doing will be in terms of what he intends to bring about, and his conception of how he is faring will be in terms of the quality of resistance met in seeking to achieve this end. This means that essentially it is one's *intentions*[6] which bring one into significant relationship with the world and it would seem to follow, therefore, that the "self" in which we are interested must be some sort of core structure of such intentions. We *are* our projects on the world, but a deeper intentional structure is required to explain the direction and coherence of more specific and limited intentions. This structure I will term the "*constitutive self*". It consists of those most general and overarching intentions by reference to which one's thoughts and actions ultimately receive felt value and intelligibility. That is to say, it constitutes a source of meaning, giving us our essential point of view on the world. Now it is important to realise that the constitutive self must have a genetic dimension (and, indeed, it is this which enables it and the structures which it motivates to be formally distinguished from other intentional structures that a person may acquire). In order *to* make intelligible at all the idea of human mental development, we must postulate a basic motivation to make sense of the world. *But this in turn presupposes certain substantive interests (intentions) which provide a certain standpoint*, for without this there would be nothing within the subject for the world to be related to. There could be nothing to receive the world for there would be nothing to inform the world. There would be nothing to initiate action upon the world. *It is the history of these primordial intentions, their development into a genealogy of overlapping intentions, which is the history of the constitutive self.* The extent to which they are unable to find expression, unable to initiate specific projects on the world, is the extent to which they remain empty and the extent to which the self is denied meaning.

R. D. Laing has investigated ways in which the denial of self can be conceptualised and used to make sense of schizoid conditions.[7] He has developed the notion of a "false self system" which stands between the world and the rejected "real self", mediating and diluting experience of the world. Such false selves are façades which are presented as a defence against a world felt to be hostile, but they have developed a certain life of their own – a certain degree of autonomy – with the consequence that the real self is weakened in proportion, being to that degree closed in upon itself, living to that degree impoverished and vicariously. For such a person full authenticity becomes impossible. So too, does full inauthenticity, for to a greater or lesser degree such a person has passed beyond the human condition. He is no longer capable of true choice, no longer responsible for action. In the terminology of the preceding paragraph, the constitutive self is no longer necessary (or perhaps necessary, but only in a very indirect way) to account for important areas of behaviour. I mention this extreme possibility here because it may provide an illuminating parallel with the sort of understanding some children are likely to acquire under compulsory curriculum, as I have defined it. I will return to this in the next section.

To conclude this and the preceding section: the suggestion has become that the pregnant sense of "own", to which reference was made earlier as being necessary to the idea of autonomy, is to be thought of in terms of a relationship which can exist between action (and, concomitantly, understanding) and the constitutive self. Actions (*and, concomitantly, understanding*) *can appropriately be said to be owned in this pregnant sense when the choices they involve are motivated by and are internally related to the constitutive self.* 'Motivation', here, not signifying determination, but the *conditioning* of choice in the sense that it is in terms of motives arising from the constitutive self that choices are made. On this account, then, choices, and bits of understanding, may be thought of as existing in the following three modes:

1   They are *authentic* when they are conditioned by the constitutive self in the way described above.
2   They are *inauthentic* when they are in *conflict* with (*including obtrusively irrelevant to*) the constitutive self, i.e. they are "dissonant" with authentic choices, actions and understanding.
3   They are *non-authentic* to the extent that either (a) they are a matter of *indifference* to the constitutive self, or (b) the constitutive self has ceased to function, as in ways suggested by Laing, for example.

Authenticity and compulsory curriculum

I have previously characterised a compulsory curriculum as one in which children are compelled to participate in certain activities regardless of their personal motivations. Thus, for White, a child should be compelled to engage in mathematics, science, philosophy, history, economics, etc., with the aim that he be enabled to perceive the world through these various perspectives, having internalised the relevant conceptual frameworks and the values (e.g. concern for consistency, relevance, humility before the facts) which may be implicit in them. In the light of the thesis that I have attempted to sketch in this paper, two criticisms arise.

First, for the child whose personal motivations are counter to studying one or more of these areas, compulsion (in so far as there is a distinction – a point to which I will return at the end of this paper) will amount to coercion. If successful, the child will be forced into living through structures which are either irrelevant to, or in conflict with, his constitutive self. They will be inauthentic structures, and therefore, for him, hollow and essentially not understood. Encountered in this way they cannot become part of what is truly him. This is to say that in terms of the aim which I have just attributed to White, when compulsion becomes coercion – as is likely in a number of cases – the exercise is self-defeating. Its outcome is likely to be boredom, verbalism, and possibly rebellion.

Related to this criticism is a second, more pervasive one levelled at all situations where a pupil's learning is directed (rather than guided) by a teacher. In situations where children are made to feel that it is of overriding importance to attend to objects which are either not pertinent to their personal directions of interest, or are beyond their capacity to understand, it seems that this could only be conducive to fostering an inner sense of lack of security and lack of self-worth. Now in teacher-directed learning, this undesirable consequence seems likely in the very nature of the case, for however well intentioned the teacher, he cannot ensure an ideal match (or "mis-match") between learner and task. As John Holt has pointed out,[8] since it is difficult to see how the teacher can possibly know precisely what a child needs next in order to make sense of the world in his own terms, it is hard to see how he can avoid confronting the child with what, for the child at least, will be senseless, ambiguous and contradictory. Where, by this means, children are forced to live in objects which are relatively meaningless to them – either through lack of interest or lack of understanding – Holt's suggestion that we teach children to be stupid, to be afraid to gamble, try the difficult, experiment, would seem to have some justification. In the circumstances, the child is too likely to fail according to canons he does not fully grasp.

It should be noted that the above considerations are not just a poor sort of arm-chair psychology, they are *conceptual* considerations. For example, while it may be possible that for some people, being confronted by the meaningless, the ambiguous, and the contradictory could lead to their acquiring a deep understanding of a subject, this could not be the normal case. We have to give some kind of special explanation in cases where this occurs. If this were not so, terms such as "meaning-less", "ambiguous" and "contradictory" could not have the meanings they have. Similarly, if we accept the premise of a "self" composed of certain directions of thought (intentions), it is not a merely empirical matter that to have these directions of thought ignored, or positively discriminated against, by those taken as being authorities on what is worthwhile will, in the normal case, lead to a sense of insecurity and lack of self-worth. Having one's fundamental aspirations consistently ignored or belittled by people whose opinions one respects is a *criterion* of situations which cause loss of sense of self-worth.

To summarise the argument at this point: in the context of successful compulsory curriculum (i.e. a curriculum that does compel), when the child's ends and the ends of the teacher as perceived by the child are not at one, the result is that the child is compelled to live through structures which are inauthentic and therefore of no real value for him. He is required to become committed to objects which at that time have only the significance of obstacle to what he really wants to do, what he really is. He is invited to deny himself, and the sad thing is that in the circumstances, he may accept the invitation. To recall Dewey on this point:[9]

> 'Tis an old story that through custom we finally embrace what at first wore a hideous mien. Unpleasant, because meaningless, activities may get agreeable if long enough persisted in ... I frequently hear dulling devices and empty exercises defended and extolled because "the children take such an 'interest' in them". Yes, that is the worst of it; the mind, shut out from worthy employ and missing the taste of adequate performance, comes down to the level of that which is left to it to know and do, and perforce takes an interest in a cabined and cramped experience.

The extent to which this occurs is the extent to which, harking back to Laing, a "false self system" with respect to understanding is interposed between the constitutive self and the world.

Conclusion

To live inauthentically is just to have life less richly, for to live through structures which are not one's own in a pregnant sense is to live at a level devoid of personal value and significance, *positive* and *felt*. If it is accepted that being authentic is the means by which a person can enter into truly meaningful relationship with the world, then it must, in general, be justified, i.e. there must be a presupposition in its favour. The onus is on the person who wishes to say that it is undesirable in a particular case to give good reasons for his claim. Hargreaves has characterised the thesis of the "New Romantics" as resting in part upon a notion of the child's "innate goodness",[10] but this is not strictly necessary to their argument (and is, anyway, probably too problematic to help it). All that need be said is that the child has a basic motivation to make sense of the world, i.e. he is committed to be *in* the world. But the child can only move out from what he already is. There is no way in which he can be beyond what he is, and therefore authentic learning (i.e. learning which is internally related to authentic action) is the only sort which has any direct value for him. This is really, perhaps, only to state truisms, but they are truisms that are in danger of being overlooked by advocates of compulsory curriculum. In the rush to get children to a position of making informed choices, they may be frustrating the possibility of them coming to make choices which are significantly their own.

What now, then, of the relationship between personal autonomy and education? Might it not be argued that if a correct and fairly full understanding of one's objective situation is not a necessary part of personal autonomy, then it seems too poor a notion to serve as an educational ideal? I suggest that such an argument should be accepted. But to do so does not detract from the importance of a regard for personal autonomy in educational practice. It will mean only that the regard takes on a different orientation. In a strictly educational context (as contrasted, for example, with a therapeutic one), the general regard for personal autonomy will become conceived of less in terms of something to be eventually *achieved by* pupils, and rather more in terms of something to be respected and *maintained in* pupils. It is true that certain general reasoning powers, and self-knowledge of an appropriate kind are necessary to autonomy; education may help to develop these. But, in general, being knowledgeable and being autonomous overlap very little, and part of the skill of the educator, perhaps, lies in fostering the former without jeopardising the latter.

The suggestion in this paper has been that for *some* children, namely those for whom what they are compelled to do conflicts with authentic action, a compulsory curriculum is likely to be counter-productive to both the above ends. But perhaps one should go further, for in so far as the term "compulsory" has any *practical force*, this is likely to hold true for *all* children. Surely, *in a concrete situation*, the idea of compulsion is only pertinent where someone will not do something of their own volition? That is to say, concretely speaking, does not compulsion always amount to *coercion*? If so, on the view put forward in this paper, and external demands apart (e.g. "needs of society", basic requirements for the child's "survival", moral considerations), the price of knowledge gained under a compulsory curriculum is likely to be too high for any child. And external demands included, the balance must be very carefully weighed if more harm than necessary is to be avoided.

Notes and references

* Originally published in: *Cambridge Journal of Education* 6: 3, 107–121.
1 See, for example:
  Hirst, P. H. and Peters, R. S., *The Logic of Education*, Routledge, London, 1970.

Dearden, R. F., *The Philosophy of Primary Education*, Routledge, London, 1968.

Lawton, D., *Social Change, Educational Theory and Curriculum Planning*, University of London Press, 1974.

White, J. P., *Towards a Compulsory Curriculum*, Routledge, London, 1973.

2 See White, J. P., op. cit. Ch. 2, for a clear and concise account of some of the problems in this area.

3 In a paper given to the Cambridge Branch of the Philosophy of Education Society of Great Britain, February 1975.

4 Merleau-Ponty, M., *Phenomenology of Perception*, Part 3, Ch. 3, translated by Colin Smith, Routledge, London, 1962.

5 For a fuller discussion of some of the ideas touched upon in this section, see Bonnett, M. R., *A Notion of Intentionality and Its Significance for Education*, unpublished M.A. Dissertation submitted to the University of London Institute of Education, 1974.

6 Throughout this paper I use this term in a broad sense so as to include one's active purposes, interests, designs, projects, aspirations, motives, i.e. whatsoever is intentional in the sense of involving direction upon an object with a certain intent or "mindedness" which is constitutive of, or has implications for, action. Thus in so far as one considers emotions and moods to be of this character, these, too, would be included.

7 Laing, R. D., *The Divided Self*, Penguin, Harmondsworth, 1965.

8 Holt, J., *How Children Fail*, Pitman, London, 1964.

9 Dewey, J., *The Child and the Curriculum*, several editions.

10 Hargreaves, D. H., "Deschoolers and New Romantics", in *Educability, Schools and Ideology*, edited by Flude, M. and Ahier, J., Croom Helm, London, 1974.

7 Authenticity, autonomy and compulsory curriculum

A reply to Michael Bonnett

*John White**

Michael Bonnett presents his thesis on authenticity in pretty stark opposition to my views on a compulsory curriculum. I am not as convinced as he is that the two positions are irreconcilable. They may prove to be so in the end, especially if one gives the key terms a certain interpretation. But let us see first what common ground we can both accept.

We neither seem to favour coercing pupils to do things. (See my *Towards a Compulsory Curriculum* (henceforth TCC), ch. 3, note 4, p. 104.) It is obviously better that children enjoy studying than being dragooned into doing it. One may object to coercion for more than one reason. There is the moral, libertarian argument that I stressed in TCC. But there is also the psychological argument, that coercion gets in the way of learning, or at least in the way of any learning which connects what is learnt with the existing knowledge, desires and attitudes of a unified self. I take it that this is a main thesis in Bonnett's argument. It is capable of two interpretations.

It may imply, first, that if a child is coerced now, he cannot learn *now* (in the required sense of 'learn'). This might seem to be a logical truth, in that (a) for learning to occur there must be some interest in whatever is to be learned, otherwise there could be no assimilation to the unified self, but (b) if coercion is necessary, interest is lacking. But it is not a logical, but only at most a psychological truth, for it is logically possible that coercion might suddenly create a *new* interest. This may even be psychologically possible in some cases: if it is, the psychological truth in question is at most a statement of tendency merely.

The second interpretation is that coercion *now* hinders learning *later*. This is clearly an empirical claim and, again, at most a tendency-claim: there are just too many well-attested cases of children who have learned Latin or whatever in fear of their teachers but who have later come to value it for its own sake to turn the claim into anything more absolute.

So I would accept the truth in both versions of the thesis, though I doubt if Bonnett would agree with me about their logical status as empirical claims. I would accept, too, his account of a unified self as involving overarching intentions under which subordinate intentions fit and to which newly acquired intentions have to be connected. It reminds me of Gordon Allport's account of the growth of personality; and also of J. F. Herbart's account of the growth of apperception-masses (although Bonnett's notion of the progressive structuring of intentions is probably more fruitful than Herbart's talk of the interconnexions of 'ideas'). I don't think there is any dispute between us over any of these points. If this is all that is involved in talking of the 'authentic self' and 'authentic learning', I am a believer in authenticity. But I would prefer not to use the term, if it can be replaced by simpler expressions, as its meaning might get entwined with other meanings which seem to me more questionable. I suspect that Bonnett does want to write more into 'authenticity' than the vanilla-flavoured meaning I have given it so far. I shall be saying rather more about this later.

So much for the common ground between us. Where, if anywhere, do we diverge? In Bonnett's view, my insistence on a compulsory curriculum is at odds with authenticity. But is it? To answer this, we need to know what I am writing into the term 'compulsory'. A 'compulsory' curriculum, as I used the word, means more than one thing. Perhaps I can use this opportunity to make clear some ambiguities in TCC, about which I ought to have been more explicit, (a) A 'compulsory' curriculum may mean one imposed on all schools by a central authority, (b) Where there is no compulsory curriculum in sense (a), we may still ask, about any particular school, which curriculum subjects it should make compulsory for all its pupils. In both (a) and (b), a compulsory curriculum is one *insisted on*, in the first case by central authority, in the second, by a school.

A further ambiguity needs clarification. In saying that a certain curriculum should be insisted on, one might mean (x) that certain terminal objectives should be insisted on or (y) that a certain course of study should be insisted on. In TCC I was centrally concerned with (x); but since it was part of my argument that certain objectives (e.g. an understanding of mathematics) could not be reached without engaging in certain activities (e.g. mathematical thinking), I also argued for (y) in some cases (i.e. the 'Category I' activities).

There are at least these four ways, then, in which I have used the term 'compulsory curriculum'. Intellectually sinful though these shifts may be, I don't think that a demand for compulsion in any of these senses gets in the way of a demand for 'authentic learning', as so far defined. Bonnett thinks it does in some cases because he believes that a compulsory curriculum involves coercion 'for the child whose personal motivations are counter to studying one or more of these (compulsory) areas'.

But at what point in time are we considering these personal motivations? Are we considering a child at the start of his (primary or secondary) school career? Suppose at this point he hates subjects A and B, some competence in which is demanded when he leaves school as a part of a compulsory curriculum in sense (y) above. It does not follow that he will have to be *coerced* into doing A and B. All kinds of blandishments may be used to entice him towards them. Every good teacher, parent or professional, knows the importance of coaxing children, often by the most unobvious of means, into forms of learning which they might otherwise have found off-putting. I am not making the familiar reply to Bonnett that there are carrots as well as sticks. Carrot-learning, we may both agree, is best avoided since it endangers authenticity. This is, rather, the point of view of the better kind of 'child-centred' educator – the kind who trusts more to the arts of seduction than to laissez-faire.

But perhaps Bonnett has in mind not a pupil beginning school but one who has already been at school some time, has experienced subjects A and B and still finds them repugnant. If A and B are to be insisted on, one must find some way of getting him to do them. Suppose, further, that all kinds of positive inducements, both of the carrot and the seduction type, have been unsuccessful over a long period of time. What is there left but the stick?

I would not myself follow through to this conclusion. No education system is going to be perfect. Where past failures have been as abject as this, I would follow Ray Elliott's advice and set the pupil on to something more profitable to him.[1] My argument for a compulsory curriculum is an argument for getting clear about those objectives on which we should insist in general. It is compatible with a modicum of failure, just as the existence of psychopaths does not nullify attempts to work out what minimum standards of morality should be generally expected.

So I do not see why a compulsory curriculum in any of my senses need endanger Bonnett's authentic self. We have still failed to find any significant difference of opinion between us. There is, however, a further thesis in his article which does give more promise of a rift, if it is rifts that we are looking for. He suggests that my compulsory curriculum puts too much stress on information and too little on the growth of authenticity. He has a good point here, though to put it in terms of 'information' might suggest I am more old-fashioned than I am. I emphasise as an educational objective the acquisition of understanding about various activities and ways of life. This is too narrow. I do gesture in places towards something more – towards the need for integration of what is learned (*TCC*, pp. 50ff.) and towards the development of permanent dispositions (pp. 84ff.). Since I wrote *TCC*, I have become increasingly drawn to the Herbartian view that morality is the chief end of education. This, too, implies a shift in the direction of dispositions as well as understanding. Since Bonnett's 'constitutive self' consists of developing hierarchies of action-tendencies (intentions), he might find more room for agreement with me. In any case, I never saw my theory of a compulsory curriculum as *complete*: the 'Towards' in the title was a deliberate choice. Bonnett writes at times as if my stress on understanding is *at odds with* his stress on authenticity. The truth is, rather, that I *presupposed* something like the latter all along. I was assuming that the educated person would be a unified self who had not been doctored into having certain wants like a gamma in *Brave New World*: I quite agree that I would have made a better case if I had exposed these assumptions and justified them.

Where I think a *real* rift may open up between us is where 'authenticity' is given a richer sense than that ascribed to it so far. Bonnett talks of a child's 'basic motivation to make sense of the world', describing this as a 'genetic dimension' of the constitutive self. He suggests that the 'New Romantics' would do better to insist on *this* form of innateness rather than on the child's innate goodness. There are hints in all this of a strong form of child-centredness which I do not find acceptable. A reconstruction of this stronger thesis would go something like this. Whatever a child learns should be connected with his unified self: it should be his own, not something external to him. Learning must be a development, therefore, of what is already within. But unless the child is equipped at birth with a self-fuelling disposition to learn, learning is impossible. Since learning exists the innate disposition must also exist. Hence a lack of interest in defining curricular objectives: the child powers his own development, towards innately determined ends.

This neo-romanticism, backed today by phenomenological existentialism just as that of earlier generations was backed by Piaget, E. G. A. Holmes, Froebel or Rousseau, is open to the central objection that it fails to do justice to the social nature of man. The *completely* autonomous individual, accepting nothing on the authority of anyone else, is a myth, as Quinton, following in the long line of recent opponents of atomistic individualism, has recently shown.[2] I have no space to develop this critique in greater detail. If I had, it would be partly on the same lines as Langford's and Hirst's objections to Elliott's similar developmentalism in his lecture on 'Education and Human Being'.[3] But since it is in any case not altogether clear just how firmly Bonnett *is* committed to this stronger thesis, I might, after all, find myself wasting ink.

Notes and references

* Originally published in: *Cambridge Journal of Education* 6: 3, 122–126.
1 Elliott, R. K., 'Education and Human Being I' in Brown, S. C. (ed.) *Philosophers discuss Education*, Macmillan, London, 1975, p. 70.
2 Quinton, A., 'Authority and Autonomy in Knowledge' in *Proceedings of Philosophy of Education Society*, Vol. V, No. 2, July 1971.
3 In Brown, S. C. op. cit.

8   The idea of a pastoral curriculum

*Terence H. McLaughlin**[*][†]*

One of the most obvious and widespread manifestations of the growing involvement of schools in the area of Social and Personal development has been the emergence both in educational discourse and in the practice of schools of the notion of "Pastoral Care". It is now being increasingly suggested that a "Pastoral Curriculum" should be an integral part of "Pastoral Care". This idea has been advocated by several prominent figures working in the field,[1] and the practical implementation of the notion has been assisted by the development and publication of structured teaching and learning material for use in the "tutor period" situation.[2]

Elsewhere[3] 1 have drawn attention to the need for the concept of "Pastoral Care" in schools – and in an educational context generally – to be subjected to careful critical analysis. It seems clear that the concept of a "Pastoral Curriculum" also stands in need of the same kind of treatment. In this paper, therefore, I shall seek to raise several fundamental questions of a primarily philosophical kind about the notion. There are, of course, many *practical* questions arising, but here I shall confine myself to a consideration of *principles*.

I shall seek to address several issues:

a   What is meant by the notion of a "Pastoral Curriculum"?
b   Principles for determining the character of the "Pastoral Curriculum".
c   Should the school be concerned with the "Pastoral Curriculum"?

a What is meant by the notion of a "Pastoral Curriculum"?

The basic idea underlying the notion seems to be that "Pastoral Care" in the sense of help and advice given to individuals needs to be supplemented by a programme of planned learning activities – things to be learned and skills to be acquired – which should become part of the formal curriculum of the school and have distinctively "pastoral" objectives. The recent HMI Secondary Survey noted that the overwhelming majority of schools sought to achieve their "pastoral" objectives by care rather than by curricula provision[4] and this was a state of affairs they criticised. What arguments are generally advanced for supplementing "Pastoral Care" by a distinctively "Pastoral" element of the curriculum?

The most commonly used argument seems to be in terms of extending the effectiveness of the Pastoral Care offered by the school. Care offered to individuals, runs the argument, can only respond to particular problems as they arise. What is needed is systematic and general treatment of a range of relevant issues in a "Pastoral Curriculum" so that the pupils are equipped with necessary knowledge and skills in this area. In this vein, Marland writes:

> unless we have an agreed background curriculum, we are depending upon children having crises before we can offer any help; that way we don't know their problem until they know their problem – and often they don't know their problem until it is too late to help them with their problem.[5]

There seems to me to be a further – and neglected – argument in favour of some of the activity going on in "Pastoral Care" taking the form of planned learning and teaching. I have drawn attention elsewhere[6] to the danger of "Pastoral Care" becoming manipulatory, indoctrinatory, unconnected with the central educational tasks of the school and damaging in a range of other ways. At least if the advice and help given to individuals is set against a background of agreed and justifiable curriculum content then these various dangers are diminished.

The term "Pastoral" is an extremely vague, unhelpful – and indeed a possibly misleading and dangerous – one. In my view it is necessary to look behind the term at exactly what we mean by the objectives and practices being advocated in its name – and this task of critical scrutiny applies to the "Pastoral Curriculum" as much as to "Pastoral Care" itself.

What precisely is involved in the notion of a "Pastoral Curriculum"? Two statements in the early part of a recent paper by Michael Marland are good examples of the kind of remark which leave the notion excessively general and vague. Thus he writes – "The Curriculum components which relate especially to individual and personal growth I would call the Pastoral Curriculum".[7] and that the aim of such a curriculum is to – "establish the concepts, attitudes, facts and skills which are necessary to the individual".[8] Although statements such as these hint at a determinate sense for the term "Pastoral Curriculum" they are imprecise and do not provide a clear enough criterion for distinguishing the "Pastoral" element of the curriculum from its other elements. Is not Liberal Education – the broad and non-instrumental initiation of the pupil into the various domains of knowledge – also related to "individual and personal growth"? Liberal Education implies much more than the acquisition of inert knowledge which is merely "stuck on". Langford, writing of the changes which occur when a person becomes educated claims – "They change the kind of person he is, making him in a real sense a different person; he is not simply the same person of whom certain things happen to be true".[9] And are not the concepts, attitudes, facts and skills developed in Liberal Education also "necessary to the individual" *in some sense?*

Marland begins to be more precise in his outline of the notion of the "Pastoral Curriculum" when he writes that it is concerned solely with – "the personal needs of the pupil resolving his individual problems, making informed decisions and taking his place in his personal and social world".[10] and that any item of content in this area should be determined by what is – "essential for the personal growth of individuals, for their learning growth ... not ... because it is part of the logic of a subject".[11] He expands this further:

> it is quite right ... that at a certain point in mathematics, negative numbers must be tackled. Negative numbers are tackled because they are part of the logic of the mathematical structure. That is proper. But I am suggesting that we have to have a check-list also for that which should be there because it is necessary for the growth of the individual.[12]

Now these remarks are more useful. They help us towards a formulation of the general character of the *aims* and *content* that might be said to be distinctive of the "Pastoral Curriculum". The aim of this part of the curriculum is clearly *instrumental* and *utilitarian* in character: it is concerned with stimulating learning which is related to the ability of the individual to deal with a range of adjustments and decisions facing him in various aspects of his life. The precise character of this aim requires further analysis and elucidation – and we shall return to this shortly. But even as it stands it is clearly distinguishable from the aims of other elements of the curriculum. One of the major elements of the curriculum is in my view concerned with "Liberal Education". Now no one clear sense can be attached to this notion and nor can it be regarded as unproblematic in itself.[13] For the purposes of this paper, however, it might be valuable to employ a rather crude characterisation of Liberal Education which lays particular emphasis on two features commonly stressed in accounts of the notion, namely *Generality* and *Non-instrumentality*. This procedure might perhaps be useful in sharpening up our attention on the distinctive features of the "pastoral curriculum", although I am conscious that leaving unexamined the central notion of "Liberal Education" may perhaps lead to the making of distinctions between the various elements of the curriculum, which are oversimple. Subsequent discussion can perhaps allow a fuller exploration of issues such as these. The primary aim of the Liberal Education component of the curriculum as I have crudely characterised it is to introduce pupils into the range of different kinds of knowledge not for the sake of helping individuals to face any particular problems they may be confronted with, but for the sake of the development of understanding. Similarly, the aim of the "Pastoral Curriculum" can be distinguished from that of "Academic Education" where this is seen as the systematic and detailed study of a particular discipline aiming at the production of specialists (in some sense) in that discipline. Now both "liberal" and "academic" education obviously have a *bearing* on the "decisions and adjustments facing the individual" which is the major concern of the "Pastoral" curriculum. But unlike the latter, their primary *aim* is not to equip pupils to handle them.

The *content* implications deriving from these distinct aims is clear. In Liberal Education, that which is to be learned is governed not by relevance to any particular "decisions and adjustments" facing the pupils but by considerations relating to the nature of knowledge alone. There will be an attempt to introduce the pupil to – "a study of at least paradigm examples of all the various forms of knowledge".[14] In "Academic Education" the criteria for content will be derived from the character of the particular discipline or disciplines to be mastered. In the case of the

"Pastoral Curriculum" however, content is delimited by reference to some account and analysis of "the kinds of decisions and adjustments thought to be likely to confront the individual".

What has emerged so far from this analysis is a still rather vague curriculum area, the aims and content of which are distinctive in that they are related to promoting learning which is concerned with helping the individual to deal with a range of as yet unspecified "decisions and adjustments" in his life. I want to suggest that this area represents the ground covered by the term "the Pastoral Curriculum". (In using this term I am not necessarily implying that work in this area should only – or indeed necessarily – take place in "pastoral" periods, namely "Tutor periods".)

Now at this point several questions might be raised. First, why should one want to call this part of the curriculum the pastoral curriculum? It seems to me that nothing hangs on excessively long analyses of the word "pastoral" and its applicability to a particular area of the curriculum. Perhaps the notion of equipping pupils to deal with *personal* decisions and adjustments leads to the term "pastoral" being used in this context. The name given to the area is not of great significance: no doubt a more appropriate and less misleading name can be found for it. What seems clear however is that the area marked out by the term "Pastoral Curriculum" as I have interpreted it is a distinctive area whose claims on the curriculum time and resources of schools are worthy of consideration. The crucial task is not one of adequately naming the area but of clarifying what it entails and assessing its importance and significance. I shall continue to use the term "Pastoral Curriculum" in this paper for convenience and without implying that there is any particular value in naming the area in this way.

Second, in tying "Pastoral Curriculum" to the notion of preparing pupils for various "decisions and adjustments facing them in their lives", is a rather restrictive definition of the term being proposed? Could not – and is not – the term used to refer to wider aspects of Social and Personal Education within the school, where there is no immediate stress on the rather utilitarian preparation I have associated with the "Pastoral Curriculum". The answer to this question is that there is no one *clear* usage of the term "Pastoral Curriculum". In a sense I have offered a stipulative definition of the term for the purpose of this paper. I would argue that this definition is persuasive in that it corresponds very closely to the way in which the term is currently used and that it makes useful and important distinctions possible.

I am not suggesting that the term "Pastoral Curriculum" in the way I have specifically defined it covers *all* the curriculum components concerned with Social and Personal Education. In my view the "Pastoral Curriculum" is only *part* of this broader area. I shall have something to say about the relationship between the "Pastoral Curriculum" and other elements of the curriculum at the end of the next section of this paper.

b Principles for determining the character of the "Pastoral Curriculum"

There are a range of questions which Philosophers of Education – quite apart from teachers and other educationists – need to ask in relation to this issue. For example, what principles can be invoked to determine the particular "problems, decisions and adjustments facing the individual" which should be selected as requiring attention by the school in the "Pastoral Curriculum"? What is the relationship between this element of the curriculum and the other elements? How is it related to "Pastoral Care"? What is the relative importance of all the various elements of the curriculum? Should the area covered by the term "Pastoral Curriculum" be the responsibility of the school at all?

Philosophers of Education have, as Jane Roland Martin has recently argued,[15] tended to concentrate their attention on the Liberal Education element of the curriculum, somewhat to the neglect of the other elements. There is much in her plea that – "Philosophical investigation of curriculum must go beyond Liberal Education".[16] She claims that – "Philosophers of Education today never ask the question 'What is left over when we subtract a Liberal Education from the whole of Education?'"[17] Now this is clearly an over-exaggeration, but it has to be admitted that more sustained philosophical attention is needed in relation to areas of the curriculum such as the "Pastoral Curriculum".

In this section of the paper I shall address two issues:

i   Principles determining the scope and content of the "Pastoral Curriculum",
ii The relationship between the "Pastoral Curriculum" and other elements of the curriculum: a crucial problem.

i Principles determining the scope and content of the "Pastoral Curriculum"

The first point to notice in relation to this question is that the scope of the "Pastoral Curriculum" is potentially unlimited. A look at the "Active Tutorial Work" programme[18] makes one aware of the wide-ranging and heterogeneous character of the kinds of objectives being attempted. They span diverse areas such as adjusting to life in school, developing study skills and practices, general social development, coping with specific aspects of life such as relationships with others, health, sex, moral decision and so on.

Faced with the potential *vastness* of what could be entailed in terms of curriculum content relevant to the aim of – "the personal needs of the pupil resolving his individual problems, making informed decisions and taking his place in his personal and social world",[19] some principles or criteria for the selection of objectives and content are needed. Much more thought needs to be devoted to this task. I suggest tentatively for consideration the following as an outline of the kinds of principles I judge to be appropriate here.

1   That the child should be equipped to deal with a range of problems, decisions and adjustments that are general in the sense of likely to face any person leading a life in our society. The strongest candidates for inclusion here are those problems, decisions and adjustments that are in some sense *unavoidable*.

2   That the school should concern itself with the kinds of problems, decisions

and adjustments outlined in (1) subject to satisfaction of the following additional criteria:

i   That the learning required is unlikely to be adequately brought about by any other means namely: by the family, by experience of life etc.

ii That the school is in a position to offer some expertise in relation to the necessary learning.

iii That dealing with these issues does not hinder the central educational task of the school, either because of an *incompatibility* between work being done in this area and that task or because of lack of resources of time, staff or money.

A comment on these three additional criteria might be appropriate. i. excludes unnecessary treatment of issues much better left to other agencies or to life itself. In Maurice Holt's recent satirical treatment of the "Pastoral Curriculum" in "Headmaster's Diary"[20] Arnold Bogwin, the cynical First Deputy, is sceptical when his colleague Sybil Fordyce returns from a course run by a county adviser keen to introduce a programme of "Planned Pastoral Progress" into the school. In response to Sybil's plea that – "Pupils must be encouraged to interact with each other, and explore each other's feelings" Arnold replies "What do kids do now all day long, then: sit and contemplate their navels?" His attitude – not without reason a common enough one – stems from the belief that the school is wasting its time in meddling with something much better left to the natural course of events. It certainly seems to me that it is incumbent upon advocates of the Pastoral Curriculum to show that the learning being stimulated under this heading really is justifiably treated in this way in the light of a criterion such as i. ii. straightforwardly excludes the school becoming involved in areas in which it lacks appropriate expertise, whilst iii. points out the fact that, in my view, the "Pastoral Curriculum" is not the *most important* thing that the school is concerned with. It could not have *priority* over what I have referred to as – "the central educational task of the school". My conception of this "central task" should become clearer as the paper proceeds.

Now it seems to me that we have not begun to analyse exactly what is involved in terms of objectives and content for the "Pastoral Curriculum" in the light of the application of a set of principles such as these. This urgently needs to be done. Hirst approaches this question by referring to the need to develop competence in all the various "zones of living" which will necessarily face somebody in a society such as ours[21] and Marland[22] has outlined a range of suggested content for this part of the curriculum.

Now this kind of content can be unpacked in many different ways. What I offer here is just *one* way of outlining what the justifiable content of the "Pastoral Curriculum" might be argued to be in the light of the principles developed above.

a The Self	Physical and psychological aspects of the self. Growing up – "How to assess, under-

stand and cope with physical and emotional well-being".[23]

b   Relationships with others — Kinds of relationships. Getting on with people. Societal conventions regarding relationships. Relationships and responsibility. Skills in relation to all these areas.

c   Living in society — Awareness of services, facilities and institutions of society and how to use them, namely: Money/Finance, Political, Legal and Health systems, etc.

d   Living in the Physical World — Skills in relation to physical aspects of our environment, namely: mending a fuse, car maintenance, basic carpentry etc.

e   Education — Awareness of the structure of the school in which the pupil is studying and the courses it offers. Study skills, the examination system, future educational opportunities, etc.[24]

f   Work — Awareness of different ways of earning a living. Skills in relation to applying for jobs. Attitudes to unions etc.

g   Constructing a lifestyle — Ways of life. Priorities in life, Hobbies/Recreation, etc.

Now something like the account offered above – where the treatment of all the issues is focussed fairly hard on equipping the pupils to make practical decisions, judgements and adjustments for themselves and their own lives – represents what I think is a coherent unpacking of the notion of a – "Pastoral Curriculum".

ii The relationship between the "Pastoral Curriculum" and other elements of the curriculum: a crucial problem

In my view, the problem I shall draw attention to in this sub-section of the paper is a crucial one which both embodies a vital educational principle and presents the school attempting to introduce an adequate "Pastoral Curriculum" with a major planning and organisational task.

It is perhaps appropriate to approach this problem by looking at one way in which a "Pastoral Curriculum" such as the one I have outlined above might be criticised. Richard Pring, referring generally to interpretations of the notion of Social Education has written – "There is more than a suggestion that what we are offering is a limited diet of social training, acquisition of the values and skills which prevail in … society, anticipation of the situations which the child will soon meet in his or her milieu, competence to deal with practical difficulties when they arise."[25] Pring refers to such a programme as a "limitation of vision" and a "Narrowing of horizons". Now of course this is a criticism which can be made against the "Pastoral Curriculum" as I have outlined it.

This kind of criticism calls on two major kinds of support. First, the criticism proceeds, this kind of programme is mere "socialisation" rather than education. Pring again writes:

> education would seem to imply at least developing the capacity to look critically at values and beliefs, to weigh evidence and acquire standards of comparison and power of discrimination. But so long as one's knowledge is limited to the familiar and the immediate, one will not arrive at standards of comparison or at the critical questioning which is the mark of the educated man.[26]

Second, appeal is made *to* the fact that since we live in a Democracy the notion of "preparing pupils for life in our society" involves much more than the acquisition of a body of information and the ability to survive in the society. As R. S. Peters points out – "Democracy is concerned more with principles for proceeding than with a determinate destination and aims of education in a democracy should emphasise the qualities of mind essential for such a shared journey."[27] In Democracy we place great emphasis on individuals – at least to some extent – making up their own minds about what they will believe and how they will act. This makes an Education aiming at "relevance for life" into a very complex affair since the individual in a Democracy must be in a position *to* determine for himself large areas of his life. As Peters again points out, this means that much *of* education should be – "concerned not with answering practical problems but with mapping the contours of the general conditions within which such problems arise".[28] Something like a "knowledge of the human condition", to use Peters' phrase, is necessary for preparing people for life in a Democracy. This latter involves nothing less than the development of individuals who are rationally *autonomous*.

Now it is not difficult to see how these kinds of criticism can be pressed against the "Pastoral Curriculum". A look at the brief outline of suggested content shows how every aspect is capable of being seen as involving the need for reflective thought against a background of wide knowledge and understanding. None of the elements of content are wholly lacking in controversy. For example, in the section on "relationships with others" what attitude is the child going to be encouraged to take with regard to, say, equality of the sexes or institutions like marriage? Are the "societal conventions regarding relationships" to be questioned at all? With regard to choosing a job, can the child avoid issues like – "Is work of this kind radically de-humanising?" and similar kinds of controversial questions in this area to which John Elliott has drawn attention.[29]

The element of the "Pastoral Curriculum" most obviously "open" in this kind of way is the final section – (g) – in my outline – "constructing a lifestyle". Now in no sense can the business of constructing a lifestyle be plausibly seen as assembling and ordering a series of items in a value-free way. Major decisions on complex and general issues of an evaluative kind are involved. A look at the examples of "ways of life" and "life ideals" given by John White in his book – *Towards a Compulsory Curriculum* brings out the generality and complexity of the judgements necessary in deciding which "way of life" to follow. White's examples include: "A way of life devoted to the pursuit of truth" ... "A way of life devoted to others' good" ... "A religious way of life, premised on the belief that this life is only a preparation for an after life" ... "A way of life devoted to domesticity" ... and so on.[30] Now what kind of Education is necessary to equip pupils to reasonably construct their own lifestyle in the light of the complexity of the evaluative issues involved? It seems clear that much more than what has been outlined above in the "Pastoral Curriculum" is involved – something much more like the wide-ranging educational task described by White in his book.

Now what does this line of criticism amount to? I think that all that it shows is that the "Pastoral Curriculum" as I have outlined it – a kind of equipping of the child with a basic set of knowledge and skills necessary for survival in our society is *by itself not* adequate as an approach to what could be justifiably called "Education" in this area. It is *important*; something *currently neglected*; something *worth doing* – but it is not *enough* in this area. The "Pastoral Curriculum" is necessary but not sufficient.

What more is required? It seems to me that the "Pastoral Curriculum" must be linked in some way with the rest of the curriculum of the school if the kinds of criticisms we have been examining are to be met. The drawing up of however ingenious and well planned a series of curriculum materials for use in tutor period time is perhaps important and valuable – but this is not enough. What is needed is some attempt to co-ordinate or link what is being done in the "Pastoral Curriculum" with other areas of the curriculum so that *depth of understanding* and *perspective* on the issues being discussed can be obtained.

Thus work on "The Self" needs to be connected on the physical side with work being done in Biology and Health Education, whilst the psychological side requires linking with curriculum areas concerned with literature and, say, religious studies. The relevance of literature to the area of "relationships with others" seems clear, as does that of History, Sociology, etc. to "Societal Conventions regarding relationships". A vigorous Humanities course where there is a serious attempt to grapple with the depth and complexity of the evaluative issues involved also seems a necessary background to many areas of the "Pastoral Curriculum". With regard to "constructing a lifestyle" almost the whole of the educational enterprise seems relevant.

What I am suggesting then is that the "Pastoral Curriculum" necessarily *focuses* upon a range of specified "decisions and adjustments" facing the individual. For this reason, the stress of the programme "Active Tutorial Work" upon clearly specified objectives is laudable.[31] But I have claimed that many – if not all – of the elements of the "Pastoral Curriculum" as I have outlined them call for consideration against a broad background of knowledge and understanding – and for this reason some kind of rather complicated co-ordinatory activity with the rest of the curriculum is called for. The "Pastoral Curriculum" then – to be taken seriously – involves more than a self-contained exercise in planning within a delimited area. It involves nothing less than an involvement with the whole of the rest of the curriculum.

In more detail, I am suggesting:

i   That the whole of the curriculum be closely looked at from the perspective of Social and Personal Education generally (The "Pastoral Curriculum", I have suggested, is only *one* part of this broader area.) This analysis should discover exactly what is being done in the various elements of the curriculum with regard to key concepts and issues relevant to Social and Personal Education. Is there duplication of treatment of issues? Are issues being systematically covered? Are concepts being progressively developed and refined? Some kind of *co-ordinatory* activity here is clearly called for.

ii   That with regard specifically to the "Pastoral Curriculum" there is a need to ensure that the material being covered is linked in with the co-ordinated material outlined in (i), particularly so that the depth and complexity of treatment in the background area can be brought to bear on the more specifically focussed area. This will have implications for, amongst other things, the location and distribution of topics in the "Pastoral Curriculum".

This "Linking" and "co-ordination" of the "Pastoral Curriculum" with the rest of the curriculum seems to me to be a major task of great complexity facing schools. What it involves *in practice* requires a great deal of thought and planning, in the context of particular institutions. What I hope to have established here is the *principle* that this task of linking and co-ordination is vital.

c Should the school be concerned with the "Pastoral Curriculum"?

The discussion so far has proceeded on the assumption that the curriculum area I have identified as the "Pastoral Curriculum" *should be* one which is the responsibility of schools. Certainly recent documents on the curriculum seen to suggest that it is,[32] and Philosophers of Education have recently been making similar claims.[33] But *should* schools take responsibility in this area? Could it not be plausibly argued, for example, that schools have quite enough to do already in providing pupils with a broad, general education and that they should concentrate on this, handing other responsibilities over to other agencies? Now there is something in this line of argument. In the previous section of this paper I argued that the "Pastoral Curriculum" could not be seen as *the prime* responsibility of schools and that the "central educational task" of the school has priority. Granted this, however, I want to offer several arguments in support of the claim that the "Pastoral Curriculum" *is* an area which should be developed and worked out properly in schools.

The first argument stems from the realisation that the kind of preparation for life outlined under the heading of the "Pastoral Curriculum" is a valuable activity from the point of view of the upbringing of our children. Now schools are in a good position to assume responsibility for this activity because they have custody of the children for large sections of the day, have access to a certain range of resources and so on. But these considerations are not conclusive. Perhaps, it might be argued, we need to develop new institutions to undertake this work. A much more conclusive consideration emerges from what has been said above about the necessity for the "Pastoral Curriculum" as I have characterised it to be related to a broad and deep background of knowledge and understanding – indeed the central educational thrust of the school. Although the "linking" and "co-ordination" I have called for is a difficult exercise, it would be an impossible one if responsibility for the "Pastoral Curriculum" were handed over to some other agency. There is a good chance that the result of such a move would be the kind of narrow socialisation about which concern has been expressed. At least if the school undertakes the kind of work distinctive of the "Pastoral Curriculum" the "linking" and "co-ordination" I have referred to should be at least possible.

A second argument is that much of what is attempted under the heading of the "Pastoral Curriculum" is a facilitator – or in some cases a precondition – of the ability of the school to undertake its central educational tasks. For example, a child who feels that the school – in at least part of its activity – is preparing him for aspects of his future life is likely to view the whole of the schooling and educational enterprise in a more positive light.

There is, however, in my view a third and particularly strong argument supporting the claim that schools should be concerned with the "Pastoral Curriculum" as I have characterised it. This is because this element of the curriculum is essential to the achievement of a very widely agreed educational aim – the development of rationally autonomous individuals.[34] A person who has received a liberal education as I have briefly and crudely characterised it is not in virtue of that alone a rationally autonomous person. More is needed. Rational autonomy is also connected to the ability to actually make decisions and to *act* in the light of them. This notion of the development of *executive capacity* is absent both from liberal education and from academic education. There are two elements which combine to make a person rationally autonomous. There is a *cognitive* element (supplied by areas of the curriculum such as liberal education), and a *practical* element (supplied by other aspects of the child's education). I shall argue that much of what I have included under the heading of the "Pastoral Curriculum" is vital to this latter element.

John White has stressed this notion of "practical knowledge" in the development of rational autonomy. Writing of a person who has passed through a "compulsory curriculum" of the kind he advocates, White claims that at a certain point if he is to become rationally autonomous – "He must ... come to see that his understanding of different activities is intended to widen his options, to give him the material for his choices, and that his insight into different ways of life is intended to give him patterns of organising this material, patterns from which he may select his own way of life, or which, if he rejects them all, at least will make him aware of the need to adopt a way of life and help him to construct his own".[35] What is needed, claims White, is the realisation that at a certain point in Education the focus should not be on – "a way of life in general, but this boy's way of life or that girl's".[36] This seems to amount to the claim that the child must actually *apply* what he has learnt in school to *himself*; his own decisions; his own life. And further claims White, the child must be given *practical* knowledge so that he can see how he can actually *achieve* his wants. He writes:

> it is not enough to have got one's ends into some kind of order: to be more than a dreamer, one has to have some idea of how these ends may be attained, of the obstacles in their way, of how these obstacles may be overcome, and of which ends are impracticable since the obstacles in their way are insurmountable.[37]

By "practical" subjects and activities White means – "those which help one to understand means to ends, obstacles and ways round them".[38] Thus Physical skills (for example in woodwork) is not seen by White as a central example of what he is intending here. A better example is "Economics," included in the "practical" category by White because it can acquaint the child with important practical realities in life.

White outlines rather embryonically[39] the curricula implications of his account of practical understanding. He makes the basic point that it is necessary that the student know something about a wide range of practical activities. He suggests that an understanding of different job opportunities, social, legal and political institutions, economic affairs, elementary human psychology etc. (to give some examples) might be needed in an account of a "basic minimum" in this area.

Now although White does not develop what he has in mind here, it seems clear that a great deal of what he is advocating is identical with the area I have referred to as the "Pastoral Curriculum" – an element of the curriculum designed to help the child to make certain kinds of decisions, adjustments and choices of a practical nature. A rationally autonomous person is precisely one who can make his own decisions, adjustments and choices of this kind. The "Pastoral Curriculum" can therefore be seen as an important element in the development and achievement of one of the most commonly agreed and well-justified aims in Education: the development of rationally autonomous individuals.

Conclusion

In this paper I have attempted to clarify what might be meant by the notion of a "Pastoral Curriculum" and have tried to examine some of the principles which might be employed in detailed planning of what should be done in this area. I have also tried to argue that the area *is* one which should justifiably claim the serious attention of schools.

What I hope has emerged from this paper is the clear need for both Philosophers of Education and those responsible for curriculum planning in Social and Personal Education to collaborate in the vital task of clarifying, elaborating and justifying the notion of the "Pastoral Curriculum" – and in the equally vital task of planning its effective implementation.

Acknowledgements

I would like to thank all the members of the conference for their very helpful discussion of this paper. I would like to similarly thank the members of a meeting of the Cambridge branch of the Philosophy of Education Society of Great Britain in October 1981 at which this paper was also read.

Notes and references

* T. H. McLaughlin is a Lecturer in Education in the University of Cambridge Department of Education and is a Fellow of St Edmund's House, Cambridge.

† Originally published in: *Cambridge Journal of Education* 12: 1, 34–52.

1 See for example: Marland, M. (1980) – "The Pastoral Curriculum" in Best, R., Jarvis, C. and Ribbins, P. (eds) – *Perspectives on Pastoral Care* (London: Heinemann Educational). Douglas Hamblin's approach to Pastoral Care through the notion of "critical incidents" is also a call for a kind of "pastoral curriculum". See Hamblin, D. (1978) *The Teacher and Pastoral Care* (Oxford: Basil Blackwell).

2 See for example: Baldwin, J. and Wells, H. (eds) *Active Tutorial Work* (1979) Bks 1 and 2, (1980) Bks 3 and 4, (1981) Bk 5 (Oxford: Basil Blackwell).

3 McLaughlin, T. H. (1980) – "Pastoral Care in schools: A philosophical perspective". Paper read to a conference on "Controversies in Philosophy and Education" at Homerton College, Cambridge. September, 1980 (unpublished).

4 (1979) *Aspects of Secondary Education in England*. A survey by HM Inspectors of Schools (HMSO) Ch. 9, para. 2.2.

5 Marland, M. op. cit. p. 153.

6 McLaughlin, T. H. op. cit. For a collection of essays giving a critical examination of the theory and practice of Pastoral Care in Schools see Best, R. *et al.* op. cit.

7 Marland, M. op. cit. p. 154.

8 Marland, M. op. cit. p. 153.

9 Langford, G. (1979) – "Education is of the whole man" in *Journal of Philosophy of Education*, Vol. 13, p. 66.

10 Marland, M. op. cit. p. 157.

11 Marland, M. op. cit. p. 156.

12 Marland, M. op. cit. p. 156.

13 In this connection, see Peters, R. S. (1977) "Ambiguities in Liberal Education and the problem of its content" and "Dilemmas in Liberal Education" in *Education and the Education of Teachers*. London: Routledge and Kegan Paul.

14 Hirst, P. H. (1974) – "Liberal Education and the Nature of Knowledge" reprinted in *Knowledge and the Curriculum* (London: Routledge and Kegan Paul) p. 48.

15 Martin, J. R. (1981) – "Needed: A paradigm for Liberal Education" in National Society for the Study of Education Eightieth Year book Pt. 1 (Soltis, J. F. (ed.)) *Philosophy and Education* (Chicago: NSSE).

16 Martin, J. R. op. cit. p. 41.

17 Martin, J. R. op. cit. p. 43.

18 Baldwin, J. and Wells, H. (eds) op. cit.

19 Marland, M. op. cit. p. 157.

20 Holt, M. (1981) "Headmaster's Diary" *The Times Educational Supplement*. London. 21st August.

21 Hirst, P. H. in a lecture series "Aims and content of the curriculum" given to students for the Education Tripos in the University of Cambridge, Lent and Easter Terms, 1980. I am indebted to Hirst for several ideas developed in this paper.

22 Marland, M. op. cit. pp. 161–168.

23 Marland, M. op. cit. p. 162.

24 Marland, M. has unpacked this quite fully. See pp. 163–164.

25 Pring, R. (1975) – "Socialisation as an Aim of Education" in Elliott, J. and Pring, R. (eds) – *Social Education and Social Understanding* (London: University of London Press) p. 16.

26 Pring, R. op., cit. p. 17.

27 Peters, R. S. (1981) – "Democratic values and Educational aims" in *Essays on Educators* (London: George Allen and Unwin) p. 49.

28 Peters, R. S. (1981) op. cit. p. 45.

29 Elliott, J. (1975) – "The Humanities project on 'People and work' and the concept of Vocational guidance" in Elliott, J. and Pring, R. (eds) op. cit.

30 White, J. (1973) – *Towards a Compulsory Curriculum* (London: Routledge and Kegan Paul) p. 44.

31 See Baldwin, J. and Wells, H. (eds) op. cit. Bk 1, pp. xv–xvi. For a critique of the notion

of designing Social Education courses according to the "Behavioural objectives" model, see Sockett, H. (1975) – "Aims and Objectives in a Social Education Curriculum" in Elliott, J. and Pring, R. (eds) op. cit.

32 See for examples (1980) *A View of the Curriculum* (HMSO) proposition 12, Ch. 3, p. 18. (1981) *The School Curriculum* (HMSO) para. 53. (1981) *The Practical Curriculum: Schools Council Working Paper 70.* (London: Methuen) v. Ch. 1, p. 15.

33 See, for example, O'Hear, A. (1981) *Education, Society and Human Nature* (London: Routledge and Kegan Paul) especially Ch. 2. O'Hear claims that one of our educational aims should be the development of pupils who are capable of "supporting themselves" in life, and under this heading he includes not only an element of vocational training but also – "General knowledge of a practical kind" – "presupposed by any reasonably competent person" – much of which could be – "easily and economically imparted in formal lessons" (pp. 49–50). Of this area of schooling, O'Hear writes – "…only an unreasonable bias in favour of academic education could exclude a small but significant amount of school time being spent on such lessons, particularly where there is little evidence that parents do or can impart this knowledge to their children" – (p. 50). See also Barrow, R. (1981) *The Philosophy of Schooling* (Brighton: Wheatsheaf) especially Ch. 2. Elaborating the notion of schooling and what it involves, Barrow claims that much of what we have identified by the label "the Pastoral Curriculum" should be tackled in schools.

Peters, R. S. (1981) op. cit. has also claimed that our thought about Education has neglected – "the role of practical knowledge in education that is not part of training for a particular job." (p. 44).

34 For an account of what is involved in the notion of rational autonomy see, for example, Dearden, R. F. (1972) "Autonomy and Education" in Dearden, R. F., Hirst, P. H. and Peters, R. S. (eds) *Education and the Development of Reason* (London: Routledge and Kegan Paul).

35 White, J. op. cit. p. 50.

36 White, J. op. cit. p. 51.

37 White, J. op. cit. p. 55.

38 White, J. op. cit. p. 55.

39 White, J. op. cit. pp. 56–58.

9 Curriculum reform and curriculum theory

A case of historical amnesia

Ivor Goodson*†

The school curriculum is a social artefact, conceived of and made for deliberate human purposes. It is therefore a supreme paradox that in many accounts of schooling the written curriculum, this most manifest of social constructions, has been treated as a given. Moreover the problem has been compounded by the fact that it has often been treated as a *neutral* given embedded in an otherwise meaningful and complex situation. Yet in our own schooling we know very well that while we loved some subjects, topics or lessons, we hated others. Some we learnt easily and willingly, others we rejected whole-heartedly. Sometimes the variable was the teacher, or the time, or the room, or us, but often it was the form or content of the curriculum itself. Of course beyond such individualistic responses there were, and are, significant collective responses to curriculum, and again when patterns can be discerned it suggests this is far from a 'neutral' factor.

Why then, has so little attention been given to the making of curriculum? We have a social construction which sits at the heart of the process by which we educate our children. Yet in spite of the patchy exhortations of sociologists, sociologists of knowledge in particular, one looks in vain for serious study of the process of social construction which emanates as curriculum.

The reasons for this lacuna in our educational studies can be focused on two specific aspects: first, the nature of curriculum as a *source* for study, and second, associated with this, questions relating to the *methods* we employ in approaching the study of curriculum.

In this article I shall deal with some of the problems involved in employing curriculum as a source. Part of the problem has already been mentioned: namely that many accounts of schooling accept the curriculum as a given, an inevitable and essentially unimportant variable. Of course, some important work in the fields of curriculum studies and sociology of knowledge have provided a continuing challenge to this kind of curriculum myopia.

But once it accepted that the curriculum itself is an important source for study a number of further problems surface. For 'the curriculum' is a perennially elusive and multi-faceted concept. The curriculum is such a slippery concept because it is defined, redefined and negotiated at a number of levels and in a number of arenas. It would be impossible to arbitrate over which points in the ongoing negotiations were critical. In addition, the terrain differs substantially according to local or national structures and patterns. In such a shifting and unfocused terrain it is plainly problematic to try to define common ground for our study. After all, if there is a lacuna in our study it is likely to be for good reasons.

The substantial difficulties do not however mean, as has often been the case to date, that we should ignore the area of curriculum completely or focus on 'minute particulars' that are amenable to focused study. Part of the problem is, I believe, resolvable. This resolution turns on identifying common ground or, conceptualised another way, some areas of stability within the apparent fluidity and flux of curriculum.

We should remember that a great deal of the most important scholarship on curriculum, certainly on curriculum as a social construction, took place in the 1960s and early 1970s. This was, however, a period of unusual change and flux everywhere in the Western world: and nowhere more so than in the world of schooling in general and curriculum in particular. For such a burgeoning of critical curriculum scholarship to happen during such times was both encouraging and, in a sense, symptomatic. The emergence of a field of study of curriculum as social construction was an important new direction. But, while itself symptomatic of a period of social questioning and criticism, this burgeoning of critical scholarship was not without its down-side.

I believe that down-side has two aspects which are important as we begin to reconstitute our study of schooling and curriculum. First, influential scholars in the field often took a value position which assumed that schooling should be reformed, root and branch 'revolutionised', the 'maps of learning redrawn'. Second, this scholarship took place at a time when a wide range of curriculum reform movements were seeking to do precisely this, 'to revolutionise school curricula' on both grounds. Therefore it was unlikely that such scholars would wish to focus upon, let alone concede, the areas of stability, of unchallengeable 'high ground' that may have existed within the school curriculum.

In the 1960s one might characterise curriculum reform as a sort of 'tidal wave'. Everywhere the waves created turbulence and activity but actually they only engulfed a few small islands, more substantial land masses were hardly affected at all, and on dry land the mountains and high ground remained completely untouched. As the tide now rapidly recedes the high ground can be seen in stark silhouette. If nothing else, our scrutiny of the curriculum reform should allow recognition that there is not only high ground but common ground in the world of curriculum.

Standing out more clearly than ever on the new horizon is the school subject, the 'basic' or 'traditional' subjects. Throughout the Western world there is exhortation but also evidence about a 'return to basics', a re-embrace of 'traditional subjects'. In England, for instance, the new National Curriculum defines a range of subjects to be taught as a 'core' curriculum in all schools. The subjects thereby instated bear an uncanny resemblance to the list which generally defined secondary school subjects in the 1904 Regulations. *The Times Educational Supplement* commented about this reassertion of traditional subject dominance: 'The first thing to say about this whole exercise is that it unwinds 80 years of English (and Welsh) educational history. It is a case of go back to go.' In the early years of the nineteenth century the first state secondary schools were organised. Their curriculum was presented by the National Board of Education under the detailed guidance of Sir Robert Morant:

> The course should provide for instruction in the English Language and Literature, at least one Language other than English, Geography, History, Mathematics, Science and Drawing, with due provision for Manual Work and Physical Exercises, and in a girls' school for Housewifery. Not less than $4\frac{1}{2}$ hours per week must be allotted to English Geography and History; not less than $3\frac{1}{2}$ hours to the Language where one is taken or less than 6 hours where two are taken; and not less than $7\frac{1}{2}$ hours to Science and Mathematics, of which at least 3 must be for Science.

But in looking at the new 1987 National Curricula, we find that: 'The 8–10 Subject timetable which the discussion paper draws up has as academic a look to it as anything Sir Robert Morant could have dreamed up.'[1] Likewise, in scrutinising curriculum history in the US high school, Kliebard has pointed to the saliency of the 'traditional' school subjects in the face of waves of curriculum reform initiatives from earlier decades. He characterises the school subject within the US high school curriculum as 'The Impregnable Fortress'.[2]

But let us return to the conceptualisation of curriculum as our source of study for it remains elusive and slippery, even in these times of centrality and tradition where we return to basics. In the 1960s and 1970s critical studies of curriculum as social construction pointed to the school classroom as the site wherein the curriculum was negotiated and realised. The classroom was the 'centre of action', 'the arena of resistance'. By this view what went on in the classroom *was* the curriculum. The definition of curriculum – the view from the 'high ground' and the mountains – was, it was thought, not just subject to redefinition at classroom level but quite simply irrelevant.

Such a view, and such a standpoint from which to begin to study curriculum, is, I think, now unsustainable. Certainly the high ground of the written curriculum is subject to renegotiation at lower levels, notably the classroom. But the view, common in the 1960s, that it is therefore irrelevant is, I think, less common nowadays. Once again, I would suspect the view is gaining currency that the high ground, our common ground in this article, is of importance. In the high ground what is to be 'basic' and 'traditional' is reconstituted and reinvented. The 'given' status of school subject knowledge is therein reinvented and reasserted. But this is more than political manoeuvring or rhetoric: such reassertion affects the discourse about schooling and relates to the 'parameters to practice'. In the 1980s it would, I think, be folly to ignore the central importance of the redefinition of the written curriculum. In a significant sense the written curriculum is the visible and public testimony of selected rationales and legitimating rhetoric for schooling. In England and Wales I have argued elsewhere that the written curriculum

> both promulgates and underpins certain basic intentions of schooling as they are operationalised in structures and institutions. To take a common convention in preactive curriculum, the school subject: while the written curriculum

defines the rationales and rhetoric of the subject, this is the only tangible aspect of a patterning of resources, finances and examinations and associated material and career interests. In this symbiosis, it is as though the written curriculum provides a guide to the legitimating rhetoric of schooling as they are promoted through patterns of resource allocation, status attribution and career distribution. In short, the written curriculum provides us with a testimony, a documentary source, a changing map of the terrain: it is also one of the best official guide books to the institutionalised structure of schooling.[3]

What is most important to stress is that the written curriculum, notably the convention of the school subject, has, in this instance, both symbolic but also practical significance. Symbolic – in that certain intentions for schooling are thereby publicly signified and legitimated; practical – in that these written conventions are rewarded with finance and resource allocation and with the associated work and career benefits.

Our study of the written curriculum should afford a range of insights into schooling. But it is important to stress that such study must be allied to other kinds of study – in particular studies of school process, of school texts and of the history of pedagogy. For schooling is comprised of the interlinked matrix of these, and indeed, other vital ingredients. With regard to schooling and to curriculum in particular, the final question is 'Who gets what and what do they do with it?'

The definition of written curriculum is part of this story. And that is not the same as asserting a direct or easily discernible relationship between the practical definition of written curriculum and its interactive realisation in classrooms. It is, however, to assert that the written curriculum most often sets important parameters for classroom practice (not always, not at all times, not in all classrooms, but 'most often'). The study of written curriculum will first increase our understanding of the influences and interests active at the preactive level. Second, this understanding will further our knowledge of the values and purposes represented in schooling and the manner in which preactive definition, notwithstanding individual and local variations, may set parameters for interactive realisation and negotiation in the classroom and school.

Studies of the preactive in relationship to the interactive are, then, where we should end. But for the moment, so neglected is the study of the preactive definition of written curriculum that no such marriage of methodologies could be consummated. The first step is plainly to undertake a range of studies of the definitions of written curriculum and, in particular, to focus on the 'impregnable fortress' of the school subject.

Reconstituting school subjects: the example of England and Wales in the 1980s

Traditionally in England and Wales those stressing 'the basics' have referred to the three R's – reading, writing and arithmetic. In the 1980s it would be fair to say that those with curriculum power have been following a new version of the three R's – rehabilitation, reinvention and reconstruction. Often the rehabilitation strategy for school subjects in the 1980s takes the form of arguing that good teaching is in t good *subject* teaching. This is to seek to draw a veil over the whole experience the 1960s, to seek to forget why many curriculum reforms were developed to try to provide antidotes to the perceived failures and inadequacies of conventional subject teaching. The rehabilitation strategy is itself in this sense quintessentially ahistorical but paradoxically it is also a reminder of the power of 'vestiges of the past' to survive, revive and reproduce.

In England the 'reinvention' of 'traditional' subjects began in 1969 with the issue of the first collection of *Black Papers*.[4] The writers in this collection argued that teachers had been too greatly influenced by progressive theories of education like the integration of subjects, mixed ability teaching, inquiry and discovery teaching. This resulted in neglect of subject and basic skill teaching and led to reduced standards of pupil achievement and school discipline; the traditional subject was thereby equated with social and moral discipline. The rehabilitation of the traditional subject promised the re-establishment of discipline in both these causes. The Black Papers were taken up by politicians and in 1976 the Labour Prime Minister, James Callaghan, embraced many of their themes in his Ruskin Speech. Specific recommendations soon followed. In 1979, for instance, following a survey of secondary schools in England and Wales, Her Majesty's Inspectorate (HMI) drew attention to what they judged to be evidence of an insufficient match in many schools between the qualifications and experience of teachers and the work they were undertaking: later in a survey of middle schools they found that when they examined,

> the proportion of teaching which was undertaken by teachers who had studied the subjects they taught as main subjects in initial training ... higher standards of work overall were associated with a greater degree of use of subject teachers.[5]

These perceptions provided a background to the Department of Education pamphlet *Teaching Quality*. The Secretaries of State for Education listed the criteria for initial teacher training courses. The first criteria imposed the following requirement: 'that the higher education and initial training of all qualified teachers should include at least two full years' course time devoted to subject studies at a level appropriate to higher education'. This requirement therefore: 'would recognise teachers' needs for subject expertise if they are to have the confidence and ability to enthuse pupils and respond to their curiosity in their chosen subject fields'.[6]

This final sentence is curiously circular. Obviously if the pupils choose subjects then it is probable that teachers will require subject expertise. But this is to foreclose a whole debate about *whether* they should choose subjects as an educational vehicle. Instead, we have a practical *fait accompli* presented as choice. In fact the students have no choice except to embrace 'their chosen subject fields'. The political rehabilitation of subjects by political diktat is presented as pupil choice.

In *Teachers' Quality*, the issue of the match between the teachers' qualifications and their work with pupils first raised in the 1979 HMI document is again employed. We learn that 'the Government attach high priority to improving the fit between teachers' qualifications and their tasks as one means of improving the quality of education'. The criteria for such a fit is based on a clear belief in the sequential and hierarchical pattern of subject learning.

All specialist subject teaching during the secondary phase requires teachers whose study of the subject concerned was at a level appropriate to higher education, represented a substantial part of the higher education and training period, and built on a suitable A level basic.

The beginning of subject specialisation is best evidenced where the issue of non-subject based work in schools is scrutinised. Many aspects of school work take place outside (or beside) subject work – studies of school process have indeed shown how integrated pastoral and remedial work originates because pupils for one reason or another do not achieve in traditional subjects. Far from accepting the subject as an educational vehicle with severe limits if the intention is to educate all pupils, the document seeks to rehabilitate subjects even in those domains which often originate from subject 'fall-out':

> Secondary teaching is not all subject based, and initial training and qualifications cannot provide an adequate preparation for the whole range of secondary school work. For example, teachers engaged in careers or remedial work or in providing group courses of vocational preparation, and those given the responsibility for meeting 'special needs' in ordinary schools, need to undertake these tasks not only on the basis of initial qualifications but after experience of teaching a specialist subject and preferably after appropriate post-experience training. Work of this kind and the teaching of interdisciplinary studies are normally best shared among teachers with varied and appropriate specialist qualifications and expertise.[7]

The rehabilitation of school subjects has become the mainstay of Government thinking about the school curriculum. In many ways the governmental and structural support offered to school subjects as the organising device for secondary schooling is reaching unprecedented levels. Hargreaves has judged that 'more than at any time previously, it seems, the subject is to take an overriding importance in the background preparation and curricular responsibility of secondary school teachers'. But the preferred policy sits alongside a major change in the style of governance of education for Hargreaves argues that,

> nor does that intention on the part of HMI and DES amount to just a dishing out of vague advice. Rather, in a style of centralized policy intervention and review with which we in Britain are becoming increasingly familiar in the 1980s, it is supported by strong and dear declarations of intent to build the achievement of subject match into the criteria for approval (or not) of teacher training courses, and to undertake five yearly reviews of selected secondary schools to ensure that subject match is being improved within them and is being reflected in the pattern of teacher appointments.[8]

The associated issue of increasingly centralised control is also raised in a recent DES publication on *Education 8 to 12 in Combined and Middle Schools*.[9] Again, the rehabilitation of school subjects is rehearsed in a section on the need to 'extend teachers' subject knowledge'. Rowland has seen the document as 'part of an attempt to bring a degree of centralized control over education'. He states that:

> *Education 8 to 12* may well be interpreted by teachers and others as recommending yet another means in the trend towards a more schematicized approach to learning in which the focus is placed even more firmly on the subject matter rather than the child.

He adds cryptically that 'the evidence it produces, however, points to the need to move in quite the opposite direction'.[10] His reservations about the effects of rehabilitating school subjects are widely shared. Another scholar has noted that one effect of the strategy 'will be to reinforce the existing culture of secondary teaching and thereby inhibit curricular and pedagogic innovation on a school-wide front'.[11]

The various Government initiatives and reports since 1976 have shown a consistent tendency to return to 'basics', to re-embrace 'traditional' subjects. This Government project which spans both Labour and Conservative administrations has culminated in the 'new' National Curriculum. The curriculum was defined in a consultation document, the *National Curriculum 5–16*. This was rapidly followed in the wake of the Conservatives' third election victory in succession by the introduction of the Education Reform Bill into the House of Commons in November 1987. The Bill defines certain common curricular elements which are to be offered to pupils of compulsory school age, which will be known as 'the National Curricular'.

Whilst presented as a striking new political initiative, comparison with the 1904 Regulations shows a remarkable degree of historical continuity. The National Curriculum comprises

- the 'core' subjects of mathematics, English and science,
- the 'foundation' subjects of history, geography, technology, music, art, physical education and (for secondary pupils) a modern foreign language.[12]

Historical amnesia allows curriculum reconstruction to be presented as curriculum revolution, as Orwell noted he (or in this case she) 'who controls the past, controls the future'.

Developing historical perspectives

In this article, I have argued that following the frustrating results of curriculum reform efforts in the 1960s and their substantial dismantling and reversal in the 1980s, the arguments for historical study are now considerable indeed. The contemporary power of those 'vestiges of the past', traditional school subjects, has been evidenced at some length with instances drawn from Great Britain. To argue for curricular change strategies which ignored history would surely be improbable, if not impossible, in the current situation. Yet as we have seen, this has been the dominant posture of curricular activists and theorists in the twentieth century. It is time to place historical study at the centre of the curriculum enterprise, to exhume the early work on curricular history, and the spasmodic subsequent work, and to systematically rehabilitate the historical study of school subjects.

In the first section, the written curriculum was identified as a major yet neglected historical source with which to develop our investigations of schooling. It becomes clear that just as the search for new sources moves us into neglected territory, so too the search for an associated modality of study will require methods seldom used or at least seldom integrated in the study of schooling. Methods are required which allow us to study curriculum as it impinges on individual experiences of schooling as well as those experiences and social activities of social groups. Exploring curriculum as a focus allows us to study, indeed exposes us to the study of, the intersection of individual biography and social structure. The emergence of curriculum as a concept came from a concern to direct and control individual teachers' and pupils' classroom activities. The definition of curriculum developed over time as part of an institutionalised and structural pattern of state schooling. Our methods therefore have to cover the analysis of individual lives and biographies as well as of social groups and structures.

For this reason we should employ a range of methods from life histories of individual teachers through to histories of school subjects where the interplay of groups and structures are scrutinised.

Biography, history, society

What C. Wright Mills argues is the case for sociology is substantially what is followed here for studies of schooling and curriculum:

> Social science deals with problems of biography of history and of their intersections within social structures. That these three – biography, history, society, are the coordinate points of the proper study of man has been a major platform on which I have stood when criticising several current schools of sociology whose practitioners have abandoned this classic tradition.[13]

The relationship between individual and collective (as between action and structure) is perennially elusive. But our studies may either accept, or exacerbate, fragmentation or seek integration. Life history study pursued alongside the study of more collective groupings and milieux might promote better integration. The problem of integration is of course partly a problem of dealing with modes and levels of consciousness. The life history penetrates the individual subject's consciousness and attempts also to map the changes in that consciousness over the life cycle. But at the individual level, as at other levels, we must note that change is structured, but that structures change. The relationship between the individual and wider structures is central to our investigations, but again it is through historical studies that such investigations can be profitably pursued: 'our chance to understand how smaller milieux and larger structures interact, and our chance to understand the larger causes at work in these limited milieux, thus require us to deal with historical materials'.[14]

The difficulties of elucidating the symbiosis of the individual and the social structure can be seen in assessing the broad goals of curriculum or schooling. The discerning of 'regularities', 'recurrences' or patterns is particularly elusive at the level of the individual life (and consciousness). Feinberg has commented that

> once we understand that a goal is identified in terms of something that is reasonably distinctive and that establishes relevance by postulating a continuity to otherwise discrete acts then we can see that goals may belong to individuals, but they may also belong to individuals as they are related to each other in acts or institutions.

He gives the example of people in America moving westwards, 'colonising the west', which they did for many reasons:

> Some went to escape debt, others to make a fortune; some went to farm, others to pan gold, or to sell merchandise; some went as soldiers, others as trappers and hunters. Whereas it is perfectly proper to speak about the continuity of any series of acts performed by an individual in terms of a goal it is equally appropriate to speak of a whole series of acts performed by different individuals along with the acts of the government that supported them, such as the Homestead Act and the building of railroads, in terms of the *general* goal of settling the west. It is this way of speaking that allows us to make sense of all these acts and to see them as forming some kind of continuous meaningful event.

The dangers of 'abstraction' to the general level are evidential and can be seen when Feinberg adds:

> moreover, it is equally appropriate to speak of the goal as beginning with the movement of the first settlers west, even though these people may not have had a whisper of an idea about the overall historical significance of their act.[15]

In these terms structural change provides a facilitating arena for a range of individual actions which then feed into and act upon this initial change. Consciousness of the significance of the action differs according to the time period in question and to the level of scrutiny – hence a series of individual 'dreams' and actions build up into a movement to 'colonise' a vast territory. Likewise, with schooling and curriculum discerning regularities, recurrences and patterns allow analysis and assessment of goals and intentions.

> To begin to characterise these goals by looking back to the origins of the school system itself is not necessarily to claim that the goals were fully understood at the time. It is simply to say that in the light of these goals we can understand some of the major lines of continuity between the activity of the past and the activity of the present.

Developing our studies of curriculum at individual and collective levels demands that our historical analyses work across the levels of individual lives and group action and assess relations between individuals, between groups and between individuals and groups. Such work is reminiscent of Esland's early exhortations to develop frameworks 'for the analysis of the knowledge which constitutes the life world of teachers and pupils in particular educational institutions, and the epistemological traditions in which they collectively participate'. The intentions are very similar:

> in trying to focus the individual biography in its socio historical context is in a very real sense attempting to penetrate the symbolic drift of school knowledge, and the consequences for the individuals who are caught up in it and attempting to construct their reality through it.[16]

Histories of the symbolic drift of school knowledge raise questions about the patterns of evolution through which subjects pass. There is a growing body of work on the history of school subjects. In *School Subjects and Curriculum Change*[17] I have looked at geography, biology and environmental studies but other monographs in the series of books *Studies in Curriculum History* have looked at science and technology (McCulloch *et al.*, 1985), mathematics (Cooper, 1985; Moon, 1985) and physics (Woolnough, 1987).[18] In *Social Histories of the Secondary Curriculum*, work is collected together on a wide range of other subjects, classics (Stray), English (Ball), science (Waring, who had written an earlier seminal study on Nuffield science), domestic subjects (Purvis), religious education (Bell), social studies (Franklin & Whitty) and modern languages (Radford).[19] These studies reflect a growing interest in the history of curriculum and besides elucidating the symbolic drift of school knowledge raise central questions about past and current 'explanations' of school subjects whether they be sociological or philosophical.

Above all, these studies begin to illustrate the historical emergence and construction of the political economy of curriculum. The structuring of resources and finance, the attribution of status and careers are linked to a system that has developed since the foundation of state schooling, and in particular since the establishment of secondary schooling regulations in the early years of this century. This structure impinges on both individual intentions and collective aspirations. By focusing our studies on the historical emergence and evolution of structures and the ongoing activities of individuals and groups we would begin to alleviate our current amnesia.

Notes

* Ivor Goodson is Professor in the Faculty of Education, University of Western Ontario.
† Originally published in: *Cambridge Journal of Education* 19: 2, 131–141.
1 1904 and all that, *The Times Educational Supplement*, 31/7/87, p. 2.
2 H. Kliebard (1986) *The Struggle for the American Curriculum 1893–1958*, p. 269 (New York, Routledge & Kegan Paul).
3 I. F. Goodson (1988) *The Making of Curriculum – collected essays*, p. 16 (Lewes, Falmer Press).

4 C. B. Cox and A. E. Dyson (Eds) (1969) *Fight for Education: a Black Paper* (London, The Critical Quarterly Society 1969). Followed by C. B. Cox and R. Boyson (eds) (1975) *The Black Paper 1975* (London, Dent).

5 Her Majesty's Inspectorate (1983), para. 3.19.

6 Department of Education and Science (1983) *Teaching Quality*.

7 Her Majesty's Inspectorate, op. cit., para. 3.40.

8 A. Hargreaves (1984) Curricular policy and the culture of teaching: some prospects for the future *(jnimeo)*.

9 DES (1985) *Education 8 to 12 in Combined and Middle Schools: an HMI Survey* (London, HMSO).

10 S. Rowland (1987) Where is primary education going? *Journal of Curricular Studies*, Vol. 19, No. 1, January, February, p. 90.

11 Hargreaves, op. cit.

12 DES (1987) *The National Curriculum 5–16* (London, HMSO).

13 C. Wright Mills (1970) *The Sociological Imagination*, p. 159 (London, Penguin).

14 Mills, op. cit., p. 165.

15 W. Feinberg (1983) *Understanding Education: towards a reconstruction of educational enquiry*, p. 86 (Cambridge, Cambridge University Press).

16 G. M. Esland (1971) Teaching and learning as the organisation of knowledge, in: M. F. D. Young (ed.) *Knowledge and Control: new directions for the sociology of education*, p. 111 (London, Collier Macmillan).

17 I. F. Goodson (1987) *School Subjects and Curriculum Change: studies in curriculum history* (London, Falmer).

18 Studies in Curriculum History comprises:

I. F. Goodson (ed.) *Social Histories of the Secondary Curriculum: subjects for study*.

G. McCulloch, E. Jenkins and D. Layton (1985) *Technological Revolution? The Politics of School Science and Technology in England and Wales Since 1945*.

B. Cooper (1985) *Renegotiating Secondary School Mathematics: a study of curriculum change and stability*.

B. Franklin *Building the American Community: social control and curriculum*.

B. Moon (1985) *The 'New Maths' Curriculum Controversy: an international story*.

I. F. Goodson *School Subjects and Curriculum Change*.

T. S. Popkewitz (ed.) *The Formation of School Subjects: the struggle for creating an American institution*.

B. E. Woolnough (1987) *Physics Teaching in Schools 1960–85: of people, policy and power*.

I. F. Goodson *The Making of Curriculum: collected essays*.

19 I. F. Goodson (ed.) (1985) *Social Histories of the Secondary Curriculum: subjects for study* (Lewes, Falmer Press).

Part II

New orders of experience

10 Teaching through small group discussion

Formality, rules, and authority

Lawrence Stenhouse[*][†]

Small group discussion, with its related activities including role play, simulations and educational games and problems, is essentially co-operative and essentially participatory. The basic principle is to place all the resources available within the group at the disposal of all the individuals within it. The group must feel that everyone's needs count.

This is not easy to achieve within the competitive assumptions of our educational system. Nor is co-operative working typical of most spontaneous groups, at least in our society. Accordingly, tutors generally have to teach students to work in groups, to value different styles and types of participation and to resist the temptation to commandeer the group to serve one's own needs. The problem of developing satisfactory small group work depends as much on student training as on teacher training.

I wish to argue here that successful participant small groups in education are likely to be formal rather than informal. They call for rules and conventions. Many seminars fail because tutors see them as informal occasions.

A spontaneous example of the development of conventions is reported by Bjerstadt.

> It was demonstrated by Beck that groups solving problems often showed initial phases where dominant individuals played an important role followed by phases where this dominance was replaced by some kind of regulated 'division of labour': each individual was expected to try in turn (Reihum-Phanomen). As ability to do the task in question developed, the dominance rank order (in certain respects comparable to the pecking order of hens) was thus replaced by rules of procedure; to express it more picturesquely, but also more loosely: 'right of strength' was followed by 'right of law'.

Small groups develop as part of their sub-cultures principles of procedure which have the status of conventions or rules. Successful teaching in participatory small groups depends on the establishment of procedures appropriate to educational aims, and this can best be done if conventions and rules are made explicit by the tutor. Usually he will be able to propose a number of rules and conventions at the outset, but others will have to be evolved in the group. In the latter case they should still be made explicit and clearly related to the group's task.

The intrusion of the tutor into the small group now needs to be considered. When he enters the group, he is immediately located in a position of authority and leadership, and he carries two types of authority. R. S. Peters has distinguished these as being 'in authority' and being 'an authority'. The teacher is 'in authority' in so far as he is the representative of 'an impersonal normative order or value system which regulates behaviour basically because of acceptance of it on the part of those who comply'. He is 'an authority' by virtue of 'his special competence, training or insight'.

The teacher in higher education is in authority as a representative of his institution, and in this respect his authority is heavily reinforced by his position as internal examiner. This authority is consciously present to his students: he is seen as defining the task and the situation in which it will be tackled.

The teacher is *an* authority by virtue of his knowledge of the subject. Most students regard most teachers as experts, and the teacher is seen as a man of knowledge. There is also a sense in which the teacher is in authority within his role as an authority. He can be seen as adding to his own knowledge of the subject a grasp of 'the impersonal normative order or value system' which represents the subject as a discipline. He is familiar and at home with both academic institutions – conferences, journals, personnel – and the criteria and norms accepted in his academic field.

The consequence of this authority position of the teacher is that students brought up in our system expect him to play the role of instructor in the sense that they expect him *to* take responsibility for their learning. They assume an attitude of dependence. Now there are occasions – even in small groups – when instruction is appropriate. But there are also many occasions when students have to accept responsibility for their own learning, to develop autonomy as scholars, and hence to learn to use the tutor as a consultant and guide rather than as an instructor. It is in this context that participatory small groups are appropriate.

Yet the tutor cannot simply and easily renounce the authority which leads students to believe that the initiative and effort should come primarily from him. He enters the small group trailing with him the authority of his own knowledge of the university or college of which he is a delegate and of the academic field of which he is a representative. This authority may be reinforced by personal charisma and by the authority of age. All in all the teacher cannot escape the responsibilities of a leadership position and the problems in the area of authority-dependency which this sets up.

If a teacher handles his authority unselfconsciously as a matter of personal habit, he usually induces a relatively passive dependency relationship.

Students are reluctant to participate and anxious to interpret the rules of the situation. If he does not make the conventions explicit, his students can interpret them only by observing the tutor. Their task is to study his behaviour in order to understand the situation in which they are placed. He is for them an experimental subject. Unless they can develop from observation consistent theories about what he is up to, his authority will appear arbitrary. The need of the students to develop such theories will reinforce the teacher's position as centre of interest in the group. The students will be teacher-oriented rather than task-oriented.

Sometimes when a teacher is attempting to convey to the group procedures of thinking, he can find no way of defining them except through his authority. Such is the method of Socrates in the Platonic dialogues; and it accounts for their one-sidedness. I would argue that in small group situations he should avoid this if he can; and this suggests that he should explicitly confine his authority in the group by rules and conventions.

I have argued that participatory small group situations, which are often seen by tutors as spontaneous and informal, are likely to be most effective as educational enterprises when they are relatively structured and formal. The group needs to adopt explicitly rules and conventions governing procedures and the role of the tutor in the group also requires some formal definition accessible to the students. If I am right, this is an encouraging position for teachers since it suggests that competence in small group teaching is to a large extent capable of being learnt. It is not some personal or intuitive possession in the absence of which the teacher cannot be effective.

The next step is to examine what rules, conventions and roles are 'appropriate'.

Here there are two areas of consideration; the logic of the task and the psychology of groups. Crudely, we might regard the first as the message and the second as the medium; and we should immediately blur the distinction and say that medium and message are inextricably entangled. For example, a group dependent on the authority of persons is not likely to learn effectively the authority of research procedures.

Educational tasks are concerned with the promotion of learning. The task is often defined in terms of an aim; and aims are often analysed as cognitive, affective or psycho-motor. This seems to me a laboratory distinction rather than a teaching distinction, and I prefer to distinguish knowledge, application, understanding, and skills.

By knowledge I mean sheer information. The distinction cannot be rigidly maintained, but most teachers will be able to give the concept meaning in their subjects. In teaching the need for knowledge expresses itself as concern for 'coverage'. Every teacher is familiar with a feeling of concern about covering the ground, and students feel this too. I do not believe that participatory small group teaching is an effective way of providing coverage. What is required is individual study, individualised learning programmes and/or lectures. (These do also have other functions). Nothing is more destructive of participatory small group teaching than concern for coverage in this sense; and any such teaching must take place in a context of coverage supplied by other experiences.

By application, I mean the application of principles to particular cases. The principles may have been learnt as knowledge or may be taught through application. They are at a higher level of generalisation than cases, but gather their strength from their effectiveness in application to cases. The task of application is a suitable one for small group teaching.

Understanding is essentially relational. It consists in establishing significant relationships of knowledge or of knowledge and skills. Application is one such relationship. The essential point about understanding is that it is both personal and public. An understanding implies a grasp of a relationship on the part of an individual. It is an experience leading the individual to claim 'I understand'. Understanding in this sense is opposed to not understanding. But it is characteristic of education that it is concerned with public criteria by which understanding can be assessed. A personal understanding must be tried out against such criteria. In this sense, understanding is opposed to misunderstanding. The promotion of understanding is a suitable task for small group teaching.

Skills are performances which are generalisable to some degree. That is to say they can be practised. One problem in this is that they may be practised as exercises in situations which are relatively meaningless. The application of skills, like the application of principles, is a suitable task for small group teaching.

Participatory small group teaching is thus effective as a critical exchange in which significant relationships are suggested and explored in order to promote an understanding of the structure and logic of knowledge or a grasp of the problems of applying knowledge or skills in various situations.

Tasks which would be suitable for small groups might be, for example, applying engineering principles to the design of a particular bridge, promoting an understanding of the wave/particle duality of electrons or of *Hamlet*, or applying skills in the design of electronic apparatus to an experimental problem in psychology.

Now, given any such educational tasks as these, it is possible, though challenging, to work out the logic of the task in terms of rules for the group and roles for the teacher. But it is also possible so to push the logic that we fail to take account of the psychology of the group. This is an important failing in an educational setting since the group is there to learn, that is, the task is there for the sake of the group, not the group for the sake of the task. In a real-life situation, the test is whether the bridge stays up. In an educational situation the test is whether *all* members of the group learned in designing it. Moreover, lack of attention to the psychology of the group can lead to crises and even problems of control.

Now, of course, sensitivity to groups is important, even vital. But it is also helpful to recognise that there are certain patterns of small group work which have stood the test of experience and obviously help us in finding a ground-base of rules and roles which harmonise the logic of the task and the psychology of groups. Many such patterns have been reported in the literature, for example, by Abercrombie, Collier, Nisbet and Richardson in this country. My concern here is to argue that a pattern appropriate to the logic of the task needs to be adopted, rules and roles need to be denned as explicitly as possible within that pattern and the proceedings need to be handled with faithful adherence to those rules and with sensitivity.

In summary, the position I am advancing is as follows:

1   Effective group work depends upon the establishment of rules and conventions – it is formal.
2   The teacher will be most effective if he defines his role and thereby makes his use of authority also rule-governed, and his areas of initiative clear. Small group work is not forwarded by the renunciation of authority, but by its definition. Effective leadership is relatively formal.
3   Both group rules and teaching roles need to be logically consonant with the demands of an explicit task.

4   Group rules and teaching roles need to take account of the psychology of groups.
5   A variety of reports of patterns of small group teaching exist and provide a range of choices which have some claim to meet the demands of 3 and 4 above.
6   Given that effective small group teaching is relatively formal and that reported patterns offer precedents, it is possible to increase one's effectiveness in working with groups by learning, i.e., effectiveness is not merely a function of personality supported by mystique.

Notes and references

* Lawrence Stenhouse is Director of the Centre for Applied Research in Education, University of East Anglia.

† Originally published in: *Cambridge Journal of Education* 2: 1, 18–24.

Abercrombie, M. L. J., *Aims and Techniques of Group Teaching*, A.R.H.E., 2nd edition, 1971.

Abercrombie, M. L. J., 'Teaching in Small Groups', from *Higher Education in the Seventies*, edited by H. J. Butcher and E. Rudd.

Abercrombie, M. L. J., Terry, P. M. *et al.* 'Whatever happened to Group Dynamics?' in the *Proceedings of the Conference on Small Group Teaching*, University of London Institute of Education, 4–5 January 1971.

Brameld, T. 'Ethics of Leadership' *Adult Leadership*, 4, 1955, pp. 5–8.

British Columbia Teachers' Federation, *The Use of Discussion Groups for Exploration of Purposes*, offset litho pamphlet, 1970.

Collier, K. G., 'Syndicate Methods: further evidence and comments', *Universities Quarterly*, Autumn, 1969, pp. 431–436.

French, Arthur, *Parameters of Group Work* typescript, no date.

Great Books Foundation, various pamphlets and plans of course for discussion leaders.

The Humanities Project: an Introduction, Heinemann Educational Books, 1970.

Nisbet, Stanley, 'A Method for Advanced Seminars', *Universities Quarterly*, June 1966, pp. 349–355.

Richardson, E., *Group Study for Teachers*, Routledge & Kegan Paul, 1967.

Scarfe, N. V., *Lectures and Seminars*, typescript, University of British Columbia Faculty of Education, no date.

Woodings, R. B., 'The Seminar is the Message', UEA *Bulletin*, February 1969, pp. 58–62.

11 The concept of the neutral teacher

*John Elliott**[†]

Over the last three years the most controversial aspect of the Schools Council Humanities Project's controversial issues programme for upper Secondary students has been that 'the teacher accepts the need to submit his teaching to the criterion of neutrality at this stage of education'.[1]

Much of the opposition to this premise arises, I think, from misunderstandings about how the concept of neutrality is applied in the Project's thinking.

Some criticisms, either explicitly or implicitly, suggest that the Project's idea of neutrality is based upon a particular meta-ethical theory. In one form or another this theory stresses the subjective nature of practical judgements and gives an extremely limited role, if any, to reason and objectivity. Moral, social and political judgements are mere expressions or reports of emotions. There are no criteria of rationality which can provide a basis for discriminating between good and bad reasons. In other words, there is a logical gap between fact and value. Two people accepting the same set of facts can evaluate the significance of these facts differently. Such a theory would seem to contradict the normal use of evaluative terms in moral, political and religious discourse. We do ask for reasons 'for doing this rather than that' or for 'why X action is good rather than bad?'

A more sophisticated version of this emotivist theory is the prescriptivist theory of R. M. Hare.[2] He argues that there is a criterion for differentiating between good and bad reasons. But this is merely a formal requirement appropriate to all forms of reason; namely, the principle of universalisation emphasising the necessity to be consistent in one's application of reasons. Apart from this logical requirement there are no substantive principles which make one reason more relevant than another. Thus it remains possible for individuals to arrive at different evaluative judgements on the basis of the same facts.

If the Humanities Project's idea of neutrality is based on an emotivist or pre-scriptivist theory it obviously excludes those teachers who are committed to rationality in the area of values i.e. to the view that factual statements are relevant for evaluative judgements. Keith Thompson[3] has suggested that the Project's strategy of discussion based on evidence is incompatible with the idea of teacher neutrality. The former assumes that information and the giving of reasons is important, while the latter is 'itself based on the importance of the fact/value distinction. It is because a value position cannot in the last resort be logically defended, Stenhouse argues, that the teacher must adopt this position.'

If Thompson is right about the Project's idea of neutrality there is the implication that moral, social, and political issues have to be handled differently from other areas of the curriculum. Since there are no logically valid criteria of rationality, other than merely formal ones of coherence and consistency, the teacher has no authority to express his personal views. I believe that Thompson's argument is based on a misunderstanding of a particular passage in Stenhouse's article 'Open-minded Teaching'. Stenhouse actually says: 'our strategy must renounce the position of the teacher as an "expert" capable of solving by authority all issues about values that arise in discussion – because this position cannot be logically justified'.[4] The misunderstanding lies in Stenhouse's use of the word 'expert'. R. S. Peters[5] has drawn attention to the distinction between 'traditional authority' and 'legal-rational authority'. The former assumes prescriptions ought to be obeyed merely because they are given by someone in authority. The latter assumes the prescriptions of an authority ought to be obeyed because they are based on impartial considerations which reasonable men will acknowledge to be relevant. Thompson 'understands' Stenhouse to be referring to the latter conception of authority, with the implication that there are no substantive criteria of rationality in morals. But Stenhouse is actually referring to the former conception. He is arguing that the position of 'the teacher as an "expert" capable of solving by authority all issues about values' cannot be logically justified because it implies that value issues can be solved on the authority of persons rather than on rational criteria. Stenhouse is attempting to do the opposite of what Thompson implies. Whereas in other areas of the curriculum teachers have at least paid lip service to standards of rationality, in the moral, social and political spheres they have all too frequently assumed that issues can be resolved by resort to a 'traditional' conception of authority. Stenhouse is making the same kind of logical point about practical discourse as Peters[6] does in his 'justification of worthwhile activities'. Peters argues that if a man asks '"Why do this rather than that?" he must already have a serious concern for truth built into his consciousness'. Controversial issues are justified in the curriculum because, although there may be disagreement about the best course of action to take, the logic of practical discourse presupposes the importance of factual considerations.

It ought to be as possible for teachers to submit their teaching to the principle of impartiality in these areas as it is in other areas of the curriculum because people do proceed on the presupposition that there are substantive criteria which can enable one to distinguish between good and bad reasons. For example, Peters has argued that practical discourse, in which people ask for reasons for 'doing this rather than that', presupposes second-order principles which serve as criteria of relevance, e.g. freedom, fairness, and consideration towards the interests of others. It is a factual matter whether people pursue their own ends without interference, are treated impartially and given opportunities to act according to their lights. Thus agreement about these kinds of facts in concrete human situations is relevant to the making of practical judgements. The teacher in a controversial issues programme has a number of criteria for establishing the facts about human situations and acts. These are provided by disciplines such as history, sociology and psychology. Literature and art provide the criteria for imaginatively exploring a situation or act from the standpoint of one involved, thus giving the facts emotional significance. If I argue 'that pacifism was the correct attitude to adopt in relation to World War Two', historical investigation can unveil why Britain entered the war and what people felt was at stake. The imaginative exploration of autobiographies, letters, war literature and poetry can reveal the human significance of national freedom. Through the disciplines of the humanities facts can be established which serve as relevant reasons for making a particular practical judgement. A boy once said to me:

> Before I studied war in the classroom I was a pacifist and could not understand that anyone else could reasonably hold any other position. I am still a pacifist but now appreciate that others can differ from me and have good reasons for doing so.

He was not saying that any practical judgement is as good as any other. But he was implying that in this particular situation alternative judgements can be made on the basis of reasons which are relevant. In relation to concrete situations our second-order criteria of rationality often conflict. Two people equally committed to rationality and sharing the same set of criteria will weigh them differently and so disagree. The boy himself may have given a greater weighting to unconditional love (the active consideration of the interests of the enemy) than to freedom. But his decision in favour of the latter does not mean he has to deny that those who opposed Germany with force had relevant reasons for doing so. The problem in making practical judgements is not so much that we do not have criteria of relevance for the reasons we offer, but that reasons equally relevant may conflict. It is here that rational men have discovered no criterion by which they can agree on the relative weightings to be given to conflicting relevant reasons.

Let us suppose the boy I mentioned had a teacher who used his authority position to promote his belief that the pacifist attitude was the *only* morally valid one to adopt in response to the threat of Nazi Germany. Such a position could not be defended by resort to impartial criteria. If he was impartial he would have to admit that alternative judgements could be made on equally valid grounds. The educationally defensible position for him to adopt is to allow the principle of impartiality to demarcate the parameter of his authority. He certainly has a duty to get his students to test the relevance of their reasons by submitting them to criteria of relevance. But he has no rational grounds for using his authority to promote judgements about situations and acts which go beyond these criteria and involve individual judgement.

The criterion of neutrality is not an alternative to impartiality as Thompson I think implies. The Humanities Project's strategy renounces the position of the teacher as an 'expert' capable of solving by authority all issues about values that arise in discussion because he ought to see his authority in terms of a commitment to rationality and the application of impartial criteria. His authority ought to be based on a procedural impartiality. Procedural neutrality is entailed by procedural impartiality in publicly controversial areas. Impartiality is the criterion which guides the way a teacher treats other people's views. Neutrality is the criterion which guides the way he handles his own. Procedural neutrality expresses a teacher's commitment to not using his authority to promote judgements which go beyond impartial criteria of rationality. Within the field of controversial value issues such a commitment is synonymous with a commitment to democracy as a worthwhile form of life. For implicit in such a form of life is the belief that practical issues are reasonable through reason rather than coercion and force, and that where differences are based on relevant reasons they should have the right to disagree. The values presupposed by practical reasoning are the foundations of democracy, i.e. freedom, fairness, consideration of other's interests. These are the second order principles which function as criteria of relevance for practical reasoning. Thus any teacher committed to rationality and democratic values could not, without contradicting himself, attempt to use his authority to promote his particular commitment when others can make alternative commitments on equally relevant grounds. He is obliged to respect the rights of colleagues, parents, and students to disagree with him. The carrying out of such an obligation in relation to the rights of others is expressed in the use of the idea of neutrality as a criterion of teaching in publically controversial areas. The problem of handling values in the classroom does not arise out of an absence of rational criteria. It arises out of the need to base teaching strategies on rational criteria (the second-order values of democracy presupposed in rationality) rather than on 'traditional' conceptions of authority. Stenhouse articulated this problem cogently in a later paper when he denned it as one of:

> Central concern to any democracy which emphasises and values the responsibility of its citizens. This is the problem of handling, within the curriculum, areas of study which involve highly controversial social, ethical or political values. In short, how is a democracy in its schools, to handle controversial issues.[7]

The idea of procedural neutrality posed as an answer to this problem is a value-position based on rational criteria.

Tied in with the misunderstanding that neutrality involves a view which casts doubt on the logical status of rational criteria are objections such as it 'emasculates the teacher', or 'reduces the teacher to something less than human'. Behind these criticisms lies the implication that neutrality means 'the teacher feeling neutral about controversial issues', that he ought to be value-free because values are purely subjective and not the mark of a rational man. For such objectors, a man in the fullest sense is one who acts in the light of considerations he feels important, i.e. in the light of values. Neutrality seems to contradict that which is most human. The same misunderstanding may lead a teacher to think that neutrality prevents him from fulfilling his obligations as a teacher, i.e. to pass on the values of his society to his students. But neutrality becomes far less objectionable if we see it as an expression of educational and political values, e.g. based on the importance of rationality, and where criteria of rationality conflict in particular situations the importance of respecting the divergent judgements which they entail. The Humanities Project has always asked teachers in experimental schools to explain to students exactly why they were being neutral. This involves making clear the value-criteria on which neutrality is based. The teacher explains that he is not value-neutral; not un-committed to a position in controversial areas. He is attempting to be procedurally neutral; not using his authority to promote his own commitment as if it were the only one that could be rationally justified, because to do so might prevent them from making judgements on equally relevant considerations. In other words it is precisely because the teacher has a commitment in a controversial area that he is neutral; not because he is 'value-neutral!' He is making clear to students the limits of his authority in publicly controversial areas, by explaining that his procedures are based on a respect for rationality and the value-criteria it presupposes.

Another related objection to neutrality in controversial areas is made on the grounds that it implies dishonesty and pretence. A recent Schools Council publication asserts: 'Teachers must be intelligently aware of the controversial issues, but must be honest in their expressions of opinion. Boys and girls are quick to detect pretence and to respect candour'.[8] But the neutral role of the teacher does not necessarily involve either. As I have suggested, the teacher is not pretending to be uncommitted about the issues under discussion. He is not 'neutral about...', but 'procedurally neutral in relation to...' situations and acts which are publicly controversial. His neutrality is procedural and this does not involve pretending he is uncommitted. It involves not promoting his own view as if it were the only rationally defensible one. His authority is limited by his commitment to criteria of rationality. This is a value-position rather than a value-free one. There is also no necessary contradiction between procedural neutrality and the expression of a teacher's personal commitment. The criteria of neutrality reminds the teacher that if he expresses his personal view certain conditions must be satisfied. Since his authority is based on criteria of rationality he would have to ensure:

1   that in controversial areas he did not promote his commitment as the only reasonable one. He would therefore have to take steps to divorce his procedural authority from the expression of this commitment, e.g. by stepping down from the chair;
2   that his own views were impartially subjected to the same critical standards as he would apply to his students;
3   that his students did not confuse the expression of his views with his authority position. An example of this would be where students saw the discussion merely as a matter of agreeing or disagreeing with the teacher (authority) rather than critically examining a perspective.

Surely this does not involve the teacher in dishonesty and pretence. In fact, not to apply neutrality as a criterion of teaching, by allowing students to think that his personal view was the only rational one, would most certainly be dishonesty and pretence. It is obviously dangerous, for it encourages the student to accept the teacher's word as the ultimate source of authority, rather than to subject judgements to critical standards (impartial criteria).

A teacher is not only responsible for the purity of his intentions. He is also responsible for the effects of his behaviour on his students. Although there is no necessary contradiction between the expression of personal views and procedural neutrality, there may be practical difficulties in actual educational contexts. Years of educational conditioning may make it extremely difficult for students to understand and accept the teacher's abdication from being the source of all wisdom, so ingrained is the notion that he is its fount. It may also be difficult for the teacher to resist this. He is so used to seeing himself in an educational situation as the one who knows. He can easily deceive himself into believing that students are not ascribing authority to his views, when in fact they are. In actual educational situations the teacher may not be able to express his personal view and remain procedurally neutral. If his students persist in ascribing an uncritical authority to his views, then some kind of closure is put on the range and depth of viewpoints explored. The development of understanding is prevented. If the teacher does not even attempt seriously to find out what the effects of his behaviour are, or if he does find out but refrains from taking effective measures to change these effects, then we have grounds for assuming that he is not using the notion of procedural neutrality as a criterion in his teaching.

Thus whether the teacher ought to give his opinion at all in a classroom discussion on controversial matters is to be decided by experiment. The project team have encouraged the sceptical teacher who argues that his personal views are not in practice incompatible with a respect for alternative views expressed by his students. They have asked him to adopt an experimental attitude to his teaching and offered this hypothesis for him to test: 'Refraining from expressing your personal views in the classroom is more likely to facilitate the development of understanding than expressing it.'

Notes and references

* John Elliott is Senior Research Associate in the Schools Council Humanities Project Centre for Applied Research in Education at the University of East Anglia.
† Originally published in: *Cambridge Journal of Education* 1: 2, 60–67.
1 'The Humanities Project: An Introduction'; Heinemann Educational, 1970.
2 Hare, R. M. 'The Language of Morals'. O.U.P., 1964.
3 Thompson, Keith. 'Philosophy of Education and Educational Practice'. Proc. Phil. of Ed. Soc. of G.B., 1970.
4 Stenhouse, L. 'Open-Minded Teaching'. New Society, 24 July 1969.
5 Peters, R. S. 'Ethics and Education'. Allen & Unwin, 1966.
6 Op. cit., 5.
7 Stenhouse, L. 'Controversial Value Issues in the Classroom'. Values and the Curriculum, Nat. Ed. Ass. Centre for Instruction, Washington, D.C., 1970.
8 'Humanities for the Young School Leaver – an approach through religious education.' Schools Council. Evans/Methuen Educational, 1969.

12 Rationality, democracy and the neutral teacher

Charles Bailey*†

This chapter collects together some thoughts about the bases of the Schools Council Humanities Project in general, and about John Elliott's paper 'The Concept of the Neutral Teacher' in particular. I shall try to argue that whilst any teacher who sees his task largely in terms of the development of rational understanding is bound to sympathise strongly with the aspirations of the Project, nevertheless there are features of the underlying arguments that are by no means clear, and about which there should be much further discussion.

The Project is clearly to be supported because of its strong emphasis on the professional necessity of the teacher to avoid the temptations of indoctrination. Whilst most teachers subscribe to the belief that indoctrination (establishing beliefs in non-evidential ways) is anti-educational, all too few have really grasped the point of the close connection between indoctrination and the teacher's traditional authority position. The Project team has looked closely at the implications of this connection and make it quite plain that in order to help pupils achieve certain kinds of understanding the teacher must abstain from whatever is likely to encourage pupils to base their beliefs on the teacher's authority *alone*. My conviction is that large numbers of pupils pass through our education system having failed to grasp what criteria of judgement, what tests of truth and falsity, apply in their areas of study. In however sophisticated a way they remain at the level of believing what a teacher or a textbook has said, and find it difficult to pass beyond this. Our teaching methods still depend far too much on authority based utterances and the Project's attempt to change this in one important part of the curriculum deserves all our support.

My subsequent arguments, then, are those of a friend of the Project, as it were. I seek only to engage in the same kind of critical analysis that the Project does so splendidly within its own team and seeks to engender in both teacher and student.

First, then, are we really clear what a controversial issue is, because much flows from distinctions made at this point? Controversies are largely social phenomena: that is, they are those topics and issues about which numbers of people are observed to disagree. Controversies, seen like this, can occur in any area of knowledge and experience. There can be controversies about scientific matters, aesthetic matters, historical matters, controversies about religion and about cosmology as well as about morals, society and politics. At one time the expressed aim of the Project was 'to help pupils to develop their understanding of a number of controversial areas of universal human concern'. This at least separated out some controversies from others and directed attention upon those held to be of universal human concern. These, presumably because they involve some kind of interaction between people seen totally as persons, thereby essentially characterise what we call 'the humanities'. The description of the Project in the Schools Council Report 1969/70 refers to 'developing strategies for the teaching of controversial human issues to pupils of average and below average ability'. This seems to move back to some kind of valuing of controversy because it is controversy, and lacks the justification of the added 'universal human concern'. This would be an over-nice point to make if it was not the case that valuing controversy for its own sake does seem to dictate the Project's concern for 'protecting diversity', as I shall try to show later.

The final version of aims which appears in the published Handbook of the Project reads: 'to develop an understanding of social situations and human acts and of the controversial value issues which they raise'. Now this, it seems to me, separates out what the Project is mainly concerned about, namely, value issues. Controversy is to be considered as about values. Since controversies are patently and demonstrably sometimes about issues other than values (e.g. did Bacon write some plays attributed to Shakespeare?) then we could read this interpretation of controversies as essentially valuative in two different ways. First, as saying that certainly there are non-valuative controversies but insofar as these are non-valuative they are not the concern of the humanities. Second, the stronger thesis which I believe the Project is claiming, that insofar as a controversy is about human action it is only understandable if valuative considerations are included. That is, any attempt to explain the controversy, to oneself or to others, that leaves out value positions will fall short of being an acceptable explanation or a coherent understanding.

This view of understanding human action has, of course, been controversial itself. Some explanation of human action seeks only to satisfy the observer. It is possible to construct conceptual and logical frameworks to make sense of what I, the observer, witness. I can do this as a behaviourist psychologist, perhaps as an economist or a sociologist. The emphasis will be upon observable behaviour and any move away from this will be seen as a move away from the much-to-be-desired objective of being scientific. As against this, however, we are reminded by people like P. Winch or A. R. Louch that the very thing we are trying to understand is *human* behaviour, and that this is essentially characterised by people acting as agents, that is with intentions, reasons, purposes and values. To view people simply as observable objects of science is, on this account, to fish for mackerel and come up with crabs.[1] There seem to be good grounds, then, for supposing the Project to be right to claim that to get pupils understanding human action, controversial or not, must involve dealing constantly with valuative positions. So far I do not see myself differing very much with John Elliott or the Project.

The next moves, however, are interesting. Given that we are committed to viewing human action as understandable only in some valuative framework, what is our conception of values to be? Now Elliott argues that in all his teaching the only authority the teacher has any right to claim is that based on what Weber called legal/rational authority. In the context of teaching I take this to mean partly that the teacher's authority rests in him being appointed by higher authorities to teach; and, further, that it is assumed that he will get his pupils involved in the various forms of rational understanding by rational procedures. The first of these would be widely accepted; the second has far-reaching implications, would not necessarily meet with universal consent, but is nevertheless, I believe, a sound assumption which has been well justified by others.[2] As far as the Project's aims and intentions are concerned, then, the teacher is committed to teaching pupils those rational forms of understanding concerned with values in a rational way. He cannot, therefore, merely pronounce from a position of traditional authority, for that would be indoctrinatory and non-rational. Is he, then, committed to neutrality in the Project's sense?

Now at this point in the argument it is usual to give some attention to the fact that we teach in a democracy. Elliott shows this concern when he says that commitment to procedural neutrality is 'synonymous with commitment to democracy as a worthwhile form of life'. He refers later to 'any teacher committed to rationality and democratic values'. Now this is an odd and indicative description which implies that democracy, like rationality, is some ultimate resting position, some basic starting ground for subsequent beliefs, stances and positions. It also implies that it is different from rationality and supports rationality as a ground for certain strategies in the Project. Surely the truth is that whilst rationality *is* a necessary presupposition, without which questions about what I ought to believe and what I ought to do become meaningless, democracy *is not* a basic ground of this order. In fact the notion of democracy only makes sense as being distinctive of that form of government least hindering the rational life. In other words, democracy itself is grounded in a presupposition of the necessary value of rationality. To ground the Project's strategy in democratic processes is therefore unnecessary if they are already supposed to be grounded in rationality. The only *necessary* connection between democracy and education is that they both work out the implications of valuing rationality. In the one case in connection with answering the question about what kind of political institutions and processes we ought to have; and in the other case in connection with answering the questions about what we ought to teach and how we ought to teach it. There are, of course, plenty of contingent connections, but what can be derived from those?

Leaving democracy to one side, then, what follows if we are committed to teaching pupils that form (or those forms) of rational understanding connected with values? The Project's answer is that the teacher must undertake the duties of procedural neutrality.[3]

Now some objections to this are indeed misunderstandings or beside the point, and Elliott is right to point these out. But it remains the case that one can believe that a teacher ought to be committed to rationality, and that he should try to increase his pupils' understanding of valuative matters, without believing that this leads to quite the same kind of neutrality as advocated by the Project. What it does lead to, certainly, is *impartiality*. That all is subject to argument, that no person counts for more than his argument counts, even the teacher, and that *all* statements are subject to rational criticism – all this is part of the rational commitment, but this is picked out by the concept of impartiality. Contrary to Elliott's assertion, impartiality is *not* merely the way I treat other people's views. To be impartial about other people's views and put mine in some special category would be to make a mockery of the notion of impartiality. Insofar as the notion of impartiality enters into reasoning and morality it is precisely about the way I see my views as against other people's, my interests as against other people's. To be impartial is to consider views and interests in the light of all possible criticisms and counter claims, and to ignore any kind of special pleading, whether from authority or whatever, about myself or whosoever.

A further point is that impartiality is compatible with truth, indeed it is a necessity of truth-seeking. Now truth has not so far entered into this discussion and it is time it did. For the teacher is not only committed to rationality in the discussion of values but also to truth. What is the point of discussion and rational procedures if we do not expect them to lead to truth? What is the point, in education, of bringing about understanding in some psychological sense, if we do not also believe that there is a sense in which some understandings are more correct than others? The trouble with the term 'neutrality' is that it sounds as though we want the teacher detached from these concerns, that it does not matter what kind of understanding is achieved in the pupil's mind as long as it is an understanding.

Elliott does not make it clear, in dealing with Thompson's arguments, what the connection between rationality and values is supposed to be. Certainly the teacher has no authority to express his personal views as indubitably true, but then nobody seriously suggests that he should. The point is whether in being committed to rationality a teacher might not have good grounds for thinking some value positions more rational than others, and some statements about values true and others false. His commitment then would provide good grounds for intervention in a discussion to demonstrate such differences. This would not only be compatible with his commitment to rationality but, indeed, necessitated by it. This does not, however, seem to be in accord with the Project's conception of neutrality. This is the contradiction I believe Keith Thompson to have spotted, and this is no misunderstanding. This is the point where the Project does seem by implication to be linked with some kind of subjective and relative position about ethics which is at odds with its otherwise strong commitment to rationality.

The position opposed to procedural neutrality is set up by Elliott as that where a teacher allows pupils to think that his (the teacher's) view is the only rationally defensible view. One must repeat that nobody has really suggested that he should; any serious and responsible educator would see this to be wrong as soon as stated. Teachers do such things, of course, but teachers like other human beings do many foolish and unjustifiable things. The point is whether anyone seriously advocates that they should so act. If not, then as an argument this remains an Aunt Sally. The position really opposed to that of procedural neutrality is that of the *impartial teacher*, and this is admirably described by Elliott in his three points about the teacher stepping down from the chair, subjecting his own views to impartial criticism and not letting his pupils confuse the validity of his views with his authority position.

The point about the connection between rationality and value judgements needs stressing because there is a strong and influential neo-Kantian school of moral theory which would see the connection as a close and possibly a necessary one. The argument here would be that to be committed to rationality is already to be committed to certain ways of approaching ethical judgements. For someone to appeal to intuition or emotion or relativism on this view would not merely be a display of interesting and diverse value positions, it would be wrong. I believe a neo-Kantian approach to ethics to be broadly right, but the argument must not (of course) hinge on my say so. The point to highlight is that any teacher who believes something like this must also believe that other approaches can be shown to be wrong, or at least have difficulties, inconsistencies or incoherencies about them. For him to disregard this in the service of procedural neutrality is for him to disregard truth as he sees it.

In his exercise of procedural neutrality the Project would have the teacher protect divergency of view and not try to achieve consensus. The fourth of the five major premises given in the Handbook says 'that the discussion should protect divergence of view among participants, rather than attempt to achieve consensus'. One of the principles of chairmanship offered for the neutral teacher is that he should maintain 'open enquiry' which is to be characterised by the challenging of consensus, the introduction of hitherto unconsidered views, the equal consideration of minority views and the extension rather than the limitation of the discussion. This is all excellent advice for the conduct of rational enquiry, provided that there is also the rational idea that open enquiry leads to justifiable judgement at some point. Running through the work of the Project and through Elliott's paper is the strong suggestion that coming to a conclusion on valuative matters is more than we can expect of a rational enquiry. Elliott says that the teacher 'has no rational grounds for using his authority to promote judgements about situations and acts which go beyond these criteria and involve individual judgement'. I have already argued that nobody seriously claims that the teacher should promote any position merely on his authority, but he might well want to promote certain views by demonstrating their superior reasonableness. What Elliott is saying is that rationality only takes us so far and then we have a variety of conflicting but equally rational views, all supported by relevant reasons, which can only be resolved by an individual by the exercise of his 'individual judgement'. Whatever this 'individual judgement' is, it cannot carry any conviction to another by any further use of reason. The open enquiry, then, is not to seek truth, but only to demonstrate to the sceptical the equal validity of diverse views. This does appear to rest on not only a fact-value distinction but a reason-value distinction as well, and it is not clear from Elliott's discussion of this whether he is denying this or not.

Now I remain puzzled by the position a pupil finds himself in as a result of all this. The evidence and the discussion under the auspices of the neutral teacher seem aimed at getting him to understand, that is, see the sense of, a number of diverse views. The strong implication is that these are equally rational possibilities and that reason will not help him decide which is the right one. His 'individual judgement' is therefore shown to be no more right than anyone else's. Now if this is so, why should he hold this judgement? To hold a view on good reasons must include the notion that the reasons for holding this view are better in some way than reasons for holding alternative views. To think otherwise is not rational, and we are at least agreed that we are committed to rationality. The dilemma seems unavoidable: either 'individual judgement' is to be rational, in which case consensus is desirable at least in the long run; or it is not rational and we are demonstrating to the pupil that non-rational decisions are meaningful. This is an odd conclusion for a teacher committed to rationality.

Protection of diversity, then, like neutrality, is a good idea pushed too far. In a praiseworthy endeavour to get teachers to be rationally impartial we push them into unnecessary neutrality. In a commendable attempt to get teachers not to rush discussion groups like tired committees to hasty consensus we push them to an unjustifiable valuing of divergence for its own sake. Sound advice for conducting rational discussion becomes acceptance of private, non-rational modes of coming to judgement.

Consider, to emphasise my point, Elliott's student of war and peace who said:

> Before I studied war in the classroom I was a pacifist and could not understand that anyone else could reasonably hold any other position. I am still a pacifist but now appreciate that others can differ from me but have good reasons for doing so.

Now if this boy had only meant that he still thought the reasons justifying pacifism were stronger, or better, or more valid than those supporting war, this would be fine. But Elliott introduces the strange notion of 'weighing' something like love against something like freedom. 'Rational men', he says, 'have discovered no criterion by which they can agree on the relative weighings to be given to conflicting relevant reasons'. Even if we grant that some people make judgements in something like this manner, perhaps even that we all do some of the time, we do not have to grant that these judgements are necessitated by some limitations of rationality, or that when they are thus made rationality has been worked as hard as it could have been. It is always possible to make judgements – or perhaps will to believe – in some non-rational way, but why should the educator encourage this? The driving force of the rational man is that he constantly tries to build principles like 'love' or 'freedom' into an ever more coherent framework in which one illuminates the other, or is seen to be necessitated by the other. He cannot, as a rational man, see them as free-floating alternatives from which he takes his pick, like vanilla or coffee flavouring.

It is possible to argue on the side of the Project that if all teachers were as rational and impartial as I would have them be then there would be no need for the concept of the neutral teacher or for the protection of divergence as they at present advocate. They might also argue, however, that this is unlikely to be achieved unless a clear line is drawn by something like the Project's strategy and that therefore rational expediency dictates approval of the Project's methods. My answer to this is that it might well prove very difficult indeed to improve the rational procedures of teachers by any methods short of training in procedural neutrality. But I have tried to show that there are certain important difficulties about a strategy set up in the name of rationality which leads to protection of irrationalities, and this makes me prefer the conception of a teacher somewhat less neutral than the Project advocates, but nevertheless rational and impartial in his teaching and in his handling of discussion. These difficulties lead me also to the conclusion that protection of divergence of view can only be a temporary tactic in the search for the truth, not an end in itself.

Notes and references

* Charles Bailey is Principal Lecturer in Education at Homerton College, Cambridge.

† Originally published in: *Cambridge Journal of Education* 1: 2, 68–76.

1 Winch, P. 'The Idea of a Social Science'. Routledge and Kegan Paul, 1958; Louch, A. R. 'Explanation and Human Action'. Basil Blackwell, 1966. For full discussions of the controversy see: Mischel, T. (ed.) 'Human Action: Conceptual and Empirical Issues'. Academic Press, 1969.

2 Notably, of course, in the works of P. H. Hirst and R. S. Peters.

3 I have not seen it necessary to spell out all the Project says about procedural neutrality and the protection of divergent views. This is made clear in the Handbook to the Project published by Heinemann Educational, who also publish the teaching materials for the Project.

13 The social organisation of the classroom and the philosophy of mixed ability teaching

*David Bridges**†

One part of the argument about mixed ability teaching centres upon the question whether children learn their science, social studies or maths more effectively in mixed ability or in homogeneous groups. This is manifestly an important question which deserves continuing research. It is not, however, the only question which needs asking about mixed ability teaching, nor for many teachers the most important one. Teachers' talk and teachers' writing about mixed ability teaching commonly suggest that their reasons for favouring this pattern of school or classroom organisation are related at least as much to *social* principles which they believe should govern that organisation and to the social values and *social* learning which they wish to promote as to their more specifically cognitive objectives.

There are at least three ways in which the decision as to whether or not to go for mixed ability teaching rests upon considerations of a social/political character. I shall discuss these in turn in the following sections.

1

The first argument is broadly egalitarian in character and relates to what is held to be the social and educational injustice which is perpetuated through streaming. A. V. Kelly, for example, one of the leading advocates of mixed ability teaching in the country, summarises his argument against streaming in this way: "In short, it has been regarded by many as a major obstacle to the achievement of anything approaching educational equality".[1] A. G. Young, headmaster of Northcliffe Community School, draws attention to the continuity of this concern with the earlier debate about comprehensive schooling in a comment on the underlying rationale for mixed ability teaching in his school.

> There was a general feeling among the staff at the social consequences pro-
> duced by our "sheep and goats" act. Many felt that we were guilty of extending
> the evil social division caused by the 11+ examination by our further invidious
> separations. We had bad consciences about social apartheid systems in educa-
> tion.[2]

But what, more precisely, is the nature of the egalitarian argument in this context? Basically, I think, it may be summarised as follows. There is a close relationship between socio-economic and ethnic status and student performance on currently used standardised tests. The streaming of students into roughly homogeneous groups on the basis of these standardised tests will therefore tend to separate students of different socio-economic and ethnic status. Moreover one of the effects of this streaming is to enhance the motivation and aspirations of those categorised as more able (and incidentally of their teachers) and to lower the motivation and aspirations of those categorised as less able (and their teachers). Thus the practice of streaming ability groups in schools tends to have the effects, first, of segregating groups of like socio-economic and/or ethnic character from each other; and, second, of reinforcing the correlation between high socio-economic status and high achievement as measured by school tests in such a way as to give those tests the power of self-fulfilling prophecy – and all of this to the disadvantage of those of low socio-economic status. The final stage in the argument moves from the assertion of what are claimed as matters of fact to the application of some basic social political principles and to the judgement that those tendencies are undesirable.

I shall not attempt in this context to establish the truth or falsity of the empirical or factual part of this argument. The account I have given accords with the general opinion of the research on the subject, as for example reviewed by Dominick Esposito,[3] though the research is not without its uncertainties and controversy. What I want to draw attention to are the issues of social/political principle which are raised in this part of the discussion of mixed ability teaching.

The fathers of the French Revolution were clear-minded enough to distinguish two principles which later social theorists and the advocates of mixed ability teaching have tended to blur. I refer to the principles of "equality" and "fraternity". One part of the argument I have described is indeed concerned with equality or more specifically with trying to break the vicious circle of *low socio-economic status – low school achievement – low socio-economic status* in the interests of narrowing the differentials between people's socio-economic status and between their levels of school achievement. But this is only one part of the argument. Beyond this as I understand it there is the ambition, which I associate with the neglected ideal of fraternity, which is opposed to the institutionalised segregation of different sections of the population not only because this is instrumentally associated with inequality but because it is itself intrinsically undesirable. The ideal society on this view is a community which is at least relatively unhierarchical in character; in which there is mutuality of concern and respect and cooperation in the pursuit of collective and individual good; in which there is a willing acceptance of the principle that no individual or group interest will persistently be subordinated to another – for all of which a certain kind of equality of consideration will be a necessary but not perhaps a sufficient condition. There is something of the flavour of this ideal in this extract from a paper contributed by John Wadham to the series of meetings on Mixed Ability Teaching held at Homerton Curriculum Development Centre.

> Our election to teach RE – or, in our case, RS – in Mixed Ability groups was an expression of the belief that children with widely different levels of intellectual ability *can (and presumably he intends "should")* interact constructively

and that an important part of growing up is learning to accept with under-standing, rather than with pride or resignation, that people are different.

Perhaps, too, the boy talking in this extract from one of Dave Ebbutt's record-ings is expressing something of the "fraternal" values to which I refer.

> If you were on your own you're going to get bored because you haven't got anyone to discuss the matter with or anything like that. Because I'm with P, if I say "How come that ... something happens to do this?", he says, "Because of this..." – and I get on well like that. Sometimes I know things that he don't know. We just get on together like that.[4]

Mixed ability teaching may be interpreted, then, as a quite deliberate attempt to *challenge* what, arguably, are or have been deeply entrenched features of our edu-cational system – the segregation of different socio-economic and (though this has been an altogether larger problem in the United States) ethnic groups and the institutionalisation, through tripartite schooling and through streaming within schools, of relatively stable social hierarchies.

2

There is a more specific sense in which a preference for mixed ability teaching rep-resents a standpoint in social philosophy. This is in the sense in which it is seen as constituting a form of classroom organisation which itself exhibits and promotes the development of desirable social attitudes, dispositions, skills or values.

Having said this, however, one is bound to notice that there is a considerable variety of classroom organisation which falls under the banner of "mixed ability teach-ing" in teachers' writing and discussion – a variety which, I shall suggest, is associated with some rather different social values. In practice teachers seem to refer to some or all of the following patterns of classroom organisation as mixed ability teaching:

A children with different levels of ability in one class working in separate groups, which are "streamed" according to ability, on work related to the level of ability of the group;
B children with different levels of ability in one class working on individually tailored assignments (following either the same scheme of work at different speeds or different schemes of work);
C children organised in mixed ability pairs or groups (usually so that the more able can help the less able) on assignments which they have in common;
D children of mixed ability working together on a common project but with individual tasks related to their different kinds or different levels of ability, e.g. (is this a caricature?) child one does the writing, child two does a picture and child three pastes the two together and pins them on the display board;
E children of mixed ability working together in a group in which tasks and responsibilities are in principle undifferentiated (as perhaps in a Humanities Curriculum Project discussion).

There are important differences between these patterns of organisation of a kind which suggest different sorts of social values or social learning. In particular it is important to separate two variables: the extent to which mixed ability teaching is interpreted as implying individualised learning or group cooperation and, within this last category, the nature and purpose of the group cooperation. Let me explain the significance of these two variables a little more fully.

Individualised learning or group cooperation

For some people, mixed ability teaching is virtually synonymous with group work and its virtue lies especially in the experience it gives in cooperative group endeavour. Thus, for example, E. M. Hoyles of Vauxhall Manor School writes:

> One of the main features of mixed ability classroom organisation is the numerous occasions on which children need to work in groups. The child has to learn to use the group activity effectively from the beginning. First of all, she needs to learn how to play her own part in the group ... In addition, she will need to grow in judgement of other people's ability and this can join the general teaching the school provides in respect for other people because, from an early stage, she will have to learn how to use other people's talents, not only for her own development but for the development of the group. It is important for her to learn how to apportion work to other members of the group so that when she becomes a leader she can use other people's talents to the full. In addition, there is a great need for learning tolerance since it will be impossible for every member of the group to fulfil exactly what the group expects and therefore, she will need to understand not only the abilities of others but also their failings and how they can best be helped.[5]

On this sort of view, mixed ability teaching is imagined to have a certain kind of value quite apart from the English, Science or whatever that is being taught – value in this case in the form of desired social skills (playing one's part, apportioning work to others, etc.), social judgement (of other people's abilities and disabilities) and social attitudes (respect for other people, loyalty to group purposes, tolerance).

Whether what is desired is actually achieved remains of course open to investigation. But at least one can see a certain *prima facie* connection between these kinds of purposes and the provision of experience in mixed ability *group* work.

However, not all patterns of mixed ability teaching give anything like this prominence to group work. Indeed Charles Bailey affirms a conception of mixed ability teaching which is in complete contrast with Hoyles'. His conception corresponds with the sort of pattern indicated in my case B. "What I mean by mixed ability teaching", he writes, "is any form of teaching which involves the teacher working with pupils as individuals rather than groups".[6] Now, clearly, where this type of organisation is set up it will provide rather different kinds of experience with rather different objectives from those envisaged by Hoyles. It is a classroom which emphasises individual rather than group responsibility for one's learning and in which satisfaction is to be gained through one's personal rather than one's collective achievement.

On the face of it, at least, these different patterns of mixed ability teaching seem likely to generate rather different outcomes in terms of the skills, values, attitudes, etc., which are developed.

Different patterns of group cooperation

Even within those cases of mixed ability teaching which are deliberately intended to encourage group cooperation, there are significant differences between the character of the cooperation which is envisaged importing different significance for social learning. In fact the three patterns of helping represented in my five types of mixed ability teaching rather neatly reflect three prominent models of society.

Case A – which is still effectively a streamed classroom in which the more able work with the more able and the least able with the least able – reflects the hierarchically divided society in which the strong/wealthy/aristocratic elite support each other in their position at the top while the weak/poor/low-born can find support and help only from those like themselves who are least able to give it. Providence (the teacher) may occasionally interfere and produce limited changes in the hierarchy, but it is at least as likely that such intervention will favour those who are already advantaged.

Case C – in which the more able assist the less able – still pre-supposes and institutionalises the divided society but seeks to make its divisions less acute and painful. It does this by encouraging the more fortunate to engage in what at its worst may be the sort of paternalistic policy of charity and mollification which the ruling classes have traditionally used to support both the reality and the righteousness of their position of privilege. At its best, however, the situation may resemble the kind of fraternal support – "from each according to his ability: to each according to his needs"(?) – once central among the ideals of British socialism.[7]

Cases D and E – in which individual contributions are made to a common group purpose envisage a genuine *mutuality* of helping in which all the children are conceived of as having in one way or another something to *contribute* to the group. This stands in important contrast to Case C in which children are divided (even if the division is not totally clear cut) into those that are expected to give and those that are expected to receive help. We have in these last cases the elements of something approaching the ideal of an intellectual commune.

I may have exaggerated the particular social significance of these different patterns of cooperation in order to highlight the contrast. I do not wish to qualify my basic point, however, which is that there would seem to be some important differences between the kinds of social learning that one would expect to issue from the different patterns of group cooperation which I have described. Moreover, it is not at all obvious that they all carry the kind of democratic egalitarian social message which is commonly associated with mixed ability teaching.

3

As I indicated at the beginning, teachers pick out two rather different kinds of concern in estimating the merits and demerits of mixed ability teaching – a concern to promote the most general and effective learning in the area of the subject, topic or form of enquiry which they are teaching, and a concern to promote certain more specifically "social" attitudes, principles or values. Potentially at least this double concern produces a dilemma for the teacher which is interpretable as a conflict of educational or social priorities. Kelly provides one illustration of the form which this dilemma may take:

> Many teachers and head-teachers are currently recognising the attraction of mixed ability groupings in Secondary schools, glimpsing in particular their possible social and behavioural advantages, but hesitate to take the plunge because of a fear of the practicalities of such a change and especially a concern with its implications for the progress of the very bright child.[8]

If it is the case that the desired social values associated with mixed ability groups may be secured only at the cost of children's achievements in mathematics; or if a vicious circle of injustice perpetuated in streaming can only be broken at the price of some loss of academic distinction; or if (cf. Eric Garner's fears in the last issue of this Journal[9]) the very survival of some subjects in the curriculum can only be secured if more thoroughgoing commitment to mixed ability teaching is rejected – then clearly the school which adopts (or indeed the school which refuses to adopt) mixed ability grouping takes a stand upon a further range of substantial and controversial evaluative social issues. In the context of widespread professional and public awareness of the alternatives, teachers cannot deny responsibility for the preference which is implicit in their practice.

Conclusion

I have tried to indicate some of the different ways in which divisions about mixed ability teaching reveal and reflect the social philosophy or social principles to which teachers are attached, or, to put it slightly differently, to indicate ways in which these decisions present problems which are rooted in social philosophy.

I have so far treated these problems as teachers' problems and these principles as the teachers' principles because it is simply a fact of our present educational system that decisions about classroom organisation lie with our teachers and head-teachers. However, it is perhaps worth asking in conclusion whether this should be the case. I have argued that decisions about mixed ability teaching involve, centrally, issues of a publicly controversial character, about social principles, social values, social attitudes and social priorities. It is not at all obvious that teachers, head-teachers or indeed any other professional educators have either the superior expertise or the natural right to determine this kind of issue on behalf of the wider community (including, importantly, the children whom it affects most directly and their parents). It seems to me therefore that the issue of whether a school should or should not adopt a pattern of mixed ability teaching is one which ought to be decided not by prerogative of the teachers, and even less head-teachers, alone but in close consultation with the wishes of at least the parents and children of the school concerned.[10]

To say this is of course itself to take a socio-political position – but it would be part of my broader argument that it is impossible to make any serious statement about education, and not just mixed ability teaching, outside the context of some such position.[11]

Notes and references

* David Bridges lectures in Education at Homerton College, Cambridge.
† Originally published in: *Cambridge Journal of Education* 6: 1, 15–23.
1 See ed. Kelly, A. V., *Case Studies in Mixed Ability Teaching*, Harper & Row, London, 1975 (p. 1).
2 Ibid. (p. 31).
3 Esposito, D., "Homogeneous and heterogeneous ability groupings: principle findings and implications for evaluating and designing more effective educational environments", *Review of Educational Research*, Vol. 43, 1973.
4 See Dave Ebbutt (*Cambridge Journal of Education* 6: 1) for the context in which this comment was made.
5 In Kelly, A. V., op. cit. (p. 61).
6 See Bailey (*Cambridge Journal of Education* 6: 1).
7 See for example Derek Digby (*Cambridge Journal of Education* 6: 1) which seems to reflect some of this fraternal support in practice.
8 Kelly, A. V., op. cit. (p. 1).
9 Writing about the way in which "modern languages appear to be especially vulnerable to hostile criticism or even outright rejection", Garner noted that "staffs committed to egalitarian policies may see French or German as elitist or divisive elements in the curriculum, resistant to child-centred, integrated or mixed-ability approaches, and inappropriate in the demands they make on pupils from less favoured socio-economic backgrounds".

   See Garner, E., "Beyond formalism: some thoughts on modern languages in the secondary school curriculum", in *Cambridge Journal of Education*, Volume 5, No. 3, Michaelmas Term 1975.
10 For development of this line of argument see Peter Scrimshaw's paper, "Should schools be participatory democracies?" and Hugh Socketts' contribution on "Parents' Rights" in ed. Bridges, D. and Scrimshaw, P., *Values and Authority in Schools*, Hodder and Stoughton, London, 1975.
11 Cf. Martin Hollis on "The Pen and the Purse" in Proceedings *of the Philosophy of Education Society of Great Britain*, Vol. V, No. 2, 1971.

14 Anti-racism and the 'new' South African educational order

Nazir Carrim*†

Introduction

The system of apartheid seriously affected the nature of educational provision and order in South Africa. It ensured that South Africans were schooled in segregated environments. This meant that every level of schooling was cast in a racial mould: educational budget provisions, the structure of educational bureaucracies, the composition of staff and pupils in schools, the kind of curriculum followed, and the ethos prevalent in schools. Transforming education in South Africa, therefore, entails effecting changes on all of these levels. This requires no less than an overhaul of the past educational order, a redefinition of the culture prevalent in schools throughout the country and a shift in mentality, from being racist, undemocratic and authoritarian to being non-racial, democratic and enabling. The task at hand is indeed a challenging one.

Using 'race' as a lens, this article concentrates on the ways in which 'new' South African educational order is being reconstructed. Given the overtly racist nature of apartheid and apartheid education, the focus on 'race' provides a useful yardstick to measure how much is in fact changing, how and why. I focus first on the national initiatives to desegregate and deracialise South African education. I then look at the ways in which some schools are undergoing this change and what the emergent patterns are, specifically within the Gauteng province of South Africa, in which Johannesburg is located.

I argue in this article that macro, national policy initiatives, whilst necessary and unavoidable, tend to homogenise and generalise issues related to 'race' and for this reason do not facilitate micro-level change in deracialising schooling in South Africa. At best, they enact a desegregation of South African schools and are structurally functionalist in orientation. Simultaneously, on the level of schools, I argue that there is a predominance of an assimilationist approach and an emerging tendency to shift from 'race' to ethnicity. However, rather than being a positive acknowledgement of difference, such a shift seems to view people's identities in fixed, stereotyped, homogenised and generalised ways – a form of 'bad' multiculturalism. Thus I suggest that on both the macro and micro levels of the 'new' South African order there is a dire need to work with complex understandings of *identity*, which would incorporate notions of *difference*, in order to ensure that an environment free of racism, and other forms of discrimination, prevails within not only South African schools, but South African society as a whole.

This article draws on empirical research carried out in some schools within the Gauteng province of South Africa only. A qualitative approach was taken, involving interviews with school-based actors and observations of daily school routines. Quantitative measures were used to determine the rate of admission of 'black' students into 'white' schools, for example. The article also analyses pertinent aspects of National Education Ministry interventions, legislated acts and policy documents.

In 1992, all 'Indian', 'coloured' and 'white' schools within the Gauteng region were surveyed with regard to their admission of students for whom their schools were previously not designated (e.g. 'blacks' in 'white' schools, 'non-coloureds' in 'coloured' schools). This survey included the rate of admission and selection procedures used. Six schools from the survey were selected for further probing. Schools were selected on two criteria: their willingness to allow us to visit and the basis of their previous racial designation and level of schooling. Two 'white' schools, two 'Indian' schools and two 'coloured' schools were selected, with a primary school and a secondary school in each pair. Three teachers, teaching different subjects and at different grades within each school were selected for interviews. Headteachers of all six schools were also interviewed. Thereafter, group interviews with students were conducted. Students were grouped only in terms of their grade levels. These students were suggested to us by their peers and the Student Representative Councils of the schools. In total, therefore, 18 teachers, six headteachers and 96 students were interviewed. The students were in groups of eight, with two group interviews being conducted in each school. This research was part of the Education Policy Unit of the University of the Witwatersrand project on desegregation of South African schools (Carrim, 1992).

During 1995 and 1996, the same survey that was used in 1992 was conducted in all 'Indian' and 'coloured' schools in the Gauteng region. The admission rates of 'non-white' students in 'white' schools were obtained from the Gauteng Department of Education's statistics. Thereafter, one primary and one secondary school in both the 'Indian' and 'coloured' schools were selected for interviews. Two teachers in each school, the headteachers and one group of students, consisting of six students, were interviewed. In total eight teachers, four headteachers and 12 students were interviewed. In addition, two teachers from 'white' schools were interviewed. They were drawn from the schools we worked with in 1992 and from one primary and one secondary school. In both research projects, notes were taken about routines in the schools, including patterns and practices on the school playing fields, movement of students into and out of classrooms and arrangements in the classrooms. No structured observations of classroom practices were conducted.

This article draws on both pieces of research. It does not claim to make generalisations. Rather, it uses the examples of the schools researched here to illuminate the nature of experiences related to processes of desegregation. At best this article notes tendencies, not trends. It also provides an account of some schools in the Gauteng province and does not imply that the same would be the case in all schools within the Gauteng province or in other schools elsewhere in the country.

The first section of this article outlines the national, macro-educational initiatives to transform South African education. The second section focuses upon some Gauteng school experiences and emergent tendencies. The third section discusses analytically the macro and micro pictures in the light of questions of *identity* and *difference*.

Changing the system

The first thing that needed to be done in the 'new' South African order was to non-racialise the educational system. In order to grasp the extent of the required changes, it is important to specify what non-racialisation meant in concrete terms.

Under apartheid, South African education was divided into 19 education departments, all of which were either racially or ethnically defined (Christie, 1986; Kallaway, 1986; Nkomo, 1990). 'White' education was controlled by the 'white' House of Assembly, so-called 'Indian' education by the 'Indian' House of Delegates, so-called 'coloured' education by the 'coloured' House of Representatives, mainly urban African education by the Department of Education and Training and African ethnically separate departments by 'homeland' educational systems. Each racially divided department was a separate educational bureaucracy, with its own regulations, laws, modes of operation, staff, contracts and history. This applied to pre-school, primary and secondary provision and in some cases to tertiary education, including universities. Establishing a single, non-racial educational system in South Africa, therefore, entails changing all these educational bureaucracies as well as their entrenched practices and personalities. This is no easy matter.

The adoption of the interim Constitution of the 'new' South Africa empowered the state to appoint a national minister of education and nine provincial ministers of education. In addition, legislation has to be passed at national and provincial levels to be effective in providing national and provincial ministers with their actual powers, duties and responsibilities. Thus, after the first non-racial and democratic election in South Africa, which instated Nelson Mandela as the first black president, all provincial and national ministries concentrated on setting up their ministries in legal terms, in terms of personnel and in the very literal sense of setting up ministerial offices. Until the enactment of such legislation, all previous apartheid educational laws were still operational. In addition, without such legislation no ministry, whether national or provincial, could officially employ staff in permanent posts. All ministries set up strategic management teams (SMTs) to assist in the processes of establishing provincial and national educational ministries. Thus the previous apartheid educational order was running in parallel with the new, fledgling education ministries.

Between May 1994 and November 1995, national and provincial legislation was passed enabling ministries to exist with real and effective powers. With this, ministers were now in the position to officially employ their staff and advertisements for posts in the departments were circulated publicly. However, the employment of people into such posts was fraught with many political land mines.

Among the considerations that were needed to characterise such employment were 'affirmative action' in terms of 'race' and gender, a balance between bureaucrats from the older order and new appointments needed to be maintained and people employed needed to be qualified for the tasks they were expected to perform. Given the negotiated nature of the settlement that propelled the changes in South Africa, a compromise agreement was also reached in which people from the old order were entitled to early retirement packages in the event of their choosing to opt out of serving within the 'new' South African system. Thus, whilst ministries were busy setting themselves up, they were also processing applications for 'golden handshakes'.

Between 1994 and 1996, the following policy documents, reports and Acts were published. They include those which integrated previously separate education departments, macro-policy bills and those focussing on specific issues and areas, such as tertiary education and school governance.

- Educators Employment Act (1994), which has an impact on the nature of teacher employment (Department of National Education, 1994a);
- Education and Training White Paper (1994, 1995), which outlines the macro principles of education (Department of National Education, 1994b, 1995a);
- National Education Policy Act (1996), which outlines the competencies of the national minister and, by implication, the powers of provinces (Department of National Education, 1995b, 1996d);
- South African Qualifications Authority Act (1995), which establishes qualification and certification authorities (Department of National Education, 1995e);
- The Hunter Commission Report (1995) on school organisation, governance and financing (Department of National Education, 1995c);
- White Paper on Organisation, Financing and Governance of Education (November 1995, February, 1996) (Department of National Education, 1995d);
- The South African Schools Act (November, 1996) (Department of National Education, 1996a, b, c, e);
- National Audit of Teacher Education, reviewing teacher training provisions and future needs;
- National Commission on Higher Education, reviewing tertiary educational provisions and needs; and
- National Management Task Team, reviewing educational management and needs.

The above list conveys the enormity of the tasks at hand in the transformation of the educational system in South Africa. Not only is the whole apartheid educational system, from pre-school to university level, being restructured, it is also being fundamentally redefined. From only serving 'white' minority interests in the past, it is being redesigned to service all South Africans in the current dispensation. In the terms of the Preamble to the South African Schools Act:

WHEREAS the achievement of democracy in South Africa has consigned to history the past system of education which was based on racial inequality and segregation; and WHEREAS this country requires a new national system for schools which will redress past injustices in educational provision, provide an education of progressively high quality for all learners and in so doing lay a strong foundation for the development of all our people's talents and capabilities, advance the democratic transformation of society, combat racism and sexism and all other forms of unfair discrimination.... WHEREAS it is necessary to set uniform norms and standards for the education of learners at schools and the organisation, governance and funding of schools throughout the Republic of South Africa.

(Department of National Education, 1996a, Preamble, p. 1)
(Original emphasis)

Consigning the past to history' entails redistributing educational resources in non-racialised ways. What follows is a more detailed analysis of the National Education Policy Act of 1996 and the educational provisions in the new Constitution of the Republic of South Africa, which was finally signed and adopted in 1996.

Macro-educational principles in the 'new' South Africa

Education, like any other sphere, is circumscribed by the provisions of the new Constitution, adopted in May 1996 and finally signed by President Mandela in December 1996. Three constitutional provisions have a direct impact on education: national and provincial educational structures; fundamental human rights clauses; those provisions concerning redressing past apartheid inequalities.

The Constitution provides for the establishment of a national ministry, as well as nine provincial education ministries. The nine provincial ministries are charged with the responsibility of educational provision in the reconfigured South African landscape, except for universities, which are considered to be national assets. The rationale behind this geographical redefinition of South Africa is to undo the segregation of South Africa into racially defined 'group areas' and 'homelands' or 'bantustans'. At the provincial level, racially different groups of people who live in physical proximity to each other are brought under the same provincial authority. Provincial provision is to be desegregated and provided in non-racial and democratic ways. At the national level, provision is intended to ensure that provincial differences are brought together in the development of a 'new nation' with a sense of national coherence, if not unity (Department of National Education, 1996d).

Provinces are granted considerable autonomy given the specificities of the conditions within their jurisdiction. For example, the Gauteng province is among the most developed of provinces in the country. What is needed, possible and viable in Gauteng will not necessarily apply in the Eastern Cape Province, which has a high level of rural settlements, is generally under-developed and is lacking in basic resources. Provincial autonomy and stark differences between provinces mean that one cannot generalise about educational developments and experiences in South Africa. Nonetheless, no province would be able to contravene the provisions of the Constitution and it is the task of the national ministry to ensure this, as well as bringing provinces 'in line' with developing a 'nation' in South Africa. Provincial autonomy, therefore, does not contradict the need for provinces to contribute towards building a 'nation' and to work within national norms. This reflects the fundamental rights clauses in the Constitution.

The second most important Constitutional provision with regard to education is that concerning fundamental human rights. The Constitution is categorical about the right to education. It states:

1   Everyone has the right:

    a   to a basic education, including adult basic education; and
    b   to further education, which the state must take reasonable measures to make progressively available and accessible.

2   Everyone has the right to receive education in the official language or languages of their choice in the public educational institutions where that education is reasonably practicable. In order to ensure access to, and implementation of, this right, the state must consider all reasonable educational alternatives, including single medium institutions, taking into account:

    a   equity;
    b   practicability; and
    c   the need to redress the results of past racially discriminatory law and practice.

(Constitution of the Republic of South Africa, 1996, p. 15)

As legislated in the National Education Policy Act (Department of National Education, 1996d, p. 6, 4(a)), no school may deny a person the right to a basic education on the basis of the human rights specified in the Constitution. The implications of these clauses are important, as was demonstrated in 1995 in the case of the Potgietusrus Primary School in the Northern Province of South Africa. The school attempted to refuse admission to 'black' students entering their school, on the basis that it was an Afrikaner only school and, as they argued, they were entitled in terms of the then Interim Constitution to maintain the Afrikaner culture, language and religion in their school. Enrolling 'black' students who were not part of this Afrikaner cultural tradition, therefore, was unacceptable. The Constitutional court, however, ruled that the Potgietusrus School acted unconstitutionally, because it acted in a way that discriminated on the basis of race, culture, language and religion of the applicant students and, more importantly, acted against the right of the applicant students to an education. The court thus ordered the school to enrol these students (Henrard, 1996; de Groof and Bray, 1996).

The Constitutional provisions on fundamental human rights therefore have profound implications for schooling in South Africa. They ensure that anti-racist measures are supported legally with the full backing of the state itself. This is indeed a milestone in the educational history of South Africa and transforms its racist nature significantly.

The Constitution states explicitly that past apartheid inequities need to be redressed in concerted ways and as a high priority (Preamble of the Constitution, 1996, p. 1). Thus, national and provincial education ministries are legally within their rights to provide for the most deprived and depressed areas in their provinces first and refuse additional provision to other more established and endowed sectors in their provinces. The 1996 campaign by the Catholic schools movement demonstrates the point. The Catholic schools in South Africa, were classified as 'independent' schools under apartheid. This meant that they were not fully 'private' schools, but were still 'independent' from government. They did, however, receive a state subsidy, according to government funding formulae in regard to semi-state, semi-private schools. In 1996, the 'new' educational ministries cut these 'independent' school budgets on the grounds that limited funds needed to be redirected to the more deprived areas. In doing so, the educational ministries were acting within their Constitutional rights to make such cuts to redress past apartheid inequalities and imbalances (Sister Kelly, 1996).

'Open' schools in South Africa

In 1990 the government in South Africa officially announced the possibility of 'white' schools legally enrolling 'black' students. This announcement was made in October 1990, by the then minister of 'white' education, Piet Clase. The announcement coincided with the unbanning of liberation organisations in South Africa, like the African National Congress (ANC), Pan Africanist Congress (PAC) and the South African Communist Party (SACP). It was also accompanied by the release from prison of political leaders such as Nelson Mandela and the subsequent return from exile of a number of South Africans. The Clase announcement, therefore, was linked inextricably to the reformist initiatives of the Nationalist government.

Clase allowed 'white' schools in South Africa to choose between three models in order to desegregate themselves. Model A allowed these state, 'white' schools to close down as state schools and to reopen as private schools. Model B allowed such schools to remain state schools, but to have an open admissions policy. Model C allowed them to convert themselves to semi-private and semi-state schools, where teachers' salaries would be paid for by the state, and all other operational expenses of the school would be borne by the school community itself. All three models allowed such schools to enrol 'black' students, where 'black' referred to people who have been classified either as so called 'Indian', 'coloured' or African. However, all of these models were subject to the same conditions:

1   all schools needed to ensure that 51 per cent of the school's student population remained 'white';
2   the cultural ethos of such schools remained intact;
3   the state and/or school were not obligated to provide any financial aid to any 'black' incoming student;
4   in the event of any 'white' parent or student refusing to remain in a school that has now begun to enrol 'black' students, and should they choose to move to another 'white' only school, the state would bear the costs of such a relocation; and
5   the school and/or the state was under no obligation to provide any 'special'

programme or support to facilitate the adaptation of 'black' students into such schools.

These conditions that accompanied the Clase announcement demonstrate clearly that the 'opening' of 'white' South African schools was done in ways intended to ensure continued 'white' privilege and security. This is not surprising because the Clase announcement was framed by the apartheid constitution itself. All apartheid education laws were still intact and the apartheid constitution was not repealed at that stage. At the same time, the Clase announcement explicitly and officially put into place an assimilationist approach. Blatant in the announcement was the assumptions that 'blacks' needed to adopt the 'white' schools' cultural ethos, to which they were also expected to adapt. Linked to this was the assumption, so consistent in 'white' supremacist logic, that the 'white' cultural ethos was superior, one that needed to be maintained and into which 'others' needed to assimilate (Carrim and Sayed, 1991, 1992; Metcalfe, 1991; Badat, 1992; Muller, 1992).

By 1992, all previously 'white' designated schools were converted to Model C schools, despite 98 per cent of all 'white' schools nationally opting to become Model B schools. This, the apartheid government argued, was unavoidable because of the inability of the state to continue to provide financially for such schools. To avoid the closure of schools and/or the retrenchment of 'white' teachers, previously 'white' only schools needed to be converted to Model C so that the financial costs of the school could be shared by the state and the school community. Stark in this development is the fact that whilst 'black' South African schools were (and in some cases still are) overcrowded and under-resourced, 'white' schools in South Africa were being under-utilised and threatened with closure. This was the case as late as 1993, and the economic rationale for the Clase announcement in the first instance.

Nonetheless, in the wake of the Clase announcement, so-called 'coloured' and 'Indian' schools in South Africa were implicitly given the green light to officially enrol students who were 'non-coloured' or 'non-Indian'. Thus, whilst the Clase announcement was targetted at 'white' school communities and applied to 'white' schools only, they did signal nationally the desegregation of all South African schools.

Under apartheid, South African schools were segregated in terms of being 'white', so-called 'Indian', so-called 'coloured' and African, with the latter being further subdivided into ethnic cultural groups, such as Tswana, Zulu and Xhosa. With the Clase announcement, one could now legally enrol non-Tswana students into a Tswana school, or a 'non-coloured' student in a 'coloured' school, and so on. Whilst such enrolments took place before the Clase announcement, they were unofficial and dependent upon the discretion of the school's principal. After the Clase announcement, however, such enrolments became public and official and increased considerably (Carrim, 1992).

Model C schools continued to exist until the end of 1996, when the South African Schools Act was passed. In this Act, the status of Model C was dissolved and all schools in South Africa are now either classified as 'public' (meaning state/government) or 'private' schools. Most previously classified Model C schools are now 'public' schools, with special provisions allowing them to maintain the character of their schools. These provisions include a high level of autonomy for school governing bodies, so that on decentralised levels they may determine the policy and nature of their schools. However, such autonomy is circumscribed by national policies and the new Constitution, which prohibits racist practices and which upholds the rights of the child to basic education. Thus, whilst schools do have autonomy, they cannot deny a child of another 'race' access to a school. They do, however, have the latitude to stipulate other selection criteria that ought to be met for enrolment into their schools (Department of National Education, 1996e).

A few points need to be noted in this historical background. First, the 'opening' of schools in South Africa is not merely a matter of 'blacks' going into 'white' schools. It has entailed desegregation of schools within the 'black' group as well. Second, an assimilationist approach to school desegregation was adopted, coinciding with the conditions that accompanied the Clase announcement. Third, and as will be shown in more detail later, the experiences of reconstructed forms of racism mean different things in the different school contexts, and these include those within 'intra-black' settings.

Some Gauteng school experiences

During 1990–1994, in the period before the first non-racial democratic elections in South Africa, school desegregation processes within the Gauteng province were characterised by distinct patterns. These trends were: the use of admission tests; a low number of 'black' student enrolments in 'white' schools, and 'non-Indian' students in 'Indian' schools and 'non-coloureds' in 'coloured' schools; the predominance of an assimilationist approach.

All Model C schools used selection tests. Seventy-seven per cent of so-called 'Indian' schools used selection tests and 39 per cent of so-called 'coloured' schools used selection tests. In the instance of Model C schools, 'Indian', 'coloured' and African students had to take selection tests. In the case of 'Indian' schools, 'coloured' and African students were tested and in 'coloured' schools African students were subjected to selection procedures. There is no record of 'white' students being admitted to either 'Indian' or 'coloured' schools or 'Indian' students to 'coloured' schools. If there were such cases, they were exceptional and not reflective of the norm.

In all cases, however, selection tests examined applicants in the areas of English and/or Afrikaans language proficiency and mathematical ability. In some instances, psychometric tests were also used. In addition, admission criteria also included the parents' ability to pay the school fees and whether students lived in areas close to the school. The latter two admission criteria also had the effect of keeping 'black' entrants to a minimum, since they favoured middle class black parents who could pay the fees (Carrim and Sayed, 1992) and, given residential segregation in 'group areas' it was unlikely that there would be many 'black' people living in or close to the areas within which 'white' schools, or for that matter 'Indian' and 'coloured' schools, were located.

The use of selection tests and other admission criteria had the effect of keeping the intake of 'black' students at a low level. In general, the total number of enrolments of students in schools previously not designated for their use amounted to between 10 and 15 per cent of the total student population of the school concerned.

The low numbers of 'others' in 'white', 'Indian' and 'coloured' schools were informed and reinforced by the assimilationist policies of such schools. Incoming students were expected to adopt and adapt to the existing cultural ethos of the schools. In addition, the normal routines of the school, including its curriculum, remained unchanged. One 'white' primary school girl said: 'I was excited about blacks coming to our school. But, I walked around the school for a week and only found one black girl in our school. Everything is still the same' ('White' primary school girl, interview, 1992).

A group of 'coloured' students said:

> So far things are alright. But once their (African students) numbers increase then things won't be the same. You see parents are already pulling out their children from our schools, and once their numbers increase this will happen more.
> (Group of 'coloured', male high school students, interview, 1992)

When an 'Indian' teacher was asked how she was coping with the changes in her school, she replied by saying: 'Oh, it's not too bad. There aren't many of them, and they seem to fit in well' (Female, 'Indian', high school teacher, interview, 1992).

These comments by teachers and students in 'Indian', 'coloured' and 'white' schools make consistent reference to an 'us' and 'them' language, which not only indicates the racially exclusivist ways in which they define their own identities, but also the predominance of assimilationism in their experiences of the desegregation of their schools. The assumption here being that 'they' are coming to 'us' and the more 'they' are like 'us' or the more 'they' become like 'us', the more acceptable 'they' become. The 'host' culture is not viewed as lacking, since deficiencies, if any, are seen to be tied inextricably only to the incoming 'other'.

Nonetheless, simultaneously with this experience were the daily pedagogical challenges that teachers faced at the chalk face. Teachers, whether 'white', 'coloured' or 'Indian', were confronted for the first time by multilingual, multiethnic and multiracial classrooms. In this, teachers could no longer do things in their normal ways. They could not use the same examples to explain things, they could not uncritically reprimand students in the same ways and they simply could not take the same things for granted. These daily pedagogical encounters pushed teachers away from assimilationist assumptions to adopting a more multicultural approach. In order to educationally reach the 'other', teachers were forced to recognise and acknowledge the 'other's' background, ways of making meaning and difference. One 'Indian' primary school teacher had this to say:

> For three months I could not get any of the black children in my class to say a word. Finally, I brought in the school caretaker to talk to them in Sotho, and

these kids began to respond. I could not deny the fact that they spoke Sotho only, and I had to reach them in Sotho. After a while, these kids began to open up and now they are coping quite well.

(Female, 'Indian' primary school teacher, interview, 1992)

Another 'white' primary school teacher pointed out:

When I allow the black kids to talk of their own home experiences, the class as a whole is amazed at what these kids actually go through on a daily basis. The whole class benefits. I could not expect them to deny their own backgrounds.

('White', female primary school teacher, interview, 1992)

Thus, pedagogically, teachers, in particular, were forced to shift from assimilationist approaches and assumptions to more multicultural ones that would acknowledge the different backgrounds and experiences incoming students were bringing with them into their schools. The policies and dominant approaches of these schools remained, nonetheless, assimilationist.

From 1994 to 1996, however, the shift from assimilationism to multiculturalism became more prevalent. This shift was also influenced by major national developments in the country as whole. First, in April 1994, the first non-racial democratic elections in South Africa took place. South Africa was now being billed as the 'rainbow nation'. Second, the new South African Constitution, interim till 1996 and then formally adopted in 1996, was in place. In this Constitution the multicultural nature of South African society was acknowledged officially, depicted most starkly in the statutory recognition of 11 official languages in South Africa. These macro developments were crucial in that they facilitated, at the micro school levels, a shift from assimilationism to multiculturalism.

The macro developments signalled officially that all people's identities and cultural or other backgrounds were equally legitimate. The developments questioned the assimilationist assumption that some cultures were superior to others and that some ways of looking at the world are necessarily and always better than others. However, it is important to note the ways in which these were experienced at the empirical level of the schools themselves. Far from being a positive acknowledgement of 'difference', the multicultural trends in schools seem to be reconstructed forms of racism itself.

When asked how multicultural her school was, one 'Indian' school teacher said: 'oh, when we have our annual school concert, the Zulu kids put up a Zulu dance in traditional Zulu costumes' (Female, 'Indian' primary school teacher, interview, 1996). When asked the same question, a 'white' school teacher said: 'I always ask the black kids what these things mean in their culture. I must admit I am always shocked when they actually don't know' (Female, 'white' primary school teacher, interview, 1996). Said another 'white' teacher: 'our parent days are like the United Nations. We have all the foods and costumes of all the cultures. We are very multicultural' ('White', male high school teacher, interview, 1996). In these teacher accounts it is evident that the types of multiculturalism at work in these schools are at best stereotypical and, at worst, caricatured. They portray student differences in stereotypical and caricatured ways, as in the case of 'Zulu kids doing Zulu dances' or parent days being like the 'United Nations' or expecting that people of particular cultural groups would necessarily know everything there is to know about their particular culture. The possibility of Zulu kids actually doing a modern dance at the school concert or Muslim kids dressing in Western-looking clothes at parents' days or 'black' kids answering questions in ways that do not tie into their supposed, and assumed, cultural backgrounds do not seem to permeate these school experiences. Instead, students are positioned in stereotypical ways, are assumed to be fixed in their identities, are portrayed as necessarily representative of and loyal to their supposed cultures and the prevalent understanding of culture seems to be narrowly defined as a reference to lifestyles, particularly with regard to dress, food and language. The effect of these is to project differences among people in negative ways and they do not erode racist practices, as the following group of 'coloured' students comments indicate:

> Oh, we do not mix really.
> Why?
> Well, you see they have their own culture and we have our own. They do things differently from us. So, they stick to themselves. And, we stick to ourselves.
> (Group of 'coloured', male high school students, interview, 1996)

One 'white' student remarked: 'it's not a question of race, you know. It is more … eh … a cultural thing. Their's is very different from our's' ('White', female high school student, interview, 1996). Not only do these comments indicate that 'differences' are perceived negatively, in that the 'difference' is rarely viewed as a strength, as the possibility of viewing the world with different eyes or broadening one's understanding of things, but they also camouflage the racial implications of such negative projections. 'White' schools are by no means culturally homogeneous. They include Afrikaners, English, Greek, Portuguese and Jews, among others. So-called 'Indians' are made up of Muslims, Hindus, Tamils and Christians. So-called 'coloureds' too are made up of Malays, Christians and Muslims. Cultural differences among these racialised groups tend to be underemphasised or ignored in these multicultural school experiences. They are only recognised in the cases of those who belong to other racial groups, leaving one with the inescapable conclusion that such forms of multiculturalism are reconstructed forms of racism.

Nonetheless, the period between 1994 and 1996 did witness a marked increase in the rate of enrolment of 'black' students into 'white' schools, 'non-Indian' students into 'Indian' schools, and 'non-coloured' students into 'coloured' schools. Existing figures indicate an increase of such student enrolments to between 30 and 50 per cent of the entire school's student population (GED Statistics, 1996). This is a more than 100 per cent increase in such enrolment rates when compared with patterns before 1994. At the same time, admission tests, whilst still administered, are now predominantly used for placement purposes, rather than admission into schools. These changes in the ways in which admission procedures work have been propelled by provincial educational legislation that stipulates that tests are to be used for placement purposes and not as mechanisms of exclusion. Thus, there is an increase in the number of 'other' students in desegregated schools within the Gauteng region, albeit characterised by racist, 'bad' multicultural practices and assumptions.

Problems with assimilationism and multiculturalism in South Africa

As the above discussion of some Gauteng schools experiences reveals, a shift from assimilationism to multiculturalism is discernable. It is equally evident that this shift entails a displacement of racial questions into foci on ethnic and cultural differences. However, rather than working with dynamic and complex senses of cultural identities, the multicultural practices that predominate in these schools' experiences tend instead to fix, stereotype and caricature people's identities. It is these that I now discuss analytically as I argue for the importance of a critical anti-racism in South Africa.

The problems with the assimilationist approach are widely known. Assimilationism denies the recognition of people's differences and the existence of cultural diversity. More so, assimilationist approaches have been found not to reduce racist practices or instances of racial abuse (Brandt, 1986; Gillborn, 1990). In the South African case, assimilationism has been found to be insufficient in actually dealing with 'mixed race' groups, since the denial of cultural diversity within assimilationism does not enable people to gain a better understanding of each other or facilitate improved relations among them (Carrim, 1992; Penny et al., 1993; Carrim et al., 1995). Furthermore, a shift from assimilationism to multiculturalism is becoming an emergent tendency.

However, the multiculturalist practices in the Gauteng schools are not without problems. As pointed out already, these practices have tended to portray people of different racial groups as being culturally different, implying a shift from 'race' to ethnicity. This is particularly evident in the fact that cultural diversity within racialised groups is denied consistently. It is easier to talk of a Zulu as being culturally different, as opposed to an Italian, in 'white' school settings, for example. This denial of cultural differences within racialised groupings lends credence to the claim that this type of multiculturalism is a reconstructed form of racism itself. In South Africa this tendency has historical precedence.

During its inception, the system of apartheid itself was justified not only in racial but in cultural terms as well. Verwoerd's infamous Senate speech in 1953, which articulated the principles of apartheid education, is well worth quoting here. Verwoerd said:

> There is no place for him (the Bantu) in the European community above the level of certain forms of labour. Within his (sic) own community however, all doors are open. For that reason it is of no avail for him to receive a training which has as its aim absorption in the European community, where he cannot be absorbed. Until now he has been subjected to a school system which drew him away from his own community and misled him in showing him the green

pastures of European society in which he was not allowed to graze. This attitude is not only uneconomic because money is spent for an education which has no specific aim but it is also dishonest to continue it. It is abundantly clear that unplanned education creates problems; disrupting the community life of the Bantu and endangering the community life of the European.

(Cited in Rose and Tunmer, 1975, p. 266)

Whereas Verwoerd used cultural differences between 'the Bantu' and 'European' as a justification for segregation and the establishment of apartheid education, the link in the argument between forms of racism and articulation of cultural differences is clear. As Cross and Mkwanazi (1992) have also argued, apartheid may be seen to be an extreme form of multiculturalism itself. The point of raising this matter here is to emphasise the following. First, linking 'race' to culture is not new within the South African context. Second, the proliferation of cultural categories is applied mainly to 'blacks'. 'Whites' are considered and projected as being ethnically homogeneous. Third, cultural differences are highlighted only when applied to inter-racial group encounters. Finally, it is clear that an uncritical acceptance of multicultural practices in South Africa could quite easily perpetuate, rather than erode, racism. Such multicultural practices take on racist connotations when they highlight selectively when and among whom cultural differences are emphasised, when they construe people's identities in certain ways and when they ignore the power dimensions to questions of racism itself.

I have already shown that the multiculturalist approach does not acknowledge the cultural differences within racialised groups. 'Whites', whether they are Greek, English, Italian or Afrikaners, tend to be projected as if they are culturally homogeneous. So-called 'Indians', who are constituted by Muslims, Tamils, Hindus and Christians, also tend to be projected as if they are culturally all the same. So-called 'coloureds' too are far from being culturally homogeneous. They are made up of Malays, Muslims and Christians. Yet, it is only when so-called 'coloureds', 'Indians' and Africans come into contact with 'whites' that cultural differences are highlighted. Or when Africans and 'coloureds' come into 'Indian' settings that cultural differences apparently become significant. Of when Africans go into 'coloured' spaces that they are important. This version of multiculturalism bears frightening resonances of the Verwoerdian manipulations of cultural diversity and the racism within it is equally stark.

Yet, these versions of multiculturalism are also fraught with problematic assumptions about the nature of people's identities. In these multiculturalist accounts, people who are perceived to be culturally different are fixed and stereotyped within their assumed identities. A Zulu student in school is assumed, as in the quotation from the interview with the 'Indian' primary school teacher cited earlier on, to be representative of and loyal to Zulu culture. The fact that this student may be living all of his/her life in an urban area, is immersed in Westernised lifestyles of rap music, denim jeans, fast foods and shopping at urban malls, get ignored, since the Zulu is not supposed to be 'into' these sorts of activities. More disturbing is the fact that the Zulu is positioned as such, as a Zulu. The gender, class, ability, sexual orientation and other characteristics of the person are ignored almost entirely. The consequence of this is that these versions of multiculturalism deny the actual ways in which people live their lives and the various dimensions of their identities. Such multicultural practices construct artificial and chimaerical changes of cultural difference that are in fact unhelpful (see also Carrim, 1995).

These multicultural practices also ignore the power dimensions of racism. This, however, is an argument that anti-racists have consistently levelled against multi-cultural approaches by pointing out that the focus within multiculturalism is on lifestyles rather than life chances or opportunities (Gillborn, 1990; Braham *et al.*, 1992; Troyna, 1993). The Gauteng schools that are discussed in this article tend to use multiculturalism to develop a 'United Nations' feel in their schools and ignore the material differences that exist among different raced students in their schools, since the emphasis is on language, food and dress habits. In these ways, the actual basis of the inequalities suffered by 'blacks' does not receive adequate, if any, atten-tion and the focus on the socially constructed nature of racism remains unex-plored. The result is that racism is displaced into consideration of different lifestyles and racist practices, processes and assumptions continue almost unabated.

It could be argued that what we have pointed to here really refers to 'bad' multi-cultural practices and that it is possible and conceivable for multicultural practices to work with non-stereotypical and dynamic senses of identity. 'Good' multicul-tural practices would overtly confront questions about the power dimensions of racism and cultural differences among all people, including those within racialised groups, would receive equal attention. This possibility of 'good' multicultural prac-tices is indeed conceivable, but we do not have evidence of them existing in any of the South African experiences, either historically or in the contemporary situ-ation, since research in this area has not been conducted. However, as I argue, this type of 'good' multiculturalism is akin to a critical anti-racism and it is to this that I now turn my attention.

A critical anti-racism

The Gauteng school experiences discussed here indicate that desegregation of South African schools is not just a 'black' versus 'white' issue. It is a matter of 'intra-black' desegregation too. This is the case because so-called 'Indian' and 'coloured' schools have also 'opened' their doors to 'non-Indian' and 'non-coloured' students. This has several implications.

First, the bipolarity between homogenised groups of 'blacks' and 'whites', so consistent within both racist and anti-racist logic, is untenable within the South African situation. Working with such a bipolarity will not equip us with the tools to investigate the 'intra-black' dynamics that are currently unfolding. This also means that one cannot work with the assumptions that all 'whites' are necessarily and only proto-racists, or that all 'blacks' are necessarily and always victims (Mac-Donald *et al.*, 1989). This is clearly not the case.

The Gauteng schools show that 'blacks' manifest racist tendencies themselves. This comes through clearly in the ways in which 'Indians' treat 'non-Indians' and 'coloureds' treat 'non-coloureds'. As such, assuming a homogenised and essential sense of 'blackness' is not only counter-factual, it is also unproductive. To capture these 'intra-black' dynamics one needs to work with a 'de-essentialised' (Hall, 1992; Rattansi and Donald, 1992) sense of what being 'black' means. Not all 'blacks' are the same and 'blacks' are actually more than just being 'black'. A 'de-essentialised conception of 'blackness' enables us to view the many ways in which people experience their 'race', the ways in which they position themselves within it and the motley of other identities that make up their person. Being 'African' in an 'Indian' or 'coloured' school is different from being 'African' in a 'white' school. Being 'African', middle class and proficient in English is very different from being 'African', working class, from a rural area and not having any English at all. Being 'Indian', female and lesbian too would have rather different implications in a 'white' school environment as opposed to being 'Indian', male and heterosexual in the same school. A 'de-essentialised' conception of identity, therefore, more accurately captures the ways in which people live their lives, the nature of the experiences they have and the ways in which their identities are actually formed (Gillborn, 1995).

The traditional anti-racist logic for us, therefore, needs to become more sophisticated to develop a complex view of people's identities in order to capture the reality of their lives. This is indispensable if we are to address the continuing and various ways in which racism is being reconstructed in the current situation. This is crucial if the anti-racist project itself is to remain viable as a future strategy. This leads to a consideration of the limitations of the structural emphases in current South African macro educational reform initiatives.

As pointed out in the first section of this article, the contemporary South African educational reforms are, out of historical necessity, aimed at enacting structural and systemic changes in the South African social order. These are of a fundamental nature. They shift South Africa away from a racist past to one of human rights and democracy. But such interventions tend to treat questions of 'race' in very generalised ways. They consistently maintain a bipolarity between 'whites' and 'blacks'; they do not effectively address 'intra-black' conflicts; they do not spell out what anti-racist practices actually entail on the levels of daily schooling routines. As a result, these macro interventions are decidedly structuralist in nature, leading to the consequent desegregation of South African schools and not necessarily to their deracialisation.

If one assumes that desegregation refers to the removal of structural mechanisms of control to prevent the entry of 'blacks' into institutions, then deracialisation would mean a situation where both 'blacks' and 'whites' may be found in the same situation and where no discriminatory practice seems to exist among them (Carrim *et al.*, 1995). What macro, structural initiatives, therefore, do is desegregate educational institutions in South Africa; they do not deracialise them. They do not deracialise such institutional settings because they do not address the complexities and specificities of 'race' and racism on the micro level of the school, as experienced by people themselves.

It is on these micro levels of people's lives that guidelines, programmes and structured interventions are needed. Yet there is no nationally instituted anti-racist programme or package which has been put into place. There are no structured, co-ordinated programmes to help teachers cope with multiracial/cultural/

lingual/ability classrooms. There are no nationally or provincially co-ordinated programmes for students to develop anti-racist, anti-sexist, anti-discrimination awareness or consciousness in the formal workings of the school. It is almost as if these are expected to occur almost entirely of their own accord. The focus, therefore, on structural, systemic changes on the macro level has had the effect of articulating anti-racist strategies in general terms. They need, however, to take into account the actual ways in which people experience their realities on the micro level. Such interventions need to 'talk to' the actual, 'on the ground' ways in which racism is perceived, understood, experienced and reconstructed. Failure to do so would frustrate these interventions and so defeat their purpose.

A critical anti-racism would ensure a 'de-essentialised' sense of people's identities, in that it would acknowledge and incorporate the notion of 'difference' within and among people. It would also pierce the bipolarity of 'whites' versus 'blacks' and thereby get to grips with the various and varying ways in which racism is experienced within and across racialised groups of people. It would also inject the necessary specificities that ought to inform macro policy formulations and interventions. At the same time a critical anti-racism would still carry with it the potency of the anti-racist emphasis on the power dimensions of racism. A critical anti-racism would maintain the focus on macro socio-economic and political forces and the ways in which they intersect with and influence people's individual lives. These anti-racist analytical strengths remain within the critical anti-racist approach, which also means that a critical anti-racism is but a sophistication and refinement of anti-racism, not a betrayal or debunking of it.

Notes

* Nazir Carrim is at the Educational Department, University of Witwatersrand, Johannesburg, South Africa.
† Originally published in: *Cambridge Journal of Education* 28: 3, 301–320.

References

Badat, S. (1992) Open schools, *New Era*, p. 28 (Cape Town, South African Research Services).

Braham, P., Rattansi, A. and Skellington, R. (eds) (1992) *Racism and Antiracism: inequalities, opportunities and policies* (London, Sage).

Brandt, G. (1986) *The Realisation of Antiracist Teaching* (Lewes, Falmer Press).

Carrim, N. (1992) *Desegregating Indian and Coloured Schools*, Education Policy Unit research report (Johannesburg, University of the Witwatersrand Press).

Carrim, N. (1995) From 'race' to 'ethnicity': shifts in the educational discourses of South Africa and Britain in the 1990s, *Compare*, 25(1), pp. 17–33.

Carrim, N. and Sayed, Y. (1991) Open schools: reform or transformation?, *Work in Progress*, 74, pp. 28–29.

Carrim, N. and Sayed, Y. (1992) Pay as you learn: Model C schools are not for working class kids, *Work in Progress/New Era*, 84, pp. 28–29.

Carrim, N., Mkwanzai-Twala, Z. and Nkomo, M. (1995) The long shadow of apartheid ideology, in: B. Bowser (ed.) *Racism and Antiracism: a world perspective* (Thousand Oaks, CA, Sage Publishers).

Christie, P. (1986) *The Right to Learn* (Johannesburg, Ravan Press).

Cross, M. and Mkwanazi, Z. (1992) The concept of multicultural education and its relevance to South Africa, unpublished National Education Policy Investigations working paper.

De Groof, J. and Bray, E. (eds) (1996) *Education under the New Constitution in South Africa* (Amerfoort, Acco Leuven).

Department of National Education (1994a) *Educators Employment Act* (Pretoria, Government Printers).

Department of National Education (1994b) *Education and Training in a Democratic South Africa: draft policy document for discussion* (Pretoria, Government Printers).

Department of National Education (1995a) *Education and Training in a Democratic South Africa: draft policy of the document for discussion* (Pretoria, Government Printers).

Department of National Education (1995b) *National Education Policy Bill* (Pretoria, Government Printers).

Department of National Education (1995c) *Report of the Committee to Review the Organisation, Governance and Funding of Schools* (Pretoria, Government Printers).

Department of National Education (1995d) *White Paper on the Organisation, Governance and Funding of Schools* (Pretoria, Government Printers).

Department of National Education (1995e) *South African Qualifications Authority Act* (Pretoria, Government Printers).

Department of National Education (1996a) *South African Schools Bill*, February (Pretoria, Government Printers).

Department of National Education (1996b) *South African Schools Bill*, April (Pretoria, Government Printers).

Department of National Education (1996c) *South African Schools Bill*, October (Pretoria, Government Printers).

Department of National Education (1996d) *National Education Policy Act* (Pretoria, Government Printers).

Department of National Education (1996e) *South African Schools Act* (Pretoria, Government Printers).

Gillborn, D. (1990) *'Race', Ethnicity and Education: teaching and learning in multiethnic schools* (London, Unwin Hyman/Routledge).

Gillborn, D. (1995) *Racism and Antiracism Real Schools* (Buckingham, Open University Press).

Hall, S. (1992) New ethnicities, in: A. Rattansi and J. Donald (eds) *'Race', Culture and Difference* (London, Sage).

Henrad, K. (1996) The equality principle and the right to education as implemented in South Africa against the background of the international law framework, in: J. De Groof and E. Bray (eds) Education under the New Constitution in South Africa (Amerfoort, Acco Leuven).

Kallaway, P. (1986) *Apartheid and Education* (Johannesburg, Ravan Press).

Kelly, M. (Sister) (1996) Input at the Catholic Institute of Education Conference, 27 May 1996, Cape Town.

MacDonald, I., Bhavnani, R., Khan, L. and John, G. (1989) *Murder in the Playground: the report of the MacDonald Inquiry into racism and racial violence in Manchester schools* (London, Longsight).

Metcalfe, M. (1991) *Desegregating Education in South Africa: white school enrolments in Johannesburg 1985–1991: update and policy analysis*, Education Policy Unit research report (Johannesburg, University of the Witwatersrand Press).

Muller, J. (1992) Open Schools, *New Era*, p. 28 (Cape Town, South African Research Services).

Nkomo, M. (1990) *Pedagogy of Domination* (Trenton, NJ, Africa World Press).

Penny, A., Appel, S., Gultig, J., Harley, K. and Muir, R. (1993) Just sort of fumbling in the dark: a case study of the advent of racial integration in South African schools, *Comparative Education Review*, 37, pp. 412–433.

Rattansi, A. and Donald, J. (eds) (1992) *'Race', Culture and Difference* (London, Sage).

Rose, B. and Tunmer, R. (1975) *Documents in South African Education*, p. 266 (Johannesburg, Donker).

Troyna, B. (1993) *Racism and Education: research perspectives* (Buckingham, Open University Press).

15 Inclusive practice in English secondary schools

Lessons learned

Lani Florian and Martyn Rouse[*†]

Introduction

Schools in England face dilemmas about how they should respond to two conflicting demands from government. The first demand is for higher academic standards and second is the call for the inclusion of children with special educational needs in mainstream schools. For some schools these demands are incompatible, but for others, policies and practices that support inclusion are emerging as the means by which they may be able to raise academic standards for all children. This paper considers how some of these schools have been able to respond to these different demands. It begins by briefly considering the context in which they are currently operating, followed by a summary of what is emerging from our work in secondary schools that are committed to inclusion.

In England the 1989 Education Reform Act introduced the principles of the market place to the education system. It introduced a series of radical changes, including increasing parental choice, competition between schools, the National Curriculum and national systems of assessment and testing. Since then the results of these national tests have been published in league tables so that the performance of different schools can be compared. More recently achievement targets have been set for schools and the cost of failing to meet these targets is high.

At the same time, the call for greater inclusion is central to many of the government's recent pronouncements about education. A Green Paper *Excellence for All Children: meeting special educational needs* appeared in 1997 (DfEE, 1997) and this has been followed by a series of other potentially important shifts in policy direction, such as the inclusion statement in the new National Curriculum (DfEE, 2000) and the recent changes to the Ofsted inspection framework for schools, which now stresses that inclusion is about raising standards *and* the achievement of all children. Although these changes are to be welcomed, the inclusion of students with special educational needs in mainstream schools has been difficult, with enormous implications for school organisation, leadership, teaching styles, curriculum, assessment, attitudes and staff development.

The problem is that whilst the government calls for more inclusion and a greater recognition of diversity, it continues to promote social and educational policies that are not supportive of the development of inclusive schools. Indeed, many of the existing market place reforms ignore diversity and stress priorities that make it hard for schools to be accepting of children who will not help them to meet their academic targets.

Effectiveness, inclusion and special educational needs

The emergence of these potentially competing strands in the current policy agenda is mirrored in two parallel areas of educational research; *school effectiveness and school improvement* on one hand and *inclusion* on the other (Slee and Weiner, 2001). The extent to which either of these fields of research has been informed by the other is questionable and when researchers with an interest in special needs and inclusion have engaged with school effectiveness research it has been to challenge its ideological, political or methodological stance (see for example Brown *et al.*, 1995; Slee *et al.*, 1998). These are serious questions because much of the work on school effectiveness has failed to recognise the significance of the context in which schools operate, particularly with regard to diversity. And yet, as Ainscow (1991, 1999) argues, there are strong reasons for each of these traditions to be better informed about the other because they are both concerned with the ways in which schools and classrooms might be improved for the benefit of all learners.

According to Teddlie and Reynolds (2000) the school effectiveness movement has evolved through a number of stages since it first began to question the widespread assumption arising from the work of Coleman *et al.* (1966) and Jencks *et al.* (1972), that 'schools make no difference'. Researchers in many countries (see for example Rutter *et al.*, 1979; Mortimore *et al.*, 1988; Smith and Tomlinson, 1989; Levine and Lezotte 1990) have been investigating the factors which make some schools more effective than others and the resulting literature on school effectiveness has been extremely influential on education policy in many countries. Not only does it describe the characteristics of effective schools, but it also provides the basis for an increasingly sophisticated and nuanced approach to school improvement. Unfortunately, in borrowing these ideas, policy makers have tended to focus only on academic achievement and underestimate the complexity of improving schools, preferring 'quick fix' solutions and approaches based on simplistic assumptions derived from management and systems theory. The reality of schools is far more complex than such 'bullet point' solutions would imply.

Although the effective schools and school improvement literature has only begun to influence the special needs debate during the past decade (Ainscow, 1991; Lipsky and Gartner, 1997; Rouse and Florian, 1996), it raises important issues for those who are struggling to create more inclusive schools because it suggests ways in which schools themselves, through the development of their own policies and practice, might become more effective at meeting the learning needs of *all* children. Such approaches require a re-conceptualisation of the special needs task so that it might emerge from being concerned only with students' cognitive, emotional or pathological problems to being seen as part of the process of school improvement. In turn, this entails the adoption of ecological perspectives which recognise, as Skrtic (1998) does, that it is the structure of schools as organisations rather than differences between individual pupils that creates special educational needs. This is not to move from blaming students for their failure to blaming their teachers or schools, but rather to acknowledge that human strengths and weaknesses can only be understood in the context in which they occur. Context is a significant factor in the construction of personal identity and the feelings that students have about themselves as learners.

Although advances in research on school improvement have produced a more refined understanding of how to enhance the capacity of schools to make them more effective for increasingly heterogeneous groups of pupils (for a review see Creemers, 1996), this literature has not specifically addressed the problem of pupils with special educational needs. As a result its relevance to the education of *all* pupils has been questioned by those who argue that high standards for all are unlikely to be achieved because of the limitations of current knowledge about effective inclusive practice (see for example McDonnell *et al.*, 1997).

Much research in special education has focused on teaching methods in an attempt to demonstrate the efficacy of individualised approaches, such as precision teaching, direct intensive structured teaching and skills-based instruction with particular 'types' of pupils (McDonnell *et al.*, 1997). These strategies have been successful in segregated settings where teacher–pupil ratios are often lower than in mainstream schools. The difficulties of implementing them in mainstream classrooms where teacher–pupil ratios are larger and, it is argued, where pedagogy is based on a different understanding of how children learn, has contributed to the belief that mainstream schools may not be the best learning environment for pupils with difficulties. Indeed, there are those who would argue that the full inclusion of all students with special educational needs is impossible because mainstream schools do not have the will, capacity or resources to do the job (Kauffman and Hallahan, 1995). It is suggested that many mainstream teachers have negative attitudes about including pupils with special educational needs (SEN) because they lack knowledge about teaching such children (Scott *et al.*, 1998). However, too much of the debate about inclusion that appears in the special education literature has been detached from broader discussions about teaching and learning. Indeed, some of it has been conducted with little knowledge of the progress made around the world in developing inclusive learning environments. In addition, it seems uninformed by the debate about whether or not there is such a 'special pedagogy' that has evolved in segregated settings that is different from pedagogy in mainstream classrooms and therefore unavailable outside special settings (Lewis and Norwich, 2001).

Equally, much work in school effectiveness and school improvement has been too narrowly focused on academic outcomes and has ignored issues of disadvantage, diversity and equity (Slee and Weiner, 2001). Rarely has it questioned the purpose and nature of schooling or considered the ways in which it may have contributed to exclusionary pressures within schools by distorting the tasks that are considered important. Yes, good test scores and examination results are necessary both for individuals and schools, but are they sufficient? Not if the future is to be more inclusive. The long and well-known history of ability testing clearly shows how standardised testing programmes consistently discriminate against vulnerable groups (Hilliard, 1990). Schools have to be more than places where children prepare for, take and pass (or fail) examinations.

Lessons learned

One strand of the inclusion literature describes and analyses attempts to implement a policy of inclusive education within mainstream schools (see for example Lipsky and Gartner, 1997; Booth and Ainscow, 1998). Other studies have examined school level variables in an attempt to identify organisational structures and practices which may be associated with facilitating or impeding inclusion (see for example Villa et al., 1992; Rouse and Florian, 1996; Ainscow, 1999). However, such research is not without its critics (Slee and Weiner, 2001) and it must be acknowledged that causal effects cannot be assumed just because some common 'factors' are present in schools that seem to be successful.

Our earlier work (Rouse and Florian, 1996) attempted to link the growing evidence from the research into effective schools with the largely descriptive accounts of the development of inclusive schools. We argued that inclusion has much in common with the movement towards effectiveness, in that they are both concerned with school improvement. However, we acknowledge the view held by many that the quest for (academic) excellence in schools may be incompatible with the extension of the principle of equity and universal access. The clash between the principles that underpin market-based reforms and the principles that underpin the development of inclusive education have produced a set of tensions between such notions as inclusion and exclusion, individuals and groups, producers and consumers and equity and excellence. Our 1997 study suggested that many schools committed to the development of inclusive practice have been able to mediate these tensions and work creatively and successfully in the current climate. These schools do not see the tensions as bipolar, either/or opposites from which they have to choose one extreme or the other. Instead, they have found pragmatic ways to mediate the potential for conflict (Rouse and Florian, 1997). A fundamental question arising from this apparent tension between equity and excellence is how can a school become both equitable (i.e. inclusive) as well as being excellent (i.e. effective as defined by policy makers and school effectiveness researchers)?

More recently our work has focused on identifying strategies which seem successful in enabling secondary schools to extend inclusive practice. It has involved ongoing work with representatives from a group of eight secondary schools who meet regularly to discuss their practice, studies of classroom practice (see for example Florian and Rouse, 1999, 2001) and evaluations of inclusive education projects (see for example Rouse and Florian, 2000). The schools in our studies are different but they share many concerns. All are educating children who in the past would have attended special schools. In the sections below we summarise some of the key findings that are emerging from our work.

Pedagogy and inclusion

As considered above, the debates about pedagogy continue, but there appears to be some general agreement across the strands of the inclusion literature about the efficacy of a number of teaching strategies thought to promote inclusive practice. These include cooperative learning, peer-mediated instruction and collaborative teaching, strategies which have been used successfully in both special and mainstream classrooms, although not necessarily to address individual learning problems. For example, cooperative learning, a strategy with great promise for mixed ability teaching, has been used to improve race relations in mainstream schools. The problem is that relatively little is known about the ways in which these and other techniques work (or do not work) in the context of a national (or core) curriculum and the demand for higher standards in classrooms which include pupils with a wide range of learning needs. Furthermore, there has been little consideration in the literature about whether such strategies are equally appropriate across all phases of education, with different size classes and in all subjects of the curriculum.

In an attempt to investigate inclusive practice in secondary schools more fully we conducted a survey of 268 teachers in five schools with a long-standing commitment to inclusive practice (Florian and Rouse, 2001). We were interested in what subject specialist teachers had to say about the strategies recommended in the inclusion literature. A list of 44 teaching strategies mentioned in the literature as helpful in promoting inclusive practice was constructed. These strategies were then organised under the broad headings of: differentiation strategies; cooperative learning strategies; classroom management strategies; teaching social skills.

Teachers reported a high degree of familiarity with and use of these strategies, however, there was variation between teachers of different subjects in the extent to which they use some of the strategies. These differences between subjects could be a function of any number of factors, including the nature and status of knowledge in a particular subject domain and whether the teachers perceive learning their subject as being related to prior learning. Mathematics and modern foreign languages tend to be seen as sequential while the humanities and English are much less so (Hallem and Ireson, 1999). The training of teachers is organised on a subject basis and most secondary schools are organised into subject departments which have different histories, varying degrees of autonomy and different priorities. All these factors produce a range of subject and department 'cultures' that may have an impact upon teacher practice and their views about what works in promoting inclusion. These differences in the use of various teaching strategies between subjects have implications for the nature and organisation of learning support within and across inclusive settings.

We found no apparent difference between schools with respect to teachers knowledge about practice, although teachers in schools with more experience in mixed ability teaching made more suggestions about what works. That they may not be able to engage in a practice is different from not knowing how to do it and some teachers made this comment when filling out the questionnaire. Clearly, organisational arrangements and resource constraints were factors that determine whether certain strategies were or were not used. For instance, it would not be possible to make use of information and communication technology if the hardware was not available.

Moreover, the schools varied with respect to the extent they engaged in streaming or setting from none at all to setting in specific subjects from particular year groups (i.e. modern foreign language in Year 8), to setting for all subjects at Key

Stage 4. In one school with a policy of setting, pupils with severe learning difficulties were included in the top set at Key Stage 3, to facilitate group work, but not at Key Stage 4 because, as one teacher explained 'everything is exam based so the curriculum is not appropriate'. Our impression was that a school or departmental policy on setting does affect the teacher's capacity to sustain inclusive practice because it makes certain strategies, such as peer tutoring or cooperative learning, less effective or impossible to organise. For example, a girl with Down syndrome lost access to her peer tutors in French when her school moved from mixed ability grouping to a policy of setting in Year 10. As a consequence, she was placed in the bottom set with other children who were struggling with the language, thus depriving her of a valuable resource for learning as well as positive role models.

Whole class teaching

In addition to the survey, eight teachers of five different subjects were observed and interviewed. Each teacher was observed on several sessions for the equivalent of two full teaching days arranged so that follow-up interviews could be held as soon after the observation as possible, often the next period. A total of 48 observations and 24 interviews were conducted. The teachers also kept 'Inclusion Journals' where they reflected on their practice. The aim was to see if we could confirm and/ or elaborate on Jordan and Stanovich's (1998) idea that teachers in inclusive classrooms 'use knowledge about the cognitive, social, emotional and self-concept characteristics of each individual in order to adapt their practice to reach [their lesson] objective' (p. 34). We read each teacher's journal and listed the themes which seemed to characterise the entries. These were then matched against the themes which emerged from the observations and interviews and the data obtained from the open-ended interview questions.

Overall, the teachers we observed were skilled in whole class teaching, presenting one lesson but offering a choice of tasks and varying expectations with respect to individual pupils. What enables these teachers to include pupils with a wide range of learning abilities seems to be the way in which they embed a responsiveness to individual need within the process of whole class teaching, a finding consistent with the Jordan and Stanovich (1998) study of inclusive practice. Teachers are constantly evaluating their performance and revising what they do in response to pupil reactions. Our observations and scrutiny of the teachers' journals highlight the fluidity and pragmatism of teachers' thinking about inclusive practice. Planning for mixed ability teaching extends beyond what individual pupils will be doing during a lesson and these plans are constantly under review during lessons in the light of pupil responses.

Teachers' knowledge and practice

There are two aspects to the debate about what teachers need to know and be able to do to sustain inclusive practice in their classrooms. The first concerns what teachers working in inclusive settings need to know about special education practice in order to include pupils who experience difficulties in learning. The second aspect is about whether successful inclusion is only about 'good teaching'.

Clearly it is impractical for every teacher to know about the educational implications of all disabilities and learning difficulties. But many reports on inclusive practice (Scott *et al.*, 1998) suggest that it is a lack of knowledge on the part of mainstream classroom teachers, attributed to lack of training, that is one of the main barriers to inclusion. Perhaps these studies have been asking the wrong questions about inclusive practice. It may be that the lack of knowledge on the part of mainstream teachers reported in some of the research literature is associated with a lack of *traditional special education* knowledge, such as information about disability types or individualised teaching approaches. In response to our questions about the nature and extent of any training (i.e. seminars, INSET or courses), 78 per cent of teachers we surveyed reported that they had received nothing relating to special educational needs within the past five years. At first we were surprised by this large number claiming to have received no training. But perhaps the teachers in our study have had relevant training but do not associate sessions on teaching and learning or classroom management with 'special needs' because the ethos of inclusive education is so embedded in these schools. Discussions with senior managers and scrutiny of documentation about training supports this interpretation.

Equally, the often quoted view that 'good teaching is good teaching wherever it occurs' may not stand up to close scrutiny when differences in the use of various teaching strategies across the various subjects of the secondary curriculum and the limits of mixed ability teaching are probed. Although there are many common features across teachers' practice in these schools, specialist teachers in secondary schools make use of different strategies, as detailed above. Therefore, we would suggest that teachers in inclusive settings are first teachers of their subject, but are capable of being responsive to the individuals they face. They are helped in this task through the frequent use of personal planners that emphasise pupil involvement in their own target setting and systems of monitoring learning that are formative in their nature.

The learning support departments in these schools are able to provide specialist knowledge on a 'need to know' basis, but more importantly they support the process of meeting 'individual need' through co-teaching arrangements and curriculum differentiation. The key point is that it is the subject teacher that is responsible for the learning of all children. Obviously this has implications for the role of learning support and the ways in which special expertise is deployed.

The changing role of learning support

To varying degrees in the schools we have been studying there has been a change of emphasis from responding to individual student needs to whole school responses to pupil diversity. The ways in which additional adult support (specialist teaching and support assistance) is used and perceived is not only a function of its availability, but depends on the focus, nature and purpose of the support. In turn this depends on whether the school sees this resource as 'special' or a means for improving classroom practice. The former is more likely if it is believed that learning difficulties arise only from personal limitations. The latter view sees additional help as a means of increasing flexibility in the classroom and the means by which teachers may receive support to employ a greater range of teaching strategies.

For example, there is an awareness that certain strategies may be associated with particular kinds of special educational need. As a result, circulating information about individual special educational needs and disabilities was seen as very important. All the schools in this study have devised mechanisms for doing this. Although the teachers expressed concern about their own capacity with respect to mixed ability teaching, they viewed the learning support departments in their respective schools as sources of knowledge and support for teaching and learning.

One example of this change involves a redefined role for learning support assistants (LSAs) so that they are reallocated from working directly with individual children to being reassigned to subject departments. There are several advantages to such an arrangement. First, it enables LSAs to learn more about the subject in which they are supporting. Second, it makes it easier for them to be part of the planning process with teachers. Third, it means they are a resource for all children in the class and it also 'unhooks' the LSA from the individual child, creating more opportunity for meaningful inclusion and reducing the child's dependency on a particular adult.

A number of other innovations in pupil support were noted as having a positive impact on inclusion. Rather than working within the traditional special education model of pulling pupils out for individual support, individual tuition is provided in creative ways. For example, in some schools learning support personnel provide help with learning tasks, through structures such as lunchtime or after school 'homework clubs', which are available for all pupils. This is particularly important for homework (or the failure to do it) is often a reason why relationships between teachers and certain students become strained.

In addition, these arrangements provide the chance to work in an inclusive environment where support is available to pupils who might otherwise be singled out for special education. Innovations such as these are an important feature of inclusive provision.

Connecting with the school

The schools in our research have made real progress in enabling all pupils to take part in extra-curricular activities, including school visits and trips, choirs, music, drama, sport and IT clubs. Because transport is provided to and from school for children who have statements of special educational need, attending rehearsals and practice after school can be difficult to organise. The schools are aware of this problem and have taken steps to overcome this by rearranging transport when possible. The provision of transport is a mixed blessing. A benefit is that the attendance and punctuality is good. However, coming to school by taxi or minibus reduces the scope for authentic learning which occurs when children use public transport or walk to school. It also restricts the opportunities for making and maintaining friendships outside school. Nevertheless, these schools provide opportunities for all pupils to feel connected to the school. A parent interviewed in one school underscored how important participation in extra-curricular activities was to the process of inclusion and its effect on pupils

Harry has higher self-esteem now. The trip on the barge was fabulous. For him to have the confidence to go was a real breakthrough. For me, I couldn't have been happier than if I won the pools. You see he was never allowed to go on any trips in his primary school.

(Parent, Year 9 pupil with 'special needs')

Emotional well-being

Teachers' concerns for the emotional well-being of pupils influences their decisions about practice. The observations of teachers, their journal entries and comments made during interviews reflected a finely tuned sensitivity to issues of particular importance in adolescence. Personal privacy, friendship and belonging were of particular concern. As one teacher reflected in her journal:

I noticed that Brian was very much left out of the small group discussions, because the boys with whom he was working were able to write down their answers much quicker than Brian could. I scribed for Brian while the LSA was working with Robert. I reminded the other boys several times that it was important that they waited for Brian and included him in the discussion. Brian's high desk (to cope with his wheelchair) acts a physical barrier when the boys huddle up to do a group activity, and Brian is physically unable to huddle with them. Disappointed that despite all the work we have recently done on disability and prejudice that the boys in my tutor group unwittingly exclude Brian. This is now something I need to discuss further with them.

(Humanities teacher)

Teachers' concerns with respect to pupil friendship and participation are consistent with other research on inclusive practice. Chang (1984) reported that pupils with SEN were often classified as unpopular by their peers. Martin *et al.* (1998) noted that pupils with SEN 'often experience significant barriers to their social inclusion' (p. 149). Although they do not say it directly, these researchers seem to suggest that friendship among pupils will not necessarily occur without some kind of intervention, a finding supported by other research (McGregor and Vogelsberg, 1998).

Shifting concepts of inclusion

Finally, we found a shift in teacher concern from individual pupil progress in the curriculum at the end of Key Stage 3 (Year 9) to group performance on national examinations, the General Certificate of Secondary Education (GCSE), in Key Stage 4 (Year 11). That teachers shift their concern from individual pupil progress to group performance on examinations was clearly evident in their practice, discussions and reflections. Field notes and journal entries were filled with references to examinations. As one teacher stated: 'the GCSE requires a lot of essays so a lot of teaching is focused on how to write an essay'. In this school the department has developed procedures such as the use of 'writing frames' to support all pupils with these tasks.

The pressure of examinations is also felt by the pupils. There were many anxious questions about revision. Pupils were not observed to take the easy way out when offered a choice of task or activity. They seemed to understand the need to challenge themselves and this was confirmed by teachers during the interviews. As one pupil told us:

> When I came here (from a special school) they didn't think I could get any GCSEs but now they think I can get them. Before I came to this school I was ungraded but now I think I will pass.
>
> (Year 11 pupil with 'moderate learning difficulties')

The point here is that many pupils, and their parents, who previously would not have had the chance to take these examinations want to be included. These schools are enabling this to happen in a meaningful way.

Discussion

Proponents of inclusive schooling have attempted to develop practice in a number of ways. One has looked at ways in which knowledge and practices developed in special settings can be transferred to the mainstream through arrangements such as outreach work from special schools or support from external specialist services, another has attempted to build on the work of those in the school improvement field by extending the definition of 'all' pupils to include pupils with learning difficulties, disabilities and other special educational needs. This latter approach entails reconceptualising difficulties in learning as dilemmas for teaching in order to provide insights into ways in which practice might be improved for the benefit of all (Hart, 1996, 2000; Clark et al., 1999).

The evidence from our research is that teachers who create inclusive classrooms often do not distinguish between 'special' and other pupils. They often hesitated when answering questions about SEN pupils because they had to remind themselves who these pupils were. This is not because these teachers were not interested in meeting their learning needs, but they had adopted a problem solving approach to inclusion. Our investigations suggest that these teachers tend to be pragmatic rather than 'pure' in their views of what works. They appear to be utilising both special and school improvement approaches to inclusion.

When they have access to a wide variety of support and teaching strategies, inclusive schools can also be effective schools as defined by current criteria. Whilst it cannot be claimed that any improvement in examination results was directly brought about by moves to inclusion, the view was expressed in interviews with teachers that the greater levels of curriculum support has enabled more effective teaching and learning strategies to be employed.

Such claims need to be interpreted with caution and more evidence would be required before we could claim that teaching methods have changed because of inclusion. What is clear is that according to the teachers and the evidence from the examination results, inclusion has not had a negative impact on the achievement levels of other pupils. However, it is still the case that the quickest and easiest way to improve the percentage of children getting the highest grades would be to remove those children with special educational needs altogether. In secondary schools we have been working with the percentage of GCSE A–C passes would be increased by at least 5 per cent if the pupils with special needs were removed from the school and, therefore, the analysis of examination results. That these schools have not done this is a testament to their commitment to inclusive practice. Fortunately, the government has now recognised that there are exclusionary forces at work in the way examination results are published and they have proposed new ways of acknowledging achievement through the adoption of so-called 'value added' measures that will be more sensitive to children's starting points. This should provide a more inclusion-friendly policy context in which to operate.

Earlier in this paper we considered two strands of research that may have an impact of the development of inclusive schools. We would propose that closer links between researchers who study inclusion and those who study school effectiveness and school improvement could prove to be mutually beneficial. A merging of these traditions may help schools to resolve some of the dilemmas that schools and teachers currently face. It might be beneficial to those with an interest in inclusive education by providing a better evidential base to inform the development of practice. It is clear that more robust and yet sensitive research designs are required to be able to explore what is happening in schools that are struggling to be more inclusive. It might also help researchers in the school effectiveness tradition to be more aware of issues of diversity and may encourage them to incorporate a broader range of outcome indicators than are currently employed.

Finally, we would argue that it is the process of becoming inclusive that makes some schools better for all children and as a result a more popular choice for parents. We would propose a conceptualisation of inclusive schools as those that meet the dual criteria of enrolling a diverse student population *and* improving academic standards for all pupils. Such schools have been struggling to resolve conflicting demands for more than a decade, but their results are beginning to speak for themselves. They have demonstrated that the inclusion project is not only possible, but it is of benefit to all. Roger Slee refers to 'resources of hope' (*Cambridge Journal of Education* 31: 3). These schools are indeed 'resources of hope' not only for the communities they serve, but also because of the lessons they have learned and the messages they have for others schools.

Notes

* Lani Florian and Martyn Rouse are at the School of Education, University of Cambridge.
† Originally published in: *Cambridge Journal of Education* 31: 3, 399–412.

References

Ainscow, M. (ed.) (1991) *Effective Schools for All* (London, David Fulton).
Ainscow, M. (1999) *Understanding the Development of Inclusive Schools* (London, Falmer Press).
Booth, T. and Ainscow, M. (eds) (1998) *From Them to Us: an international study of inclusion in education* (London, Routledge).

Brown, S., Duffield, J. and Riddell, S. (1995) School effectiveness research: the policy makers tool for school improvement?, *European Educational Research Association Bulletin*, 1(1), pp. 6–15.

Chang, H. (1984) *Adolescent Life and Ethos: an ethnography of a U.S. High School* (London, Falmer Press).

Clark, C., Dyson, A., Millward, A. and Robson, S. (1999) Inclusive education and schools as organisations, *International Journal of Inclusive Education*, 3(1), pp. 37–51.

Coleman, J. S., Campbell, E., Hobson, C., McPartland, J., Mood, A., Weinfeld, R. and York, R. (1966) *Equality of Educational Opportunity* (Washington, DC, Government Printing Office).

Creemers, B. (1996) The goal of school effectiveness and school improvement, in: D. Reynolds, R. Bollen, B. Creemers, D. Hopkins, L. Stoll and N. Lagerweij (eds) *Making Good Schools: linking school effectiveness and school improvement* (London, Routledge).

DfEE (1997) *Excellence for all Children: meeting special educational needs* (London, DfEE).

DfEE (2000) *Curriculum 2000* (London, DfEE).

Florian, L. and Rouse, M. (1999) *Investigating Effective Classroom Practice in Inclusive Education (Final Report)*, report to the University of Cambridge School of Education Research and Development Fund (Cambridge, University of Cambridge School of Education).

Florian, L. and Rouse, M. (2001) Inclusive practice in secondary schools, in: R. Rose and I. Grosvenor (eds) *Doing Research in Special Education* (London, David Fulton).

Hallam, S. and Ireson, J. (1999) Pedagogy in the secondary school, in: P. Mortimore (ed.) *Understanding Pedagogy and Its Impact on Learning* (London, Paul Chapman).

Hilliard, A. (1990) Misunderstanding and testing intelligence, in: J. I. Goodlad and P. Keating (eds) *Access to Knowledge: an agenda for our nation's schools* (New York, NY, The College Board).

Hart, S. (1996) *Beyond Special Needs: enhancing children's learning through innovative teaching* (London, Paul Chapman).

Hart, S. (2000) *Thinking Through Teaching: a framework for enhancing participation and learning* (London, David Fulton).

Jencks, C. S., Smith, M., Ackland, H., Bane, M. J., Cohen, D., Ginter, H., Heyns, B. and Michelson, S. (1972) *Inequality: a reassessment of the effect of the family and schooling in America* (New York, NY, Basic Books).

Jordan, A. and Stanovich, P. (1998) Exemplary teaching in inclusive classrooms, paper presented at the *Annual Meeting of the American Educational Research Association*, San Diego, CA, April.

Kauffman, J. M. and Hallahan, D. P. (eds) (1995) *The Illusion of Full Inclusion: a comprehensive critique of a current special education bandwagon* (Austin, TX, Pro-Ed).

Levine, D. U. and Lezotte, L. W. (1990) *Unusually Effective School: a review and analysis of research and practice* (Madison, WI, National Center for Effective School Research and Development).

Lewis, A. and Norwich, B. (2001) A critical review of systematic evidence concerning distinctive pedagogies for pupils with difficulties in learning, *Journal of Research in Special Educational Needs* [online at http://www.nasen.org.uk] (Tamworth, National Association for Special Educational Needs).

Lipsky, D. K. and Gartner, A. (1997) *Inclusion and School Reform: transforming America's classrooms* (Baltimore, Paul H. Brookes).

Martin, J., Jorgensen, C. M. and Klein, J. (1998) The promise of friendship for students with disabilities, in: C. Jorgensen (ed.) *Restructuring High Schools for All Students: taking inclusion to the next level*, pp. 209–232 (Baltimore, Paul H. Brookes).

McDonnell, L., McLaughlin, M. and Morison, P. (eds) (1997) *Educating One and All: students with disabilities and standards-based reform* (Washington, DC, National Academy Press).

McGregor, G. and Vogelsberg, R. T. (1998) *Inclusive Schooling Practices: pedagogical and research foundations* (Baltimore, Paul H. Brookes).

Mortimore, P., Sammons, P., Stoll, L., Lewis, D. and Ecob, R. (1988) *School Matters: the junior years* (Wells, Open Books; reprinted 1995 by Paul Chapman, London).

Rouse, M. and Florian, L. (1996) Effective inclusive schools: a study in two countries, *Cambridge Journal of Education*, 26(1), pp. 71–85.

Rouse, M. and Florian, L. (1997) Inclusive education in the marketplace, *International Journal of Inclusive Education*, 1(4), pp. 323–336.

Rouse, M. and Florian, L. (2000) *Developing Inclusive Education at Rawthorpe High School (Final Report of the Second Phase of the Evaluation)* (Ilford, Barnardos).

Rutter, M., Maughan, B., Mortimer, P., Ouston, J. and Smith, A. (1979) *Fifteen Thousand Hours: secondary schools and their effects on children* (London, Open Books).

Scott, B. J., Vitale, M. R. and Masten, W. G. (1998) Implementing instructional adaptations for students with disabilities in inclusive classrooms: a literature review, *Remedial and Special Education*, 19(2), pp. 106–119.

Skrtic, T. (1998) The organisational context of special education, in: E. L. Meyen and T. M. Skrtic (eds) *Exceptional Children and Youth: an introduction* (Denver, CO, Love).

Slee, R. and Weiner, G. (2001) Education reform and reconstructions as a challenge to research genres: reconsidering school effectiveness research and inclusive schooling, *School Effectiveness and School Improvement*, 12(1), pp. 83–98.

Slee, R., Weiner, G. and Tomlinson, S. (eds) (1998) *School Effectiveness for Whom? Challenges to the school effectiveness and school improvement movements* (London, Falmer Press).

Smith, D. J. and Tomlinson, S. (1989) *The School Effect. A study of multi-racial comprehensives* (London, Policy Studies Institute).

Teddlie, C. and Reynolds, D. (2000) *The International Handbook of School Effectiveness Research* (London, Falmer Press).

Villa, R. A., Thousand, J. S., Stainback, W. and Stainback, S. (eds) (1992) *Restructuring for Caring and Effective Education: an administrative guide to creating heterogeneous schools* (Baltimore, Paul H. Brookes).

16 The ecologisation of schools and its implications for educational policy

*Peter Posch**[†]*

Introduction

The Ecologisation of Schools is an international OECD project which currently involves ten countries. It is based on the 1986 Environment and School Initiatives (ENSI) project, one of the first international projects to promote development and research in ambitious, environment-oriented project instruction (OECD/CERI, 1995; Posch/Mair, 1997; Elliott, 1998, ch. 7). The Ecologisation of Schools (ECOLOG) programme currently involves 22 pilot schools in Austria, from primary to secondary technical school level. It is largely administered by the same teachers who were able to gain experiences in the ENSI project (see Appendix). In the following, I will try to discuss three issues at greater length:

- What do we understand by the ecologisation of schools?
- What is innovative in this project?
- Which framework conditions are important for the success of the project?

What do we mean by the ecologisation of schools?

Condensed to one sentence, ecologisation means shaping our interaction with the environment in an intellectual, material, spatial, social and emotional sense to achieve a lasting/sustainable quality of life for all. This concise definition clearly shows that ecologisation is not a one time affair, but an on-going task. What is more, it concerns not only schools, but all institutions within the social fabric. The term environment embraces the natural and technical environment as much as the social and intellectual environment.

What are schools doing if they strive for ecologisation? They launch initiatives at three levels, at the pedagogical, at the social/organisational and at the technical/economic level.

In initiatives at the *pedagogical level* schools aim at creating stimulating and meaningful learning experiences and at involving pupils in ecological ways of thinking, acting and feeling in school, in their family and in the community. This process is characterised by a shift of priorities:

- from the prevalence of learning tasks structured by systematic knowledge to a focus on complex, real life unstructured situations which raise controversial issues;
- from an orientation towards individual subjects to interdisciplinary inquiry;
- from passive learning of facts, rules and principles to the active generation of knowledge by pupils and teachers in the local contexts of action, to a pro-active shaping of the environment, to promoting a critical, reflective attitude towards given stocks of knowledge; and
- from top-down communication of learning requirements to active participation of pupils in negotiating the conditions of learning, to promoting individual reflection by pupils about the quality of their learning.

The focus here lies on a dynamic concept of learning according to which pupils not only acquire knowledge and experiences for the future, but shape their living and working conditions constructively in the present (Elliott, 1994).

At the *social/organisational level* schools aim at building and cultivating a culture of communication and decision making and at developing a social climate which is characterised by mutual recognition and respect. This implies a shift of priorities:

- from isolated teachers and pupils towards a team structure and social continuity;
- from the predetermination of organisational regulations to negotiating binding rules, and to assigning responsibilities to pupils; and
- from detachment from the social, cultural and economic environment towards active construction of external relations in terms of mutuality.

At the *technical/economic level* schools aim at the ecologically sound and economic use of resources. This includes measures:

- to save resources;
- to reduce waste;
- to design indoor and outdoor space in an aesthetic and ecologically viable way; and
- to promote healthy living conditions.

Ecological schools are schools which become active at all three levels. They relate pedagogical, social/organisational and technical/economic initiatives to each other in a constructive way and make the pursuance of these efforts an inherent feature of their educational philosophy. Ecologisation, in this sense, involves awareness and action, social structures and observable effects on the quality of the environment. In another sense it is an extended view of education.

What is innovative in the Ecologisation of Schools project?

Its novelty consists, first and foremost, of three long-term, educational policy developments.

At the level of the individual schools, it is *the step from temporary individual initiatives to ecologically sustainable structures and to a combination of pedagogical, social and technical/economic initiatives.* In this respect, ecologisation can be regarded as an important contribution to school development.

Many innovations at the school level are individual or group initiatives launched by committed teachers, school heads and pupils and tied to their motivation and involvement. Most innovations come to an end when commitment falters or when external support is withdrawn. Few innovations actually have a transformative impact on the culture of the institution as a whole. The ecologisation programme therefore attempts from the very outset:

- to win a 'critical number' of teachers in a school by persuasion, good example and open communication;
- to transform passive concern into active involvement and to create the necessary conditions which allow parents and pupils to take part in reflection, in planning and in decision making processes;
- to set up an organisational structure which ensures the quality and the stability of the ecologisation process;
- to pool existing initiatives, use synergies and embed them in the curriculum;
- to create mutual expectations and traditions with respect to acceptable attitudes and behaviour.

At the level of the educational system, it is *the step from pilot schools to an inherent feature of the system of education.*

This means developing a strategy to spread ecological development processes as widely as possible. Many reform initiatives are burdened by the fact that they are limited to a few rather privileged schools, particularly because the required investment in terms of counselling and resources cannot be afforded on a general scale. Therefore, a strategy is needed which stimulates and supports a dynamic development within schools, involving teachers, students, administrators, support staff such as secretaries and caretakers and parents.

There is probably no topic better suited for developing and testing such a strategy than the ecologisation of schools, for several good reasons:

- almost all schools have already taken initiatives in this area, not least because they are searching for new forms of meaningful learning;
- public interest in developments of this kind is large, ecologically driven initiatives therefore provide opportunities to establish links with external institutions (e.g. municipal administrations, cultural institutions, the business community, etc.); and
- schools which become ecologically active do not only gain status, but gain a certain influence on their environment and they are no longer at the receiving

end of social demands only, but also in a position to effectively assert demands towards society.

The development of a sound strategy for the dissemination of initiatives aiming at ecologisation is a pioneering feat whose impact would reach far beyond the specific concern of the ecologisation of schools.

At the level of competences, it is *the step from the competences of a minority of teachers and headteachers to an intrinsic professional feature of the teaching profession and of school management.*

A survey of environmental education policies in Austria has shown that innovative practice is only rarely generated in teacher training institutions, but almost exclusively in schools. Teacher training has been identified as a weak point in the educational system (House *et al.*, 1994). The second issue within the ecologisation programme therefore is teacher training. In Austria, three teacher training institutes and three university departments are developing and testing viable curricula to prepare students for a teaching practice guided by the educational philosophy of the ecologisation programme. These curricula will include *inter alia* the involvement of trainee teachers in ecologisation initiatives as part of their training and close cooperation with the schools which have taken on a leading role in this field.

Framework for the ecologisation of schools

An appropriate framework is called for if the ecologisation of schools is to become an inherent feature of the educational system. Three factors deserve particular attention in this context: the regional support system, the incentive system and the obligation of schools to engage in a self-organised development process, combined with self-evaluation.

Regional support system

Building a regional support system is a fundamental task for the coming years. In Austria, three distinct development phases have been envisioned so far (see Appendix).

- The 22 schools involved in the pilot phase (1996–1998) received direct support and guidance from the ENSI team members. Another 30 schools are loosely associated with the project and receive information about the ongoing activities.
- All schools were invited to participate in this movement through a national competition (1998–1999). Nearly 300 schools have applied and more than 200 have engaged in the required local development activities. The regional training seminars were organised by the members of the ENSI team in cooperation with teachers from the pilot schools.
- During this phase a formal regional support system has also been established to support further extension of the programme. In each of the nine provinces one

or two members of the regional In-service Education Institute have received initial training to coordinate and support the participating schools.

- The third phase will extend the ecologisation programme to a still wider range of schools than those participating in the competition. This phase and other extension phases are being developed together with the facilitators from the support system. A first medium-term goal is to reach a critical mass of about 1,000 schools (i.e. 15 per cent of all schools) by 2005.

From today's viewpoint, the support system will have one major task to fulfil: to organise further education and training and, closely connected to that, to promote the exchange of experiences between schools in order to derive maximum benefit from the pool of competence which is accumulating in the schools. In order to sustain the movement, schools must become the central agents of the further extension of the movement and must be able to develop specific profiles through their involvement. By mutual communication and support, teachers, pupils and heads of interested schools should be able to gain experiences with ecologisation processes, without having anything imposed on them. 'Innovations move along personal relationships' (House, 1974).

It is assumed that the development of professional competence in organising communication to disseminate innovation will become increasingly important, irrespective of the ecologisation programme. First experiences were gained in the programme Teachers Reporting from Practice, where teachers share their experience on innovative projects with interested colleagues in afternoon events (Piber, 1993). This programme could be further developed into a Schools Reporting from Practice programme. The development of effective means of stimulation and external support for school innovations will probably become a major area of development for regional educational infrastructures.

The incentive system

Many school-based innovations remain a one time affair because their benefits are not always immediately discernible, while the disadvantages, which are part and parcel of every innovation, attract ready attention (let alone the fact that criticism tends to be more appreciated than praise and that innovation is often considered a threat to and devaluation of the status quo).

These problems are of a general nature. Some of the more salient strategies to overcome them are:

- initiatives promoting an attitude among teachers which holds them responsible not only for their classroom teaching but also for the further development of their school;
- initiatives promoting an attitude which sees innovations as inherent features of any good school and which therefore deserve recognition per se; and
- initiatives developing a reliable and credible process for evaluating the quality of innovations in schools.

Another, more profane, reason why ecological initiatives often die away early is that schools do not benefit financially from the savings made. In Austria, a system is currently being elaborated according to which savings made in the course of ecologisation initiatives may remain fully or partly at the school (bonus system). The basic problem is how to devise a fair system which neither puts schools which have used their resources sparingly so far at a disadvantage nor reward those schools which have wasted their resources in the past.

An interesting and less complex approach to this problem has come up in a Tyrolean community: a secondary general school received an advance grant of 10,000 Austrian schillings in recognition of its pledge to use energy resources more sparingly. The actual amount of savings would then be ascertained at the end of the year. Under this concept an advance grant is given in good faith and accounted for later on.

Apart from financial incentives there are other motives that often weigh heavier than material considerations. One of the most important motives is recognition by other persons. Even if schools are entitled to keep part of the saved resources the material value may be less important than its symbolic value as an indication of public recognition. Other relevant incentives are:

- a firm belief in making a socially important contribution;
- an opportunity actively to be able to shape conditions of work and life; and
- an observable gain in the quality of life.

The demands for accountability and school development

The more autonomy schools enjoy, the more they are accountable to the general public for how they use human and material resources. It is important that schools take on this responsibility themselves and do not wait until they become dependent on external evaluation (Posch and Altrichter, 1997). In Austria, a self-evaluation concept is currently being developed which closely links evaluation and development and which leaves the individual schools with the main responsibility for quality evaluation and development. Under this concept, schools will be asked credibly to present their readiness for innovation and their achievements to the public by way of a school programme (Federal Ministry of Education and the Arts, 1997).

School programmes will become mandatory in Austria by the year 2002/2003. Under the ECOLOG Programme schools will be invited first to gain experience with linking development and evaluation by designing an ecological school programme before the mandatory period begins. The pedagogical, social/organisational and technical/economic levels of ecologisation initiatives described above will provide substantial quality criteria and the framework within which schools are supported to reflect on their aims, analyse the situation, identify challenges, draw conclusions from data for further initiatives and provide a credible account to the public.

This development process takes place under difficult conditions: schools must cope with new demands on the part of pupils and of society in times of tightening resources (Posch, 1998). The scope for local decision making has become broader. However, the schools will still have to find ways and means to exploit this scope for further development of the quality of teaching and of learning, the quality of life in schools and the quality of the local environment. The ecologisation programme could make a significant contribution to designing, shaping and stabilising these spaces of discretion.

Appendix: chronology and timetable of the programme Ecologisation of Schools (ECOLOG) in Austria

1	Since 1986	Research and development activities by the Austrian ENSI team. The team consisted of 10–12 teachers, a national coordinator and a scientific advisor.
2	1995	Conceptual development and methodological documentation for the Ecologisation of Schools programme.
3	1996	Selection of 22 pilot schools and an introductory seminar for these schools.
4	Since October 1996	Ecologisation initiatives launched by pilot schools, supervised by the ENSI team with external evaluation.
5	Since October 1997	Recruitment of regional coordinators to develop a regional infrastructure, with an introductory seminar.
6	January 1998	Invitation to tender for a competition to involve other schools.
7	1998	Ecologisation initiatives as preparation for the competition, guided by the regional coordinators and supported by the ENSI team and the pilot schools, with regional training seminars.
8	October 1998	International OECD/CERI conference on the ENSI programme in Linz.
9	January 1999	End of competition and invitation of participating schools to the network. Planning of the next phase.
10	1999/2000	Start of the third extension phase by inviting and supporting schools to design an ecological school programme.

Notes

* Peter Posch is at the University of Klagenfurt, Austria.
† Originally published in: *Cambridge Journal of Education* 29: 3, 341–348.

References

Bundesministerium für Unterricht und kulturelle Angelegenheiten (1997) *Qualitätsentwicklung mit Programm – Leitfaden. Entwurf für Pilotphase* (Wien, BMUK).

Elliott, J. (1994) Developing community-focussed environmental education through action research, in: M. Pettigrew and B. Somekh (eds) *Evaluating Innovation in Environmental Education* (Paris, OECD/CERI).

Elliott, J. (1998) *The Curriculum Experiment – Meeting the Challenge of Social Change* (Buckingham, Open University Press).

House, E. (1974) *The Politics of Educational Innovation*, (Berkley, CA, McCutchan).

House, E., Eide, K. and Kelley-Lainé, K. (1994) Umweltbildungspolitik in Österreich, in: G. Pfligersdorffer and U. Unterbruner (eds) *Umwelterziehung auf dem Prüfstand*, pp. 46–73 (Innsbruck, Studienverlag).

OECD/CERI (1995) *Environmental Education for the 21st Century* (Paris, OECD).

Piber, C. (1993) Zu zweit oder zu dritt ist es leichter – Gedanken zur Veranstaltungsreihe 'LehrerInnen berichten aus der Praxis', *Newsletter* No. 6, Department for School Development and Social Learning (Klagenfurt, Institute for Interdisciplinary Research and Continuing Education (IFF)).

Posch, P. (1998) Social change and environmental education, in: M. Ahlberg and L. Filho (eds) *Environmental Education for Sustainability: good environment, good life*, pp. 45–56 (Frankfurt, Peter Lang).

Posch, P. and Altrichter, H. (1997) *Möglichkeiten und Grenzen der Qualitätsevaluation und Qualitätsentwicklung im Schulwesen* (Innsbruck, Studienverlag).

Posch, P. and Mair, G. (1997) Dynamic networking and community collaboration – the cultural scope of educational action research, in: S. Hollingsworth (ed.) *International Action Research – a case book for educational reform*, pp. 261–271 (London, Falmer).

17 Seeing our way into learning

Shirley Brice Heath*†

Introduction

More often than educators might think possible, findings from basic research fields distant from schools and schooling come along to help us as teachers think in new ways about a daily issue or problem. Such research can be especially helpful when thinking about future directions for the curriculum. Current work in neurobiology and physics brings new understanding of just how important engaging with the visual arts can be for broadening neural circuitry involvement in the brain. This research makes sense to us because of our growing awareness of the ubiquitous power of visual images, moving and still. We have also become aware of the special demands that reading hypertext brings and of the need to grasp information that comes to us through multiple media. We somehow know schooling has to enable students to process and produce information more rapidly than ever and through simultaneous use of new forms and means. But what are reasonable ways to do so, and what can research tell us about how to go about making these decisions?

The literate eye

Only since the late 1980s have neurobiologists and physicists begun to grasp the workings of neural mechanisms through which images and symbols interact in the human brain during conscious cognition. This research tells us much about how post-retinal visual processing works and what effect focused attention on components of the visual has on neighbouring cells. What the eye sees in colour, form and depth to constitute imagistic representations interacts in a continuous recursive process with symbolic centres which in turn ground representations by returning to interact with visual projection centres of the brain. The neurodynamics, both in direct perception and spontaneous creative and inventive work, ensure interplay between visual images and symbolic interpretation for thinking and expressing with meaning. The work of that portion termed the 'visual brain' benefits from highly specialised cells (such as those that process motion, those that process colour and so on) that interact or engage with one another simultaneously in a parallel processing perceptual system (Zeki, 1998, 1999; Chao and Martin, 1999). Simply put, what amounts to visual perception carries meaning because the imagistic character of neural activity manages to link up with stored experience that gives coherence and embeddedness to primary sensory images.

Studies that use positron emission tomography (PET) help us understand what happens between certain sections of the occipital lobes and other portions of the brain that mediate perception and meaning. This research makes clear that selective attention to one feature of an object and naming of that feature, such as colour, results in increased activity in brain regions that mediate colour perception and also those that retrieve information from previous experience with colour (including the lexical form or name of a colour). Again, simply put, it would seem that seeing and attending to specific features of perceived images engage us in calling up information we have stored through prior experience and can now recall and recount verbally.

In an era increasingly dependent on the interdependence of colour, form and line used in icons, we have to be able to call up a host of meanings in connection with symbols. For example, when we depend on the Internet for information, we have to move away from the usual linear print-only expectations of 'reading'. As conditional statements such as 'if you want to know more about [thus and so], click here' guide our reading, we jump constantly across nodes of information, generally guided by our interpretation of particular icons and expectations of where they will lead us. Gaining coherence for presentation in some recall and recount of information collected from the Internet calls on multiple kinds of literacy. We must be able to go far beyond merely reading print in a linear fashion to know how to interpret colour and form in multiple icons and other visuals. We must be able to organise for recall disparate chunks of information linked in categorical orders. These categories of subdivision within a large content area do not subscribe to the 'logic' of written outlines, in that each subdivision or choice of where an icon will lead us is not parallel in significance to any other. Instead, the selection of categorical divisions on Internet material often appears to have no logic internal to the subject; in fact, categories often derive simply from types of information readily available and norms related to industry demands to website creators that they combine words and images to make a 'text' appealing.

The electronic world of information is increasingly dependent on visual images, colour and mixtures of printed text, moving images and brief 'gloss notes' that point to fuller bodies of information. Few textbooks or materials selected for use in school reflect these changes; few of us understand how to interpret the neuroscience findings noted above or the realities of electronic media in our own teaching of reading and writing. Only a few glimmers of help have yet appeared. These come in the form of radically different textbooks and innovative programmes that stress learning in the arts. For example, *Seeing Writing* (McQuade and McQuade, 2000) is a textbook on the teaching of writing and reading that stresses reading visual and verbal texts and brings to a meta-level of understanding just what is required to process multiple forms of information across media. By the early 1990s, British scholars were calling for heightened attention to 'visual literacy' and the reading of meaning in complex symbol systems beyond the alphabetic script (Kress and van Leeuwen, 1996). The Centre for New Ethnicities Research of the University of East London has moved forward to bring engagement with the real work of production and interpretation closer to school learning, particularly for youth (see Ainley et al., 1999). The 1999 report Making Movies Matter (Film Education Working Group, 1999) urges the incorporation into education of moving image industries and argues that interpretation of film, video and television constitutes a key part of literacy. The call to 'creative education' by the National Advisory Committee on Creative and Cultural Education in 1999 (Robinson, 1999) emphasises the integral role that visual images and the creative arts play in supporting literacy and numeracy as traditionally conceived. Within the USA, an increased call for study of the arts both within and beyond school stresses their relevance to adequate preparation for participation in the new economy and maintenance of a civil society (President's Committee on the Arts and Humanities, 1999).

All of these sources firmly support the expected basics of education, such as reading and writing extended texts, but they urge the potential of enhancement of learning and rapid processing that integration of the arts provides. The visual arts with accompanying focus of attention on details of features, such as colour, form and line, ensure attention to perception and engagement of the 'visual brain', which, in turn, resonates with remembered experience and linguistic representation. Manipulation of these features of the visual arts, from drawing or fingerpainting in early childhood to the complexities of creating sequences on video, provides essential opportunity for focusing joint attention, taking on numerous roles, bringing memory to external form and developing language. All of these skills are critical for academic achievement and all underlie literacy and numeracy as traditionally conceived.

But learning through and in the arts in the embodied enacted view of perception suggested by neuroscience research and the recent reports on education and the arts noted above speaks to more than may be immediately evident. Including the arts in meaningful ways in learning opportunities brings shifts in contexts as well as content of learning.

Stepping into theory building

What happens within full participation in the arts is collaborative theory building widely called for by work in the new economy as well as by those concerned about ensuring a healthy and vibrant civil society. Here again, research from unexpected sources often viewed as far afield from classrooms helps explain what happens in the joint work of creating and interpreting art, of engaging with visual literacy that is interdisciplinary, multimodal and calls for multiple forms of representation (Kress, 1997). These scholars (cognitive linguists, developmental psychologists and cognitive psychologists) almost invariably ground their interest in the learning of language and have come to the study of contexts of learning through their increased focus on just how we learn to make meaning.

Most important among their findings are the following.

1   Joint talk about specific strategies of problem development and solution enables reorganisation of cognition for sustained learning.
2   Having to make decisions collaboratively engages beliefs, experience, abstrac-

tions, argument and application – a combination of mental and linguistic processes that enable essential practice in developing theories about how the world works.

3   The line between word and image is getting harder to draw; the visual through colour, line and form enables understanding of metaphor – our ability to map interactions, experiences and cognitive operations across concepts to form images. In other words, the visual and the verbal reinforce one another in the sustained and adaptive learning necessary to increase learning from the theories of others and to build strength in one's own theories.

Let's address the first two of these to examine, with the foregoing discussion of visual image processing in mind, how these few findings from basic research on one aspect of human learning might carry suggestions for curricular development.

Talk about strategies

Psychologists who want to understand how young children develop theories about the world have long focused on how toddlers 'explain' events and states of mind (see Astington and Olson, 1995; Nelson, 1996). Implicit in this work is the need to understand early development of theory building: how is it that children observe the world and then figure out how it works and what their place is within it? A sense of strategy (how to get desired states) underlies all theory building.

The extent to which adults verbalise connections across events or between intentions and behaviours varies across cultures and socialisation patterns. However, groups whose societies place high value on formal schooling appear to stress such explanations more than those who have only recently begun to make education in schools widely available and requisite (Scribner and Cole, 1981). Adults attuned to school-based norms also make strategies explicit – not only those related to observable process but also those attributed to internal non-observable states of mind or intentions. The narrative form of shaping the self, others and events, often with highly elaborated and specific detail, appears to be universal, though with highly varied genre characteristics and attribution of mental states across cultures (see Nelson, 1989, 1996; Bruner, 1990; Kulick, 1992). In addition, groups differ greatly in the extent to which children and young people are encouraged to engage in such narratives as explanations of themselves and their behaviours.

A central curricular issue is then how can schools model and provide ample authentic practice opportunities for students who may have highly varied approaches to building theories and talking about strategies. An ease with such discourse forms comes only with multiple opportunities to play meaningful roles within groups that talk across these genres of explanation, explication and narrative and that demonstrate understanding in several modes – from dramatic improvisation to paint to photography. Hence, any curriculum must ensure extensive opportunities for students to develop explanations through different means and collaboratively with the guidance of adults and older youth. The latter are important in this socialisation process, because they illustrate peer uses of certain discourse forms and model roles that demonstrate theory building at work. The arts lend themselves most readily to creating such opportunities. Jointly composing the script for a play or interpretation of a given script, planning and painting a mural as a class or providing advertising and programme design for a school-wide musical event demand collaborative theory building and strategy development.

We expect theories to have coherence and a causal–explanatory framework and to reflect certain ontological distinctions, as well as to carry some predictive value. A sense of strategies and tactics, often imputing mental states or intentions, underlies any theory that refers to human events or actions. Observation, involvement and interpretation make possible the idea that one can, and indeed is often expected to, explain behaviour, whether past, present or future (see Wellman, 1990).

Formal education depends on theory building by students who must come to show themselves capable of 'logical' or 'scientific' reasoning and must increasingly remove their own mental state or themselves as central actor and narrative figure in theories about how things or people work. Exhibition or demonstration of this development and academic growth currently depends in large part on verbal display – generally through explanations and explications – and often in written form. Explanations focus on process and include tactics and strategies as well as reasons for their inclusion; explanations also often refer to internal states of mind to explain actions of individuals or groups. Explications frequently appear within explanations or they may stand alone; to explicate is to lay open components, stages and their scope and sequence. Both explanations and explications often incorporate brief narratives of illustration, development of future scenarios of possibility and argumentation toward one or more points.

Practice in such talk must precede development of competence in writing the many kinds of school assignments that require explanation, explication and argumentation. Addition of illustration or layering of means of representation reflect deepened understanding. At a fundamental level, an awareness of how 'all of this gets worked out in the mind' seems to help language learners not only verbalise and create images for others but also internalise such talk and images as self-guidance.

Psychologists have shown in experiments and comparative studies that guided participation that includes explicit talk about strategies, as well as introduction of problems with direct talk about how alternatives can be weighed in reaching solutions, enhance performance, particularly that associated with schooling (Rogoff et al., 1993). In experiments related to engagement with mathematical problems as well as reading, scholars have shown that making explicit strategies of what is happening in a learning situation offers measured gains over either practice-only or engaged interactive participation (see Palincsar and Brown, 1984; Schoenfeld, 1985). Such meta-talk enables individuals to retain concepts across domains of activity.

Learning to talk through the options that are possible for action on a particular problem or in a specific situation carries over not only to a similar situation repeated but also to some other situations as well. For example, young people engaged in a highly participatory arts-based programme leading to performance and product development have multiple opportunities to take part in joint problem solving and critique. In non-school organisations, where time flows beyond the usual limited number of minutes available for arts classes within schools, young people work collaboratively toward maintaining the organisation, preparing and producing the work of the group and assessing success or failure. For such groups who focus on the arts, young people who spend at least ten hours per week involved in the organisation soon begin to use language forms that echo those of adults and older youth directors. Open-ended questions ('what kind of show do you want to do this year?'), conditionals ('if we tighten that second scene, we have to cut out some lines that really drag') and development of future scenarios ('what if the exhibition space does not have mid-floor lighting?') reflect both problem posing and solving. Frequent calls for explanation as well as explication come along with the many roles that young people have in these organisations and the expectation that their joint attention goes to developing theories about 'how's it going?' Within a few weeks of beginning participation in such groups, young people reflect, even in talk and situations unrelated to the organisation or to the arts, an increased use of strategy building language (see Heath, 1999, Heath and Roach, 1999). It appears that their rapid adoption of complex language forms tied to reasoning within their arts groups also benefited from the extent of focus members of the group had to give to details of artistic products and performances under development (see Worthman, 1999).

Making decisions collaboratively

The joint talk that comes with collaboration receives the lion's share of attention in studies of early language development. Underlying this research is the view that when adult as expert and child as novice work together, the child learns joint attention skills, role taking and turn taking, as well as other conversational strategies. Reading illustrated books together, talking about them, enacting their stories and illustrating their relation with real life stands high in the view of educators as desirable preparation before children enter school.

Making decisions together follows developmentally the ability to talk jointly about either events visually present or remembered events. Decisions refer to actions that will take place in the future, and they generally rest firmly on knowledge drawn from past experience, references outside the personal and societal or institutional norms and procedures. Hence, much research has gone into showing how complicated joint decision making is and how extensively it figures in the world of adult work. Knowing how to make decisions collaboratively and to talk these through involves such complex skills as how to interrupt, latch onto the sentence of another speaker, illustrate with non-verbal means and disengage from talk (see Bilmes, 1997; Ochs and Jacoby, 1997; Szymanski, 1999). Executing these skills depends on attending to what is going on, as well as finding ways to argue, persuade and present convincing evidence to support one's points. Studies of the work of scientists, in particular, have shown that unless such skills are present within a group, the joint work cannot go forward (see Fleck, 1935; Latour and Woolgar, 1986).

The relevance for school tasks of collaborative decision making comes through the reports of high achieving students, particularly in the sciences. For example, winners of the Westinghouse Awards in Science often point out the collaborative work of study groups that worked out decisions related to their winning projects. This theme is echoed by cognitive scientists who argue for a 'situative perspective' that views learning to think as becoming an effective participant in social groups engaged in joint inquiry and interpretation. These researchers propose as ideal context for learning not an isolated individual thinker, but instead 'groups of people in animated conversations, interacting with some material that they are reasoning about and with which they are developing representations of their ideas' (Greeno and MMAP, 1997, p. 119). It is thinking within the activity of groups of people working on a collection of problems over an extended time that enables conceptual understanding, accumulation of skill in manipulating symbols and participation in practices of inquiry, such as formulating hypotheses, using evidence, making explanations and arguing toward a point.

An ideal curriculum for the future

What might schooling look like if we were to follow some of the implications from the basic research of neuroscientists, linguists and psychologists? What if schooling could take seriously the need to generate meaningful opportunities to practice collaborative theory building through multimodal creative tasks? Six factors are proposed here related to schooling that need attention in order to build a receptive context for curricular changes that would draw on the research summarised here.

The first of these is *space*. Schools would need to be central nodes within a web of learning environments for children and young people that would include museums, playgrounds, civic centres, libraries and business places. Schools would be available all year and would be open from early morning into the evening. An ecology of learning environments would be the focus, rather than schools alone. In this way, societal members would reconceive young people as learners and resources for the learning of others rather than as passive students.

Such a reconception of students would also involve re-envisioning *agents for learning and teaching*. No one would expect to learn something simply for the individual, but with an awareness that learning is to flow to younger or less expert learners. Trained teachers in specific subject fields taught in schools would know their work would be complemented and put into action by leaders within community-based organisations. For example, a general science teacher could count on project work in youth centres involving students in development of interactive exhibits at park and recreational centres used by younger children. A teacher of mathematics could count on Boy Scout troop leaders to incorporate concepts relevant to trigonometry and geometry in Scouts' work with maps, study of regional topography, etc. Teachers of language arts would know that their students would be spending time in local libraries and community centres working on puppetry and photography projects for use with younger visitors to these locations. Adults from a range of businesses and from the public sector would have responsibilities for taking part a few hours a week in working with different groups of students to enable them to understand how concepts and skills learned in school relate to the worlds of work and government.

Schools would expect *display of learning in multiple modes*. Assignments in every subject field would include a range of optional forms of displaying learning in verbal, visual, dramatic, video and schematic forms. Therefore, materials used in schools would have to include these modes, and students would be expected to learn how these contribute to explanations, explications and other genres such as narratives (for examples of such requirements, see Film Education Working Group, 1999). (In many elementary schools in Sweden, video cameras have become an expected tool for student use in preparing reports and creating projects.) Artists in the community would systematically be included within project and performance development within schools, and teachers in training would work in different arts and study learning in the arts in order to understand distinctions between coaching and instructing, facilitating and dictating, criticising and critiquing (see Heath and Langman, 1994; Soep, 1996). Platforms for display of learning and achievement by artists include studio, gallery, stage, canvas, script and storyboards. Learning to be adept in these contexts and means of presentation draws on seeing, listening, attending, creating and communicating. When several of these are at work simultaneously, a dynamism around learning takes place that helps sustain skill development and build knowledge accumulation through cultivation of specific individual talents.

Assessment would include not only customary measures of individual knowledge and skill capabilities, but also periodic evaluation of small group collaborative performances or product development by relevant individuals from local businesses and the public sector. Forms of assessment would be multiple – from written evaluations and point assignment (as in world class skating competitions) to interviews. In addition, each student would prepare once every few months some form of representation of learning achieved, along with a reflection on next steps and goals as a learner. Once each year, every student would be involved in a group project to create a unit of study in one subject field for students at a lower grade level. This unit would include multiple media as well as forms of testing and would be assessed by a teacher from a lower grade level either through a recounting of how the unit worked with younger students or by means of a written appraisal of the unit and its appropriateness, thoroughness, originality and appeal. Through the school career, a personal achievement collection of materials related to assessment would accompany each student for use in movement from one school to the next and in community organisations.

Social community for students would be achieved by keeping, to the extent possible, students together in a single group over 2–4 years. Students would move from one grade level to the next with their cohort. In addition, each cohort would include students of different grade levels, so that early primary groups would include kindergartners through fourth graders. Teachers would move with the cohort for the 2–4 years during which the group stayed together. Each cohort would ideally include between 15 and 20 students in the primary years, with incremental growth in the size of each cohort in the later years of schooling. Ideally, one or more community artists and representatives from civic government and private business would also remain with each cohort through the 2–4 years. Each group at the young level would be paired with a group of approximately the same number but in more advanced years of schooling. Together for several days at a time in different times of the year, the two groups would work in still smaller groups to prepare for a culminating performance or project (related, for example, to science, mathematics or social studies).

Opportunities to *learn through work experience* would be available for all students 14 and older. Each would take part in two, six-week work study programmes; one each in some kind of public service job and the other in any of a range of types of commercial or business enterprise. For 4–6 hours each day for these weeks, students would intern or apprentice in teams of two. Each week student teams would be expected to prepare in multiple forms with supporting documentation reports on their work week. The group would meet to analyse these reports and to focus on several key features: decision making and experimenting strategies used or called for in the workplace; kinds of uses of mathematics; language of a special register and genre. This information would be shared with both the business taking part and with future student apprentices or interns. Particular tax benefits would have to be developed in order for businesses to have an incentive for participating in such programmes.

Research for what?

It goes without saying that putting any component of this ideal into place will take altered attitudes, new expectations of children and youth and shifted conversations among parties not accustomed to playing such key roles in the learning environments of their communities. But both research and common sense about what the new economy will need would argue the merits of consideration of some aspects of this ideal. Already several components are in place in learning communities (Longworth, 1999), and more public policy spokespersons argue for understanding learning as a system and not as disparate subjects taught only during certain hours of the day and with limited means of display of knowledge and skills (Ranson, 1994). In sum, both research and policy point to the dire need for new thinking about education for a changing world and to 'learning as the major driving force for the future prosperity, stability and well-being of our citizens' (Longworth, 1999, p. 206).

In several realms of daily life, we choose courses of action and make purchases with an expectation that research supports what we do. From road maps to pharmaceuticals to automobile tyres, consumers know that serious examination has gone into development of these products. The same is true even for trivial matters that pale in comparison with what is needed for choice of travel route, course of antibiotics or tyre selection. Breakfast cereals, dyes used in clothing and projected life of light bulbs receive attention from researchers in laboratories and help determine product development and consumer information available in marketing and packaging materials.

It is curious that a similar attention to research on learning does not lie behind curricular choices; instead, these float in and out of favour, dependent largely on fashion, passion and politics. This paper has considered what research tells us about two major aspects of learning – the visual dimension and the verbal links of theory building, both of which are widely acknowledged as extremely important for citizens of the future. These findings are then applied in one possible ideal curriculum for children and youth that would build from this research. It is worth considering that seeing our way into the future will take just such leaps as those suggested here. Already many features of learning proposed here are at work in organisations of post-industrial societies: project-based product development, high valuation on people and their multiple and creative talents as a major resource and greater coordination of horizontal, rather than hierarchical, personnel structures. Most critical to achieving any of these features to a significant extent within education institutions is distributed responsibility that results from engaging human, informational and spatial resources within an integrative ecology of learning environments that moves well beyond the class room (see Bentley, 1998; Hargreaves, 1994; Mulgan, 1997).

Acknowledgement

The author wishes to acknowledge the research support of The Spencer Foundation, General Electric Fund, National Center for Research on the Gifted and Talented and Carnegie Foundation for the Advancement of Teaching towards the research upon which part of this paper are based.

Notes

* Shirley Brice Heath is at Stanford University, Stanford, California.
Preparation of this article was partially supported under the Javits Acts Program (Grant No. R206R50001) as administered by the Office of Educational Research and Improvement, US Department of Education. The opinions expressed here do not reflect the positions or policies of the Office of Educational Research and Improvement or the US Department of Education.
† Originally published in: *Cambridge Journal of Education* 30: 1, 121–132.

References

Ainley, P., Cohen, P, Hey, V. and Wengraf, T. (1999) *Studies in Learning Regeneration* (Dagenham, University of East London).

Astington, J.W. and Olson, D.R. (1995) The cognitive revolution in children's understanding of mind, *Human Development*, 38, pp. 179–189.

Bentley, T. (1998) *Learning Beyond the Classroom* (London, Routledge).

Bilmes, J. (1997) Being interrupted, *Language in Society*, 26, pp. 507–532.

Bruner, J. (1990) *Acts of Meaning* (Cambridge, MA, Harvard University Press).

Chao, L.L. and Martin, A. (1999) Cortical regions associated with perceiving, naming, and knowing about colors, *Journal of Cognitive Neuroscience*, 11(1), pp. 25–35.

Film Education Working Group (1999) *Making Movies Matter* (London, British Film Institute).

Fleck, L. (1935) *Genesis and Development of a Scientific Fact* (Chicago, IL, University of Chicago Press) [reprinted 1979].

Greeno, J. and MMAP (1997) Theories and practices of thinking and learning to think, *American Journal of Education*, 106(1), pp. 85–126.

Hargreaves, D. (1994) *The Mosaic of Learning: schools and teachers for the next century* (London, Demos).

Heath, S.B. (1999) Dimensions of language development: lessons from older children, in: A. Masten (ed.) *Minnesota Symposia on Child Psychology*, Vol. 29, *Cultural Processes in Child Development* (Mahweh, NJ, Lawrence Erlbaum).

Heath, S.B. and Langman, J. (1994) Shared teaching and the register of coaching, in: D. Biber and E. Finegan (eds) *Sociolinguistic Perspectives on Register* (Oxford, Oxford University Press).

Heath, S.B. and Roach, A. (1999) Imaginative actuality: learning in the arts during the nonschool hours, in: *Champions of Change: The impact of the arts on learning* (Washington, DC, President's Committee on the Arts and Humanities).

Kress, G. (1997) *Before Writing: rethinking the paths to literacy* (New York, NY, Routledge).

Kress, G. and Van Leeuwen, T. (1996) *Reading Images: the grammar of visual design* (London, Routledge).

Kulick, D. (1992) *Language Shift and Cultural Reproduction* (New York, NY, Cambridge University Press).

Latour, B. and Woolgar, S. (1986) *Laboratory Life: the social construction of scientific facts*, 2nd edn (Princeton, NJ, Princeton University Press).

Longworth, N. (1999) *Making Lifelong Learning Work* (London, Kogan Page).

McQuade, D. and McQuade, C. (2000) *Seeing Writing* (New York, NY, Bedford).

Mulgan, G. (1997) *Connexity: how to live in a connected world* (Boston, MA, Harvard Business School Press).

Nelson, K. (ed.) (1989) *Narratives from the Crib* (Cambridge, MA, Harvard University Press).

Nelson, K. (1996) *Language in Cognitive Development: emergence of the mediated mind* (New York, NY, Cambridge University Press).

Ochs, E. and Jacoby, S. (1997) Down to the wire: the cultural clock of physicists and the discourse of consensus, *Language in Society*, 26, pp. 479–506.

Palincsar, A.S. and Brown, A.L. (1984) Reciprocal teaching of comprehension-fostering and comprehension-monitoring activities, *Cognition and Instruction*, 1, pp. 117–175.

President's Committee on the Arts and Humanities (1999) *Champions of Change: the impact of the arts on learning* (Washington, DC, President's Committee on the Arts and Humanities).

Ranson, S. (1994) *Towards the Learning Society* (London, Cassell).

Robinson, K. (1999) *All our Futures: creativity, culture and education* (London, NACCCE).

Schoenfeld, A.H. (1985) *Mathematical Problem Solving* (New York, NY, Academic Press).

Scribner, S. and Cole, M. (1981) *The Psychology of Literacy* (Cambridge, Cambridge University Press).

Soep, E. (1996) An art in itself: youth development through critique, *New Designs for Youth Development*, 12(4), pp. 42–46.

Szymanski, M.H. (1999) Re-engaging and dis-engaging talk in activity, *Language in Society*, 28, pp. 1–24.

Wellman, H.M. (1990) *The Child's Theory of Mind* (Cambridge, MA, Bradford Books/MIT).

Worthman, C. (1999) Different eyes: imagery, interaction, and literacy development at Teenstreet, PhD dissertation, University of Illinois at Chicago.

Zeki, S. (1998) Parallel processing, asynchronous perception and a distributed system of consciousness in vision, *The Neuroscientist*, 4, pp. 365–372.

Zeki, S. (1999) Art and the brain, *Journal of Consciousness Studies*, 6/7, pp. 76–96.

18 Pupil participation and pupil perspective

'Carving a new order of experience'

*Jean Rudduck and Julia Flutter**[*†]*

Introduction

This paper explores four related observations that stem from our work on pupil participation and perspective.

- In a climate that respects the market and the consumer it is strange that pupils in school have not been seen as consumers worth consulting. We need to understand more about why we haven't taken account of the views of pupils and why the situation is now beginning to change.
- In our efforts at 'school improvement' we need to tune into what pupils can tell us about their experiences and what they think will make a difference to their commitment to learning and, in turn, to their progress and achievement. We should recognise, however, that there are difficulties in directly eliciting pupils' views of some aspects of schooling; for instance, their views of 'the curriculum'. Pupils are often ready to comment directly on 'bits and pieces' of the curriculum – content that does or does not engage them, for instance – but they have no basis for comparing the present with any earlier version of 'the curriculum' nor, usually, any systematic sense of curriculum possibilities. They may say that they would like more group work or more opportunities to use their own ideas, but for the most part pupils have little overall sense of how differently learning *might* be structured and handled and what different values alternative approaches might represent. However, there is a lot in what they say *incidentally* about particular lessons that we can recognise, and use, as a commentary on the curriculum and on the assumptions that underpin it.
- In our experience pupils do not have much to say about the curriculum as Young (1999, p. 463) defines it: 'the way knowledge is selected and organised into subjects and fields for educational purposes'. Rather, they talk about forms of teaching and learning that they find challenging or limiting and, importantly, about what we have called (Rudduck *et al.*, 1996) the *conditions of learning* in school; how regimes and relationships shape their sense of status as individual learners and as members of the community and, consequently, affect their sense of commitment to learning in school.
- We could do more to help pupils develop a language for talking about learning

and about themselves as learners so that they feel that it is legitimate for them actively to contribute to discussions about schoolwork with teachers and with each other.

Pupil perspective and pupil participation

Children's rights

In order to understand attitudes to pupil participation and pupil voice we have to look briefly at the progress of the children's rights movement. Children's rights have mainly, but not exclusively, been argued for by adults on behalf of pupils where as 'pupil participation and perspective' suggests a stronger input by pupils themselves and a readiness among adults to hear and to take seriously what they have to say. We also need to see in what arenas – social and welfare and/or education – the debates have been pursued.

The children's rights movement has 'a rich and substantial heritage' (Franklin and Franklin, 1996, p. 96). Activity has been high profile at different times and for different reasons but because, Proteus-like, the movement has changed its concerns and its constituencies, its impact has not been cumulative. The movement has been most at risk from those who hold traditional views of the place of the child in school and in society.

The first formal Declaration of the Rights of the Child in 1924 focused on support for children who lost families and homes in the 1914–1918 war; the next Declaration came 35 years later. The main concerns of such initiatives were conditions *outside* school but there have been some attempts to focus directly on young people's experiences *in school*. In the early 1970s there were two initiatives worth mentioning in this brief sketch, one taken by young people themselves. In autumn 1972 the outcome of a national conference for the National Union of School Students (NUSS, a group formed, for a short time only, within the NUS) was a policy statement which, according to Wagg (1996, p. 14) 'must rank as one of the most uncompromising and idealistic statements of liberation philosophy ever seen in British educational politics'. What is interesting, as we suggested above, is that pupils themselves focus more on aspects of school organisation than they do on curriculum. The document called for:

- The speedy abolition of corporal punishment and the prefect system, and ... an increase of student responsibility and self discipline in schools.
- All forms of discipline to be under the control of a school committee and all school rules to be published.
- The abolition of compulsory uniform..., students having the right to determine their own appearance at school.
- Free movement in and out of the school grounds and buildings during break, lunch time and free periods.
- School students of all ages to have a 'Common Room' and to have facilities of relaxation similar to those enjoyed by teachers and sixth-formers.

(in Wagg, 1996, pp. 14–15; there were 27 items in all)

It is interesting to see which proposals have been acted on and which still reflect the concerns of pupils in the 1990s.

Three years later Lawrence Stenhouse, director of the controversial Humanities Curriculum Project, drew up a statement of the 'demands' that pupils should be able to make of the school and the expectations that they could justifiably hold of it. The work was commissioned by the then Schools Council, but the Council refused to give the principles its imprimatur and it was published not by the Council but by the author some years later (Stenhouse, 1983). These are some of the items that Stenhouse thought would make a difference to young people's experience of school; they are similar in focus and spirit to those of the NUSS document:

Pupils have a right to demand:

- That the school shall treat them impartially and with respect as persons.
- That the school's aim and purposes shall be communicated to them openly, and discussed with them as the need arises.
- That the procedures and organisational arrangements of the school should be capable of rational justification and that the grounds of them should be available to them.

Pupils have a right to expect:

- That the school will offer them impartial counsel on academic matters, and if they desire it, with respect to personal problems.
- That the school will make unabated efforts to provide them with the basic skills necessary for living an autonomous life in our society.
- That the school will do its best to make available to them the major public traditions in knowledge, arts, crafts and sports, which form the basis of a rich life in an advanced society.
- That the school will enable them to achieve some understanding of our society as it stands and that it will equip them to criticise social policy and contribute to the improvement of society.

The activities of the early 1970s, characterised by Franklin and Franklin (1996, p. 96) as the struggle for 'libertarian participation rights', took schools as the arena for action and the discourse was essentially about empowering students. The International Year of the Child in 1979, according to Franklin and Franklin, re-centred the children's rights movement on child protection and relocated it in the social and welfare arena. It was the United Nations Convention on the Rights of the Child in 1989 that brought the issues of protection and participation together: the right of young people to talk about their experiences and be heard and to express a view about actions that might be taken in relation to them, was seen as a basis for protection. According to Freeman (1996, p. 36) this was 'the first convention to state that children have a right to "have a say" in processes affecting their lives'. It proposed that 'the child who is capable of forming his or her own views' should be able to 'express those views freely' in all matters affecting him or her, 'the views of the child being given due weight in accordance with their age and maturity' (see Freeman, 1996, p. 36). Freeman comments:

> The right enunciated here is significant not only for what it says, but because it recognises the child as a full human being with integrity and personality and the ability to participate freely in society. The views of children are to count (in relation to) decisions ranging from education to environment, from social security to secure accommodation, from transport to television.
>
> (1996, p. 37)

Winter and Connolly (1996, p. 40) remained sceptical, saying that the right to express an opinion was 'largely conned to social services intervention 'and could be overthrown by appeal to adult judgement on the grounds of 'acting in the best interests of the child'. And Lansdown (1994, p. 37) commented, wryly, that despite the national rhetoric of pupil voice there was no attempt to elicit the views of pupils 'about testing and the National Curriculum ... and how schools are run'.

Franklin and Franklin summed up the situation in the mid 1990s in this way:

> The UN Convention ... has offered a rallying point ... it also offers a programme of proposals designed to empower children and young people. The future of children's rights ... is uncertain in the current political climate with its emphasis on retreating from any progressive policy. But the hope must surely be that in ... the next phase, children will be the key political actors, seeking to establish their rights to protection but also their rights to participate in a range of settings which extend beyond the social and welfare arenas.... The future is open.
>
> (1996, p. 111)

We shall see if their optimism is well founded.

Constraints on the development of pupil participation and perspective

Progressivism and politics

The children's rights movement has been criticised for being tarred with the brush of progressivism – as offering young people rights without responsibility; part of the weaponry was the perceived contribution of progressive and child-centred practices to the lowering of educational standards. Hodgkin confirms the force of this perspective: '...the phrase "child-centred" has negative connotations. It has become associated with laissez-faire forms of education which ... (it is said) failed children, neither equipping them with the basic skills nor giving them a confident approach to learning' (Hodgkin, 1998, p. 11). Offering children a voice was seen, according to Wagg (1996, p. 17), as part of the leftist agenda that promoted such things as 'anti-racism, anti-sexism and "peace studies"', while traditional values and images of children were being sidelined.

It seems that governments have not seen children's rights as a vote winner. The caution of central policy makers is evidenced by Franklin and Franklin (1996, p. 103) who claim that 'when the Polish government initially suggested a Convention on Children's Rights in 1979, the British Government suggested that it was unnecessary'. And ten years later, according to Lansdown (1994, p. 37), the government was slow to endorse the recommendations of the Convention, with the then Department of Education and Science (DES) claiming that it already 'fully complied with the Convention and that there was therefore no action required to achieve compliance'. The terms of the Convention were in fact ratified in 1991, but as Franklin and Franklin (1996, p. 103) observe, 'the word should not be mistaken for the deed' for the principles were to some extent in conflict with the image of the supremacy of the family that the Tory party, then in power, was projecting: the 'emphasis on children's rights does, by default, begin to undermine the traditional familial relationship between parent and child' (Winter and Connolly, 1996, p. 36).

Ideologies of childhood

There is a legacy of public perception of childhood that has made it difficult, until recently, for people to take seriously the idea of encouraging young people to contribute to debates about things that affect them, both in and out of school. Even the 1989 Convention elicited familiar counter arguments: according to Lansdown (1994, p. 42), children were portrayed as 'lacking morality, as being out of control and lacking the experience on which to draw for effective participation'.

Freeman (1983, p. 8) reminds us that 'childhood' is a social construct. In the tenth century, he says, 'artists were unable to depict a child except as a man (*sic*) on a smaller scale' and the concept was 'invented' as a distinct period in about the seventeenth century by the upper classes 'who alone had the time and money' to support it; later, the trend 'diffused downwards through society' (Prout and James, 1997, p. 17). When 'young people' were given a form of attire that marked them out as children and that set them apart from adults, childhood became associated with ideas of innocence or natural waywardness and, consequently, with the need for formalised induction and discipline.

The most enduring assumption, and one that has shaped policy and practice in many aspects of life, has been that childhood is about dependency; what Gerald Grace (1995, p. 202) calls 'the ideology of immaturity'. Hart (1992, p. 8; cited by Holden and Clough, 1998, p. 27) saw children as 'the most photographed and the least listened to members of society'; a character in an Anthony Powell novel (quoted in Silver and Silver, 1997, p. 5) described pupils as 'uneasy, stranded beings'. And Oakley (1994, p. 23), following the sociologist Ronald Frankenburg, comments on 'the derogatory tone' of the term 'adolescence' which perpetuates the idea that teenagers, rather than being actors in their own right, are still 'people who are *becoming* adults'.

Outside school, as James and Prout (1997, p. xiv) have said, 'the conception of children as … inadequately socialised future adults, still retains a powerful hold on the social, political, cultural and economic agenda'. Morrow and others have demonstrated the selective visibility of young people in relation, for instance, to surveys of domestic labour where:

> children (are rarely mentioned) as sources of assistance in their homes ... except to a minimal extent in the literature on (girls') socialisation where such work is seen entirely as role rehearsal for future adulthood and not intrinsically useful or valuable in any way.
>
> (Morrow, 1994, p. 134)

James and Prout (1997, p. xv) offer further evidence: they mention six problems concerning the visibility of children which were highlighted in a document presented to the UN World Summit on Social Development by The Save the Children Fund:

> a failure to collect child specific information; lack of recognition of children's productive contribution; no participation of children in decision-making; the use of an inappropriate 'standard model of childhood'; the pursuit of adult interests in ways which render children passive; and lack of attention to gender and generational relationships.

In the 1980s Freeman, professor of English Law, offered a swingeing critique of the status of children in our society, pointing to the anomalies and inconsistencies that the system has constructed: 'Children have not been accorded either dignity or respect. They have been reified, denied the status of participants in the social system, labelled as a problem population...' (Freeman, 1987, quoted in Davie, 1993, p. 253).

It is time to review our notions of childhood and take account of recent work in sociology which argues that 'childhood should be regarded as a part of society and culture rather than a precursor to it; and that children should be seen as already social actors not beings in the process of becoming such' (James and Prout, 1997, p. ix). In such a framework, the idea of pupil participation and pupil perspective may be more acceptable than it has been in the past.

Pupil participation and pupil voice: its legitimacy in the 1990s

Although bruised by association with 'progressivism' and in tension with traditional notions of the child as dependent on the family and the school for socialisation into adulthood, the issue of pupil participation survives. What is giving it legitimacy at the moment?

The closely observed school studies published by Hargreaves (1967) and Lacey (1970), at a time when pupil participation issues were highly controversial, 'gave a powerful impetus to interest in children's views of their everyday life' (Prout and James, 1997, p. 19). Since then there has been a succession of studies which have attempted to highlight the importance of seeing school from the pupils' perspective. Such studies have helped to keep the issue alive. And although the force of the United Nations Convention has been relatively slight in mainstream education, it is there to be invoked as an additional source of legitimacy.

However, it is the school improvement movement that has provided the most striking opportunity for teachers, researchers and policy makers to work on a common agenda of concern and it is in this context that the issue of pupil participation and voice is being most obviously addressed.

The school improvement movement

Lateral security is provided by trends in other countries where researchers, over the last decade, have been asking some pointed questions. In the USA, Erickson and Schultz (1992, p. 476, quoted by Levin, 1995, p. 17) point out that 'virtually no research has been done that places student experience at the centre of attention'. In Canada, Fullan (1991, p. 170) has asked, in relation to school reform: 'What would happen if we treated the student as someone whose opinion mattered…?'. In Sweden, Andersson (1995, p. 5) has said that 'politicians' who decide about school reforms and the teachers who run the classrooms seldom ask how the students themselves perceive their school'. Levin (1995, p. 17), from Canada, notes that while the literature on school-based management 'advocates more important roles for teachers and parents … students are usually omitted from the discussion'. And Nieto (1994, pp. 395–396), from the USA, brings the issue of pupil perspective firmly into the school improvement frame: 'One way to begin the process of changing school policies is to listen to students' views about them; however, research that focuses on student voice is relatively recent and scarce.' She points out that pupils' perspectives have, for the most part, been missing 'in discussions concerning strategies for confronting educational problems' and she also says, importantly, that 'the voices of students are rarely heard in the debates about school failure and success' (p. 396). This view is echoed by Suzanne Soo Hoo (1993, p. 392) who says: 'Traditionally, students have been overlooked as valuable resources in the restructuring of schools'. Nieto adds a cautionary note, explaining that a focus on students 'is not meant to suggest that their ideas should be the final and conclusive word in how schools need to change'; to accept their words as the sole guide in school improvement is 'to accept a romantic view of students that is just as partial and condescending as excluding them completely from the discussions' (Nieto, 1994, p. 398).

Patricia Phelan *et al.* (1992, p. 696), also from North America, argue that it is important to give attention to students' views of things that affect their learning, not so much factors outside school but those in school that teachers and policy makers have some power to change. And in the UK we, along with other researchers, have argued that pupils are our *'expert witnesses'* in the process of school improvement (Rudduck, 1999a). This position, especially since it is commanding so much support from teachers, seems to be one that does not offer the kind of threat that derailed the movement in earlier years.

Pupils *are* observant and have a rich but often untapped understanding of processes and events; ironically, they often use their insights to devise strategies for avoiding learning, a practice which, over time, can be destructive of their progress. We need to find ways of harnessing pupils' insight in support of their learning. Pupils' accounts of their experiences of being a learner in school can lead to changes that enable pupils to feel a stronger sense of commitment to the school and to the task of learning; and commitment can lead to enhanced effort and enhanced levels of attainment. But what is our motivation? Are we 'using' pupils to serve the narrow ends of a grades-obsessed society rather than 'empowering' them by offering them greater agency in their schools?

Citizenship education

Young argues (1999, p. 463) that the curriculum is 'a way of asking questions about how ideas about knowledge and learning are linked to particular educational purposes and more broadly to ideas about society and the kind of citizens and parents we want our young people to become'. His observations are timely given the resurgence of interest in citizenship education and its potential for endorsing the idea of pupil participation and pupil perspective in school.

The recent Report of the Government's Advisory Group, *Education for Citizenship and the Teaching of Democracy in Schools*, argues the need for citizenship education to be part of the formal curriculum.

> We unanimously advise the Secretary of State that citizenship and the teaching of democracy ... is so important both for schools and the life of the nation that there must be a statutory requirement for schools to ensure that it is part of the entitlement of all pupils.
>
> (1998, p. 7)

The most challenging, and easily glossed over, dimension is the need for pupils to learn about citizenship in a structure that offers them *experience* of the principles of citizenship. The benefits of citizenship education, the Report says, will be to empower pupils to participate effectively 'in *society*' and 'in *the state*', as 'active, informed, critical and responsible citizens' (p. 9; emphasis added), but it doesn't say '*and in the school*'. Harold Dent (1930, p. 15), 70 years ago, believed that every school could offer young people 'a developed and sane comprehension of how the affairs of a community are managed'; but, he said, 'pupils will learn not by talking about civics – a futile process – but by living civics' (see Rudduck, 1999b). This view is echoed in the nineties by Hodgkin (1998, p. 11): 'Democracy ... is not something which is "taught", it is something which is practised'.

The next step is to build more opportunities for pupil participation and pupil voice into the fabric of the school's structure. But it takes time and very careful preparation to build a climate in which both teachers and pupils feel comfortable working together on a constructive review of aspects of teaching, learning and schooling. Many schools may rely on their school council but we know that these only work well if they are the centre – and symbol of – school-wide democratic practice. If the school is not ready for pupil participation then a school council can become a way of formalising and channelling students' criticisms; an exercise in damage limitation rather than an opportunity for constructive consultation. And the agenda of schools councils often do not roam far outside the charmed circle of lockers, dinners and uniform.

We should not fudge the issue by taking pupil performance in tests and examinations as proxy for school improvement but accept the simple logic that school improvement may, after all, be about *improving schools*, their organisational structures, regimes and relationships; in short, 'the conditions of learning'. This, after all, is what the pupils tell us. The changes we are talking about 'will not happen by accident, good will or establishing ad hoc projects. They require new structures, new activities, and a rethinking of the internal workings of each institution...' (Watson and Fullan, 1992, p. 219, quoted by Fullan, 1993, p. 96).

Pupils and the curriculum

As far as pupils are concerned, it is not evident that we have learned the lessons of the curriculum development movement of the 1970s. Two things became clear (see Rudduck, 1991). First, the concept of 'relevance' was invoked to persuade us that the content of the curriculum would appeal to pupils but it was often an adult view rather than a pupil view of what was meaningful for young people. Second, there was little attempt to discuss with pupils why changes to content and pedagogy were being made. Teachers went on training courses that justified and helped them to cope with the break from traditional ways of working; pupils had no such support and they could respond by using their collective power as a class to resist or subvert the innovation. An alternative to imposed change through the authority of the teacher is to explore the need for change with the pupils themselves – what Ted Aoki (1984) called 'a communal venturing forth'; the discussion of purpose, he said, was a precondition of working effectively together. In the same spirit, Stenhouse saw 'standards' not as benchmarks imposed from 'outside and up there', but as criteria developed and shared by the working group for judging what counts as quality in their work together (see Rudduck, 1997; Stenhouse, 1967).

Aoki and Stenhouse were writing about opportunities for consultation on aspects of curriculum work in the 1960s to 1980s. But what about in the 1990s? Meighan (1988, pp. 36–38) has argued that even within the framework of a National Curriculum there *are* spaces for pupils to have an input. He distinguishes between a 'consultative curriculum', a 'negotiated curriculum' and a 'democratic curriculum'. A consultative curriculum, he says, is based on an imposed programme, but regular opportunities for learners to be consulted are built in. Feedback is reflected upon by the teacher and modifications may be proposed. In the negotiated curriculum, 'the degree of power sharing increases': what emerges 'is an agreed contract ... as to the nature of the course of study to be undertaken'. The negotiation 'constitutes an attempt to link the concerns and consciousness of the learners with the world of systematic knowledge and learning'. Finally, there is the democratic curriculum, 'where a group of learners write, implement and review their own curriculum, starting out with a blank piece of paper'. The challenge is to identify opportunities for participation, at the consultative level at least, within the framework of the National Curriculum.

What lies behind Meighan's categorisation is an awareness that what matters to pupils is that they feel that they have a stake in school and are respected enough to be consulted. Teachers can often construct choices for pupils within most courses of study, but listening to what pupils have to say about the 'conditions of learning' in school is also important (see Rudduck et al., 1996). Our recent interviews with pupils in primary and secondary schools across the country (see Rudduck and Flutter, 1998; Flutter et al., 1998) confirm that pupils are interested in changing structures that cast them in a marginal role and limit their agency. Pupils of all ages ask for more autonomy, they want school to be fair and they want pupils, as individuals and as an institutional group, to be important members of the school community. Policy makers may think about school primarily in terms of lessons and formal learning, but for pupils school is a holistic experience: it is about lessons, it is about what happens between lessons and it is about the regimes that define who and what matter to the school.

From our interview data we were able to construct a model of the things that affect pupils' commitment to learning and their identity as learners (Figure 18.1). The regimes of school, which embody values operating through structures and relationships, shape pupils' attitudes to learning and their view of themselves as learners. The more that the regimes are changed to reflect the values that pupils call for (intellectual challenge, fairness, etc.), the stronger pupils' commitment to learning in school is likely to be.

When talking *directly about learning in the classroom*, as opposed to these overarching concerns, pupils also have a lot to tell us that is worth hearing. They can, for instance, explain which of their classmates they work well with in different

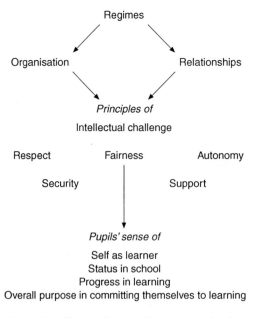

Figure 18.1 The conditions of learning in school.

subjects and which they don't like working with (and yet teachers rarely elicit and use this information). They are capable of working on the problem of noise in the classroom (pupils in a primary school came up with a set of voice levels for different situations, each colour coded for easy memorisation; they ranged from pale blue, for the quietest whisper to the teacher when others are working, to red, the playground voice). Pupils affirm the excitement of problem solving tasks and tasks that allow them to use their own ideas. They can often explain what levels of difficulty they find productive in different kinds of task.

We interviewed boys who were judged to be underperforming and they had a lot to say about changes that would help them. They told us that they *do* read but that the kind of reading that they like (technical journals, often using highly specialised vocabularies) is not valued in school. They said that they like to learn skills that can be used in everyday situations (such as map reading for family outings). Boys said that they prefer small challenges that can build up to something large (an essay, for instance, that is structured around a series of short, well-defined sections). They told us that they like to be active in class and that they like team work and work where oral contributions count and not just writing (see Rudduck and Flutter, 1998).

The pupils we interviewed seemed to be, although using very different words, as concerned as Young is about the curriculum as a product of the way in which knowledge is socially stratified. Their comments confirm Young's view that the curriculum is characterised by:

- the superiority of subject-based knowledge;
- the under-valuing of practical knowledge;
- the priority given to written as opposed to oral forms of presenting knowledge; and
- the superiority of knowledge acquired by individuals over that developed by groups of students working together.

(Young, 1999, p. 468)

Conclusion

Teachers are very aware of the difficulties of engaging all pupils in learning and know that schools have changed less in their deep structures in the last 20 or 30 years than young people have changed. As Nieto (1994, pp. 395–396) says: 'Educating students today is a far different and more complex proposition than it has been in the past'. We need to recognise the implications of this change. Out of school, many young people find themselves involved in complex relationships and situations, whether within the family or the peer group. Many carry tough responsibilities, balancing multiple roles and often finding themselves dealing with conflicting loyalties. In contrast, the structures of secondary schooling offer, on the whole, less responsibility and autonomy than many young people are accustomed to in their lives outside school, and less opportunity for learning-related tensions to be opened up and explored. This traditional exclusion of young people from the consultative process, this bracketing out of their voice, is founded upon an outdated view of childhood which fails to acknowledge children's capacity to reflect on issues affecting their lives.

We should recognise pupils' social maturity and experience by giving them responsibilities and opportunities to share in decision making. Hodgkin (1998, p. 11) recalls the lessons from industry where productivity went up as a consequence of worker participation schemes: good ideas were used, workers felt that they mattered and they understood more about the enterprise as a whole and their part in it. She concludes:

> The fact is that pupils themselves have a huge potential contribution to make, not as passive objects but as active players in the education system. Any (policy) concerning school standards will be seriously weakened if it fails to recognise the importance of that contribution.
>
> (Hodgkin, 1998, p. 11)

Policy makers are beginning to see the wisdom, or prudence, of taking account of pupils' experiences of learning (the QCA has recently commissioned work on pupil perspectives on assessment, on different curriculum subjects and on the National Curriculum; the Department for Education and Employment has emphasised the importance of the pupil perspective in many of the research projects that it is funding). Teachers up and down the country are finding ways of tuning in to pupils' accounts of learning in school, and they say that they find pupils insightful, measured and constructive. Consulting pupils need not be threatening, provided that teachers and policy makers genuinely see 'the pupils' world as worth becoming engaged with' (Sleeter and Grant, 1991, p. 67).

In conclusion, we cannot do much better than to urge readers to think about the two categories that Young offers us, Curriculum of the Past and Curriculum of the Future. Curriculum of the Future reflects the values of participation and perspective that feature so strongly in our own research on pupil voice. Young identifies the key features of the Curriculum of the Past as follows:

- it embodies a concept of knowledge and learning 'for its own sake';
- it is almost exclusively concerned with transmitting existing knowledge;
- it places a higher value on subject knowledge than on knowledge of the relationships between subjects;
- it assumes a hierarchy and a boundary between school and everyday knowledge, thereby creating the problem of the transferability of school knowledge to non-school contexts.

He invites us to contrast this with a Curriculum of the Future that expresses:

- a transformative concept of knowledge which emphasises its power to give learners a sense that they can act on the world;
- a focus on the creation of new knowledge as well as the transmission of existing knowledge;

- an emphasis on the interdependence of knowledge areas and on the relevance of school knowledge to everyday problems.

(Young, 1999, pp. 469–470)

Notes

* Jean Rudduck and Julia Flutter are at Homerton College, Cambridge, UK.
The quotation in the title is from the work of Maxine Greene.
† Originally published in: *Cambridge Journal of Education* 30: 1, 75–89.

References

Andersson, B.-E. (1995) Why am I in school?, paper presented at the *European Conference on Educational Research*, University of Bath, 14–17 September 1995.

Aoki, T. (1984) Towards a reconceptualisation of curriculum implementation, in: D. Hopkins and M. Wideen (eds) *Alternative Perspectives on School Improvement*, pp. 107–139 (Lewes, Falmer Press).

Davie, R. (1993) Listen to the child: a time for change, *The Psychologist*, June, pp. 252–257.

Dent, H. (1930) The aim: an educated democracy, *The Nineteenth Century and After*, CVII, pp. 10–16.

Erickson, F. and Schultz, J. (1992) Students' experience of the curriculum, in: P. Jackson (ed.) *Handbook of Research on Curriculum*, pp. 465–485 (New York, Macmillan).

Flutter, J., Kershner, R. and Rudduck, J. (1998) *Thinking about Learning, Talking about Learning* (Cambridge, Homerton Research Unit for Cambridgeshire LEA).

Franklin, A. and Franklin, B. (1996) Growing pains: the developing children's rights movement in the UK, in: J. Pilcher and S. Wagg (eds) *Thatcher's Children? Politics, childhood and society in the 1980s and 1990s*, pp. 94–113 (London, Falmer Press).

Freeman, M.D.A. (1983) *The Rights and the Wrongs of Children* (London, Frances Pinter).

Freeman, M.D.A. (1987) Taking children's rights seriously, *Children and Society*, 1(4), pp. 299–319.

Freeman, M.D.A. (1996) Children's education: a test case for best interests and autonomy, in: R. Davie and D. Galloway (eds) *Listening to Children in Education* (London, David Fulton).

Fullan, M. (1991) *The New Meaning of Educational Change* (New York, NY, Teachers' College Press).

Fullan, M. (1993) *Change Forces* (London, Falmer Press).

Grace, G. (1995) *School Leadership* (London, Falmer Press).

Hargreaves, D. (1967) *Social Relations in a Secondary School* (London, Routledge and Kegan Paul).

Hart, R. (1992) *Children's Participation: from tokenism to citizenship*, Innocenti Essays no. 4 (Florence, UNICEF International Child Development Centre).

Hodgkin, R. (1998) Partnership with pupils, *Children UK*, Summer.

Holden, C. and Clough, N. (1998) The child carried on the back does not know the length of the road, in: C. Holden and N. Clough (eds) *Children as Citizens: education for participation*, pp. 13–28 (London, Jessica Kingsley).

James, A. and Prout, A. (1997) Preface, in: A. James and A. Prout (eds) *Constructing and Reconstructing Childhood*, 2nd edn, pp. ix–xvii (London, Falmer Press).

Jonathan, R. (1990) Choice and control in education: parental rights, individual liberties and social justice, *British Journal of Educational Studies*, 37, pp. 321–338.

Lacey, C. (1970) *High town Grammar: the school as a social system* (Manchester, Manchester University Press).

Lansdown, G. (1994) Children's rights, in: B. Mayall (ed.) *Children's Childhoods: observed and experienced*, pp. 33–44 (London, Falmer Press).

Levin, B. (1995) Improving educational productivity through a focus on learners, *International Studies in Educational Administration*, 60, pp. 15–21.

Meighan, R. (1988) *Flexi-schooling. Education for tomorrow, starting yesterday* (Ticknall, Education Now Publishing Cooperative).

Morrow, V. (1994) Responsible children? Aspects of children's work and employment outside school in contemporary UK, in: B. Mayall (ed.) *Children's Childhoods: observed and experienced*, pp. 128–141 (London, Falmer Press).

Oakley, A. (1994) Women and children first and last: parallels and differences between children's and women's studies, in: B. Mayall (ed.) *Children's Childhoods: observed and experienced*, pp. 13–32 (London, Falmer Press).

Nieto, S. (1994) Lessons from students on creating a chance to dream, *Harvard Educational Review*, 64, pp. 392–426.

Phelan, P., Davidson, A.L. and Cao, H. (1992) Speaking up: students' perspectives on school, *Phi Delta Kappan*, 73, pp. 695–704.

Prout, A. and James A. (1997) A new paradigm for the sociology of childhood? Provenance, promise and problems, in: A. James and A. Prout (eds), *Constructing and Reconstructing Childhood*, pp. 7–33 (London, Falmer Press).

Rudduck, J. (1991) *Innovation and Change* (Milton Keynes, Open University Press).

Rudduck, J. (1997) Lawrence Stenhouse's vision of the teacher, the student and learning, talk given at the University of the Basque Country, Vitoria, May 1997.

Rudduck, J. (1999a) Teacher practice and the student voice, in: M. Lang, J. Olson, H. Hansen and W. Bunder (eds) *Changing Schools/Changing Practices: perspectives on educational reform and teacher professionalism*, pp. 41–54 (Louvain, Graant).

Rudduck, J. (1999b) 'Education for all', 'achievement for all' and pupils who are 'too good to drift' (the second Harold Dent memorial lecture), *Education Today*, 49(2), p. 3.

Rudduck, J. and Flutter, J. (1998) *The Dilemmas and Challenges of Year 8* (Cambridge, Homerton Research Unit for the Essex TEC).

Rudduck, J., Chaplain, R. and Wallace, G. (1996) *School Improvement: what can pupils tell us?* (London, David Fulton).

Silver, H. and Silver, P. (1997) *Students – changing roles, changing lives* (Buckingham, SRHE and Open University Press).

Sleeter, C.E. and Grant, C.A. (1991) Mapping terrains of power: student cultural knowledge versus classroom knowledge, in: C. Sleeter (ed.) *Empowerment through Multicultural Education* (Albany, NY, State University of New York Press).

Soo Hoo, S. (1993) Students as partners in research and restructuring schools, *The Educational Forum*, 57, pp. 386–393.

Stenhouse, L. (1967) *Culture and Education* (London, Nelson).

Stenhouse, L. (1983) The aims of the secondary school, in: L. Stenhouse (ed.) *Authority, Education and Emancipation*, pp. 153–155 (London, Heinemann Educational Books).

Wagg, S. (1996) 'Don't try to understand them': politics, childhood and the new education market, in: J. Pilcher and S. Wagg (eds) *Thatcher's Children? Politics, childhood and society in the 1980s and 1990s*, pp. 8–28 (London, Falmer Press).

Watson, N. and Fullan, M. (1992) Beyond school district university partnerships, in: M. Fullan and A. Hargreaves (eds) *Teacher Development and Educational Change*, pp. 213–242 (Lewes, Falmer Press).

Winter, K. and Connolly, P. (1996) 'Keeping it in the family': Thatcherism and the Children Act 1989, in: J. Pilcher and S. Wagg (eds) *Thatcher's Children? Politics, childhood and society in the 1980s and 1990s*, pp. 29–42 (London, Falmer Press).

Young, M. (1999) Knowledge, learning and the curriculum of the future, *British Educational Research Journal*, 25, pp. 463–477.

19 Identifying and responding to needs in education

*Nel Noddings**[*][†]

Care ethics and needs

An ethic of care is needs-based. When I am one-caring in a situation, I am attentive – I listen to whatever needs are expressed – and, if possible, I try to respond
positively (Noddings, 1984). Sometimes it is easy to do so. The one addressing me
may want only a shared moment, directions to an office on campus, or something
as simple as 'please pass the salt'. There are times, however, when I cannot respond
by meeting the expressed needs. I may not have the resources to do so, or I may
believe it is not my place to fill the need, or I may mistakenly assess the need as a
mere desire – even frivolous, or – in the worst case – I may judge the need to be
harmful or immoral. In all cases, however – even the last – I try to respond in a
way that will maintain the caring relation. It is not only the decision at hand that
must be justified but also a future that depends on what I do now. It is not enough
to make an ethically justified decision in a particular case such as firing an incom-
petent teacher or failing a lazy student. I must also consider how best to help the
person who feels hurt by my decision. An ethic of care is, in this sense, future-
oriented. Its work begins where an ethic of justice often ends.

When I am the cared-for in a situation, I hope my need will be heard and, if not
actually satisfied, at least treated with regard and understanding. My contribution
to the caring relation is to signal that the caring has been received. Without that
recognition, there is no caring relation, no matter how virtuous the carer may be in
trying to respond to me. The possible conflict between expressed and inferred
needs is apparent here. If my expressed needs are not treated positively, or at least
sensitively, I will likely not feel cared for. Attempts to care frequently misfire this
way. Would-be carers think they know what the cared-for needs and act on their
inferences in the name of caring.

As care ethicists, we do not ignore or discount rights, but we believe that rights
arise out of acknowledged needs (Noddings, 2002). There are times when people do
not want the rights that generous advocates would thrust on them; they want, instead,
to have their expressed needs heard and acknowledged. Internationally, powerful
nations have made, and continue to make, this mistake repeatedly.

How are needs to be assessed? When should we respond by trying to satisfy an
expressed need, and when should we gently try to dissuade the one who has
expressed it? As we move along in this discussion, it will become obvious that

assessing and responding to needs is one of the most difficult tasks faced by parents and teachers. When the student expresses one need and the teacher infers quite another for him or her, it can be hard to decide which need should be pursued. A teenager, for example, may express a need to learn a craft, while his parent infers a very different need for him – possibly (likely!) the need for solid preparation in academic mathematics. The underlying inferred need here is for the teenager to go to college, but the teen's own expressed need may be to become an apprentice in a field that does not require a traditional college education. A child may indicate a need to speak, while the teacher may believe that her real need is to listen. In general, teachers may infer a need for children to learn the standard school subjects, while children – through their behavior or verbalizations – express a need to learn how to live.

The distinction between expressed and inferred needs is important. An expressed need comes from the one expressing it, and it may be expressed in either words or behavior. An inferred need comes from someone other than the one said to have it. In the context of care ethics, an expressed need comes from the cared-for; an inferred need comes from one trying to care. Now, of course, there is almost always at least a low-level inference involved in interpreting an expressed need, but the sort of inferred needs in which I am interested here may be entirely independent from – even at odds with – particular expressed needs. A basic distinction has now been established, but we should refine it a bit.

Needs and wants

It is not unusual to start educational theorizing with an analysis of needs. Ralph Tyler (1949) started his influential book on curriculum and instruction with a discussion of learners' needs. Tyler says this about needs:

> Studies of the learner suggest educational objectives only when the information about the learner is compared with some desirable standards, some conception of acceptable norms, so that the difference between the present condition of the learner and the acceptable norm can be identified. This difference or gap is what is generally referred to as a need.
>
> (1949, p. 6)

Such needs are clearly inferred needs. Indeed, most of the needs identified by educators for learners may be classified as 'inferred' needs; that is, although they are said to be the 'needs of the learners', they are not needs expressed by the learners themselves.

Some needs are so nearly universal that we can safely infer them without their being expressed by any one individual, and Tyler recognizes these as a 'second type' of need. Basic or course-of-life needs (Braybrooke, 1987) are of this sort. Among such needs are food, water, shelter, safety, medical care and clothing. These, we might say, are expressed biologically. In addition to these, certain course-of-life needs arise in a particular culture. In liberal democracies, for example, the need for freedom to make life-directing choices is generally recognized.

Questions have been – and continue to be – raised about how these needs should be met and by whom, but, as we move beyond basic needs, we encounter further complications in the identification of needs. When we put together a curriculum, there is an assumption that it will somehow meet students' needs. Often in our day-to-day work, we forget about the connection between curriculum and needs or suppose it has already been established in a long-standing body of goals and objectives. All we need to do, then, is to tinker around the edges, adding things here, subtracting there, and perhaps forcing a given curriculum on students who have not studied it in the past and may have no expressed need for it. Most of the needs we infer for students – if only half-consciously – are inferred pre-actively; that is, they are inferred and written into the curriculum before we meet particular students.

Other inferred needs may be identified interactively. Working with a particular high school student, we may decide that she needs to learn how to add fractions or that she needs to learn punctuality. These are still inferred needs – needs not expressed by the student – even though they are identified with reference to a particular student. When we turn to the discussion of conflicting needs, we'll see that one possible response is to discard some inferred needs when they are challenged, but, clearly, we should not always do this. Insisting on every inferred need we have established is authoritarian. Giving way whenever such a need is challenged marks us as permissive. Neither style is characteristic of the best teachers or parents (Baumrind, 1995).

Before considering how to act on needs, however, we should consider one more distinction. Human beings are 'wanting' creatures (Brecher, 1998). Our wants seem sometimes to be limitless. If we recommend responding as positively as possible to expressed needs, are we committed to meeting every 'want' that is expressed? Not every want rises to the level of a need. It may help to consider the following criteria for deciding when a want should be recognized (or treated) as a need:

1   The want is fairly stable over a considerable period of time and/or it is intense.
2   The want is demonstrably connected to some desirable end or, at least, to one that is not harmful; further, the end is impossible or difficult to reach without the object wanted.
3   The want is in the power (within the means) of those addressed to grant it.
4   The person wanting is willing and able to contribute to the satisfaction of the want.

(Noddings, 2003, p. 61)

The last criterion suggests a form of partnership in satisfying wants. The child who wants a new bike and whose want satisfies the first three criteria, might, for example, be willing to help pay for it by saving money from his allowance. Usually, the criteria are used for cases like this – a person's desire for some material thing that may or may not be considered a need. However, with slightly refined thinking, the last criterion can also be applied to a situation familiar to educators. For example, most students want good grades; at least, most children start school eager to learn and hoping to get good grades. The student who wants good grades must be willing to work for them. But notice that, in the matter of grades, we rarely ask what the student is willing to contribute. More often, we arbitrarily set the conditions for an A, B, or passing grade. Some children just cannot meet the conditions, especially if the grades are to be awarded competitively. In failing to negotiate the conditions to meet this student want, we miss many opportunities to convert vague wants into felt needs. Instead, the vague want becomes a hopeless longing and the student gives up.

A word of caution here. A student's willingness to contribute to the satisfaction of a want or need should not be turned into a bribe. Parents often corrupt the process by making fulfillment of a want contingent on good behavior that is irrelevant to the end sought. This can be a double mistake because it offers a reward for behavior that should be an unconditional expectation in healthy family life (Kohn, 1993), and it disconnects the want or need from the effort required to satisfy it. In schools, for example, students are sometimes assured the passing grade they want in return for attending class and causing no trouble. Instead, honest teachers might present a list of relevant learning tasks students could choose to complete in order to obtain, say, a B. This approach encourages students to think about why they want a B and how hard they are willing to work for it. It also ensures that, if they complete the tasks adequately, their want will be satisfied. The much-wanted B will not depend solely on competitive test grades, or perhaps not on tests at all. Such assurance can be vitally important for youngsters who have had little success in their lives (Nichols and Thorkildsen, 1995; Michie, 1999). The testimony of many adults tells us that the failure to achieve badly wanted success in school can lead to lifelong fear of learning and of the authorities who try to teach (Shipler, 2004).

In addition to differentiating wants from needs and pre-active from interactive inferred needs, more should be said about expressed needs. Sometimes such needs are actually, verbally expressed. But many times, internal needs remain hidden – sometimes even from the one who has them. How are these different, then, from inferred needs? Educators certainly need to hypothesize and make inferences in trying to get at them. But when they are uncovered, they clearly belong to the one struggling to express them. Children may cover over the need to belong with a show of indifference, their need to be relieved of fear by avoiding any task that might induce the fear of failure, their need to succeed in school by pretending that success is unimportant to them. These hidden needs are expressed in ways that require skillful and sensitive interpretation.

Overwhelming needs

Many children today come to school (if they come at all) with overwhelming needs (Kozol, 1988, 1991; Quint, 1994; Anyon, 1997; Books, 1998). As if to confirm the point made above about children covering over their real needs, one 11-year-old said:

> Sometimes at school I just avoid teachers because they might feel sorry for me because they might see like bruises or something.... Sometimes I act bad so

they won't feel sorry for me, then if they see a bruise or something they would think I deserved it. I would rather have them think that than getting the principal or nurse.

(Quoted in Weis and Marusza, 1998, p. 38)

It is hard to imagine this youngster feeling a need to learn arithmetic when her basic needs for love and safety have not been met. She has not even had an opportunity to learn that decent, emotionally stable adults would never suppose that she deserved the beatings she has suffered. All of her energy is going into enduring, worrying, covering up and inviting new emotional wounds through the means she has chosen to cover up the physical ones. I am not arguing here for a rigid hierarchy of needs (Maslow, 1954). Often, basic needs and needs associated with self-actualization co-exist, and some deeply troubled children relieve their anxieties by immersing themselves in schoolwork. But more often, needy children simply cannot concentrate well enough to learn.

All kinds of real, pressing needs overwhelm the academic ones we so easily infer for schoolchildren. Homelessness, poverty, toothaches, faulty vision, violence, fear of rebuke or mockery, sick or missing parents, and feelings of worthlessness all get in the way of the learning deemed important by school people.

Then there is the foolishness actually taught in many classrooms, material presented without regard for either educational aims or students' expressed needs. David Shipler describes a sixth grade English lesson he observed. Students were given two sentences and asked to identify the complete subject and the simple subject in each. Here are the sentences:

1   Have you heard the new CD by Gloria Estefan?
2   Those reporters have been interviewing the mayor all day.

To the first, one child answered, 'CD'. 'No', said the teacher, 'Who are they talking to?' Student: 'You'. Teacher: 'Right'.

On the second, we hear the following interaction.

STUDENT: Those reporters.
TEACHER: Right. Damion, can you tell us what the simple subject is?
DAMION: Mayor.
TEACHER: No. Stan?
STAN: Reporters.
TEACHER: Because reporters is what we're focusing on.

(Shipler, 2004, p. 243)

Shipler assesses the teacher's explanations as 'terrible'. Terrible explanations, yes, but why did school people infer that children in a poor school (or any school) needed to learn this material? What need is met by teaching this topic? I'll come back to this in a discussion of negotiating and balancing needs.

Not only are some children overwhelmed by needs they bring with them from home, but teachers too often make things worse (Anyon, 1997). Shipler writes:

In every school, students could point to at least one or two teachers who stood out because they answered questions and showed the kids respect. More often, though, children felt deterred from asking. 'They give you a smart remark or a disrespectful answer,' said an eighth grade boy in Akron. His classmates added that they were made to feel stupid by teachers' tone of voice and body language.

(2004, p. 247)

The teachers to whom this boy referred ignored the felt need of students to ask questions and to receive a respectful response. But there are also teachers who do wonderful things with children whose expressed needs are both great and different from the needs inferred by curriculum makers (Charney, 1992; Meier, 1995; Deiro, 1996; Nieto, 1999; Bullough, 2001). The stories are many and heartening but, despite similarities, they are also quite different. Some sensitive teachers manage to teach the standard curriculum to students whom others would find impossible to teach. Some abandon the standard curriculum to teach lessons about life and relationships. Some act effectively as social workers. Some act almost as parents.

Qualitative researchers have given us vivid pictures of both wonderful and terrible teaching. However, we do not know enough about how teachers negotiate and balance needs. We know that it happens, but we know little about the decision mechanisms used by teachers, how alternative curricula are developed and justified, or how teachers persevere under the pressures of standardized testing. When teachers succeed in teaching the standard curriculum, we often are ignorant of the special conditions – such as mandatory involvement of parents – that made the success possible. Sometimes in such cases, a packaged curriculum is credited for the success only to be discredited a year or two later.

The standardization movement also raises deeper questions. If standard test scores rise, what real gain has been made? Some years ago in the US, high schools in many states instituted competency tests for graduation but, although teachers worked hard and with considerable success to get students through the tests, scores on the big national tests were unaffected. Moreover, there was some evidence that material learned for the competency tests was quickly forgotten. Might gains on the new tests produce similar results? Do we risk producing a generation of young adults whose attitude toward learning and work will be 'just tell me what to do'? We do not know the answers to these questions, but many of us fear that sacrificing expressed needs to inferred needs may indeed have a depressing effect on intrinsic motivation, creativity, initiative, and the desire for continued learning. Michael Fielding (2004) and Alfie Kohn (2004) – among many others – share my concern. In commenting on what is wrong with schools today, Kohn writes:

the way conformity is valued over curiosity and enforced with rewards and punishments, the way children are compelled to compete against one another, the way curriculum so often privileges skills over meaning, the way students are prevented from designing their own learning...

(2004, p. 570)

All of these comments relate directly to either the neglect of expressed needs or their distortion through the faulty methods instituted by policymakers. The original (sometimes intellectually valuable) expressed needs of students are converted into a mere, but keenly felt, need to pass tests.

Attending to needs

Overwhelming needs cannot be met by the usual processes of schooling. Children who are in pain, afraid, sick, or lost in worry cannot be expected to be interested in arithmetic or grammar. Many of us now believe that schools – particularly those in poor neighborhoods – should be full-service institutions. Medical and dental care, social services, childcare and parenting advice should be available on campus. People who are poor, perhaps homeless, without dependable transportation cannot afford to run all over town seeking such services, and often they don't know where to begin (Noddings, 2002).

Citing interviews with clinicians in Massachusetts, Shipler notes, 'Eating and learning, housing and health, a mother's early nurturing and a child's later brain function are connected' (2004, p. 219). Academic and social problems are interconnected (Shonkoff and Phillips, 2000), and we can't solve one without attending to others. 'That's why,' Shipler observes, 'Dr Barry Zuckerman hired attorneys to work with his staff at the Boston Medical Center's pediatrics department' (2004, p. 225). Lawyers and social workers can help families to get better housing, and better housing can prevent or relieve asthma, earaches, lead poisoning and accidents. Arguing along the same lines, Richard Rothstein (2002) suggests that attending to biological and social needs might return high dividends. Attending to dental needs, for example, should increase the possibility that children, no longer in pain, will be able to concentrate on schoolwork. 'In addition to health benefits, we might get a bigger bounce from such spending than from educational programs costing far more' (Rothstein, 2002, p. 20).

As things are today, schools are too often blamed for failing to work miracles. Like guilt-ridden flagellants, we urge ourselves on with slogans such as 'No excuses!', 'All children can learn!', 'High expectations!', and the like. After spending huge amounts on various programs of whole school reform, we are dismayed to find that academic achievement all too often is stagnant. And so it may remain unless we begin to think in an integrated fashion.

Instead of preparing teachers to educate the homeless, we should insist that no family be homeless. Instead of deploring the parenting skills of many adults, we should teach parenting in our schools. Instead of forcing academic algebra and geometry on all students, we should teach them how to avoid exploitation by check-cashing outfits that charge usurious rates (Shipler, 2004). As citizens, we should press for the day when no person who works full time at an honest job lives in poverty. And as educators, we should be ashamed to advertise education as the way out of poverty when, of course, the jobs that now pay poverty wages will still have to be done by someone. Education can be the way up for only some. A decent society should be concerned about all of its citizens.

Barbara Ehrenreich, living temporarily as a poor person and reporting on the experience, comments on the plight of poor people needing everything at once:

I need a job and an apartment, but to get a job I need an address and a phone number and to get an apartment it helps to have evidence of stable employment. The only plan I can come up with is to do everything at once …

(2001, p. 54)

Add to the problems of obtaining job, apartment and phone those of childcare, transportation, and suitable dress, and the needs really are overwhelming.

Rothstein (2002) urges us to increase experimental research in education to learn more about the effects of the total environment on children's achievement. In particular, cost–benefit analyses should be conducted to see whether non-educational interventions might be more effective than directly educational strategies. Qualitative research can both inspire such experiments and elaborate on their findings. Such research certainly can and should make the plight of the poor vivid and moving. At bottom, however, we know that, even if achievement scores are not thereby improved, a caring society should still be sure that everyone has decent housing, adequate childcare, medical insurance, and a living wage. We don't provide these things so that achievement scores will go up. We provide them because people need them, and caring people respond to the need.

Negotiating needs

If basic biological and social needs were met, it would be appropriate to give most of our attention to the educational problems over which educators have more direct control. Among these problems, balancing expressed and inferred needs is of central importance. Today we give little attention to this problem. The curriculum may undergo changes – usually to align it to standardized tests – but we rarely question whether the curriculum is persuasively connected to our larger aims and to the expressed needs of students.

'Why do we gotta study this stuff?' is a question that deserves an answer. It is a clear sign that the need we have inferred for students is not one that they are expressing or feeling. What need is expressed here? Almost certainly, it is a need for meaning. Students need to know how schooling is related to real life, how today's learning objective fits into their own interests and plans, and even whether there is any meaning to life itself. These questions – spoken or merely implied in the initial challenge – should induce deep and lively discussion. Addressing them is not a distraction or waste of time. On the contrary, such discussions are at the heart of what it means to educate. Caring teachers can help students to understand the process of socialization they are undergoing, the consequences of choices suggested by their expressed needs, and the sources to which they might turn for further knowledge. In addition to engaging in genuine education through these discussions, teachers who encourage them reap another reward – the ordinary lessons go better. Students will work on even trivial material for teachers they like and trust. Such teachers admit to their students that some subject matter is trivial and that, in a sense, we are all caught in a curriculum that offers both meaning and nonsense. The teacher's message is that we'll get through the nonsense together and work eagerly toward the construction of personal and collective meaning.

Too often, conscientious teachers have tried to come up with convincing answers that connect the lesson's objective to a practical problem, and sometimes this satisfies the student's question. But much that we teach does not have this kind of direct relevance, and some of it is simply a waste of intelligent effort. In such cases, the teacher's best answer might be, 'The powers that be say you and I have to do this'. Having to give this answer frequently should be a reason to engage in serious aims-talk. What does it mean to educate? What are the aims of education? What does the present task – the one challenged by our students – have to do with educating?

These are important educational questions, and we should spend time addressing them. The teacher who did the dreadful lesson on simple and complete subjects could not have asked herself these questions. This is not to say that they cannot be answered with respect to the topic. Although I can't think of a convincing answer and would drop the topic, reasonable people differ, and some might argue that it is significantly connected to a large aim of education. But if they could construct such an argument for the topic, they would surely suggest a better way of teaching it. Aims-talk is ultimately practical.

Researchers might try to find out how often teachers connect the day's learning objective to the aims of education and/or to the expressed needs of students. If, for example, teachers infer the need for students to learn standard English – as, say, a requirement for successful economic life in a liberal democracy – how do they go about meeting the need? Where, if at all, does identifying simple and complete subjects fit? What does such learning contribute to the aim of learning standard English? Why is it that instruction in grammar so often has little effect? And why do so many accomplished writers feel that much instruction in grammar is a waste of time? What might we do instead?

When inferred needs are challenged, the best response is to think through the whole problem carefully. What expressed need lies beneath the challenge? If the present task (supposedly designed to fill a need) is poorly connected to the major aims of education, it should be discarded. Perhaps we can substitute one that is clearly connected to both our aims and the expressed needs of our students. One can imagine, for example, a lesson in which the teacher starts by asking the students, 'Why would it be wrong to say, "Has you heard the new CD by Gloria Estefan?"' In some communities, the answer might be that there is nothing wrong with that way of asking the question, and this could lead to a lively discussion of language communities and where it is appropriate or inappropriate to use various forms. A lesson of this sort might involve history, politics, sociology, and psychology as well as language, but it would be guided by both a defensible educational aim and the expressed needs of students. A caring teacher, listening to students as they express the need to have their language respected, can show the needed respect and, at the same time, offer cogent reasons for students to learn standard forms. Certainly, if Shipler's teacher held competence in standard English as an aim, the lesson she conducted failed miserably. What was she trying to do?

Teachers and parents should be open to abandoning some inferred needs. Indeed, when we begin to think this way, much of the current curriculum seems trivial – a collection of unconnected fragments. In parenting, a lovely example of rethinking inferred needs can be found at the very end of Sinclair Lewis's *Babbitt*. Babbitt had always wanted his son to get a college degree; indeed, he and all the rest of the family had inferred that Ted needed that degree. But the boy confessed his desire to become a mechanic: 'I think I'd get to be a good inventor', he said (Lewis, 1922, p. 401). And Babbitt listens. Then he gives his enthusiastic consent, admitting: 'I've never done a single thing I've wanted to in my whole life!... Go ahead ... The world is yours!' (1922, p. 401).

Babbitt's comment on his own life is chilling. Joseph Campbell commented on it in one of his interviews with Bill Moyers. Imagine living such a life! Campbell's advice to the young: Follow your bliss! Can teachers help young people to do this and still get the education they 'need'? When we insist unreflectively on inferred needs and neglect expressed needs, we are likely to have unhappy, confused and resistant students.

But sometimes we contribute to unhappiness and cynicism by accepting expressed needs that seem to facilitate our work as teachers. For example, students who work hard for high grades please us. We know that some youngsters who are successful in achieving high grades and test scores are unhappy, and many have lost interest entirely in learning (Pope, 2001). Here our task may be to restore an inferred need – the need to engage in learning for its own sake – and de-emphasize the expressed need for high grades. After all, the need we educators infer – a real, vital engagement with learning – started out as an expressed need in our early childhood students. As schooling proceeds, too many students cease to express that need and substitute one that educators reward – the need to work hard for good grades. No wonder so many students are stressed and unhappy today. Researchers should give more attention to identifying and documenting the causes of increased depression and stress among the young. How widespread is this phenomenon? And what role do schools play in aggravating it?

Dewey once wrote: 'To find out what one is fitted to do and to secure an opportunity to do it is the key to happiness' (1916, p. 308). Do students hear that message today? My guess is that students are told repeatedly that the key to success (and, thereby, happiness) is to do well in school, go to college, and get a high-paying job. How often do they hear the story told over and over in biographies that the happiest, most successful people are almost always those who are doing what they really love? And some of these happy, successful people were not all that good at 'doing school'.

Today, in the name of equity, we force all children – regardless of interest or aptitude – into academic courses and then fight an uphill battle to motivate them to do things they do not want to do. Have we decided that it is impossible to create vital and relevant curricula around interests other that the academic? Are there no success stories that begin in vocational or highly specialized education? Because academic courses are often the only choice, many students drop out entirely. With excellent vocational training – chosen, not coerced – many more young people might be prepared for gainful employment that they would actually enjoy. In the past, children – too often children of color – were assigned to tracks considered lower than the revered academic. But if these tracks offered rich curricula and highly skilled teachers and if they could be freely chosen by any interested student, the stigma of the past could be lifted. Forcing everyone into one narrow and increasingly watered-down curriculum is hardly equitable.

A basic need for everyone – especially for people living in post-industrial liberal democracies – is to satisfy at least some personal interests. Our interests instigate and help us to form purposes. In discussing purposes, Dewey wrote:

> There is, I think, no point in the philosophy of progressive education which is sounder than its emphasis on the importance of the participation of the learner in the formation of the purposes which direct his activities in the learning process...
>
> (1938, p. 67)

That all legitimate interests and talents should be nurtured seems indisputable, but educators should not discard every inferred need that is challenged. Sometimes, after thinking things through critically, we may stand by the initial need. Preceding his remark on the importance of the learner's participation in the formation of purposes, Dewey said: 'Plato once defined a slave as the person who executes the purposes of another, and ... a person is also a slave who is enslaved to his own blind desires' (1938, p. 67).

Teachers and parents do sometimes know what is best. In the face of challenge, boredom, or overt antagonism, teachers must find a way to move toward the satisfaction of needs not yet expressed by students. To develop this theme fully would take a volume – perhaps several volumes. Suffice it to say here that the resolution requires critical thinking and dialogue directed to mutual understanding of both expressed and inferred needs. In this dialogue, caring teachers show that they are willing to rethink inferred needs, and students should be encouraged to criticize and re-evaluate their own interests, wants, and purposes. It is acceptable and understandable, for example, to want high marks, and good teachers are committed to helping in this quest. But what aims motivate this desire? What does the student want to learn, create, do, or be? It should not be enough simply to want high grades.

The need for this dialogue suggests that not every class session should be directed or dominated by a specific learning objective. Many significant class periods should be given to the development of care and trust, the search for connections among interests and aims, the identification of learning objectives (that may vary from student to student), and free gifts of intellectual material that students may pick up and use to satisfy their own needs. How often is this happening?

I have suggested here that educational researchers give more attention to the expressed needs of students, to how teachers try to balance expressed and inferred needs, and to how unsatisfied needs work against success in school. We are not going to overcome poverty and misery by a bootstrap operation in schools. We need to remind ourselves that conditions in the larger society need much improvement and also that the aims of education include far more than getting high grades and test scores. Continual reflection on aims should help us in the task of balancing expressed and inferred needs.

Notes

* Nel Noddings is at Stanford University, USA.
† Originally publishd in: *Cambridge Journal of Education* 35: 2, 147–159.

References

Anyon, J. (1997) *Ghetto schooling* (New York, Teachers College Press).

Baumrind, D. (1995) *Child maltreatment and optimal caregiving in social contexts* (New York, Garland).

Books, S. (ed.) (1998) *Invisible children in the society and its schools* (Mahwah, NJ, Lawrence Erlbaum).

Braybrooke, D. (1987) *Meeting needs* (Princeton, Princeton University Press).

Brecher, B. (1998) *Getting what you want?* (London, Routledge).

Bullough, R. V. Jr. (2000) *Life on the other side of the teacher's desk: stories of children at risk* (New York, Teachers College Press).

Charney, R. (1992) *Teaching children to care* (Greenfield, MA, Northeast Foundation for Children).

Deiro, J. (1996) *Teaching with heart* (Thousand Oaks, CA, Corwin Press).

Dewey, J. (1916) *Democracy and education* (New York, Macmillan).

Dewey, J. (1963) *Experience and education* (New York, Collier Books). (Original work published 1938.)

Ehrenreich, B. (2001) *Nickel and dimed* (New York, Metropolitan Books).

Fielding, M. (2004) Philosophy and the end of educational organization, paper presented to the Philosophy of Education Society of Great Britain, New College, Oxford.

Kohn, A. (1993) *Punished by rewards: the trouble with gold stars, incentive plans, A's praise and other bribes* (Boston: Houghton Mifflin).

Kohn, A. (2004) Test today, privatize tomorrow: using accountability to 'reform' schools to death, *Phi Delta Kappan*, April, 569–577.

Kozol, J. (1988) *Rachel and her children* (New York, Crown).

Kozol, J. (1991) *Savage inequalities* (New York, Crown).

Lewis, S. (1922) *Babbitt* (New York, Harcourt, Brace).

Maslow, A. (1954) *Motivation and personality* (New York, Harper & Row).

Meier, D. (1995) *The power of their ideas: lessons for America from a small school in Harlem* (Boston, Beacon Press).

Michie, G. (1999) *Holler if you hear me* (New York, Teachers College Press).

Mosteller, F. and Moynihan, D. P. (1972) A pathbreaking report, in: F. Mosteller and D. P. Moynihan (Eds) *On equal educational opportunity* (New York, Random House), 3–66.

Nicholls, J. B. and Thorkildsen, T. A. (1995) *Reasons for learning* (New York, Teachers College Press).

Nieto, S. (1999) *The light in their eyes: creating multicultural learning communities* (New York, Teachers College Press).

Noddings, N. (1984) *Caring: a feminine approach to ethics and moral education* (Berkeley, University of California Press).

Noddings, N. (2002) *Starting at home: caring and social policy* (Berkeley, University of California Press).

Noddings, N. (2003) *Happiness and education* (Cambridge, Cambridge University Press).

Pope, D. C. (2001) *'Doing school': how we are creating a generation of stressed out, materialistic, and miseducated students* (New Haven, Yale University Press).

Quint, S. (1994) *Schooling homeless children* (New York, Teachers College Press).

Rothstein, R. (2002) *Out of balance: our understanding of how schools affect society and how society affects schools* (Chicago, Spencer Foundation).

Shipler, D. K. (2004) *The working poor: invisible in America* (New York, Alfred A. Knopf).

Shonkoff, J. P. and Phillips, D. A. (eds) (2000) *From neurons to neighborhoods: the science of early childhood development* (Washington, DC, National Academy Press).

Tyler, R. W. (1949) *Basic principles of curriculum and instruction* (Chicago, University of Chicago Press).

Weis, L. and Marusza, J. (1998) Living with violence: white working-class girls and women talk, in: S. Books (ed.) *Invisible children in society and its schools* (Mahwah, NJ, Lawrence Erlbaum), 23–46.

20 A curriculum for the future

*Gunther Kress**[*][†]*

Introduction

In this paper I will briefly outline some thoughts on a curriculum for the future. I address the question of the present curriculum, largely inherited from the nineteenth century, the disintegration of the frames which had given it its shape and purposes and then move on to ask about the broad outline characteristics of curricula relevant for the near future. In particular, I suggest that the presently existing curriculum still assumes that it is educating young people into older dispositions, whereas the coming era demands an education for instability. I conclude with a brief sketch of how this might look in relation to a specific curriculum subject area, English.

In periods of relative social and economic stability it is possible to see the curriculum as a means for cultural reproduction: as a process whereby values, skills and knowledges are made available to enable the young to make themselves in the image of their culture. The period from the middle of the last century to the middle of this can be seen as one such period, despite the cataclysmic events that have characterised it. In important ways, the social mores, cultural values, forms of the economy and the social organisations of 1955 had more affinity with those of 1855 than they have with those of 1995. It is possible to see, with hindsight, that from about the mid 1950s on, the inevitable, constant, gradual changes which marked the preceding 100 years began to act together, producing change at an increasing pace, so that by the end of our millennium many of the significant, taken for granted features of that previous period are now (nearly) swept away, are under challenge or coming to be changed out of recognition.

'Reproduction' is no longer a plausible metaphor for institutional education and its curricula. When tomorrow is unlikely to be like today and when the day after tomorrow is definitely going to be unlike yesterday, curricular aims and guiding metaphors have to be reset. The metaphor that I have chosen for myself, for some time now (Kress, 1995), is that of 'design': curriculum as a design for the future. That then leaves the task of attempting to establish as securely as one might what the outlines of that future are likely to be like, in order to begin to think about the shapes of a curriculum for that future. What remains constant is the fundamental aim of all serious education: to provide those skills, knowledges, aptitudes and dispositions which would allow the young who are experiencing that curriculum to lead productive lives in the societies of their adult periods.

The agendas of education in the current period and in the near future

It is clear to any dispassionate bystander that institutional education is in deep crisis, and not only because politicians, media pundits and gurus of various sorts tell us that it is so. By and large, the curricula of the school in 'Western' societies – not all, not everywhere, but most – remain the curricula of the nineteenth century school. That curriculum had developed to serve the needs of the nineteenth century nation state – with its desire for a homogeneously conceived citizen for that state, a citizen who was 'French' or 'German' or 'British', and the need for a labour force and the professions – of the economy of that state. The school's task was to produce both and, by and large, it managed to perform that task well enough. This environment had provided strong framings of values and of know-ledges, framings which had become relatively invisible. Now, in the present period of radical instability, the former framings are becoming visible, particularly in the absence of new framings, for the moment at any rate.

What is clear is that the new circumstances demand a response: new goals and new curricula which are appropriate to these new goals. It is becoming possible now both to see the dissolution, the break-up, of the former framings and tenta-tively, hazily, the emergence of new configurations of frames. The latter are unlikely to be stable for a considerable period to come, but what there is may be useful as indicators of directions in which 'things' are moving. To show, con-cretely, the processes of the dissolution of former frames and the emergence of new framings, I will briefly consider an innocuous but real text, reproduced below. It fluttered through the letterbox of our house in North London early in June 1998.

In its less than 200 words it encapsulates most of the criterial features of the current environment for education and it exhibits the dissolution of the frames which had held institutional education, its values, knowledge, authority and pur-poses, in a relatively stable state for most of the preceding 100 years. To draw out just some of these frames, briefly and without detailed debate, there are: (a) the frame around the institution of education itself; (b) the frame around the site of education; (c) the frame around the time of education; (d) the frame around the educational audience; (e) the frame around educational knowledge; (f) the framing between education-as-work and education-as-pleasure; (g) the frame between state and market; (h) the frame around locations of authority. There may be others, but these will serve to make the points which I wish to make.

a   The frame which is dissolved here is that between one specific type of educa-tional institution, the university, and local government in the shape of its amenities department, 'the Play and Youth Service' of a local authority. The causes of this dissolution, as of all the others, are complex (and usually inter-connected with the others). This university is, I assume, responding to a number of factors: for instance a felt or expressed need to integrate itself more with the 'local community'. This itself has two market-driven origins, one being a kind of 'accountability' to the community in its guise as 'taxpayers'; the other being more directly linked to the market, namely a felt need to build

Islington Summer University

In partnership with Islington Play & Youth Service

1st June 98

Dear Parent/Guardian,

This summer Islington's Play & Youth Service in partnership with the University of North London are organising and running a Summer University. The programme will run from 17th to 21st and 24th to 28th August 98 inclusive.

The University is targeting two groups of young people:-

1. Those young people who are moving from Primary to Secondary school in September, (which is why you are in receipt of this letter.)
2. Those young people who are taking their GCSEs in spring 99.

The Venues:- University of North London, Holloway Road.
Islington Boat Club, Graham Street.
J.V.C. Centre, Arsenal Stadium, Avenell Road.
E.C.1. Music Project, White Cross Street.

All onsite courses are FREE, however at this point the programme has not been finalised but the following activities will definitely be included:-

Rap & Scratch courses
Dance
Maths GCSE revision
Womens football
Fabric painting
Canoeing
African dance & drumming
Making music through computers
Drama
Art
Vocals/singing classes
Sailing
Discussion groups
Music technology & recording skills

Computer courses, beginners through to introduction to the internet AND MANY MORE EXCITING COURSES

Please discuss with your child if she/he would like to attend. If they do please complete and return the attached form to ensure a programme and enrolment form are forwarded to you once the details have been finalised.

Yours sincerely

Steve Clarke

Steve Clarke

Figure 20.1 Islington Summer University.

its local clientele, to entrench itself in and to capture its local 'market'. This itself is a consequence of a decline in direct government support, which means that the university has to operate as an institution in and of the market.

b Until quite recently institutionalised education was tied to and identified with its 'own' geographical site, a campus, a building or sets of buildings. These buildings were dedicated educational buildings: for instance, they would (and still do to a large extent) stand empty in vacation time. Here the university has decided not only to locate its courses off site, but to choose sites (with one exception) associated with everyday and decidedly non-educational activities. In fact this shift is metaphorically/ideologically highly potent: it is a move from (sites of) education to (sites of) leisure; a change in relation between institution and community, from making the community 'come to you', to going out to the community.

c   These courses are offered outside the school year and the university term. It is thus a weakening of the temporal frame of education. As such the weakening of this frame can be seen as the extension both of the university and of the school year and as the extension of learning time as such (i.e. of organised/institutionally controlled time dedicated to education for young people). This is in line with current slogans about 'life-long' learning.

d   The offer made here by the Summer University abolishes the temporal/ developmental framings between the hitherto firmly bounded/framed sectors of education: between primary, secondary and tertiary education. The leaflet appeals to young people in their transitional period between primary and secondary school and equally to those in the latter years of secondary schooling. Inviting them to attend courses at a 'university' abolishes all these frames. Of course, this has its very real causes: again, notions of life-long learning, the need to develop an 'audience' and a market. Its effect is nevertheless to make a formerly stable system radically unstable and to make formerly fixed boundaries fluid.

e   Equally, the framings around what counts as educational knowledge are here unmade: for the university and its curricula as much as for the secondary (and even the primary) school. This blurs or abolishes quite decisively the boundary between knowledge sanctioned in educational institutions and the knowledge of the everyday. In effect, it undoes a boundary between sacred (or at least the 'revered') and profane (or at least everyday) forms of knowledge.

f   The dissolution of the frame around educational time proceeds under the banner of education-as-leisure, and in that it has a long tradition, a long antecedent, certainly of 20 or so years in the shape of hobby courses, etc. But the fact that this university is offering these courses will have a reciprocal effect on what the university does and will do: it is making a promise (of course already frequently repeated in the more recent marketing of universities – one university situated in London advertised itself, some while ago, as being only '40 minutes from London's exciting West End') that learning is fun, that the knowledge which it offers, is fun, that 'doing a course' at university is like leisure time activity more than like work time activity.

g   As mentioned, all or most of these are in some way related to changing relations between the state and the market. This is latently there in this university's appeal to a 'client base'; in the changed relation of work, leisure and pleasure. In this text it appears overtly in the statement that 'All onsite courses are FREE', an appeal which both invokes a prior period when education was free and a statement evoked by the present situation where it no longer is and where, as with other commodities, some educational commodities are offered for free as a marketing ploy.

h Lastly, the framing (location) of authority. The activities offered by the Islington Summer University are not just free, they are not obligatory: you attend
them if 'you would like to attend'. You, as an adult, are asked to 'please discuss
with your child'…; and 'if they do', you are asked to complete the form. This
is not the authority relation or the authority location of the traditional school
(or university, which until very recently stood *in loco parentis*. This is not the
authority which had supported the regulative discourse of Bernstein's schema).
Power has decidedly shifted to the learner, who is now conceived of as a con-
sumer/client and not, as before, as a 'pupil' or 'student'. The move to relations
of consumption is of course of one piece with the relations which properly
obtain in the market. Authority relations in the school as an institution of the
market are deeply different to those of the traditional school, which stood in
place of the state and its relation to its subjects (or citizens). If there is regulation here, its source of authority is not as before.

Several frames which are not mentioned, invoked or more or less directly
implied here are nevertheless causally involved: they are the frames of the globalisation of finance capital; the changing frames of transport, whether of physical
entities (commodities and people) or of information (though the latter is directly
mentioned); and the changing frames of a society being transformed willy-nilly
from a conception of a homogeneously monocultural society to a decisively pluri-
cultural one.

All of these are having the profoundest effects on what education can plausibly
be (as on what it can no longer plausibly be) and what new conceptions can, need
and should be developed. The demands of the nation state and of its economy had
provided an overarching frame of coherence through its authority and its needs.
This frame is becoming less available as a stable point of reference and is being
replaced by far less stable, less predictable contingencies and requirements. The
relative stabilities of the class societies of industrialised states, with their
economies founded on industrial mass production, are being replaced, or at the
very least overlaid, by the highly fluid arrangements of lifestyle groupings. The
demands generated in this new arrangement are diverse and the new curricula consequently have no immediately available, secure basis for broadly integrative principles of coherence.

If before the present period the education systems of industrial nations had the
task of educating a population for stability, the new arrangements seem to demand
an education for a period of fluidity, for instability. What are the features of an
education for instability? This of course touches decisively on the question of identity and its relations to pedagogy and knowledge.

In all this I have not mentioned the issue which for me is central, namely that
of the changing landscapes of representation and communication. It is this which
both has the most radically transformative effects on knowledge and ties in most
directly to the new forms of the economy. Associated with this are the new media
of communication and, in particular, a shift (paralleling all those already discussed) from the era of mass communication to the era of individuated communication, a shift from unidirectional communication, from a powerful source at the

centre to the mass, to multidirectional communication from many directions/locations, a shift from the 'passive audience' (however ideological that notion had always been) to the interactive audience. All these have direct and profound consequences on the plausible and the necessary forms of education for now and for the near future.

Education for instability

The changes in the environments in education are making new demands on education, demands to which institutional education, in its form as school or university, has barely begun to respond. The new demands are at bottom demands for a different kind of social subject. The social subject educated, in my somewhat pessimistic phrase, for an era of social and economic instability is deeply different to the social subject of the preceding era: a citizen/worker/professional who was educated toward the stabilities of well-defined citizenship or equally stable subjectivities as a participant in stable economies. There is of course a positive way of expressing 'instability' and a positive response to such demands, and that is to invoke notions such as creativity, innovativeness, adaptability, ease with difference and comfortableness with change. These will form the bedrock values in my own educational vision (in my idea of education for utopia).

In the meantime, however, the stable environmental arrangements of the former period have come asunder: the homologies between the purposes of the nation state and the values of the school, the needs of the economy and the forms of knowledge and pedagogic practices of the school and the values of the school and the values of the media, all these have come adrift. One means of assessing this is to look at 'lifeworlds': the manner in which socio-cultural groups arrange (or have arranged for them!) vastly webbed systems of practices, values, objects and meanings. To speak too generally, it is possible to say, nevertheless, that the sets of arrangements around specific forms of work provided by and characteristic of the economies of the Fordist era – tight boundaries of hierarchy, tightly classified, highly segmented and closely enforced work practices (whether of trade or profession) – were expressed in cultural terms as high valuations of well-understood traditions, high valuations of loyalty, dependability, expertise in a specific or even narrow range, and so on.

Work and its lifeworld, itself an effect of forms of the economy, produced 'leisure' – that time which was left over from work (for those whose work was defined by the formal economy; for those who were outside that, 'leisure' usually did not exist). The structuring of leisure was largely homologous with that of work, even if at times by a negation or inversion. But work also produced, in a not too highly mediated form, the structures of the school, as has been pointed out before, for instance in E.P. Thompson's definitive *The Making of the English Working Class*. Whether as the organisation of time in accordance with the rhythms of the working day, the structurings of authority relations (as relations to knowledge), the shape and content of the curriculum itself or in the inculcations of clear value systems, the school stood in a closely homologous relation to work and to the economy more broadly.

So what are the essential features of this world and how can a new curriculum hope to respond to them? Stability has been, or will be, replaced by instability. Locality will become 'virtual': knowledge, with the new ICTs, is or will be accessible anywhere. It no longer needs either the site of the school or of the library. The world of communication is multimodal, no longer reliant on language-as-speech or on language-as-writing alone. The social world is no longer monocultural; the economic world has moved from the era of mass production to the era of niche production, with its different requirements (innovative, changing, individuated), and to the world of an economy of services and information.

The curriculum which was serviceable for that former world and the social and material organisations and structures built around it will no longer suffice. What is required is a thoroughgoing review of what the features of this new world are likely to be and what curricular and pedagogic responses are likely to be possible and most useful. The curriculum of the most recent past, and still present in schools, had a particular orientation to knowledge and was marked by particular selections of knowledge. Knowledge was 'there', produced elsewhere, authoritative and to be acquired. Its presence in the curriculum was justified by its relevance in and for 'the world'. Science made available a specific take on the natural world, namely that that which was invisible in the world could be made visible in 'laws'; English provided access to that which was regarded as the aesthetically outstanding in the domain of literature, and much else besides; Mathematics and its allies showed that the world of disorder could be brought to order by high level abstraction and regularity. Art provided means of recording that which was judged salient via conventionalised representational practices. And so on.

Underpinning this curriculum were, of course, notions of social order which themselves appeared as givens in curriculum and in pedagogy: attitudes to authority and notions of individual agency (or the limitations on or of agency). And these notions appeared in theories and approaches to teaching and learning: teaching as transmission, learning as acquisition. In that structure learning was not a domain of individual creative agency; individual agency as work of acquisition, yes, individual agency as reshaping, no. 'To learn' was not supposed to mean 'to change': authority relations attempted to guarantee the unchanged replication of knowledge in learning. The link between the school subjects, on the one hand, and work and professions, on the other, was also clear: theoretical elaboration for those who went beyond the years of compulsory schooling, practical training for those whose trajectories would take them into the world of manual, physical labour.

Economies founded on services and information do not (necessarily) need the knowledge of the subjects of the older curriculum. Instead of attitudes and dispositions to fixed knowledge, both the economy of services and the economy of information demand the ability to design: to design objects (whether as texts or as commodity of any kind) and to design processes (whether in entertainment, in business or in education). The ability to design, an aptitude in using the resources available for making (whether the making of representations for communication or the making of objects for consumption) differs fundamentally from the aptitudes and dispositions previously needed, prized and rewarded.

'Design' rests on agency; it takes agency for granted, still as work, but no longer as acquisition but now definitely as 'shaping work'. In this, design proceeds on the basis of a full knowledge of the resources available to the designer and the capacity of the designer to assemble these materials into designs expressing her/his intentions and interests in relation to particular demands.

This suggests a very different curriculum, a very different pedagogy and a fundamentally different notion of learning. It sees the learner as fully agentive, as becoming fully aware of the potentials, capacities and affordances of the materials to be used in the designs. It sees design as the making of signs (whatever the materiality in which they appear: material/three-dimensional, spoken/temporal, written/-two-dimensional) whether in the science classroom, in English or in art. Of course, this is a fundamental realignment of the curriculum: a realignment from a curriculum focused on knowledge as a stable, even if complex, 'entity', to a curriculum focused on uses of knowledge-as-information in relation to specific domains of application.

'Design' as a central category of the school curriculum and as a goal of its purposes places the student-as-learner very differently to the place he or she occupied in the traditional curriculum. There competence in relation to the 'making' of knowledge was central, and 'learning' was seen in the light of that. Design makes the learner agentive in relation to her/his interests in a specific environment and in relation to the resources available for the production of that design. He or she is transformative, creative and innovative. Design asks for production of the new rather than replication of the old. Thus putting 'design' at the centre of the curriculum and of its purposes is to redefine the goal of education as the making of individual dispositions oriented towards innovation, creativity, transformation and change. In my view these are the dispositions which will be essential to meet the demands of the new forms of the economy and of the now culturally plural societies and the conditions of globalising capital. They are also, somewhat paradoxically, dispositions which would in any case recognise the real potentials of humans as always creative, always innovative, always transformative.

Let me make one last point here before I discuss, briefly and very generally, what this might look like in relation to a curriculum subject such as English. That point concerns the effects of globalisation of capital on the curriculum. The curriculum has always had a more or less direct relation to the economy. The globalisation of finance capital means that the conditions of labour are becoming globally uniform, and any curriculum has to be designed with that in view. If someone seeks work in a sector of the economy which has become globalised (say in working for a transnational company) then it is the conditions of the global economy which will make their demands on the curriculum. At the 'lower end' of the employment scale, the exporting and importing of jobs means that the conditions of and demands made of labour in any one locality on the globe in effect become the conditions and demands of labour everywhere. The curriculum in any locality will have to be attuned to these global demands; what is taught and how it is taught will need to take the globe not just as the relevant but as the necessary domain of thinking and practice. Of course, there are always local inflections: the 'global' appears in Corsica and in Bangladesh and it is transformed by Corsicans and

Bangladeshis in the environment of local histories, values, dispositions and contingencies. And of course, as a reciprocal effect of globalisation there will be (the possibility of) a newly intense concern with the local. Within the European Union this is manifesting itself in the form of the (re)emergence of regions and nations, whether the Toscana or Burgundy or Scotland. That too will have to be accommodated in the curriculum of the future.

A new curriculum of communication

The new requirements made by globalisation of education and its curricula are the basis of the work of the New London Group and its work on 'Multiliteracies' (New London Group, 1996). Here I will briefly sketch just some of the features of the curriculum that would take the place of the English curriculum in England. For me it is clear that, whatever it might be called, and for the time being the name and label English is perhaps the one that needs to stay, this has to be a full, rich curriculum of communication. To discuss that I will use the notions of 'multiliteracy' and of 'communicational webs'. As responsibility for education shifts from the state to the market, a whole new set of questions arises around values and ethics, and I will make a comment on that, in relation to the categories of style and aesthetics as essential underpinnings of the purposes of a curriculum of communication.

The term 'multiliteracies' was coined by members of the New London Group (1996) (New London after the town in New Hampshire where the group held its first meeting). It is a term which attempts to capture and recognize the multiple forms, the multiple sites and the multiple purposes of communication, to show them in their social/cultural environments, link them to the demands of the society and its economy and to show them as the effects of the agentive, creative, transformative, designing action of individuals communicating in their social lives. A focus on multiliteracies at once moves away from concern with language alone, whether as speech or as writing, and focuses instead on the ensembles of communicational modes which are in use in a particular situation, on a particular occasion of communication, and on the shaping/designing action of those producing their communicational ensemble, and on their purposes. This approach does not privilege any one of the modes of representation which are in use, but rather focuses on what goes on and on the purposes of what is going on. This rhetorical approach of course has to be attuned to the effects of power in communication. It is also the necessary approach in culturally plural settings: by focusing on what actually goes on and why, by not privileging image over language or gesture over sound or action over a three-dimensional model, it is an approach which is, potentially at least, culturally 'open': it is open to the varying communicational practices of any group.

'Design' is central to this approach, i.e. the recognition that in all communication we work with culturally already shaped material (as 'semiotic modes' with grammars: writing, image, gesture, speech, music), but in working with these materials constantly reshape them, remake them, in line with the characteristics of our designs. In this way the approach puts forward a quite new, radically different theory of meaning, of semiosis, in which the individual is always shaping (the etymology of the word points to both 'creating' and to 'work', both present in the

German word 'schaffen') and never simply 'using', as in 'language users'. This provides the necessary theory of meaning and of learning for the new curriculum of communication, and indeed for other curricula as well.

Multimodality is a given in the Multiliteracies approach; the task then is to uncover, describe and theorise what the different modes are which appear in communication and what meaning potentials they make available to those who integrate them and draw on them in their designs. (Some work is now available on this; see for instance Kress and van Leeuwen, 1996; van Leeuwen, 1999; Kress, 1999). Designs speak of choices: choices which reflect the interests of their designer, choices of mode: 'I will represent and communicate this element or these elements in image, these elements in writing, to produce this ensemble'. Choice is action which represents the interests of the chooser (or the constraints under which the chooser chooses). In a society in which the state has begun to lose (or cede) power to the market, choice in any case becomes the criterial principle of action. In the nineteenth-century nation state, with its clear (even if often not clearly, overtly, articulated) value systems, choice was not the issue, and often hardly possible. The taken-for-grantedness of social forms had made them seem natural and, hence, not amenable to choice and to change through choice. Adaptation to, fitting into, the structures of the society supported by the state was the required disposition, mirrored, of course, in so many ways by the curriculum of that era (and present still, as I said earlier, in so many ways, in the backward looking and backward moving curriculum of today).

Now communication happens in new communicational webs. The 12 year old boy who spends much of his leisure time either by himself or with friends in front of a PlayStation, lives in a communicational web structured by a variety of media of communication and of modes of communication. In that, the 'screen' may be becoming dominant, whether that of the TV or of the PC, and may be coming to restructure the 'page'. The visual mode may be coming to have priority over the written, while language-as-speech has new functions in relation to all of these. The media in this web would be TV, PC, PlayStation, magazine, book, talk and Internet websites. The modes of communication would be, probably dominantly, image, then writing, then talk. In contrast, the 12 year old's ten-year-old sister is likely to live in a quite differently structured communicational web; yes TV and PC figure, but quite differently. Instead of the books on science fiction (derived from PlayStation games) or books on games themselves, there might be much more conventional narratives, and the magazines might be absent. Talk would figure more prominently, as would play of a self-initiated kind.

The communicational webs of school and beyond school would also differ, more so for the 12 year old than for his sister. The notion of the 'communicational web' would allow us to look at sites of work and sites of leisure and at the fit or lack of it between the school and the world beyond the school. That would allow the new curriculum to (re)connect with the world of its domain.

The state's purpose for the education system was to produce citizens and the requisite labour force for its economy. The demands of the market are to produce consumers, first and foremost, and perhaps a labour force for its economies, though that aim is a much more diffuse one for the market. The structures of the nation state and of its economy had provided the means of constructing identities for individuals, via their place in its structures: 'I am working class', 'I am an academic', 'I am a welder', 'I am…', etc. The market provides for those who have the means to participate, the possibility of identity making via choice-in-consumption: 'we prefer French brie', 'I like wearing Gap clothes', 'we always buy a French car'. The still active realities of 'class' give way in this environment to the metaphor of 'lifestyle', and lifestyle is constructed out of the work of choice in the market of commodities (those who cannot participate in consumption in the market cease to matter, for the market at any rate). Choice-in-consumption is the expression of the individual's interest (shaped, of course, in the environment of the society and its market) and becomes the expression of an individual aesthetic (shaped, of course, and met by the aesthetic of the market). Style-as-aesthetics is now the condition of all of those in consumer capitalism who are not excluded from consumption. That has moved the domain of aesthetics from its reference to the objects of the elite to all practices of the everyday. Communication is no exception: the look of the newspaper which I read relates to the look of the supermarket that I shop in and that relates to the clothes that I wear to go to work in or for leisure, etc. Texts, whether linguistic or linguistic and visual or musical, texts of every kind and certainly not just the texts of the canon of the elite, are entirely related to consumption of commodities of all kinds. Contemporary school textbooks, in England as around the globe, are also subject to the same aesthetic demands.

Which school subject is likely to deal with this as an issue, both as an issue of preparing the young appropriately for their societies and as an issue of making overt the principles of design which suffuse every aspect of the aesthetics of the market? For me the answer is quite clear: if the subject English in the English school curriculum does not do so, then there is nowhere else at the moment where this will happen. But it is an issue which is both essential for the design of a new form of communication and for the understanding of life in a consumer (i.e. market dominated) society.

As I said, whether this newly (re)conceived subject remains English or becomes, much more appropriately, 'communication' (or something else entirely, as in the new curriculum 2005 in South Africa, where it has become language, communication and literature), the *tasks* for that subject remain. Preparing young people for their lives in a society dominated by consumption structured by the market demands that aesthetics, as the politics of style (itself the result of work by individuals), whether of the banal text or the valued texts of the elite, be at the core and as the foundation of that curriculum. Aesthetics as the politics of taste, whether of the everyday or the exceptional, or the bringing together of the two, allows and entails the development of notions of the potentials of individuals, of representational resources, of agency, of the transformative action of design, of innovation, of a taken-for-granted creativity of all communicational action/work. Implicit in it is the notion of critique, i.e. full awareness of the representational and communicational potentials of forms of communication will always allow the recipients of 'texts' to hypothesize in informed fashion as to what the interests and intentions of the makers of the text might have been.

In the world of market-dominated consumption, as much as in the world of an economy of information and services, meaning resides in commodities of all kinds, both because commodities have been constructed as signs and because commodities are taken as signs by those who construct their identity through choice-in-consumption. Meaning is therefore no longer conned or connable to 'texts' in a traditional sense, nor is communication. A curriculum of communication which is to be adequate to the needs of the young cannot afford to remain with older notions of text as valued literary object, as the present English curriculum still does, by and large.

Conclusion

I have not discussed one of the most burning issues – will there be a school at all in 30 years time or will ICTs become such that framings of site, time and authority have become superfluous or irrelevant? I have assumed the continued existence of the school, even if in greatly changed form, but the school will only retain its place if it, or those who are responsible for it, face the question of the fit between curriculum and the new shapes of work and leisure around the school and if the question of wider purposes for each subject in the curriculum can be satisfactorily answered.

Notes

* Gunther Kress is at the Institute of Education, University of London, London.
† Originally published in: *Cambridge Journal of Education* 30: 1, 133–145.

References

Cope, B. and Kalantzis, M. (1999) *Multiliteracies* (London, Routledge).

Gee, J.P, Hull, G. and Lankshear, C. (1996) *The New Work Order: behind the language of the new capitalism* (Boulder, CO, Westview).

Kress, G.R. (1995) *Writing the Future: English and the making of a culture of innovation* (Sheffield, National Association of Teachers of English).

Kress, G.R. (1997) *Before Writing: rethinking the paths to literacy* (London, Routledge).

Kress, G.R. (1999) *Early Spelling: between convention and creativity* (London, Routledge).

Kress, G.R. and Van Leeuwen, T. (1996) *Reading Images: the grammar of visual design* (London, Routledge).

New London Group (1996) A pedagogy of multiliteracies, *Harvard Educational Review*, 60(1), pp. 66–92.

Van Leeuwen, T. (1999) *Speech Music Sound* (London, Macmillan).

Part III
Teachers and teaching

21 Review essays

'The Pain Must Go On' and 'The Highs and Lows of Teaching: 60 years of Research Revisited'

Mary Jane Drummond* and Marilyn Osborn[†]

This Review section of this special issue follows a slightly different format. Mary Jane Drummond and Marilyn Osborn were invited to prepare essay reviews of a total of seven books published between 1932 and 1989. These books, which span more than 60 years, have all made a valuable contribution to our knowledge of the emotions in teaching and are as vibrant now as they were on publication.

THE PAIN MUST GO ON

When Teachers Face Themselves
Arthur T. Jersild, 1955
New York, Teachers College Press

An Analysis of the Emotional Problems of the Teacher in the Classroom
John Gabriel, 1957
London, Angus & Robertson

The Emotional Experience of Learning and Teaching
Isca Salzberger-Wittenberg, Gianna Henry and Elsie Osborne, 1983
London, Routledge & Kegan Paul

The publication dates of these three books span nearly 30 years of writing and thinking – and feeling – about 'the emotions in teaching'. Let us begin in 1948–1949: those were the days! John Gabriel was there and was grateful: 'I beg to state that this enquiry has been aided by a grant of £65, awarded from the Research Fund of the University of London'. He goes on to thank the 900 teachers who, during 1948–1949 responded to his questionnaires, a colleague who lent him a 'tabulating machine' and the academics who supported him as he wrote up his data for a PhD. In 1957 his work appeared as a book, *An Analysis of the Emotional Problems of the Teacher in the Classroom*. His definition of the territory to be surveyed is succinct; emotional problems are those 'which give rise to negative feelings of worry or strain, annoyance or concern'. His approach is direct: teachers in primary and secondary modern schools were asked to list all the types of children's behaviour 'which tend to frustrate you, and which you, therefore find annoying (omit no item, however trivial it may first appear)'. To balance the picture Gabriel asked for two further lists: occasions for elation and occasions for depression. (Even so, some of his respondents spotted his bias. 'This questionnaire is difficult because I like teaching.' 'I have had twenty splendid years of teaching.')

The teachers' detailed responses, reeking of classroom life, were used to construct a second questionnaire, with a closed structure and a 5 point scale on which to indicate the degree of worry and strain, degree of pleasure and degree of concern, caused by each of a long list of specific behaviours and classroom conditions. Out of this mass of data, Gabriel constructs his analysis, both quantitative (pages of painstaking percentages) and qualitative.

The quantitative data has little to offer us today, but the reflections and conclusions that Gabriel draws from them are rewarding in several ways. First, for a sense of history; the recent past is here revealed in pungent bites of classroom life. The reader can almost smell the dinners – and some of the children – and hear the clamour of the unruly 'ink-splashing, cutting desks, pen-nib breaking, playing darts with pens'. (I had forgotten how much ink there used to be in schools, until Gabriel reminded me; his vivid definition of a bad day includes spilled milk *and* ink.) Second, Gabriel's organising categories include some that are powerful reminders of the essential provisionality of human thought. For example, there is an extended discussion of the severe emotional problems (for teachers) connected with the education of 'backward children'. There is no evidence of any unease on Gabriel's part as he argues that the effective teaching of backward children requires a change of attitude in teachers. They must learn to accept a programme which includes the teaching of craftwork, such as weaving and making mats, because these activities entail 'simple repetitive movements at which backward children can become skilled' (p. 151).

Forty years on, such a position would be viewed as unforgivable, as a breach of fundamental assumptions about entitlement and inclusion. Which of our own currently acceptable categories, I wonder, will be refrained and reconceptualised in another 40 years? Which of our present enthusiasms will date as quickly as Gabriel's advocacy of basket work?

For all this historical interest, there are also lasting insights. For example, Gabriel traces the connection between discipline problems and the degree to which teachers are free from inner feelings of doubt. The teacher in a state of inner doubt experiences uneasiness, irritability, hostility and discomfiture. At such times, speculates Gabriel 'the child's joke, the slamming of a desk or door, and, indeed, any untoward events' may contribute to a sense of being psychologically overwhelmed. This experience, he notes, 'is not a pleasant one'.

In another penetrating passage, writing of children's vitality, enthusiasm and excitement, Gabriel notes how exhausting these traits may be for adults. Then, going deeper, with a sure thrust of the scalpel, he dissects out a more disconcerting possibility: that children's exuberance contrasts painfully with our own lack of it in adulthood. 'Unbeknown to ourselves, we may envy children this capacity and resent them for it. If this is so, we may react with severity to quell its expression' (p. 135). In this discussion, Gabriel is doing more than reporting the deeply felt details of what his teachers told him; here, his work is interpretative. His contribution to our thinking is to bring together, in a new synthesis, material about the emotional experiences of adults *and of children*. As these two pieces of the puzzle slip sweetly into place, we can, for a moment, see more of the picture, come closer to getting a sense of the whole domain of the 'emotions in teaching'.

For a fuller picture still, we can turn to a more recent account, *The Emotional Experience of Learning and Teaching*, first published in 1983, reprinted three times and still in print. This too is a study with an empirical basis; the authors draw on their experiences (as psychotherapists and psychologists) of working with teachers on a course called 'Aspects of Counselling' at the Tavistock Clinic, London. The central theme that unites their contributions is the interconnectedness of teaching and learning. The subject matter to be investigated is the emotional domain in which these processes occur: the intrapsychic and intrapersonal relationships between teacher and learner, adult and child and, indeed, psychotherapist and adult student. The outcomes of this investigation, the authors reason, will be more fruitful relationships, for both students and their teachers.

The text is enriched with copious illustrations from the course members' own classrooms – case study material they discussed with the course tutors and with each other – and with the course leader's (Isca Salzberger-Wittenberg's) reflections on her own emotional responses and personal relationships with these same teachers. Much of this material is presented verbatim, in the first person singular; these voices on the page are extremely moving. An emotional response from the reader who is also a teacher is thereby guaranteed; it is impossible to read a page without being drawn in, without starting to investigate oneself. The reader cannot but ask: Is this *me*, she's writing about? Has she been listening at keyholes? Do I do this? Do *my* students/pupils/children see *me* this way? Do *they* feel rejection, blame or guilt?

Such questions are both an expression of anxiety, an emotion endemic to teachers, and also a form of sensitivity to criticism. All learners are continuously conscious of being judged, argues Salzberger-Wittenberg, and interpret their teacher's every comment as implying either praise or blame. The relationship between these authors and their unknown readers parallels that between teacher and learner; the text recreates, in a sense, especially for readers who are teachers, the emotional conditions of a classroom. Just as learning in classrooms exacts an emotional price, so too does an attentive reading of this book. And this is part of its strength and authenticity.

The framework within which the case material is presented and discussed is psycho-analytic. The work of Wilfred Bion and Melanie Klein, in particular, has been influential in shaping Salzberger-Wittenberg's formulation of the tasks of the teacher. One of these tasks resembles the work of the child's parents in infancy: containing the destructive and painful emotions that every child experiences. In the same way, a teacher has to act as a 'temporary container' for the excessive anxieties of the learner. In the process, the teacher will experience at first hand 'some of the mental pain associated with learning'. In spite of this pain, the teacher's task is to maintain 'curiosity in the face of chaos, love of truth in the face of terror of the unknown, and hope in the face of despair' (p. 60). If this can be done, the student will learn to tolerate the uncertainties and anxieties of being a learner.

A further task, again derived from the work of Bion (on the concept of 'reverie') is for the teacher to act as a reflective and thinking person: 'not only a container of feelings but a mind that can hold thoughts ... the teacher's capacity to be thoughtful and reflective rather than producing ready made answers enables the learner to internalise a thinking person' (p. 60).

These two central tasks make many demands on teachers and Salzberger-Wittenberg spells them out: attentiveness, openness, receptiveness. This description of what it is to be a teacher has much in common with some of the writings of the French philosopher and religious genius Simone Weil, in particular her account of what it is to be fully human. In the beautiful essay *On Human Personality*, written in the last year of her life, she broods on the page over the concept of attention and its relation to human affliction. As she describes it, 'attention' is more than listening, more than seeing vaguely from a distance. It is an act of putting oneself in the afflicted one's place; it can only be achieved in the spirit of justice and the spirit of truth – 'The spirit of justice and truth is nothing else but a certain kind of attention, which is pure love' (Miles, 1986). It is remarkable how effortlessly, but reverently, the words truth, justice, beauty and love drop from Weil's pen.[1]

Salzberger-Wittenberg, in contrast, though she writes of the teacher's love of truth and, following Klein, of the mother's loving response to her child's pain, does not speak of love between teacher and pupil. Her understanding of the principle of containment is, indeed, lovingly conveyed and the ways in which teachers show how much they care about their pupils are evident throughout the case studies presented for discussion by the teachers themselves. Yet the word 'love' does not appear in this context. In a discussion of the dangers of 'idealised relationships', where all positive feelings come to be (unrealistically) lodged in one person, Salzberger-Wittenberg offers teachers a choice. We have to choose in our relationships, she suggests, between 'comfort and development'. If a comfortable existence, free from pain and anxiety, is what we opt for, we may close the door on the possibility of growth and development. Opting for development is the less comfortable – or comforting – decision, but it will be more productive in the long term. Weil's concept of love seems to me to have something to add to these rather arid possibilities, suggesting a fuller meaning, a deeper significance for productive human relationships. Our understanding of what such relationships might be like is enriched and extended by Weil's understanding of what this attentive love can do, for those who love, for those who are beloved. 'Love is not consolation, it is light' (Miles, 1986).

There are other emotions, and virtues, that Salzberger-Wittenberg does weave into her exploration. She describes movingly, for example, how the emotional development of students stems from their teachers' emotional responses to the lives they lead together in schools and classrooms. From a trusting teacher, she argues, children learn to trust, and from a courageous teacher, courage. (We may note here that Froebel claimed that the young child learns the meaning of love from living with two parents who love one another; Liebschner, 1992).

The reciprocity of the emotional relationship between teacher and learner has some less positive consequences, which are worth thinking about. Salzberger-Wittenberg does not, in this text, write of what pupils might learn from teachers who are locked in what she calls 'denigratory relationships' with one another or who act rejectingly towards one another. But it is certainly possible, perhaps even probable, that pupils who seem to reject their teachers, and their schoolmates, are saying in effect: yours is a society of which I do not desire to be a member. Perhaps the behaviour of students that finally leads them to be excluded can sometimes be understood as an extreme example of this desire not to be part of an unjust or rejecting whole. The appalling report of the MacDonald Enquiry into the death of a pupil at Burnage High School (MacDonald Committee, 1989) clearly suggested that the breakdown in communication between members of staff, and the vicious circle of mistrust and misunderstanding that characterised staff relationships in that school, played an important part in the events leading up to and immediately following the murder. Incidentally, it has long interested me how readily, as a profession, we have chosen to forget or repress the whole incident and how few teachers I meet in the course of my work who have read the full report or even know of its existence. Perhaps this is a case of a lack of the openness and receptivity that Saltzberger-Wittenberg so convincingly advocates. It may just be too painful for us to be open and receptive to the emotions aroused by the MacDonald report.

And yet Salzberger-Wittenberg is clear that we

> must be prepared to *have* an emotional experience What makes the painful experience bearable is an interest and ability to think about the feelings evoked in us. We may need space and time to consider the nature of the pain and appreciate what it is about.
>
> (p. 63, author's italics)

For those privileged teachers who attended the course at the Tavistock Clinic, the necessary space and time were provided, organised into their lives, valued as part of their professional development. For the rest of us, this book offers, through the printed page, the opportunity to do some of the same work, the thinking, the rethinking, the coming to understand. From his prison cell in Bedford, John Bunyan wrote 'Believing is sweating work' (Hill, 1988); the thinking work that Salzberger-Wittenberg and her colleagues invite us to do will be just as demanding.

'We may need space and time…' reflects Salzberger-Wittenberg; our third author, A.T. Jersild is never so tentative. *When Teachers Face Themselves*, first published in 1955 and reprinted 13 times by 1969, is shot through with the urgency of the task he sets out in the title. Jersild's enterprise is on the grand scale: to explore the relationship between self-understanding and education as a whole and, in particular, what the concepts of self-understanding and self-acceptance mean for teachers. Jersild's account of this exploration, like the other two, draws on a large empirical study and deals with two areas of pervasive concern in his respondents' lives. These are the teacher's search for intimate and personal meaning, and the difficulties that accompany that search, the teacher's burden of loneliness, hostility and anxiety. Especially anxiety: Jersild takes the position that *'the concept of anxiety should be regarded as an essential topic in all teacher training programmes'* (p. 7, author's italics).

The question of meaning is, Jersild recognises, as old as the human race. The questions teachers ask themselves are fundamental: who and what and why am I? We are a long way, in this enquiry, from the irritations of classroom life, the sounds and smells of school, so painstakingly annotated by Gabriel. Jersild emphasises the privacy of the teacher, as well as the crowds that inhabit the school and its corridors. He reminds us of D.H. Lawrence's image:

> What we know of ourselves may only be a little clearing in the forest.... But a little clearing is infinitely greater than no clearing at all, and it is better ... to dwell in such a clearing, and to work in it, with things that count, than just to go through the motions.
>
> (p. 7)

The date of publication may be 1955, but the messages are, like the questions they stem from, timeless, universal and, in post-Dearing Britain, deeply political. Meaninglessness, argues Jersild, is a common condition in teaching and learning. The only solution is:

> to conduct education in depth – to move towards something that is personally significant beyond the facade of facts, subject matter, logic, and reason ... (by making) an effort to overcome the prevailing tendency in education to encourage the learner to understand everything except himself.... It means also that the process of learning will not be used as a means of competing with others and gaining power over them.
>
> (pp. 80–81)

Jersild is equally clear-headed about the reason for the chronic condition of meaninglessness in education. It is because 'we have assumed that knowledge has value apart from its meaning for the one who acquires it'. In this assumption, we are gravely mistaken; the personal implications of what we learn and teach must be direct, immediate, pressing and vivid. Every subject must be deeply charged with meaning for both teachers and learners. And what must be done for this to be possible?: 'To help a pupil to have meaningful experiences, a teacher must know the pupil as a person. This means that the teacher must strive to know himself' (p. 82).

This, then, is the task – to face oneself. And its corollaries are: to face the role of feeling in thinking, to face the personal implications of ideas, to face the connection between the idea, the theory and one's own life. These tasks are, in Jersild's view, compulsory. And this is the essential difference between his work and the two other books considered here.

Gabriel documents the negative emotions, both powerful and trivial, that teachers experience daily. He treats them as inevitable occupational hazards, which could be alleviated, though not abolished, by smaller classes, more effective and longer pre-service training and improvements in classroom conditions. Salzberger-Wittenberg and her colleagues go a little further; they stress the centrality, in teaching, of the emotional relationship between teacher and learner and recommend that teachers develop the qualities of attentiveness and receptiveness. They recognise that this is likely to be an emotionally demanding task in itself. But Jersild insists on a more radical reappraisal of the tasks of teachers. The search for meaning, which is at the heart of human existence, is also, for Jersild, at the heart of everything that teachers do in the name of education. A necessary part of this work, he argues, is the search for self. He represents this search, not as a process of reaching out, a voyage of exploration, in which the adventurous individual charts unknown waters and undiscovered islands, but as a process of looking in, facing oneself and one's experience in its totality. The quest for self requires a mirror, not a compass. Teachers facing themselves face their humanity, and its most tremendous events, birth, death and sex.

Jersild does not deny the inevitable emotional costs of the search that he is urging us all to undertake. Many who responded to his questionnaires and took part in interviews revealed deep suffering. Jersild sympathetically catalogues their emotions; teachers facing themselves feel lonely, homeless and hopeless; they feel anxiety, fear and hostility. There are parts of the search that they are reluctant to pursue; in a brief chapter on 'Sex', for example, Jersild notes that teachers tend to avoid the subject, even though it is of vital concern to all people. This avoidance, he concludes, is damaging: 'As long as we evade the issue of sex in education – in the education of teachers and in the education of the children they teach – we are play-acting'. The alternative Jersild proposes is a reiteration of his central theme: 'call it what we will, sex, Eros, the emotion tied to life's passion to renew life, cannot be denied ... we must face its power ... if we would take the first steps toward accepting or understanding ourselves' (p. 105). The search must go on, in spite of the pain and suffering it entails. But, Jersild insists, the search for selfhood is not only painful but healing. Although people who undertake it are likely to feel worse before they feel better, it is work that has to be done. It is a hard struggle, but brings great rewards, of which the greatest, Jersild promises, is growth in compassion.

Compassion is the theme of the final chapter, which seems to come as a reward in itself, a reward, as it were, to the readers who have 'faced themselves' through the harrowing chapters on anxiety, homelessness and hostility. In these closing pages, in strikingly poetical passages of clarity and tenderness, Jersild extols the virtue of compassion.

> Compassion is stronger than anger, mightier than love, more powerful than fear. It gives the measure of a person's strength as a human being. It is not the emotion of the weak. It is the hard-gotten property of the strong.
>
> (p. 126)

Compassion incorporates the self and the other; it involves both self-acceptance and acceptance of others: 'Hatred of self is linked to hatred of others; without healthy love of self there can be no genuine love for anyone else' (p. 131). In this, compassion is distinct from sacrifice and self-denial. Jersild is at pains to demolish the notion that it is only by self-denial that one can be of service to others. Self-denial, in Jersild's view, may be a means of escaping anxiety or atoning for guilt; it also constitutes a refusal to face the self and so to become an accepting and compassionate person. The compassionate teacher feels with others by drawing on the strength of his or her own feelings.

The penultimate page of the book is almost incantatory – a hymn to the self, the citadel and stronghold of one's being and worth: 'Here in this self – my self, your self – is where time touches on the eternal. Here the finite and the infinite are joined' (p. 135). And then, in the nick of time, just as the mystical language begins to cloy and the incantation is about to turn to syrup, Jersild plunges back to earth, to practising teachers who must search for meaning in their work. With a resounding thud of conviction, he touches ground again and reasserts the fundamental task. We must continuously ask, of everything we say and do in the name of education, of everything we seek to learn and of everything that is taught, two piercing questions: What does it mean? What difference does it make?

This is a brave conclusion to an important, frightening and compassionate book. Jersild's final questions constitute a kind of razor, with which we may slice away diseased or superfluous growths on the body of practices that we call education. The 'emotions in teaching' play a part in those practices – but the essence of what teachers and learners do is the search for meaning. This search is driven by the absolute and passionate necessity of finding ourselves and, in so doing, helping others in their search.

Notes

* Originally published in: *Cambridge Journal of Education* 26: 3, 449–464.
1 Weil's close friend, Gustave Thibon saw her for the last time towards the end of April 1942, in Marseilles, just before she sailed for the USA. They talked all night. Thibon wrote:

> I can still hear Simone Weil's voice in the deserted streets of Marseilles as she took me back to my hotel in the early hours of the morning; she was speaking of the Gospel; her mouth uttered thoughts as a tree gives its fruit.
>
> (Quoted in McLellan, 1989)

References

Hill, C. (1988) *A Turbulent, Seditious, and Factious People: John Bunyan and his church 1628–1688*, p. 176 (Oxford, Clarendon Press).
Liebschner, J. (1992) *A Child's Work: freedom and play in Froebel's educational theory and practice* (Cambridge, Lutterworth Press).
MacDonald Committee (1989) *Murder in the Playground, The Burnage Report* (London, Longsight Press).
McLellan, D. (1989) *Simone Weil: Utopian pessimist* (London, Macmillan).
Miles, S. (ed.) (1986) *Simone Weil: an anthology*, p. 92 (London, Virago).

Mary Jane Drummond
Tutor, University of Cambridge
Institute of Education

THE HIGHS AND LOWS OF TEACHING: 60 YEARS OF RESEARCH REVISITED

The Sociology of Teaching
Willard Waller, 1932
New York, Wiley

Life in Classrooms
Philip Jackson, 1968
New York, Holt, Rinehart and Winston (re-issued 1990 with a new introduction)
New York, Teachers College Press

Schoolteacher: a sociological study
Dan C. Lortie, 1975
Chicago, University of Chicago Press

Primary Teachers Talking: a study of teaching and work
Jennifer Nias, 1989
London, Routledge

One of the qualities of a classic book is that it continues to illuminate and to give insights to readers many years after it has been written. In different ways this is true of all the four books reviewed here. Each of them has a timeless quality, giving rich descriptive insights into the social world of school, insights which emphasise the central importance of human interaction in teaching and learning. Each of them adopts a qualitative and narrative approach which has enduring relevance. When I reread them for this review, I was immediately struck with how revealing a revisiting of some of their central themes could be in illuminating and increasing understanding of current developments in education. At a time when school systems are being restructured to meet ever-increasing demands for accountability, for greater rationality and for technical competencies in teaching; in a climate of postmodernism characterised by accelerating change, scientific uncertainty and lack of stability and security there is a particular need to consider again the central argument of all these books which is that effective teaching and learning is necessarily *affective*, that it involves human interaction and that the quality of teacher–pupil relationships is vitally important to the learning process.

The situation of teachers has been radically altered since these books were first written; in England and Wales by the introduction of a National Curriculum and national assessment and of a system of teacher appraisal and school inspection by Ofsted, as well as by the infiltration of the values of the marketplace into education. There have been similar moves towards greater control of teachers and greater accountability in many other Westernised countries. On the one hand, these developments lead to the intensification of teachers' work and are seen as deskilling teachers (Apple, 1986; Densmore, 1987); on the other hand, they may also be viewed as increasing opportunities for creativity in teaching (Hargreaves, 1994).

Why then are these books still relevant? In part, it is because all the recent innovations have had a tendency to impersonalise or even to depersonalise teaching and learning. It is easy for new developments in education to come to be seen as ends in themselves, as educational goals which it is sufficient to achieve, rather than simply a possible means for achieving a better human environment for learning. These books all reassert a vital message; the importance of human relationships in schools. As Waller argues 'Let no one be deceived, the important things that happen in the schools result from the interaction of personalities'.

Waller's was one of the first books to take the commonplace, taken-for-granted events in the life of the school and to make them 'strange', to hold them up for examination and to set the stage for a study of the school as a social institution. In many ways, his was a very grim view of teaching. He emphasised the harm a teaching career can do to teachers by institutionalising them, making them 'unbending creatures of routine', cut off from real creativity and from any vital contact with pupils. Teaching, he argued, deadened the intellect, paralysed the personality and inhibited creativity. The teachers he described were not dissimilar from those portrayed by D.H. Lawrence in *The Rainbow*, encountered by Ursula in her first teaching job; unbending, inflexible and wielding extreme power. Some of the things he had to say about women teachers, who he saw as sex-starved spinsters, about whom 'the moral order tightly coiled', were extremely derogatory, but, as Acker (1995) points out, his characterisations of men were hardly more flattering.

However, unlike Waller's remarks about spinster teachers, his comments about the institutionalisation of teaching and the demands of the education system cutting teachers off from real contact with their pupils have a great deal of relevance for teachers now. It is clear that current developments in teaching have given these arguments a new force and that new generations of teachers might find a relevant message here, as well as much that is of historic interest. The dangers of the current technocratisation of teaching are similar to the institutionalisation described by Waller; teachers may find it much harder to take the time to develop a strong affective learning relationship with their pupils, subject as they now are to a conflicting array of obligations and objectives imposed by external demands. Recent research in English primary schools carried out by the PACE project (Primary Assessment, Curriculum and Experience) (Pollard et al., 1994) showed that teachers were taking on an increasing range of objectives and that this pressure to meet a wider range of goals, both externally imposed and self-imposed, may be a major cause of stress and anxiety for teachers, contributing significantly to intensification of workload.

To counteract such institutionalisation, Waller argued that teachers and pupils needed to work out the social order of the school for themselves in a developing situation which resulted 'from the spontaneous, inevitable, and whole-hearted interaction of personalities'. For teachers to be able to resist such institutional dominance required strong and independent teachers 'who have no need of barriers between themselves and their students'.

This is very resonant of recent developments in education which Waller could not have foreseen in 1932, but which clearly threaten to dominate teaching in the same way and to depersonalise the relationship between teachers and children. At present some strong teachers are fighting against this and trying to work out a new and more creative order in the classroom for themselves while protecting their relationship with children (Osborn *et al.*, 1992, 1996; Pollard *et al.*, 1994).

One of the key issues now, as in Waller's time, is for teachers to have the confidence and motivation to put their values into practice, to make choices and to see alternatives. They want to avoid, as one PACE teacher described it 'becoming a machine for carrying out a prescribed curriculum'. Waller used very similar terminology. Teachers and pupils, as he says, are not 'instructing machines' or 'learning machines', but whole human beings interlocked in a network of human relationships. It is the quality of these relationships which determines much of the outcomes of education.

As at the time when Waller was writing, there is a danger now that this will be forgotten in a climate of increased external demands, constraints and accountability and that new developments in curriculum, assessment and accountability will be seen as educational goals in themselves, rather than simply a possible means for making learning more effective and meaningful. This perspective from the past has a freshness and force about it, when viewed in the light of current developments, which makes a library copy of Waller (it is now unfortunately out of print) eminently rereadable, or readable for the first time by a new generation of educators and researchers.

A continuing thread concerning the importance of human relationships and the emotional component in teaching runs strongly through the other three books I review here, although elaborated and developed in rather different ways. Philip Jackson reasserts the significance of a strong emotional component in teaching and emphasises the way in which teachers' satisfactions derive from a focus on 'immediacy, informality, autonomy, and individuality'. The 'immediacy' and 'informality' of classrooms was, he argued, characterised by a here-and-now urgency and spontaneous quality which brought excitement and variety to the teacher's work, although it might also contribute to the fatigue felt by teachers at the end of the day. Many of the satisfactions and 'joys' (a word used by many of them) of Jackson's sample of teachers were derived from this and from 'individuality', a sense that it is what happens to individual children which is important, seeing an individual child develop and progress, gaining a sense of excitement from surprising and unexpected classroom events.

In emphasising the importance of autonomy, Jackson's teachers perceived threats to this from a possible future scenario which might include the imposition of an inflexible curriculum, an emphasis on the observation and evaluation of their work and from possible future requirements to plan a term or more in advance. To some extent, he argued, the teachers in his sample were 'present-oriented teachers in future-oriented institutions'. On the other hand, they were not arguing for a return to isolation and total independence, but rather for a freedom to retain room for spontaneity and the exercise of professional judgement and to work within broad guidelines, rather than a prescriptive, imposed curriculum.

With remarkable foresight, Jackson predicted that these values and concerns might become a source of discomfort for teachers in the future. In fact, many of these teachers' concerns *were* echoed by the PACE sample of teachers in the wake of multiple education reforms in England. They welcomed the guidelines and framework provided by the National Curriculum, but not its over-prescriptive nature. They experienced their work as far more stressful than it had been and regretted the decrease in their professional autonomy and the loss of spontaneity in their work with children.

These themes are taken up and expanded by Lortie, whose teachers also gained many of their satisfactions from the affective dimension of their work and from their relationship with pupils. The main rewards in teaching came from classroom events, from students responding well and from being influenced by their teaching. Once again the 'joys of teaching' came from 'knowing that I have reached students and they have learned'. For the teachers in Jennifer Nias' sample also, the key professional 'satisfiers' came from the affective rewards of being with children, 'giving and receiving affection, talking and laughing together, sharing common interests, enjoying shared activities', followed closely by the importance of 'helping children learn'.

For Lortie's teachers, like Jackson's, some degree of autonomy was also important. They 'accepted the legitimacy of the prescribed curriculum' but saw their role as more than just implementing this. They were 'moral agents' as well, emphasising the social and personal development of children and the importance of making emotional connections between the children and their learning. Teachers emphasised the central importance of 'psychic rewards, instructional goals, and evocative relationships', just as Nias' teachers emphasised 'intrinsic rewards'.

Lortie echoed Jackson in talking of the 'presentism', 'conservatism' and 'individualism' of teachers. He argued that the 'way in which teachers see their tasks reinforces a conservative frame of mind – a preference for doing things as they have been done in the past'. Together with a focus on 'individualism' this could mean that teachers relied on personal convictions, obtaining high satisfaction from outcomes that were less than universalistic, deriving rewards even when only a limited number of students learned. The values of 'presentism' and 'individualism' in teachers, he argued could contribute to 'a lack of enthusiasm teachers show in working together to build a stronger technical culture'. These values meant that teachers worked too much in isolation, rather than working collegially to improve occupational knowledge. Later work, in particular that of Nias et al. (1989) in the English context, does not support this view. On the contrary, strongly collaborative cultures have been shown to be a feature of some English primary schools, although the evidence from other countries, such as France, is more mixed.

Lortie has been criticised for his emphasis on a deficit model of teachers, particularly women teachers (Casey and Apple, 1989) and for an over-emphasis on the importance to teachers of technical knowledge (Alexandersson, 1994). His model of teaching does not locate itself explicitly enough in a situational constraints model as Jackson's does. Jackson shows how teachers' commitment to what appear short-term concerns are a result of the constraints within which they work in the classroom and of their desire to protect children.

Both Jackson and Lortie were writing at a time when much educational research tended to emphasise a 'blame the teacher' or deficit model of teachers, rather than seeing them as trying to cope with situational constraints. In this respect Jackson has the advantage, as his 1990 foreword to the re-issued edition makes this explicit; he is able to reflect on the role of the researcher and on the research climate in which the original book was written. Here he emphasises the importance of seeing 'beyond praise and blame' and seeking neutrality, although many readers will query whether the latter is attainable in research.

Nias starts from a very different point in her discussion of teachers' rewards and satisfactions and the emotions which are important in teaching. Although much research has been done to explore teachers' actions and strategies, their beliefs and perspectives, there has not been a consistent body of work on teachers' feelings. Waller, Jackson, and Lortie only begin to touch upon this. Gabriel (1957), Jersild (1952), who points out that teachers 'face themselves' as well as their pupils, and Salzberger-Wittenberg *et al.* (1983) are among the few writers who particularly emphasise emotions in teaching. Nias, however, addresses the emotions of teaching from the starting point of how teachers themselves talk about this dimension of their work. Her teachers are given a distinctive voice and she shows very clearly how the theoretical concepts which emerge from the interviews are grounded in these voices.

In *Primary Teachers Talking* she brings the issue of the teacher's self and its realisation to the top of the agenda. Drawing upon symbolic interactionism, she makes a distinction between the 'substantial' self, an inner unchanging core, and 'situational selves', which are adaptations to particular situations. Many of her teachers had invested their personal sense of identity in their work. They emphasised verbally and non-verbally the importance of 'wholeness' as a teacher, sometimes achieved by blurring the boundaries between their personal and professional lives, sometimes experienced as a sense of unity which they were achieving in the classroom. Without exception, when displaying what Biklen (1986) called a 'passion for teaching', they 'cupped their hands or made enfolding movements with hands and arms' to explain what it meant to feel at one with a group of children.

This may sound as if it has little place in the technical–rationalist, market-oriented reforms of the early 1990s. Yet these sentiments were echoed by teachers studied by the PACE team between 1990 and 1995, who accepted some of the reforms as improving the overall situation for childrens' learning, but nevertheless experienced a sense of loss on their own behalf as well as that of children. In particular, they mourned the loss of spontaneity in teaching and a warm, relaxed relationship with children. Nias has referred elsewhere to this feeling of loss as being strong enough to constitute 'bereavement' on the part of many teachers (Nias, 1993).

This sense of loss experienced by English primary teachers post-ERA is strongly bound up with another strong emotion in primary teaching: a 'commitment to caring'. This is a strong theme, particularly in Nias' work, but also a feature of Jackson's, Lottie's and, to some extent, Waller's work. Jackson talked of teachers caring about children, missing them when they were not there and opening their personalities to children. Nias' teachers expressed caring in terms of warmth, love, affection for children and protecting childrens' self-esteem. However, none of these writers made a particularly explicit link between an ethic of care and gender issues. Jackson linked this level of emotional attachment with a blurring of the role of teacher and the role of mother. Yet this did not lead on to a discussion of the feminisation of teaching at primary level and whether a commitment to caring has any relationship with this. Lortie has been criticised on the more general count of ignoring women teachers and gender as a specific issue (Casey and Apple, 1989). Nias sees caring as part of the teacher's self. Her work and that of Lee (1973) suggested that a commitment to caring may be characteristic of both men and women in the conditions of primary teaching, since they are both influenced by similar ideologies and structures of schooling. As Acker (1995) points out, 'the place of caring in teachers' work remains deeply contradictory, simultaneously the moral high ground of the teaching task and a prime site of women's oppression'.

There is a persistent notion that good teaching means sacrificing the self and the risk of such sacrifice is stronger now amongst primary teachers in England, who are at tempting to combine their commitment to caring with new rational technocratic demands for increased accountability and intensification. One teacher in the PACE study memorably likened the intensity of the caring ethic to religious commitment. Is it possible that some teachers may care *too* much (Hargreaves, 1994)? This was not the case for most of the teachers in Nias' study, who appeared to be able to put caring into perspective alongside other commitments and saw themselves 'as interested in educational ideas as well as the practicalities of teaching'. For them caring was 'not a soft option'.

Indeed, the evidence suggests that caring is an essential condition for pupil achievement. A strong care orientation is closely linked with positive school climates which foster pupil achievement, but only when accompanied by high expectations, challenging work and a clear focus on teaching and learning (National Commission on Education, 1993, 1996). However, for some teachers facing particular pressures, it is possible for a strong commitment to caring to take over too much from teaching. Comparative studies of French and English primary teachers carried out before and after recent educational reforms found evidence that before the reforms, some teachers working with disadvantaged children in England had such a strong commitment to caring, 'rescuing' and providing a safe haven for children that their academic expectations were not as high as those of primary teachers in similar schools in France. The latter, on the other hand, felt so constrained in their role that they paid very little attention to the affective dimension in learning (Broadfoot and Osborn, 1993). After reforms in both countries, there appeared to be some shift in the perspectives of both sets of teachers (Osborn, 1996).

Caring can be strongly linked with guilt, stress, and with a feeling that one is facing an impossible task. In France, as the above study showed, the task of teaching was narrowly defined and teachers could feel that they had completed what was required of them. They reported higher levels of satisfaction with their work than teachers in England, whose role was defined very broadly, in social and emotional terms as well as academic ones. English teachers felt that they were striving after a perfection which it was impossible to achieve. The recent educational reforms simply led them to take on an increased range of objectives, both affective and academic, as they strove to cope with the proliferation of curriculum and assessment demands embodied in the new National Curriculum (Pollard et al., 1994), leading to increased intensification and stress. This is a case where too much caring or 'over-conscientiousness' (Campbell and Neill, 1994) is harmful to teachers themselves and can make it difficult for them to develop coping strategies (Pollard, 1985) to limit their task to a realistic level. Those teachers who 'survived' (Woods, 1977) the reforms and were able to become 'creative mediators' had not given up caring, but were learning to protect children and themselves by being selective in their priorities and yet emerging with something creative (Pollard *et al.*, 1994; Croll, 1996; Osborn, 1996; Osborn *et al.*, 1996). Others felt unable to do this and suffered unprecedented levels of stress and dropout.

In this respect, Nias' point that being a primary teacher in England involves living with paradox and contradiction is just as true in 1996 as it was when her book was published. As she described the feelings of her teachers, in their own words, to be a successful primary teacher you have to:

> be prepared to be someone you dislike in order to gain anything. To be ful-filled by the job you have to be depleted by its demands. You need to be both egocentric and selfless – you can't care for children as individuals if you don't value yourself.

Lortie and Jackson made similar points in their references to individualism and to 'present-oriented teachers in future-oriented' institutions. It is certainly still the case that English primary teachers are setting themselves and being set goals that they cannot possibly meet and at the same time trying to meet conflicting demands from government, parents, heads and children.

All these books, but particularly the latter three, should still be of considerable interest to a new generation of researchers and teachers. Those who, like me, read them in the past will find that they continue to have resonance in the light of current developments in education in Europe and North America and that they are well worth rereading. The emotions of teaching identified here, including commit-ment, enjoyment, pride in teaching, affection, satisfaction, perfectionism, conscien-tiousness and even loss and bereavement, are likely to continue to play an important part to a greater or lesser degree in teachers' work and careers in the future.

Notes and references

† Originally published in: *Cambridge Journal of Education* 26: 3, 449–464.

Acker, S. (1995) Gender and teachers' work, in: M. Apple (ed.) *Review of Research in Educa-tion*, Vol. 21 (Washington, DC, American Education Research Association).

Alexandersson, M. (1994) Focusing teacher consciousness: what do teachers direct their consciousness towards during their teaching?, in: I. Carlgren, G. Handal and S. Vaage (eds) *Teachers' Minds and Actions* (London, Falmer Press).

Apple, M. (1986) *Teachers and Texts: a political economy of class and gender relations in educa-tion* (London, Routledge).

Biklen, S.K. (1986) I have always worked: elementary school teaching as a career, *Phi Delta Kappa*, March, pp. 504–508.

Broadfoot, P. and Osborn, M. (1988) What professional responsibility means to teachers: national contexts and classroom constants, *British Journal of Sociology of Education*, 9, pp. 265–287.

Broadfoot, P.M. and Osborn, M.J. (1993) *Perceptions of Teaching: primary school teachers in England and France* (London, Cassell).

Campbell, J. and Neill, S. (1994) *Curriculum Reform at Key Stage 2* (London, Longman).

Casey, K. and Apple, M. (1989) Gender and the conditions of teachers' work: the development of understanding in America, in: S. Acker (ed.) *Teachers, Gender and Careers*, pp. 171–86 (Lewes, Falmer Press).

Croll, P. (ed.) (1996) *Teachers, Pupils and Primary Schooling: continuity and change* (London, Cassell).

Densmore, K. (1987) Professionalism, proletarianization and teachers' work, in: T. Popkewitz (ed.) *Critical Studies in Teacher Education* (Lewes, Falmer Press).

Gabriel, J. (1957) *An Analysis of the Emotional Problems of the Teacher in the Classroom* (London, Angus and Robertson).

Hargreaves, A. (1994) *Changing Teachers, Changing Times* (London, Cassell).

Jersild, A. (1952) *When Teachers Face Themselves* (Columbia, Teachers College Press).

Lee, P. (1973) Male and female teachers in elementary schools: an ecological analysis, *Teachers College Record*, 75, pp. 79–98.

National Commission on Education (1993) *Learning to Succeed* (London, Heinemann).

National Commission on Education (1996) *Success Against the Odds* (London, Routledge).

Nias, J. (1993) Changing times and changing identities: grieving for a lost self, in: R. Burgess (ed.) *Educational Research and Evaluation for Policy and Practice* (London, Falmer Press).

Nias, J., Southworth, G. and Yeomans, R. (1989) *Staff Relationships in the Primary School: a study of organizational cultures* (London, Cassell).

Osborn, M. (1996) Social class, educational opportunity and equal entitlement: dilemmas of schooling in England and France, paper presented at the American Education Research Association Annual Conference, New York.

Osborn, M., Broadfoot, P., Abbot, D., Croll, P. and Pollard, A. (1992) The impact of current changes in English primary schools on teacher professionalism, *Teachers College Record*, Fall.

Osborn, M., Croll, P., Broadfoot, P., Pollard, A., McNess, E. and Triggs, P. (1996) Policy into practice and practice into policy: creative mediation in the primary classroom, in: G. Helsby and G. McCulloch (eds) *Teachers and the National Curriculum* (London, Cassell).

Pollard, A. (1985) *The Social World of the Primary School* (London, Holt, Rinehart and Winston).

Pollard, A., Broadfoot, P., Croll, P., Osborn, M. and Abbott, D. (1994) *Changing English Primary Schools?* (London, Cassell).

Salzberger-Wittenberg, I., Henry, G. and Osborne, E. (1983) *The Emotional Experience of Teaching and Learning* (London, Routledge and Keegan Paul).

Woods, P. (1977) Teaching for survival, in: P. Woods and M. Hammersley (eds) *School Experience* (New York, St Martin's Press).

Woods, P. (1995) *Creative Teachers in Primary Schools* (Buckingham, Open University Press).

Marilyn Osborn
Research Fellow, University of Bristol School of Education

22 Teaching and the self

*Jennifer Nias**

The claim that teaching is a personal activity is often advanced as a reason why it cannot be systematically taught to others or fully brought into the public domain. Yet this claim is seldom explicated or justified, to the detriment of mutual understanding among people inside and outside the profession. In this article, I argue that to be a teacher in the primary (and often the middle) schools of England is to work in a historically determined context that encourages individualism, isolation, a belief in one's own autonomy and the investment of personal resources. Each of these conditions stresses the importance in teaching of the teacher as a person (as distinct from, though not as opposed to, the teacher as the possessor of occupational knowledge and skills). In other words, the self is a crucial element in the way teachers themselves construe the nature of their job. In turn, this directs attention to theoretical formulations of the self, a hypothetical construct which has been explored by, among others, poets, philosophers, psychologists, social psychologists and sociologists. In this article, I focus upon the sociological and psychological perspectives provided by symbolic interactionism and psychoanalysis (especially self-psychology), and in particular upon the distinctions which may be made between the self as 'me', the self as 'I' and the notion of 'identity'.

Most obviously, teaching is a personal activity because the manner in which each teacher behaves is unique. Teaching, like learning, has a perceptual basis. The minute-by-minute decisions teachers make within the shifting, unpredictable, capricious world of the classroom and the judgements they reach when they are reflecting on their work depend upon how they perceive particular events, behaviours, materials, persons. In turn, these perceptions are determined by schemata ('persistent, deep-rooted and well-organised classifications of ways of perceiving, thinking and behaving' which are also 'living and flexible', Vernon, 1955, p. 181) or basic assumptions ('schemata ... organised in more generalised, vague or ill-defined patterns', Abercrombie, 1969, p. 641) which help us to order and make sense of the world around us. Schemata and assumptions are learned; they are slowly built up as, from birth, we develop and exercise the skill of seeing (or hearing, smelling, tasting, touching). They are modified by experience and activity. Since no two people have the same life experiences, we all learn to perceive the world and ourselves as part of it in different ways. So teachers, as people, 'see' and interpret their pupils and the latter's actions and reactions according to perceptual patterns which are unique to themselves. No matter how pervasive particular aspects of a shared social or occupational culture may be or how well individuals are socialised into it, the attitudes and actions of each teacher are rooted in his/her own ways of perceiving the world.

This biological explanation for teachers' individualism exists side by side with a pervasive historical tradition which emphasises the teacher's personality. In his study of American elementary school teachers Lortie (1975, p. 79) has pointed to an unchallenged orthodoxy, that 'personal predispositions are not only relevant but, in fact, stand at the core of becoming a teacher'; and more recently, in the United Kingdom the same view has been expressed not only by writers such as Woods (1981) and Sikes *et al.* (1985) but also by HMI and the DES. In 1982, the DES Report on *The New Teacher in School* (DES, 1982, 6.2) claimed: 'HMI found that the personal qualities of the teachers were in many cases the decisive factor in their effectiveness. A similar view was put forward by schools'; and the government White Paper *Teaching Quality* (DES, 1983, p. 26) argued: 'Personality, character and commitment are as important as the specific knowledge and skills that are used in the day to day tasks of teaching.' Small wonder, then, that practitioners themselves perpetuate a largely unquestioned assumption that 'what gets taught is the teacher'.

This stress upon personality is encouraged by allegiance to philosophical traditions which see the personal relationship between teacher and learner as central to the educational process. Two centuries ago Rousseau wrote *Emile*, an imaginary account of the education of one child by his tutor. On to this Romantic preoccupation with the individual, practising educationalists grafted the Christian tradition, expressed by Froebel and Pestalozzi as respect and concern for the whole child and by Buber as the 'I–Thou' relationship (in which the teacher as a person becomes a resource for the self-activated development of the learner). Still today many primary school teachers see the personal relationship which they have with individual children not just as a means of establishing control and increasing motivation but also as the means by which education itself takes place (Nias, forthcoming; Woods, forthcoming).

Moreover, throughout their professional education and socialisation, teachers are led to believe that they are capable of 'knowing' not just one child, but all the pupils in their care (Alexander, 1984). When Kay Shuttleworth set up the first teacher training college in England at St John's, Battersea, he took many of his ideas from Pestalozzi's work in Switzerland. Among them were the notions that teaching should be inspired by love and that teachers should therefore live and work among their pupils. This aspiration was itself drawn partially from Froebel's metaphysical concern for the centrality of unity and wholeness and his consequent belief that education should be an organic process, free of artificial and damaging divisions. Teachers socialised into this tradition tend to identify with their classes, to talk of themselves in relationship to their pupils as 'we'. Indeed, many teachers derive intense satisfaction from feeling 'natural' and 'whole' in their relationship with children and from creating a sense of community within classes and schools (Nias, forthcoming).

The centrality of the personal relationship between teacher and pupils is further emphasised by the solitary nature of much primary teaching. Until recently the architectural design of most primary schools in the UK has unquestioningly followed the tradition, established in urban elementary schools in the nineteenth century, that instruction is best carried out in 'box' classrooms occupied by one teacher and a group of 30 to 40 children. These classrooms are cut off from one another, though they are usually linked by a corridor, a staircase, or, in older schools, a central hall. In addition, windows are often placed so that it is difficult for passing teachers to see into one another's rooms. The isolation imposed by architecture has helped to foster an occupational context from which teachers learn to expect that much of their working lives will be spent with children not adults. Further, initial teacher education provides students with relatively few chances to observe their more experienced colleagues in action and, except in open plan schools, the latter seldom see one another teaching. This lack of opportunity to 'sit by Nellie' encourages students and probationers to feel that they must survive by their own efforts and to believe in an occupational 'rite de passage' which equates the establishment of competence with suffering (Nias, 1987a). Altogether, as Lortie (1975) and Hargreaves (1980) have argued, teachers have little opportunity or incentive to develop shared professional knowledge or a collegial sense of the 'state of the art'. Teacher education, experience and conventional wisdom continually underline the uniqueness of the individual, the specificity of context and the primacy of the person.

These tendencies have been encouraged by the relative freedom from political control which primary teachers have until recently taken for granted (although, as Broadfoot and Osborn, 1986, point out in a comparative study of French and English teachers, the latter's freedom is restricted in practice by the power of their headteachers). For much of the past 100 years, teachers in Britain have felt it was their responsibility to make far-reaching decisions about the curriculum and teaching methods which they will use in their classes, to the point in some schools that there is little continuity, communication or agreement between classes in the same school. Teachers often learn to depend upon their own knowledge, interests and preferences in making pedagogic and curriculum decisions. Indeed, this freedom from external constraints and collegial influence is, for some teachers, one of the main attractions of the job (though others deplore the sense of incoherence which it sometimes gives to their work, Nias, 1980).

A sense of autonomy in matters of curriculum and pedagogy is closely related to the ideological freedom which most British primary teachers enjoy. This is particularly important because few of them are satisfied with imparting only knowledge or skills to their pupils. Rather they have always been chosen, or have selected themselves, in part for their concern with religious, moral, political or social values (Rich, 1933; Tropp, 1957). Indeed, in the past many have seen themselves as 'missionaries' or 'crusaders' (Floud, 1962), a tradition which still persists (Nias, 1981). The study by Ashton et al. (1975) of primary teachers' aims found that the majority thought that aims relating to social and moral education were more important than those which were concerned with intellectual, physical or aesthetic education, while Lortie (1975), Lacey (1977), Woods (1981) and Nias et al. (forthcoming) have all highlighted the continuing existence within the profession of individuals with strong dedication to religious, political or humanitarian ideals.

Kay Shuttleworth's vision of a band of 'intelligent Christian men entering on the instruction of the poor with religious devotion to their work' (quoted in Rich, 1933) is still, mutatis mutandis, a recognisable one in many schools.

However, as studies such as those by Ashton et al. (1975) and Hartley (1985) demonstrate, there is little agreement, even within single schools, on which moral or educational values should be transmitted. Indeed, given the different social and curricular traditions (Blyth, 1967) which have shaped the primary system and into which its teachers are socialised it would be surprising if there were. Educational writers such as Alexander (1984) and Kelly (1986) have drawn attention to the persistence of this plurality, arguing that conflicting views of the nature of knowledge, and thus of teaching and learning, still bedevil primary schools. The epistemological confusion which such authors describe does however allow those teachers and headteachers who have a coherent philosophy to pursue it with relative impunity. Despite recent political developments, the English system still offers plenty of scope to individuals who wish to propagate particular views of the educational process.

Teachers' freedom to make many of the decisions which closely affect their work and to select within broad limits the values which they seek to transmit has also been protected in the past few decades by attempts to define teaching as a profession and therefore to regard it as self-governing. Although political decisions taken in 1986 and 1987 have undermined these efforts in the UK and tend to reduce teaching to, at best, the level of a 'semi-profession' (Etzioni, 1969), habits of autonomy are likely to die hard. Teachers will probably go on expecting to enjoy large measures of personal choice and discretion in matters relating to the conduct of their classrooms.

Finally, there are some teachers who, consciously or unconsciously, reduce the boundaries between their occupational and other lives. For them, teaching is very 'inclusive' (Argyris, 1964), that is, it absorbs much of their time and energy and makes use of many of their talents, skills or abilities. For such people, teaching is particularly personal in the double sense that it draws upon interests and capacities which might, in other occupations, be reserved for non-work activities and that it allows little space for the development of alternative lives. Indeed, the more demanding it becomes of imagination, insight, problem-solving and professional skills, the more it offers an outlet for creative potential, thereby reducing individuals' need to seek the latter elsewhere. Similarly, when teaching is conceptualised as a relationship between two or more people, rather than as an instrumental activity, it becomes possible for teachers to find personal and emotional satisfactions within their working lives instead of outside them. I have further explored the implications for individuals of undertaking a highly 'inclusive' occupation in Nias (forthcoming).

The fact that teaching as an occupation is potentially inclusive is compounded by the chronic scarcity of resources from which it suffers. By definition, no teacher ever has enough time, energy and material resources to meet all the learning and personal demands of a large class of young children. To this shortage are now added recent expenditure cuts at both local and national levels. So, as an occupation, teaching has a bottomless appetite for 'commitment' (i.e. 'a readiness to allocate scarce personal resources', Lortie, 1975, p. 89). As a result, teachers are easily trapped. The more they identify with their jobs, the greater the satisfaction they receive from their personal relationship with individuals and classes, the more outlet they find in their work for varied talents and abilities, the greater the incentive that exists for them to invest their own personal and material resources in their teaching. They are, in short, beset by the paradox that the personal rewards to be found in their work come only from self-investment in it.

Primary teaching is, then, an activity which for psychological, philosophical and historical reasons can be regarded as individualistic, solitary and personal, inviting and in some senses requiring a high level of self-expenditure. It follows that any understanding of primary teachers' actions and reactions must be based upon knowledge of them as people.

However, this line of thinking leads into poorly charted territory. Surprisingly, an occupation which has for nearly 200 years attached great importance to the idea of knowing and catering for the individual child has paid little formal attention to the concept of the individual teacher. Particular primary teachers have attracted some largely unflattering attention from fiction writers, (see, for example, Biklen, 1986), but very little from academics or from teachers themselves. There have been a few attempts (notably Elbaz, 1983) to examine the professional or craft knowledge of individuals, to portray their 'ideologies' (Hartley, 1985) or personal constructs (Ingvarson and Greenway, 1984), or to record their feelings (e.g. Hannam *et al.*, 1976; Huggett, 1986). One or two life histories exist (e.g. Aspinwall, 1987) but there has so far been no work on individuals' lives and careers comparable to that carried out by Sikes *et al.* (1985) or Connell (1985) on secondary teachers. Individuals feature in the work of King (1978), Berlak and Berlak (1981) and Pollard (1985), but their opinions and activities are treated as if they were representatives of groups or sub-cultures. Moreover, studies such as these make more use of observation and questionnaires than of interviews. Few attempts, other than that of Nias (forthcoming) and Nias *et al.* (forthcoming) have been made to present a detailed portrayal of the subjective reality of teaching from the standpoint of and, as far as possible, in the words of teachers themselves. There is a gap here waiting to be filled.

To emphasise the personal nature of teaching is also to draw attention to the notion of the 'self'. Yet although terms such as 'self-concept', 'identity', 'self esteem', 'the ideal self' have multiplied in educational writings, they are, like the notion of the 'self' itself, hypothetical constructs which do not refer to anything tangible or directly observable. Any choice of explanatory system for them is therefore to some extent arbitrary.

One such system which offers many productive insights is symbolic interactionism, a set of ideas primarily associated with two Americans, Charles H. Cooley and George H. Mead. Although the psychologist William James made the distinction in the 1890s between 'I' and 'me', it was Cooley (1902, 1983 edition) who argued that through interaction with people to whose behaviour we attach symbolic meanings we learn to take other people's perspectives and so to see ourselves as we think they see us. In doing so we come to have an awareness of ourselves as objects. Mead (1934) elaborated this idea, claiming that the self can be an object to itself (that is, 'I' (ego) can observe, be aware of and think about 'me' (alter)). We experience ourselves in the same way that we experience the people and things with which we come in contact. More than that, by interacting (Mead argued by talking) with others we become aware of the attitudes they hold toward us and this in turn shapes the way we see ourselves. Our 'selves' are inescapably social. Deprived of interaction with others we would have no sense of self for 'selves can only exist in definite relationships with other selves' (Mead, 1934, p. 164).

This is not to claim that all interactions are equally important in determining the way we see ourselves. Social psychologists now generally accept that 'significant others' (the idea, though not the term, was coined by Cooley) have a particularly powerful effect upon our self-concept. For, as Cooley (1902, 1983 edition, p. 175) argues: 'In the presence of one whom we feel to be of importance, there is a tendency to enter into and adopt, by sympathy, his judgement of myself.' Mead built upon this idea when he introduced the concept of the 'generalised other'. His suggestion was that, in time and through repeated interactions, we internalise the attitudes not just of particular people but also of organised social groups (for instance, churches, political parties, community groups, workforces). When we do this, we supplement with new influences the forms of internal regulation we have acquired through identification with significant others. Our behaviour as adults is therefore likely to vary not just in relation to the social context of which we are immediately a part but also according to the 'reference group' (Newcomb, 1950) whom we have in-mind in any particular situation. In other words, Mead set the scene for the development of the notion of 'multiple selves', each sustained and regulated by reference to different 'generalised others'.

Yet few social psychologists would wish to defend a totally situational view of the self. Katz (1960) suggested that each individual develops through contact with significant others an inner self or core. Writing as a biologist, Abercrombie (1969) put forward similar views, arguing that through the processes of perception, individuals begin to develop at birth assumptions about the world and themselves as part of it. The most potent schemata or assumptions (including those which are self-referential) are established by close physical contact between the infant and growing child and those who care for him/her. Because they are formed before the child can talk, and 'having been made non-verbally are very difficult to talk about' (Abercrombie, 1969, p. 73), it is particularly hard for individuals to uncover the fundamental assumptions they have about themselves. These therefore remain relatively impervious to change.

Ball (1972) used the term 'substantial' to distinguish this inner core, which, he argued, is persistently defended and highly resistant to change. It comprises the most highly prized aspects of our self-concept and the attitudes and values which are salient to them. This idea, that we most strongly protect from challenge those attitudes which are expressive of the values by which we define ourselves, finds support from other theoretical perspectives. Rogers (1982) argued from his experience as a psychotherapist and educationalist that individuals need to maintain consistent self-concepts and will reject new ideas which they do not perceive as compatible with the latter. Festinger (1957), observing that people often find it psychologically uncomfortable to hold views which are mutually incompatible or to act in ways which are inconsistent with one or more of them, suggested that we resolve the resulting 'cognitive dissonance' by changing our views or actions so as to bring them into line with one another. Rokeach (1973) went further, claiming that the dissonances most likely to precipitate change in an individual arise not at the level of views but of beliefs and values. By implication, it is against dissonance in values or between values and actions that we most strongly protect ourselves. The group psychotherapist, Foulkes, was also of this opinion. He argued that 'the nuclear family imbues and impregnates the individual from his earliest phase of life and even before birth, with the total value system of the culture of which this family is part' (1975, p. 60). We become habituated to the patterns of behaviour derived from these values and very skilled in their defence, to the extent that in new situations we try to recreate the relationships which sustain and perpetuate the values from which our view of ourselves derives. There is then support from different disciplines for the idea that we each develop a relatively impervious 'substantial self which can be distinguished from our 'situational selves' and which incorporates those beliefs, values and attitudes which we feel to be most self-defining.

Two further distinctions need to be made with respect to the self as 'me'. The first is between self-concept and self-esteem. It is easy to envisage circumstances under which people are not happy with or proud of the image which they have of themselves. Though the evidence is inconclusive (Hargreaves *et al.*, 1975), it seems in general to support the idea that when there is a conflict between the two, people act so as to maintain a stable self-image, even though this image may not be the one they wish they had. This may be in part because self-perceivers have access to 'privileged information' (Hampson, 1982, p. 192), that is to knowledge of past and present experience which is denied to their partners in the interaction. Such knowledge may affect their perceptions of themselves and also of the messages being transmitted by their partners. The second distinction is related: social psychologists often distinguish between people's image of themselves as they would like to be ('ideal') and as they think that they are ('real'). However, if one is guided by Thomas' (1931) well-known dictum that 'what people believe to be true is true in its consequences', this distinction becomes blurred. Unless people make it clear when they are speaking self-referentially, that they are making a distinction between their 'ideal' and 'real' selves, it may be helpful to assume that they have the latter in mind.

So far, the discussion has been of the self as 'me'. Symbolic interactionists also however conceptualise the self as 'I', the active subject which initiates and innovates as well as responding to the messages about 'me' that it receives from others. As a concept the self as subject is however even more elusive than that of the self as object because 'I' turns into 'me' as soon as the actor is self-conscious, as soon, that is, as his/her actions become the object of reflexive thought. As Mead said, 'The "I" of this moment is present in the "me" of the next moment ... I cannot turn round quick enough to catch myself' (Mead, 1934, p. 174).

Nevertheless the 'I' is important because it is:

> that part of the self which is relatively free of social constraints: it is impulsive
> and capable of inventing new ideas or meanings not sent in by the 'others'. It

is that most private core of inner experience which has a degree of autonomy ... The 'me' cannot be anything but conformist ... (but when we realise) that in some respect we acted against the grain of society, such a realisation is awareness of the 'I' and its capacities.

(Introduction to Sociology Course Team, 1981)

In other words, Mead's notion of the 'ego' makes it possible for us to reject the concept of a self which is entirely the product of social conditioning.

But accepting that the self exists as subject as well as object brings us no closer to knowing how we should conceptualise or characterise the 'ego'. This may in part be because, as Holland (1977) has so clearly shown, attempts from Mead onwards to explain the social self have been unable (or unwilling) to come to terms with the powerful, instinctual forces of the human personality to which Freud drew attention over a century ago. Freud's analysis of personality structure provided two hypothetical constructs – the superego (the controlling 'conscience' provided by internalised values) and the ego (the conscious actor in touch with the daily realities of living) – which fitted in relatively well with the idea of a socially constructed self. It also, however, presented us with the id (the unconscious, a potentially explosive mixture of instincts and repressed memories). This aspect of the self is, by definition, resistant to investigation but because of the forces which are contained within it, it continually influences every aspect of human thought, feeling and behaviour. It is obviously difficult to accommodate within a view of the self which emphasises socialisation, continuity and conformity rather than individuality, conflict and change.

Yet the 'I' is an inescapable part of education. Books such as those by Jersild (1952) remind us that the encounter between teachers and learners is an emotional experience. Richardson (1967; 1973) and Salzberger-Wittenberg et al. (1983) have both used an explicitly Freudian perspective to explore the actions and reactions of student teachers and teachers in relation to their pupils and colleagues. Abercrombie carried her work on the unconscious nature of perception into higher education, seeking to increase the autonomy and responsibility of adult learners by helping 'each participant to understand his own behaviour and acquire better control over it' (1981, p. 52). Her first project, with medical students, is reported in Abercrombie (1969); the second, with architecture students, in Abercrombie (1974); the third, on improving small-group teaching in universities, in Abercrombie and Terry (1978, 1979). In addition accounts of her work with teachers, guided by the same insights, appear in Abercrombie and Terry (1979) and Lintott (1986). In short, there is growing evidence that teachers' attitudes, actions and responses are influenced by their unconscious as well as their conscious selves, by the parts of themselves which they have rejected or 'split off' (Holland, 1977) as well as by those which they accept.

However, not all psychoanalysts adopt a view of the 'I' which involves the denial and repression of parts of it. Rather, self-psychology (Kohut, 1971) stresses the continuation into adulthood of self-love or narcissism, seeing it as the means by which many admirable human qualities are developed. Kohut presents a view of the self which, drawing upon infants' apparent inability to distinguish in early life between self and others, argues that nurturant figures in their environments become what he calls 'selfobjects' (Kohut, 1971, p. 27). Since young children are inescapably self-regarding, these extensions of self mirror back to them their own sense of 'narcissistic grandiosity' (Kohut, 1971, p. 25). Infants also expect to be able to control these 'selfobjects' as if they were themselves. With the passage of time, they learn to differentiate self and environment and they realise the limits both of the care provided by their nurturant figures and of their own controlling powers. As this happens, Kohut argues, the qualities detected as missing from their nurturing 'selfobjects' are incorporated into their own egos and adopted as their own ideals. At the same time, their self-love and self-importance become less extreme and unrealistic and are integrated into the ego as conventional aims and forms of ambition. So, early care-providers fulfil both a mirroring and an idealising function for young children. As these functions are gradually internalised, individuals develop a stable capacity for self-regard and self-regulation and a mature ability to love people and things that exist independently of themselves.

However, as adults they retain their early tendency to relate to the world and people in it as if these were part of themselves. Indeed, Kohut argues, self-love develops into culturally valuable attributes such as creativity, the ability to be empathetic, a sense of humour and wisdom. This development is accompanied and is in some senses sustained by the fact that we do not lose our need, especially in periods of intellectual, biological or social change, for relationships which mirror or affirm our sense of self-esteem and present us with an idealised picture of strength and concern for others. The fact that we are able to revert at times of stress and confusion to infantile levels of narcissism enables us to treat these as transitional periods during which we can reshape or rebuild ourselves in a manner more in tune than previously with the external circumstances that caused our distress.

This account of the ego differs from that of classical psychoanalytic theory, in positing separate development in individuals of the capacities to relate to their environments both as part of themselves and as independent of them (as opposed to the Freudian view that the normal individual develops beyond narcissism and that the persistence of the former is a sign of regression or dysfunctional dependence on a mother figure). Now, widespread acceptance of Freudian notions has resulted in a socially defined view of the ego, and thus of the individual teacher, from which not only negative emotions but also self-love are largely banished. Yet the persistent self-referentialism of teachers, their tendency to treat their pupils as 'selfobjects' and thus to seek simultaneously to control and to look to them for reinforcement of their self-esteem (Nias, forthcoming) suggests that Pajak (1981) may be right in pressing for fuller understanding among educationalists of Kohut's views. It may well be that a continuing capacity for narcissism underpins the development of many aspirations and qualities which teachers, as adults, display. Certainly, any view of the 'I' which discounts self-love is as incomplete as one which ignores the controlling superego and the instinctual drives of the id.

Notwithstanding lack of agreement among psychologists and social psychologists about the nature of the 'I', many teachers are intuitively aware of its existence (Nias, forthcoming). They and others may well recognise this expression of it, described by William James in a letter to his wife (quoted in Erikson, 1968, p. 19):

> A man's character is discernible in the mental and moral attitude in which, when it came upon him, he felt himself most deeply and intensely active and alive. At such moments there is a voice inside which speaks and says, 'This is the real me'!

James does not offer a definition of the 'I' and his description contains no criteria for its recognition by anyone other than himself. Nevertheless, his is an experience of which writers from diverse fields (ranging from poetry to psychology) are aware. Despite the many specific and general meanings which they, and others, have attached to the term 'identity', it may be useful to retain its use for those occasions when the 'I' speaks most deeply of the 'real me'.

None of this however is to argue for a static view of the self. To be sure, the heart of the 'I' (a sense of identity), and the core of the 'me' (the substantial self) are hard to reach even by reflexive activity (e.g. introspection and self-examination), are well defended and difficult to change. Yet, as I have argued in Nias (1987b) both are open to modification, development and even (as St Paul's experience on the road to Damascus suggests) radical redefinition. However, as the work of Marris (1958, 1974) shows, changes in self-definition reduce an individual's sense of control over self and environment. They are, in consequence, accompanied by feelings of loss, anxiety and anger, particularly when (for example, in bereavement, tribal dislocation, redundancy) they threaten fundamental aspects of the self. In such cases, accommodation to them will be painful and conflictual. It is clear from the work of Woods (1981), Nias (1984, 1985) and Pollard (1985) that, being people, teachers too are threatened by the prospect of changes in self-definition, that many of the gratifications and dissatisfactions of teaching are related to the maintenance of an individual's self-image, self-esteem and identity, and that they develop situationally specific strategies to protect themselves from the need to alter the ways in which they perceive themselves.

There are then good reasons for regarding teaching as an occupation which makes calls upon the personality, experience, preferences, skills, attitudes, beliefs, values, interpersonal qualities and ideas of the individual practitioner. The culture and physical context of schools, together with the historical and philosophical traditions of primary teaching and the resulting way in which the activity is often defined all create a situation in which who and what people perceive themselves to be matters as much as what they can do. There are a growing number of classroom studies which illuminate the latter but as yet virtually no information about the former. To assist preliminary steps in this direction, the theoretical frameworks provided by symbolic interactionism and self-psychology have much to offer.

I have used these perspectives to throw light on 150 interviews made as part of a longitudinal study of early and mid-career teachers in primary and middle schools (Nias, forthcoming), looking in particular at the subjective realities of teaching, job-satisfaction and dissatisfaction, motivation, staff relationships and the extent to which teaching as a career is compatible with notions of adult development. In this article I have attempted to establish the basis on which the arguments there are constructed, suggesting that in trying to understand what teachers say and do, we must be aware of the ways in which theirs is personal activity in which the self is often heavily invested.

Note

* Originally published in: *Cambridge Journal of Education* 17: 3, 178–185.

References

Abercrombie, M. L. J. (1969) *The Anatomy of Judgement: an Investigation into the Processes of Perception and Reasoning*. Harmondsworth: Penguin.

Abercrombie, M. L. J. (1974) Improving the education of architects. In Collier, K. (ed.) *Innovation in Higher Education*. London: NFER.

Abercrombie, M. L. J. (1981) Changing basic assumptions about teaching and learning. In Boud, D. (ed.) *Developing Student Autonomy in Learning*. London: Kogan Page.

Abercrombie, M. L. J. and Terry, P. M. (1978) *Talking to Learn*. Guildford: Society for Research into Higher Education.

Abercrombie, M. L. J. and Terry, P. M. (1979) *Aims and Techniques of Group Teaching*. 4th edn. Guildford: Society for Research into Higher Education.

Alexander, R. (1984) *Primary Teaching*. London: Holt, Rinehart and Winston.

Argyris, C. (1964) *Integrating the Individual and the Organisation*. New York: Wiley.

Ashton, P. *et al.* (1975) *The Aims of Education: a Study of Teacher Opinions*. London: Macmillan.

Aspinwall, K. (1986) Teacher biography: the in-service potential. *Cambridge Journal of Education*. Vol. 16, No. 3, 210–215.

Ball, S. (1972) Self and identity in the context of deviance: the case of criminal abortion. In Scott, R. and Douglas, J. (eds) *Theoretical Perspectives on Deviance*. New York: Basic Books.

Berlak, A. and Berlak, H. (1981) *The Dilemmas of Schooling*. London: Methuen.

Biklen, S. K. (1986) Good morning, Miss Mundy: Fictional portrayals of young female teachers. Paper presented at AERA Conference, San Francisco.

Blyth, W. A. (1967) (2nd edn) *English Primary Education*. Vol. II. London: Routledge and Kegan Paul.

Broadfoot, P. and Osborn, M. (1986) Teachers' conceptions of their professional responsibility: some international comparisons. Paper presented to BERA Conference, Bristol.

Connell, R. (1985) *Teachers' Work*. London: Allen and Unwin.

Cooley, C. (1902) (1983 edn) *Human Nature and the Social Order*. New Brunswick, New Jersey: Transaction Books.

DES, (1982) *The New Teacher in School*. HMI Series: Matters for Discussion 15. London: HMSO.

DES (1983) *Teaching Quality*. London: HMSO.

Elbaz, F. (1983) *Teacher Thinking: a Study of Practical Knowledge*. London: Croom Helm.

Erikson, E. (1968) (1983 edn) *Identity: Youth and Crisis*. London: Faber and Faber.

Etzioni, A. (ed.) (1969) *The Semi-Professions and their Organization*. New York: Free Press.

Festinger, L. (1957) *A Theory of Cognitive Dissonance*. Stanford, California: Stanford University Press.

Floud, J. (1962) Teaching the affluent society. *Brit. J. Soc.* 13, 299–308.

Foulkes, S. H. (1975) A short outline of the therapeutic processes in group-analytic psychotherapy. *Group Analysis*, 8, 59–63.

Hampson, S. (1982) The construction of personality. In Barnes, P. *et al.* (eds) (1984) *Personality, Development and Learning*. London: Hodder and Stoughton/The Open University.

Hannam, C. *et al.* (1971) *The First Year of Teaching*. Harmondsworth: Penguin.

Hargreaves, D. (1980) The occupational culture of teachers. In Woods, P. (ed.) *Teacher Strategies: Explorations in the Sociology of the School*. London: Croom Helm.

Hargreaves, D. *et al.* (1975) *Deviance in the Classroom*. London: Routledge and Kegan Paul.

Hartley, D. (1985) *Understanding the Primary School as an Organisation*. London: Croom Helm.

Holland, R. (1977) *Self and Social Context*. London: Macmillan.

Huggett, F. (1986) *Teachers*. London: Weidenfeld and Nicholson.

Ingvarson, L. and Greenway, P. (1984) Portrayals of teacher development. *Australian Journal of Education* 28 (1), 45–65.

Introduction to Sociology Course Team (1981) *Self in Social Context*. Milton Keynes: Open University.

Jcrsild. A. (1952) *When Teachers Face Themselves'*. Columbia: Teachers College Press.

Katz, D. (1960) The functional approach to the study of attitude change. *Public Opinion Quarterly*, 24, 163–204.

Kelly, A. (1986) *Knowledge and Curriculum Planning*. London: Harper and Row.

King, R. (1978) *All Things Bright and Beautiful: a Sociological Study of Infant Schools*. Chichester: Wiley.

Kohut, H. (1971) The analysis of the self; a systematic approach to the psychoanalytic treatment of narcissistic personality disorders. (Psychoanalytic study of the child. Monograph No. 4) Int. Univ. Press.

Lacey, C. (1977) *The Socialisation of Teachers*. London: Methuen.

Lintott, B. (1986) Group work in a course for teachers. Mimeo, Cambridge: Cambridge Institute of Education.

Lortie, D. (1975) *School Teacher*. Chicago: University of Chicago Press.

Marris, P. (1958) *Widows and Their Families*. London: Routledge and Kegan Paul.

Marris, P. (1974) *Loss and Change*. London: Routledge and Kegan Paul.

Mead, G. H. (1934) *Mind, Self and Society*. Chicago: University of Chicago Press.

Newcomb, T. (1950) *Social Psychology*. New York: Dryden.

Nias, J. (1980) Leadership styles and job satisfaction in primary schools. In Bush, T. *et al.* (eds) *Approaches to School Management*. London: Harper and Row.

Nias, J. (1981) Commitment and motivation in primary school teachers. *Educational Review* 33, 181–190.

Nias, J. (1984) Definition and maintenance of self in primary education. *Brit. J. Soc. Ed.* 5 (3), 267–280.

Nias, J. (1985) A more distant drummer: teacher development as the development of self. In Barton, L. and Walker, S. (eds) *Social Change and Education*. London: Croom Helm.

Nias, J. (1987a) Learning the job while playing a part: staff development in the early years of teaching. In Southworth, G. (ed.) *Readings in Primary Management*. Lewes: Falmer Press.

Nias, J. (1987b) *Seeing Anew: Teachers' Theories of Action*. Geelong: Deakin University.

Nias, J. (forthcoming) *On Becoming and Being a Teacher (provisional title)*. London: Methuen.

Nias, J., Southworth, G. and Yeomans, R. (forthcoming) *Knowing the School as an Organisation* (provisional title). London: Cassell.

Pajak, E. (1981) Teaching and the psychology of self. *Am. J. Ed.* 9, 1–13.

Pollard, A. (1985) *The Social World of the Primary School*. London: Holt, Rinehart and Winston.

Rich, R. (1933) *The Training of Teachers in England and Wales in the Nineteenth Century*. London: Cambridge University Press.

Richardson, J. E. (1967) *Croup Study for Teachers*. London: Routledge and Kegan Paul.

Richardson, J. E. (1973) *The Teacher, the Task and the School*. London: Methuen.

Rogers, C. (1982) *A Social Psychology of Schooling*. London: Routledge and Kegan Paul.

Rokeach, M. (1983) *The Nature of Human Values*. New York: Free Press.

Salzburger-Wittenburg, I. *et al.* (1983) *The Emotional Experience of Learning and Teaching*. London: Routledge and Kegan Paul.

Sikes, P. *et al.* (1985) *Teachers' Careers*. Lewes: Falmer.

Thomas, W. (1931) The relation of research to the social process. In *Essays on Research in Social Science*. Washington: Brookings Ins.

Tropp, A. (1957) *The Schoolteachers*. London: Heinemann.

Vernon, M. (1955) The functions of schemata in perceiving. *Psychological Review* 62 (3), 180–193.

Woods, P. (1981) Strategies, commitment and identity: making and breaking the teacher role. In Barton, L. and Walker, S. (eds) *School, Teachers and Teaching*. Barcombe: Falmer.

Woods, P. (forthcoming) The art of teaching in primary school. In Delamont, S. (ed.) *The Primary School Teacher*. Lewes: Falmer.

23 The emotional contours and career trajectories of (disappointed) reform enthusiasts

*Judith Warren Little**[*][†]

Introduction

For the past several years, I have explored the locally situated meanings that teachers and others attach to large-scale 'school restructuring' in the USA. More than in any prior studies of teachers' work lives, I have found myself drained at the end of each day of observation and interviewing. I attribute this state not simply to the intellectual concentration and physical stamina required for extended field research, but to the emotional range and intensity I confront at every turn. Amid well-wrought narratives and cogent analyses of school life, teachers weave vivid tales of exhilaration and despair, anticipation and disappointment, intimacy and loss. Emotions lie very near the surface in these schools. As teachers reach the four year point in a five year funded program of school change, they more frequently employ the language of 'burnout' to describe themselves or their colleagues. Teachers report to us and to one another that they are 'pulling back', 'hanging in' or 'moving on', signaling not only turning points in relation to particular reforms, but also certain shifts in the contours of their teaching lives and careers.

In this paper, I examine the intersection of heightened emotionality and shifting career contours among teachers engaged in large-scale reform movements in US secondary schools. The significance of this analysis lies not in demonstrating once again the social and intellectual demands associated with innovation, but in investigating the power of ambitious reforms to influence teachers' career trajectories and professional commitments.

Although this work might be seen broadly as contributing to research on conditions of teachers' work and the dynamics of school change, it responds most directly to a theoretical and practical problem framed by Michael Huberman's analysis of teachers' career experiences. In his study of the career trajectories of Swiss secondary teachers, Huberman (1989, 1993) reports that teachers who engaged in large scale or 'big idea' reforms were likely to end their careers less satisfied than those who had simply tended the gardens of their individual classrooms. Those who became disillusioned or fatalistic later in their careers often pointed to their earlier disappointment in the conduct or consequences of some major innovation. Huberman (1989) summarizes:

Teachers who steered clear of reforms or other multiple-classroom innovations but who invested consistently in classroom-level experiments ... were more likely to be satisfied later on in their career ... [H]eavy involvement in school-wide innovation was a fairly strong predictor of disenchantment after 20–25 years of teaching.

(pp. 50–51)

Huberman's conception is consistent with that of organizational theorists who define career not simply in relation to organizational structure, as a sequence of formal posts and promotions, but in social and personal relationship to the work undertaken. (In the US, this perspective originates in the work of Everett Hughes in the 1930s, but see especially van Maanen and Barley, 1984.) Such a perspective acknowledges the 'flatness' of teaching careers with regard to formal promotional opportunities, but takes serious account of other structures of organizational opportunity (e.g. teaching assignment) and other sources of career satisfaction. Further, its focus on the meanings that persons attach to work, work conditions and work relations enables us to theorize more precisely about the relationship between organizational context and career experience.

My purpose here is to begin to specify more fully the sources of long-term optimism or fatalism that reside in teachers' periodic encounters with reform movements. Of practical import are questions regarding the scope and conditions of school reform and related questions regarding the sources of teacher engagement and commitment. Would one scale back the quest for institutional reform in the interest of courting career satisfaction? How do teachers' experiences with large-scale reform breed disappointment and how might the factors contributing to disappointment be modified? What are the classroom and career consequences of disillusionment?

This analysis focuses on the experience of self-described reform enthusiasts during the first three years of a five year program of school restructuring in US comprehensive high schools. Specifically, it concentrates on those whose efforts have resulted in some form of personal defeat and career regress during that period. In major structural reforms, the stakes are often large and teachers may stand to win or lose in important ways. In the Swiss case, the creation of the middle school and the introduction of co-educational classes in the upper school 'modified the career of a great number of teachers in a direct way' (Huberman, 1993, p. 247). In the UK, the comprehensivization movement of the 1960s disrupted the careers of many secondary modern teachers – hence Beynon's (1985) portrait of the 'embittered Mr Pickwick' – and engendered conflicts over school purpose, curriculum and pedagogy (Ball, 1987). Although the reforms undertaken in these US schools do not approximate the scale or permanence of the Swiss or British structural reforms of the 1960s, they do implicate central features of school organization, curricular and instructional values and teachers' work conditions.

The reform agenda – reinventing the high school

Ambitious reforms have the capacity to engage teachers deeply while also challenging the 'fundamental grammar of schooling' (Tyack and Tobin, 1994). The ambitious secondary school reforms of the past decade respond to a litany of criticisms, many of them voiced by teachers as well as outside observers. In a series of studies completed in the early 1980s, critics charged that the high school curriculum was superficial and fragmented, sacrificing rigor and coherence to other compelling interests – most prominently, the interest in maintaining school attendance and social order (see especially Cusick, 1983; Powell et al., 1985). These and other studies challenged what Engstrom (1991) has called the 'encapsulation' of school knowledge in a curriculum far removed from out-of-school domains of knowledge use and production. Schools were also faulted for failures of equity and social justice, particularly those stemming from curricular tracking, for bureaucratic controls that curtailed teachers' professional discretion and for large size that bred anonymity, indifference and isolation. Portraits of teaching highlighted a few stellar examples against a more uniform backdrop of sterile pedagogy (see Boyer, 1983; Sizer, 1984; McNeil, 1986).

During the 1980s and early 1990s, reform advocates (including groups of activist teachers) sought remedies in a broadly defined campaign to 'reinvent' or 'restructure' the high school. The major reform documents and initiatives echo certain common refrains. They argue for more depth and meaning in the subject curriculum, often accompanied by efforts to develop an integrated or interdisciplinary curriculum. They seek greater 'personalization' in the teacher–student relationship through the development of advisory (pastoral) roles, smaller schools or smaller units within large high schools. They shape new roles and organizational structures that entail shared responsibility for students and a higher degree of interdependence among teachers. Reformers advocate more 'authentic' forms of instruction grounded in constructivist theories of learning. Some urge closer ties between academic study and work education and between school and community. And finally, they envision new professional roles in leadership and decision making, joined to new forms of governance that sometimes involve parents, students or community members.

Each of these strands of reform implicates long-established features of secondary teaching. Especially at issue are teachers' conceptions of their subject fields and their affiliation with departments and other professional communities, their perspective on the purposes of schooling, their expressed curricular priorities and preferred instructional approaches, the norms and values surrounding collegial relationships in and out of school and their view of the legitimate bases of leadership. The significance of each for teachers' work is well documented and each in some manner has bearing on teachers' conception of work and engagement in it (see for example, Little, 1995a, b; Siskin, 1994b; Talbert and McLaughlin, 1994). Each strand of reform thus introduces the prospect that fundamental beliefs about teaching and learning will be challenged and deep-seated facets of identity and professional community somehow altered.

These multiple strands of reform coincide in programs of state-funded school restructuring in California, giving rise to the cases I examine here. The selection of cases is pragmatic – they are among the more fully analyzed cases from two sites in which field work first began and where the problem of emotionality and career trajectory first became apparent. Eventually, the data will encompass teachers, administrators and other staff, students and parents from more than ten comprehensive high schools and will form the basis of an analysis that reaches more deeply to the origins and consequences of teachers' involvement in school-wide reform. In both of these early-stage schools, we conducted interviews and observations with a wide range of teachers – veterans and newcomers; teachers of core academics and teachers in vocational and elective fields, those in formal leadership positions and those who say they are 'regular classroom teachers', those who embrace the reform ideas and those who oppose them or are simply indifferent. We also interviewed a diverse group of students (from honors to 'at risk'), counselors or other specialists and administrators.

The exact proportion of reform supporters in the combined staff of approximately 140 cannot be determined from our data, as we did not reach every individual in these two sites. However, interviews yield a pool of approximately 50 teachers who vividly and explicitly expressed support for one or more of the fundamental premises of the reform and who might reasonably have been labeled 'enthusiasts' in the first year of the study. Of these, fully 80 percent had suffered serious setbacks or stresses by the end of the second year and about 20 percent had left altogether; of those that remained, many scaled back their involvement, investing energy in the work of a small team or special project. Teachers' emotional contours in these two schools tended more often toward increasing frustration, disappointment or cynicism. At issue, then, are the consequences for individuals and institutions when enthusiasm turns to disaffection on a sizable scale.[1]

Emotional contours, career moments and reform experience: three cases

However broad and comprehensive any school-wide agenda for reform, teachers establish the meaning of broad principles in the context of specific social relations and against the backdrop of personal histories, i.e. *school-wide* reform ideas unfold in quite localized *within-school* settings. The following three cases illuminate these within-school contexts and dynamics of school-wide reform and the ways in which they influence teachers' emotional equilibrium and career disposition. These cases are consistent with the larger body of preliminary data, reflecting the frequent pattern of diminished faith in reform among those who begin as enthusiasts.

Case 1: Vivian Michaels

Vivian Michaels is a founding member of a graphic arts 'academy' that embodies one strand of her school's broad reform agenda – its proclaimed interest in strengthening the ties between academic and vocational education. In the first year of this configuration, Vivian describes her passionate endorsement of the school's reform agenda and her own particular mission in the academy ('absolutely the way to go for kids'). To Vivian, teaching in the academy seems a perfect career move. She came to high school teaching from a previous career in nursing and her own educational background disposed her to be a subject generalist. Like many others in this school, she now teaches a combined program of social studies and

English (titled 'humanities'). Vivian's colleagues in the academy during its first year include a graphic arts specialist and a teacher of math and science. For her, the assignment to this team is a good fit: 'I have a good background in science and a fairly good background in maths. As far as (curriculum) integration, it all looks integrated to me'. She and her two co-founders speak in glowing terms of their role in launching a venture that the school and community have deemed significant.

Over the two years that followed, Vivian sustained her belief in the educational premises of the career academy but recorded a precipitous decline in the web of social and institutional supports that helped feed her initial enthusiasm. Expectations for program development intensified, with pressure from administrators and funders to establish well-structured work internships, create a series of appropriate assessment methods, expand the supply of integrated curriculum units and extend the entire program to an additional grade level. At the same time, administrative support began to dwindle – reduction in paid summer planning time and the threat of eliminating the teachers' common preparation time. As the program expanded, the school recruited two new academic teachers to join the team, but these teachers soon began to express ambivalence about the academy's vocational focus and a reluctance to alter their basic curriculum in the interest of cross-subject projects. Distressed about what she deemed a compromise of the academy's core values, Vivian pressed her case in team meetings that often turned stormy. For the first time since her arrival, she experienced classroom difficulties and her confidence as a 'great teacher' was shaken. After a series of bitter encounters with colleagues, administrators and the academy's external partners, Vivian announced that she was resigning to take a new post in another state.

Case 2: Meredith Hunt

Meredith Hunt had taught mathematics in the same school for nearly 20 years and was serving as chair of the maths department when the school's new principal launched a restructuring campaign. Meredith identified herself as an advocate and veteran of change who boasted a long record of innovations in mathematics, instructional methods and school desegregation. She was an early supporter of the restructuring agenda, attracted by its public commitment to improving the performance of the school's increasingly diverse student population and, more centrally, by the promise of a more open structure of governance and decision making. But the devil lay in the details, as she and the principal clashed over the latter's decision to abolish all remedial maths courses and to modify the scoring of basic math proficiency examinations so that lower scores would be considered 'passing'. From Meredith's perspective, restructuring quickly developed along lines that constituted an assault on the integrity of the academic subjects. At the same time, Meredith's opportunities to confront such issues in a public forum quickly diminished. The school's new organizational plan reduced the influence of departments and department chairs in favor of interdisciplinary groups (houses) led by 'head teachers'.

Over a two year period, Meredith developed a tale of disillusionment and loss, of being displaced in several respects: from a leadership role as department chair and mentor to new teachers; from a position of influence over teacher hiring, curriculum priorities and classroom practice; from the company of good and talented colleagues who resigned or retired; from her classroom (and even her parking place) and her preferred schedule of classes and planning times; overall, from what felt like 'her school'. She said that she and others had been subject to administrative retribution or 'vengeance' in response to their criticisms of changes in curriculum and assessment priorities. At the time of our last visit, she was campaigning for presidency of the local teachers' union while fulfilling a teaching assignment outside her primary field.

Case 3: Barrie Everett

Barrie Everett was among the experienced teachers who formed the first cohort of teachers at her school when it opened less than a decade ago. The school adopted an explicit plan to transform the high school experience, with equity achieved by heterogeneous grouping of students and collegiality fostered by interdisciplinary teams of teachers. Teachers who sought positions at the school in those early days did so in large part because they were advocates for the reform agenda. For most of the time that she has taught history and government here, Barrie has worked in partnership with an English teacher whom she credits with having been her mentor and intellectual companion. Throughout our study, Barrie was highly visible as a member of committees, co-founder of an interdisciplinary program in the eleventh and twelfth grades, grade-level interdisciplinary coordinator and facilitator of a teacher research group.

Barrie's descriptions of the school's development are both incisively analytic and intensely personal. Employing a metaphor of 'the pioneers and the settlers', she charts the changes in staff composition and professional orientation. The pioneers shared a conception of the school and relied upon teacher partnerships and administrative flexibility to translate broad principles into action. At the same time, they 'staked out territory' that was both conceptual and social, forming the basis of eventual divisions among the growing staff. Staff were divided about the value of heterogeneous grouping; partnerships increasingly took the form of 'arranged marriages' that had little meaning for teachers and left little mark in the classroom. With greater size came the tendency to formalize expectations and relationships. Barrie recorded her growing disappointment in the routinization of innovation and criticized teacher leaders who have pushed for uniformity rather than defending experimentation. Her teaching partnership began to unravel, troubled by disagreements over the amount of 'give and take' required to create an integrated curriculum. She began to speak of relinquishing some of her organizational responsibilities, confining her activity more to her own classroom ('I'm regrouping. I'm pulling back'). Over time, she expanded her professional activity outside the school – enrolling in a PhD program, participating in professional conferences and becoming a teacher education supervisor. She began to envision life and career beyond this school, although 'I don't see myself as being a very viable researcher or teacher educator if I don't continue to teach'. Among the options she was considering was her own 'charter school' under the auspices of a state-funded program, an opportunity she saw as once again 'pioneering'.

In some respects, these constitute highly individual tales. Teachers vary in their teaching knowledge, experience and values. They differ in the formal positions they occupy as the reform begins and in what they stand to lose or gain by the success of the reform effort. They embrace the proposed reforms for quite different reasons and encounter quite different constellations of institutional and social support. Finally, they vary in the intensity of their involvement and in the significance of that involvement in shaping career meaning and direction. Of the three cases, Meredith alone brings to reform certain firmly developed commitments to traditional conceptions of subject and traditional practices of teaching. In her early enthusiasm for shared decision making and improved student performance, Meredith did not anticipate the ways in which restructuring would effectively undermine a central tenet of her professional self – that of subject specialist. Neither Vivian nor Barrie placed the same value on subject specialism, but both described a personal stake in some aspect of work that was implicated in the restructuring. It is precisely the differences among these cases that call attention to the intersection of individual biography and institutional reform and that cast doubt upon reform strategies that do not take explicit account of individual history, context and perspective.

In other respects, these tales are linked by what they reveal of the collective aspects of teachers' experience in restructuring high schools. Most vividly, perhaps, they establish that active engagement in school-wide reform may constitute an emotional investment of some magnitude – an aspect of collective experience that remains, nonetheless, collectively unexamined. In addition, the cases locate individuals in relation to various long-standing traditions and contexts of high school teaching. Although the individual teachers vary in their affiliation with subjects and subject departments (Meredith being the most closely affiliated and Vivian the least), each case underscores the salience of subject specialism and departmental organization. Each case points to within-school teams, partnerships and departments that form the collegial environments in which the meaning of reform is discovered. Administrators' symbolic and material support – for what, for whom and for how long – figures prominently in each of the stories. In one way or another, external relationships to professional or public communities play a part in teachers' resilience or defeat.

The contexts of heightened emotionality

By teachers' accounts, large scale school restructuring is both ambitious and difficult. Yet with few exceptions, it is not the failure of promising ideas that gives rise to the emotional sub-text so prominent in these teachers' talk and in the interactions that we witnessed between them and their colleagues. Rather, it is the relentless negotiation of principle-as-practice and the reshaping of workplace conditions and relationships that deplete or restore teachers' emotional energy. Whatever the power of broad principles to excite interest and motivate action, teachers nonetheless experience reform at closer quarters – in the small niches of particular teams or partnerships, with particular cohorts of students, through responsibility for this or that curriculum. These cases point to certain contextual conditions that intensify teachers' emotional experience and that might plausibly account for lasting effects on career satisfaction.

First, emotionality rises most noticeably in relation to work *outside* the classroom with colleagues, administrators and other adults (parents, community representatives). Adult relationships supply much of the emotional content of teachers' interviews. Indeed, all three of these cases alert us to the possibility that the reform environment will draw emotional energy away from the teacher–student relationship and invest it in the adult work required to make the reform 'school-wide' or even 'team-wide'. Vivian speaks frequently and eloquently about her new-found professional ties and spends a large share of her out-of-class time with colleagues; Barrie occupies several leadership roles in the school and much of her intellectual energy goes toward making sense of reform as it unfolds; even Meredith is preoccupied with restoring the influence of the department heads and finding a way to exert influence on curricular decision making.

When these professional exchanges go well, they yield great satisfaction. In a brief passage in which she employs some variant of the word 'excite' seven times, Vivian recalls,

> The highlight of my two years in the academy was the synergism – the professional synergism. That to me was the ultimate.... To see the ideas bubble and grow and just go with it, and then to be able to implement it right away and do it.... I mean, it was just so exciting!

When the same exchanges engender conflict or when team efforts fail, they expose teachers' differences or uncertainties more publicly than do failed experiments in the classroom. In the second year of the academy, Vivian was charged by her team colleagues with attempting to 'railroad' her own ideas, ignoring the new teachers' reservations about curriculum integration. The team conflicts spilled over into meetings that involved administrators, industry partners and researchers. Barrie found herself choosing between competing loyalties when her partner objected to the agreements about curriculum and student assessment sought by the twelfth grade teachers. When the partners absented themselves from the regularly scheduled twelfth grade meetings, their colleagues voiced their resentment. Meredith erupted with anger when she recalled the principal's moves to assert control over the maths program in ways that she believed would 'water it down'. Her anger and frustration were evident in the infrequent department head meetings, but equally evident was her failure to move her own agenda. Such experiences acquire special significance not only because they are public, but also because they display the 'disagreeable passions' – anger, shame, bitterness, hatred, jealousy – that threaten the social fabric (see Burack, 1994). Public conflict, humiliation or defeat could be expected to leave a lasting mark on teachers' career interests and memories.

A second contributor to heightened emotionality is the convergence of multiple pressures or the simultaneous loss of several sources of support. Among the three cases, Vivian's speaks most clearly of the problem of an escalation of demands and corresponding erosion of support. Asked about her decision to seek a new post, Vivian

emphasized that it was a 'combination of things'. The bases of Vivian's initial excitement, as she told it, are threefold: the philosophical appeal of joining academic and
work education and the observed responsiveness of her students; the internal dynamics of a cohesive and energetic teacher team; the external supply of resources and
recognition. In effect, each of the pillars of Vivian's enthusiasm was irretrievably
weakened by the end of the second year: the program philosophy questioned by newly
hired members of the team and the synergy of the team thus disrupted; valued organizational support threatened or withdrawn; the approbation of the external community
diminished. Asked in an interview to describe the year 'in a few words', Vivian's colleague Adam retorted: 'It was hell. Is that too many words?'. One of the newcomers to
the team added: 'You couldn't speak your mind without hurting somebody's feelings
or somebody huffing off in a fit of rage.... I was hours away from quitting'. In this case
especially, and in the other cases to a lesser extent, heightened levels of emotional distress served to attenuate collegial bonds and isolate individuals.

How does this emotional intensity bear upon teachers' classroom work? At the
positive extreme, teachers suggest that shared intellectual and emotional excitement among the adults in turn enhances the rewards of the classroom. Harmonious
and active teams describe classroom benefits – responsive students, more uniform
attendance and progress across classes, the pleasure of teaching a richer curriculum
– that are at least partially confirmed by our classroom observations and by interviews with students. But teachers embroiled in conflicts with colleagues or others
suggest that those preoccupations diminish the quality of classroom planning and
instruction in ways that are evident to students. Again, the academy case is the
most vivid. In a meeting involving the teachers, administrators, and community
members, the teachers reported that students were complaining of 'broken
promises' – internships that had not materialized, field trips not made, ordinary
classroom assignments instead of cross-subject projects. Vivian finally expostulated:

> I'm seriously wondering how much longer I can go on. I'm serious. I'm losing
> it. I'm losing it ... I had my hands full today. She (the researcher) watched
> me. Just handling my class, I have never had as bad a day as what you saw.
> And I'm a great teacher. And I'm not getting to teach. I'm not!

Career trajectories and turning points

A broadened conception of career acknowledges *both* the opportunity for formal
advancement and the more informal opportunities for career position and movement afforded by specific teaching assignments, collegial arrangements, resource
configurations, management strategies and the like. School-wide plans for 'restructuring' formally advantage some teachers and disadvantage others in these schools.
Meredith's position as department head had been devalued, but others in the same
school had seen their fortunes elevated by promotion to newly-defined leadership
positions (see Little, 1995a). Of the five teachers selected as house heads (i.e.
heads of newly created interdisciplinary teams), four sustained their emotional
enthusiasm throughout the period of the study and increasingly adopted an administrative persona when they described future career possibilities.

For most of the early reform enthusiasts, however, the career significance attached to restructuring lies not in the prospects for promotion but in other dimensions of school life. As choices and controversies unfold, teachers discover or create new configurations of career advantage and disadvantage. The political face of the school changes. For example, the degree of authority granted to various teacher *groups* (for example, departments versus houses or grade levels versus within-grade teams) permits *individual* teachers greater or lesser influence, autonomy and scope for pursuing their teaching values. In Barrie Everett's school, controversies develop over the level of autonomy to be enjoyed by the several partnerships that make up each grade level team and over the rights of departments to place limits on interdisciplinary endeavors. Individual teachers must choose among loyalties. Barrie complied with her department's insistence on an end-of-year final examination in US history, but supported her partner in resisting grade-level agreements that the partner believed would compromise the values she brought to the English curriculum (specifically, agreements to link the senior English curriculum to the economics and government courses).

In these cases at least, emotional intensity is at its most extreme and career dislocations most evident where the personal and career stakes in reform are highest. In each of these cases, those stakes lie not in formal promotion, but in attaining a Utopian vision or in preserving valued traditions. Perhaps because Vivian's state comes closest to the emotional exhaustion and 'depersonalization' associated with burnout (Maslach and Leiter, 1996), her case illuminates this point most clearly. Describing her first year in the career academy, Vivian's language was laced with hyperbole: 'wonderful', 'joyful', 'exciting', 'thrilling'. Vivian believed she had found a perfect fit within the career academy and that her own career was on an upward trajectory; in an early interview she exclaimed that 'This particular academy and this school ... is a very exciting place to work, if you're interested in progressing in your profession'. Yet when the vision proved vulnerable and relationships soured, she saw no career options within the mainstream program of the school. By the end of the second year, the excitement had drained from Vivian's language:

> the energy level that this takes – I don't know, I can't go on indefinitely trying to do this. It's a wonderful idea, it's great for the kids, but it's not so great for teachers. This year was extremely traumatic.

Similarly, Meredith embraced restructuring with optimism, but subsequently felt betrayed: 'I'm a born teacher, damn it! And this is what I've always wanted to do. And when I heard somebody say we're going to keep what works and change what doesn't, I believed it. But we're not keeping anything that's working'.

Disruptions and discontinuities mark the careers of these reform enthusiasts, some more consequential than others. In two of the three focus cases, career situations and satisfactions had declined precipitously by the third year of restructuring. Vivian's departure followed a year of trauma in which she both resisted and mourned what she interpreted to be a failed dream; two other members of the five member team also left. Meredith's losses were many, ranging from her formal position as department head to more informal but crucial support for career satisfaction, including her preferred teaching assignment. Among three of Meredith's veteran colleagues to whom we spoke (one in her own department and two in other departments), all spoke of damage done to curricular programs they had taken years to build. Having invested more than 20 years there, all had anticipated ending their careers happily at this school. During the period of our study, one of the three colleagues accepted a position in a neighboring district (at considerable financial sacrifice), one took early retirement and the third attempted unsuccessfully to transfer to another school within the district. By their own accounts, Meredith and her veteran colleagues became steadily more isolated and all have suffered some form of career regress.

Unlike Meredith and Vivian, Barrie responded to her growing doubts and scepticism by gradually cultivating alternative career options. She continued to participate in committees and projects within the school, preserving her influence in that arena. However, she also actively opened new doors outside by enrolling in a doctoral program and participating in external research projects. In a sense, she was simultaneously 'pulling back', 'hanging in' and 'moving on'.

Together, these cases illuminate the complexities that arise when one considers the intersection of emotionality and career trajectory. The relationship in these cases is not isomorphic – eroding enthusiasm is not uniformly matched to career regress. Nor does it appear that the career movement experienced during restructuring was all of a piece; rather, teachers may be variously advantaged and disadvantaged, satisfied and disappointed, at different points in time and by different elements of a reform initiative. Some apparent setbacks open new opportunities. Vivian's new position placed her in charge of an experimental program employing high technology in remote rural schools; Barrie's interdisciplinary experiments with her partner, though fleeting, led her to new contacts with the university.

The teachers' capacity to recover from disappointment or to restore career momentum may rest partly on structural avenues for influence within the school and partly on perceived opportunities for job mobility. By comparison with the others, Meredith appears to be the most thoroughly defeated, both emotionally and instrumentally. Her long years of service in the school reduce her options to move elsewhere; her structural marginality as deposed department head limits her influence among administrators and many of her colleagues. These comparisons recall Hirschman's (1970) analysis of individuals' responses to conditions of decline in firms, organizations and other polities. In the Hirschman model, 'exit' and 'voice' constitute alternative resources on which individuals or groups rely in responding to conditions that erode organizational loyalty. In the case of teaching, 'exit' may presumably take the form of actual departure or the withdrawal of effort from classroom and colleagues; the possibilities for 'voice' (protest, complaint, organizing opposition) reside both inside and outside the school – hence the significance of Meredith's bid for union presidency – and seem contingent on degrees of social isolation. Assessing the broader utility of the Hirschman model of 'exit, voice, and loyalty' must await a larger body of cases, but clearly the resources of voice and exit are differentially available within and across these three cases.

Conclusion

A small set of individual cases illuminates a relatively unexamined aspect of teachers' participation in large scale reform – teachers' experience of heightened emotionality and its relationship to career discontinuity or career risk. Although the specific relationship between teachers' emotional contours and their career trajectories will require more thorough investigation than these preliminary cases afford, the cases do help to frame a more systematic analysis of a large body of data that seems heavily populated by disappointed reform enthusiasts. In this way they begin to probe the possible roots of Huberman's reported phenomenon – the long-term career dissatisfaction of reform activists.

First, the cases focus attention on the conditions of optimism or pessimism that reside in the organizational niches of professional communities where structures (e.g. departments, grade levels or staff assignments), cultures (shared beliefs) and individual biographies coincide. Analyses that take the individual and the whole-school environment as their twin points of departure risk overlooking the most salient contexts in which the teaching career acquires meaning and in which professional commitments are forged or unraveled (on this point, see also Casey, 1992; Siskin, 1994a; Talbert, 1995). In addition, these meaningful localized contexts extend to professional affiliations that remain independent of formal organizational structures and that may extend or reside entirely beyond the school, as exemplified by informal networks of subject specialists.

Second, this analysis locates individuals in relationship to multiple sources of pressure or support, both inside and outside the school. These cases illustrate the convergence of these multiple social and institutional contexts in shaping the rise and fall of reform enthusiasm. To a greater or lesser extent, teachers' various relationships with students, colleagues, administrators and others – all reconfigured in some manner by the restructuring initiatives – may feed career satisfaction or career distress. I did not incorporate the role of family and friends in this analysis, but might productively have done so. In the two cases of greatest career decline or discontinuity (Meredith and Vivian), teachers found themselves increasingly unable to derive support from any quarter; in the third case (Barrie), conflicts in some arenas were offset by supports in others and internal career uncertainties were matched by a growing number of external career options.

Finally, several aspects of reform implementation operated to erode reform optimism in one or more of the cases, thus calling attention to the context-specific dynamics of reform work in schools. In these cases, careers were affected directly by: (1) steep and rapid escalation of institutional demands for reform progress, intensifying the work of individuals and groups; (2) increasing visibility of cracks in the reform facade – internal contradictions in the reform vision or conflicts among the reform advocates for which there existed no organizational remedy; (3) inconsistency of symbolic and material support afforded to teachers by administrators and others who wield formal power and authority. The last of these – precarious and unpredictable support – drew the most fire from teachers, but each suggests both a source of career crisis and a corresponding avenue by which teachers' reform energies might be sustained.

Taken together, these cases reveal the affective side of reform activism and point to the possible intersections of heightened emotionality and significant career turning points. In doing so, they underscore the limitations of inquiries in which 'reform' is conceived principally as a problem of organizational structure or individual knowledge and skill (though it may be those as well), granting little attention to context-specific aspects of teachers' identity and professional community. Considerable promise resides in a more probing and systematic investigation of the emotional dimensions and career consequences of teachers' reform activism.

Acknowledgments

The research reported here was supported by the School Restructuring Study at the University of California, Berkeley, with funds from the Stuart Foundations and the Hewlett Foundation, and by the National Center for Research in Vocational Education, with funds from the US Department of Education. Thanks are due to Jennifer Nias and two anonymous reviewers for their comments on an earlier draft.

Notes

* Judith Warren Little is Professor of Education, University of California, Berkeley.
† Originally published in: *Cambridge Journal of Education* 26: 3, 345–359.
1 For related investigations of the problem of conflict and strain in the pursuit of ambitious innovation see Bartunek & Reid (1992) and Muncey & McQuillan (1993).

References

Ball, S.J. (1987) *The Micro-politics of the School: towards a theory of school organization* (London, Methuen).

Bartunek, J. and Reid, R. (1992) The role of conflict in a second order change attempt, in: D. Kolb and J. Bartunek (eds) *Hidden Conflict in Organizations: uncovering behind-the-scenes disputes*, pp. 116–142 (London, Sage).

Beynon, J. (1985) Institutional change and career histories in a comprehensive school, in: S.J. Ball and I.F. Goodson (eds) *Teachers' Lives and Careers*, pp. 158–179 (London, Falmer Press).

Boyer, E.L. (1983) *High School: a report on secondary education in America* (New York, Harper and Row).

Burack, C. (1994) *The Problem of the Passions: feminism, psychoanalysis, and social theory* (New York, New York University Press).

Casey, K. (1992) Why do progressive women activists leave teaching?, in: I.G. Goodson (ed.) *Studying Teachers' Lives*, pp. 187–208 (New York, Teachers College Press).

Cusick, P. (1983) *The Egalitarian Ideal and the American High School* (New York, Longman).

Engestrom, Y. (1991) *Non Scolae sed Vitae Discimus: toward overcoming the encapsulation of school learning* (San Diego, Laboratory of Comparative Human Cognition, University of California, San Diego).

Hirschman, A.O. (1970) *Exit, Voice, and Loyalty: responses to decline in firms, organizations, and states* (Cambridge, MA, Harvard University Press).

Huberman, M. (1989) The professional life cycle of teachers, *Teachers College Record*, 91, pp. 31–57.

Huberman, M. (1993) *The Lives of Teachers* (translated by J. Neufeld) (New York, Teachers College Press).

Little, J.W. (1995a) Contested ground: the basis of teacher leadership in restructured high schools. Special issue on teacher leadership, *Elementary School Journal*, 96, pp. 47–63.

Little, J.W. (1995b) Subject affiliation in high schools that restructure, in: L.S. Siskin and J.W. Little (eds) *The Subjects in Question: departmental organization and the high school*, pp. 172–200 (New York, Teachers College Press).

Maslach, C. and Leiter, M. (1996) Classroom context and student consequences of teacher burnout, paper presented at the *Invitational Conference on Teacher Burnout*, Marbach, Germany (Berkeley, University of California, Berkeley).

McNeil, L.M. (1986) *Contradictions of Control: school structure and school knowledge* (New York, Routledge and Kegan Paul).

Muncey, D.E. and McQuillan, P.J. (1993) Preliminary findings from a five-year study of the Coalition of Essential Schools, *Phi Delta Kappa*, February, pp. 486–489.

Powell, A.G., Farrar, E. and Cohen, D.K. (1935) *The Shopping Mall High School: winners and losers in the educational marketplace* (Boston, Houghton Mifflin).

Siskin, L.S. (1994a) Is the school the unit of change? Internal and external contexts of restructuring, in: P. Grimmett and J. Neufeld (eds) *Teacher Development and the Struggle for Authenticity: professional growth and restructuring in the context of change*, pp. 121–140 (New York, Teachers College Press).

Siskin, L.S. (1994b) *Realms of Knowledge: academic departments in secondary schools* (London, Falmer Press).

Sizer, T. (1984) *Horace's Compromise: the dilemma of the American high school* (Boston, Houghton Mifflin).

Talbert, J. (1995) Boundaries of teachers' professional communities in U.S. high schools: power and precariousness of the subject department, in: L.S. Siskin and J.W. Little (eds) *The Subjects in Question: departmental organization and the high school*, pp. 68–94 (New York, Teachers College Press).

Talbert, J.E. and McLaughlin, M.W. (1994) Teacher professionalism in local school contexts, *American Journal of Education*, 102, pp. 123–153.

Tyack, D. and Tobin, W. (1994) The 'grammar' of schooling: why has it been so hard to change?, *American Educational Research Journal*, 31, pp. 453–479.

Van Maanen, J. and Barley, S.R. (1984) Occupational communities: culture and control in organizations, *Research in Organizational Behavior*, 6, pp. 287–365.

24 Voice

The search for a feminist rhetoric for educational studies

Madeleine R. Grumet[*][†]

> It was her voice that made
> The sky acutest at its vanishing.
> She measured to the hour its solitude.
> She was the single artificer of the world
> In which she sang. And when she sang, the sea,
> Whatever self it had, became the self
> That was her song, for she was the maker. Then we,
> As we beheld her striding there alone,
> Knew there never was a world for her
> Except the one she sang and, singing made.[1]

The world she sang and singing made. Once this verse of Wallace Stevens's was sufficient to reassure me that expression and creation and order could coincide. This mellifluous image of rhetoric recapitulates the ancient conception of its efficacy. Then rhetoric was not considered to be mere social exhortation. Discourse that shaped the *polis* was thought to be the expression of both a divine order of the universe as well as the full realization of human possibility. As the song of Stevens's singer defines the boundaries of time, of space, and of meaning, it too appears to extend rhetoric's promise of coherence. Once I identified with the singer. Now I am not so sure. Then I was more comfortable with the voice of feminist theory and pedagogy than I am now. Then I was more comfortable with voice as a metaphor for feminist theory and pedagogy than I am now. Now I stand on the beach with the others watching her, striding there, on the boundary of the world that she sang, and singing made.

In 1976 I gave the title 'Another voice' to the final chapter of *Toward a Poor Curriculum*, a book that William Pinar and I wrote to develop the rationale for autobiographical studies of educational experience.[2] This final chapter was an autobiographical account of a seminar for student teachers. The chapter received that title because it shifted the theoretical and discursive mood of the preceding chapters to narrative, where my identity as teacher of the seminar and writer of the chapter coincided.

This use of 'voice' to denote a shift from the expected discourse reappeared in 1977 in Carol Gilligan's essay, 'In a different voice: women's conceptions of self and morality', published in the *Harvard Educational Review*, and was echoed again when her book was published in 1982. Gilligan also used voice to mark the distinction between the research on the development of conceptions of morality derived from studies of male subjects from that drawn from studies of women subjects.

I can't speak for Gilligan, but I can say that my use of voice as a marker to differentiate my work from male work and my text from male text allowed me to express my ambivalence as I joined the procession of 'educated men' in the late 1970s.[3] Voice promised presence, contact, and relations that would take place within range of another's hearing. And in that proximity the sound of the voice, the movement of breath, of teeth and tongue and lips carried the promise of speech. After all, consciousness raising was never a silent levitation but always grounded in talk, and in the relations of women who 'opened up to each other' and through 'disclosure'. And so, in the 1970s voice carried with it the promise of cultural transformation, as it announced resistance to a distant, universalistic knowledge, and as it provided conversations that generated collective action.

But voice has carried only some of us only so far. For those of us whose daily labor is the welding of words in texts and lectures, discussions and analyses, voice has sounded in the new scholarship on women and in the critique of the methods of the disciplines. It has challenged the methods of social science, literary criticism and history, of scientific method by reminding us all that texts are generated by speakers hoping to be heard by imagined listeners. Drawn from the body and associated with gender, voice splinters the fiction of an androgynous speaker as we hear rhythms, relations, sounds, stories, and style that we identify as male or female.

I suspect that the metaphor of voice has been most persuasive when it has been used to challenge another speaker, thus discriminating that speaker from another. It may be most discernible against a background of other sounds, against which it discriminates itself. This figure/ground *gestalt* frames both the salience as well as the subordination of the feminist voice in the academy.

In *The Acoustic Mirror* Kaja Silverman studies the presence of women's voices in film.[4] She describes the interplay of male and female voices common to traditional films of the 1940s and 1950s, an acoustic politic that I hear echoed in the rhetoric of educational discourse. She points out that male voices often provide the totalizing narratives often heard in voice-overs. I remember those voices. We heard them at the beginning of historical films as they read the text of the yellowed parchment displayed on the screen, that for some reason would curl up in flames signalling the start of the action. The anonymity of those voices was their appeal.

To this day my husband is tracking the voice of Superman from his radio childhood. Most recently he heard its resonance in the voice of the announcer for Thompson's water seal, exulting less in the announcer's fall from glory than in his own ability to crack the code and determine identity and history in the sound designed to speak timeless and ubiquitous power and authority.

Silverman points out that women rarely speak the voice-over narratives. Instead the female voice is located in the interior of the film, often lodged in its recesses. Silverman argues that the female voice in films is often intertwined with images of the female body, emphasizing female sexuality. If the voice is the medium for the projection of meaning, then woman as a meaning maker is undermined by the visual emphasis on her body as an object of display and desire. The interaction of image and voice is, as I have argued elsewhere, implicated in pedagogy.[5] Positioned in the front of the room, receiving, if not demanding, the gaze of the student, the female teacher receives a gaze that the *mise en scene* of the classroom had originally directed toward the pastor whose position vis-a-vis his congregation is the blueprint for the theatre of the contemporary classroom. If he projected the gaze as accuser or interrogator, she receives it, and I suspect, uses speech to deflect it. Teacher talk is then a defensive move deployed to assert her subjectivity in the face of the objectifying gaze.

Pointing to films where the woman's voice provides much of the narrative, Silverman shows us that this speaking is often elicited by drugs or therapy, so that the narrative is seen as elicited by men who ultimately control it and the female speaker. Silverman also suggests that these female narratives are often confessions, exposing private and hidden histories to public reception. These exposures carry the connotation of sexual penetration, as if they have been drawn from the dark internal continent of female sexuality, and Silverman points to the screams and cries that punctuate female vocalization in pornographic and sexually sadistic films, as vocal ejaculations designed to present involuntary female expressions of agony or terror as sounds of sexual release and pleasure.

Once we are no longer satisfied with just being heard and address the politics of our utterances, we find that the rhetoric of discourse in education is not exempt from the politics that the more explicitly erotic medium of film displays. For decades the voice-over of educational research and discourse was dominated by quantitative measures of learning and schooling. Statistical analyses that obscure individual experience have given ground in the last decade to qualitative studies employing history, literature, anthropology, and journalism to convey a subject's sense of educational experience. The voices of these subjects are frequently drawn from the recesses of the school, pulled out from behind the classroom door, they too disclose what has been hidden from the normative discourse of the curriculum.

In contrast to the language of administration, curriculum, educational psychology, and research, these voices of schoolteachers and students are discernible because of their texture, their presence, their connection to the bodies that schools sequester in gym lockers and teachers' lounges. And frequently those voices are elicited in interviews that recapitulate the 'talking cures' of the films Silverman describes, leaving ethnographers to apologize for the theft of another's subjectivity even as they subordinate the confession to the theory for which it is an example.

If the narrative or autobiographical voices in educational discourse echo the female interiority that Silverman hears in film, and if the male discourse of education is located as an exterior, generalizing over-voice, then it is possible that all we have established is an appeal for recognition that petitions phallocentric discourse but does not challenge its control. The expressivity of the female voice may recapitulate the hysteric's flashy subterfuge that constructs a facade of affect and expression to conceal ambivalence and an avoidance of real contact or action.

There is another interpretation available to us, however. One that hears the narrative voice not as a petitioning appeal or exhibitionistic gesture, but as a stream of negativity, constantly challenging the generalizing, hegemonic discourse with the inflections, images and sounds reminiscent of preoedipal or what Kristeva calls 'semiotic' discourse. In this version the female voice is an echo of the maternal voice, the sonorous envelope within which we come to consciousness, from which we differentiate as ego grows into identity. While this version of the female voice may seem stronger than the masochistic speaker whom Silverman hears in dominant film, it is not without its complexities.

> Listen again to the maternal voice:
> And when she sang, the sea,
> Whatever self if had, become the self
> That was her song, for she was the maker.

This portrayal of dissolving boundaries, as identity passes from the singer to the sea. The situation just described is one where the object has as yet no externality, since it is no sooner identified than it is assimilated by the child. Nor, since the subject lacks boundaries, does it as yet have anything approximating an interiority. However, the foundations for what will later function as identity are marked out by these primitive encounters with the outer world, encounters which occur along the axis of the mother's voice. Since the child's economy is organized around incorporation, and since what is incorporated is the auditory field articulated by the maternal voice, the child could be said to hear itself initially through that voice – to first 'recognize' itself in the vocal 'mirror' supplied by the mother.[6]

Julia Kristeva's concept of the *chora* is a name for this amalgam of space and sound and sense of existence.[7] She has argued that our sense of connection to the maternal voice and to the world it sang us into never disappears, but lingers in language, in culture and in fantasy as human possibility, always erupting to undermine the grip of language, of paternal law and symbolic code. Nevertheless, in Lacan's version of ego development, the mother's voice is, according to Silverman, a metaphor for the child's appropriation of identity. Like her breast, once experienced as part of the infant's self, voice is differentiated as belonging to her and not to the infant, and the infant gives up not only that which belonged to another but some strata of its subjectivity as well. Lacan argues that this preoedipal separation castrates all who achieve ego identity by requiring them to amputate their earliest sense of world and self, a sense of connection and loss that lingers like a phantom limb.[8]

Silverman presents Rosolato's reminder that however powerful the *chora* and its semiotic echoes may seem to us as we imagine what we can barely remember, we know it from our place within the symbolic from which the maternal voice speaks to us of lost loves, lost selves, and lost worlds.

Thus burdened by nostalgia, the maternal voice in educational discourse is prey to sentimentality and to an audience that consigns its melodies to fantasy, no matter how compelling. And these are not necessarily comforting fantasies, as Odysseus can tell you. The sirens, whose sweet songs lured seamen to their death, were located between Circe's island and Scylla's rock, hardly refuges. Odysseus escapes their call by binding himself to the mast of his ship and by filling the ears of his crew with wax. Hear no evil.

Despite her criticism, Silverman recuperates the *chora* of Kristeva as a positive icon of female collectivity, as a 'powerful image of women's unity and necessary separatism'.[9] She chastises Kristeva for consigning the maternal voice to singing only, and argues appropriately that the mother is also the person who introduces the child to language, to objects, to self. In *Bitter Milk: women and teaching*[5] I discussed at some length the ways in which psychoanalytic theory projects connection and symbiosis on the mother, appropriating knowledge, ego and ultimately subjectivity for the father. How can we rescue voice from such an adoring, yet finally patronizing and trivializing score?

One escape is found in the chorus that is our own voice. As difficult as it may be for us to stretch our identities across multiple discourses we are both the writers and readers of our own stories, and we diminish our experience and our rhetoric if we limit ourselves to only one voice. We need not dissolve identity in order to acknowledge that identity is a choral and not a solo performance. Structures of this choral self are usually organized in three parts. Roy Schafer's *A New Language for Psychoanalysis* presented the trio of self as object, agent, and place. 'The processes of reflection that yield self-as-object inform a creative and free will, self-as-agent, who then acts through self-as-place'.[10] In *Beyond Feminist Aesthetics*, Rita Felski points to Gidden's tripartite model of the subject that distinguishes practical consciousness, discursive consciousness, and the unconscious.[11] A triad is also summoned by Habermas in *The Theory of Communicative Action*. He argues that in standard speech acts we take up a pragmatic relation

> – to something in the objective world (as the totality of entities about which true statements are possible); or – to something in the social world (as the totality of legitimately regulated interpersonal relations); or – to something in the subjective world (as the totality of experiences to which a speaker has privileged access and which he can express before a public): such that what the speech act refers to appears to the speaker as something objective, normative or subjective.[12]

Let me suggest a similar triad for the voices of educational theory. Let our songs have three parts, situation, narrative, and interpretation. The first, situation, acknowledges that we tell our story as a speech event that involves the social, cultural and political relations in and to which we speak. Narrative, or narratives as I prefer, invites all the specificity, presence and power that the symbolic and semiotic registers of our speaking can provide. And interpretation provides another voice, a reflexive and more distant one, the exterior voice-over in Silverman's acoustics. What is essential is that all three voices usher from one speaker and that each becomes a location through which the other is heard. None is privileged.

This trio may save us from the objectification of 'identity politics'[13] by recognizing the dynamic process through which identity is grounded in history, and desire, subjected to description and reflection and constantly presented to and negotiated with other people. A dynamic, reflective, and finally collaborative version of voice is required if the projects of teacher empowerment and school based management will generate new ways of teaching and schooling. The assertion of an individual history and passion is necessary if instruction is once again to be a valid sharing of a meaningful world. Reflection is necessary if that vision is to acknowledge its own partiality and assume the irony that challenges its own dogma and invites another view. Collaboration is the foundation for the transformation of the space, time, and politics of schooling and yet it must constantly be challenged by another voice, if collaboration is not to degenerate into a coerced consensus. There is no 'single artificer of the world', nor will there be a world for us but for the one that *we* sing and singing make.

Notes

* Madeleine R. Grumet is at the School of Education, Brooklyn College.
† Originally published in: *Cambridge Journal of Education* 20: 3, 277–282.
1 Wallace Stevens (1954) *The Collected Poems of Wallace Stevens* . . . 'The Idea of Order at Key West', pp. 129–130 (New York, Vintage).
2 Madeleine Grumet (1976) Another voice, in: *Toward a Poor Curriculum* (with William Pinar) (Dubuque, IA, Kendall/Hunt).
3 The phrase is Virginia Woolf's.
4 Kaja Silverman (1988) *The Acoustic Mirror: the female voice in psychoanalysis and cinema* (Bloomington, IN, University of Indiana Press).
5 See Madeleine Grumet (1988) *Bitter Milk: women and teaching* (Amherst, MA, University of Massachusetts Press); see 'My face in thine eye, thine in mine appeares; the look in parenting and pedagogy'.
6 Silverman, p. 80.
7 Julia Kristeva (1980) *Desire in Language* (ed. by Leon S. Roudiez; trans, by Thomas Gora, Alice Jardine & Leon S. Roudiez) (New York, Columbia University Press).
8 Silverman, p. 85.
9 See Silverman, p. 125.
10 See Madeleine Grumet (1976) Toward a poor curriculum, in: *Toward a Poor Curriculum* (with William Pinar, p. 69) (Dubuque, IA, Kendall/Hunt) for a discussion of Schafer's model on consciousness and the process of autobiography.
11 Rita Felski (1989) *Beyond Feminist Aesthetics*, p. 57 (Cambridge, MA, Harvard University Press).
12 Jurgen Habermas (1981) *The Theory of Communicative Action*, Vol. II, p. 120 (trans, by Thomas McCarthy) (Boston, MA, Beacon Press).
13 See Hank Bromley (1989) Identity politics and critical pedagogy, *Educational Theory*, 38, pp. 207–224.

25 Reflective writing and the spirit of inquiry

Mary Louise Holly*†

Writing, like life itself, is a voyage of discovery.

(Henry Miller)

Journal writing can be a powerful means for teachers to explore practice; to document classroom life as it unfolds and to reflect on experiences past, their life histories and the social, historical and educational conditions that ushered in the present. Capturing words while the action is fresh, the author is often provoked to question "why?"

> I think in writing ... we are questioning ourselves.... And I think there is very little precedent set for us to do that. Yet I think when we look at the whole concept of professional growth, that's a piece of it. Yes, you have to do it.
>
> (Jerry Johnson, primary teacher, journal excerpt, 1982)

This voyage, like others which cover the most intriguing terrains, is not smooth. "Custom is second nature", wrote Plutarch (AD 46–120), and deliberately setting off to explore what has become custom is not without its risks and discomforts as truths are challenged and the taken-for-granted is questioned, and often found to be problematic. Writing also taps the unconscious; it can make the implicit explicit, and therefore, open to analysis: "Writing stimulates this interchange [between the conscious and unconscious] and allows us to observe, direct, and understand it" (Ferrucci, 1982, p. 41). Keeping a personal, professional journal enables the author to develop an educational archive which serves as an evolving database for gaining understanding and insights which inform and enrich professional judgement. Keeping a journal enables the writer to explore what Virginia Woolf describes as (multiple) realities which only time and different perspectives make possible. It makes possible new ways of theorizing, reflecting on and coming to know one's self and one's profession. The journal documents the many voices which shape practice, including the author's, and the multiple realities, selves and minds that teach.

Inquiry in teaching and the cultures of practice

> People in other cultures than our own not only act differently, but they have a different basis for their behavior. They act upon different premises, they perceive differently, and codify it differently.
>
> (Lee, 1949, pp. 406–407)

Dorothy Demetracopoulon Lee, an anthropologist, acknowledged that she was viewing those she studied (the Trobriand) "through the eyes of my own culture, relationally, seeing them according to what they were unlike, and so stressing the absence of concepts which have no relevance to their thought" (Lee, 1949, pp. 406–407). With few exceptions (Lucy Sprague-Mitchell, Sylvia Ashton Warner, for example) research on teaching and teachers has traditionally been conducted by outsiders, by academic researchers whose cultures and premises differed from those they attempted to describe, explain and understand. Differences in perspective, purpose and language can account for many of the difficulties one group has in interpreting and understanding the experiences and motives of the other group. While researchers call attention to a lack in teachers' use of theory to ground their teaching, teachers voice regret at a lack of researchers' real-world description and applications of their findings. It has been argued that teachers are not a-theoretical (Bussi *et al.*, 1975; Elbaz, 1983, 1988; Holly and Walley, 1988) and that problems arise in the lenses researchers use to view teachers and teaching, that these lenses are often too theory-bound and do not permit the researcher to be open to the subtle (and sometimes not so subtle) and complex nuances that are indications of teachers' theories-in-use (Schon, 1983). Researchers, more simply, overlook teachers' theories because they do not understand the language of classrooms, of the bases for teachers' behaviour.

Over the last decade there has been a shift from academics' research on teaching to research with teachers, to research by teachers. As this shift takes place it marks the increasing communication between and among cultures – the growing overlap and understandings of perceptual fields (Combs and Snygg, 1959). Since the advent of "the teacher as researcher" (Stenhouse, 1975) the focus of research in classrooms and schools underscores the importance of teachers' work, both as it relates to the quality of education for young people and also as it contributes to knowledge about teaching and learning for the profession. As Stenhouse noted, it is not enough for researchers to study teachers' work "they [teachers] need to study it themselves". The "extended professionalism" he advocated included:

> The commitment to systematic questioning of one's own teaching as a basis for development; the commitment and the skills to study one's own teaching; the concern to question and to test theory in practice by the use of those skills.
>
> (Ibid., pp. 143–144)

Research was "systematic, self-critical enquiry",

> founded in curiosity and a desire to understand; but it is a stable, not a fleeting curiosity, systematic in the sense of being sustained by critical principles, a doubt not only about the received and comfortable answers, but also about one's own hypotheses.
>
> (Stenhouse, 1981, in Ruddock and Hopkins, 1985, p. 8)

Along with the slowly expanding notion of teacher inquiry, there have been changes in the contexts, methods and resources for teaching. With the accountability movement has come competency testing (for children and their teachers) and concomitant standardization of curricula and teaching. So, while teachers have an increasingly important role in studying practice, they have less latitude in exercising professional judgement. The range of their responsibilities is both broadened (research) and narrowed (restricted professional prerogatives) in teaching and curriculum development. With more emphasis on the immediate products of teaching, resources are directed to explain and control the curriculum and classroom procedures. As a result, we have (inadvertently perhaps) shackled the spirit, and, therefore, school and classroom culture. Schools, it can be argued, are becoming less like "human cultures" and more like "standardized civilizations" (Earle, 1976) with primary schools becoming "skill and drill factories" (Haberman, 1988). With the goal of becoming more efficient and "scientific", objectivism and protection from the personal, subjective, and intuitive is advocated – a hard science approach, empirical, visible and linear, or in Schön's (1983) terms, a system based upon principles of technical rationality.

In many schools, culture is shaped not by the spirit of those who would define it (and comprise it) but by outside forces which are manifested in mandated curricula and testing. Knowing is defined in specified universals (reaching for the "knowledge base" which is approximated, if implicitly, through competency testing) rather than, and to the exclusion of teachers' own theories, knowledge and intuition. The spirit, the force which brings life to life, according to Earle (1976), has three main functions: to concern itself with itself, to become lucid and finally to manifest itself. When the spirit is free to function in these ways, it creates culture. When teachers are free to theorize, the spirit is engaged – it focuses its concern, the mind focuses on setting problems and inquiring into possible solutions: the teacher theorizes. Several teachers theorizing together influence and shape culture. Developing school cultures, where the minds and spirits of participants are alive and active is the knowledge base for teaching. In this way teachers use public theories (Piaget's theory of cognitive development, for example) and private theories (those intuitions, explanations, concepts and frameworks which inform their practice) to theorize (speculate, try out, hypothesize and test).

Calling for an "emancipatory psychology" to shape school culture, Sullivan (1984) writes,

> an emancipatory interest in human freedom rests on the assumption that part of all human action is creative and on the assumption that humans create

their world while, at the same time, being determined by it. The human ir
tions that can motivate human actions are history making. We call the latter
function "culture". Up to this point, the psychological enterprise has been, we
might say, "uncultured" [blocking rather than accepting subjectivity] ... add a
cultural dimension as the essential location where human freedom operates.

(p. xi)

Creativity, the self and professional development

Whether we approach the person who teaches from the standpoint of spirit, the
self, creativity or psychological maturity, there are inter-relationships and intersections among them. All are related to biology and human development, and, of
interest here, to how minds operate (and why reflective writing is a potent means
for theorizing).

Nias (1988) has shown how important the teacher's self is to teaching, how, in
order to understand teachers, we must understand how they view themselves (their
identities) as teachers and what teaching does to influence this self. Combs and
Snygg (1959) refer to this self as the phenomenal self which is at the center of the
perceptual field of the teacher. When called upon to present a lesson, for example,
there can be varying amounts of licence to the teacher's creative expression, none,
little, or a lot, depending on the lesson and the teacher's roles and responsibilities. In
general, the more standardized the lesson, the less opportunity and likelihood that
the teacher will engage the spirit and rely on his/her own resourcefulness and creativity. The more threatened and constrained the teacher feels, the less permeable the
teacher's mental constructs (Kelly, 1955), and the more guarded and rule-governed
the teaching. Conversely, the more opportunity the teacher has to create and adapt
the lesson, the more chance there is to engage the spirit and strengthen self-affirming
aspects of the self (or selves).

According to Woods (1988, p. 8), "In order for teachers to be creative, teachers
need to be in control, and not, for example, being dictated to by higher authority
... they also need this for their own realization of self as teachers". He suggests that
"Creativity involves innovation, ownership, control and relevance" (p. 7), and
that there are abundant examples of creative teaching though these are rarely the
focus of attention in research and educational discourse. "Characteristics attending
creative teaching include imagination, that is the ability to take the role of the
other.... This process is accompanied by adaptability, flexibility, and a willingness
and facility for improvisation and experimentation" (ibid., p. 9). Creativity is often
characterized by playfulness, a child-like quality of interest and engagement, even
immersion, perseverance and confidence (necessary to being different), the ability
to withhold judgement, to juxtapose the everyday with the novel, and to bringing
closure when it is indicated by an aesthetic sense of completion.

Inherent in this discussion of the active spirit and creativity is psychological
maturity and health: the secure self that is open to experience, daring to risk and
to view circumstances from multiple perspectives, taking into account diverse and
seemingly disparate kinds of experience: to view the world in highly differentiated
dimensions. Effective teachers have been described as cognitively complex (Oja,

1988), and thus able to take multiple perspectives, self-accepting and compassion-ate (Jersild, 1955), personally adequate (Combs and Snygg, 1959), and flexible (Sprinthall, 1980).

Journal writing and the many voices and minds of teaching

Socrates' advice to "know thyself" remains salient and challenging for today's edu-cator, especially if dominant sociological perspectives characterizing teachers have any credibility. Teachers, research suggests, are isolated, lacking a professional lexicon, conservative, present-oriented, reluctant to take risks, moralistic rather than analytical and self-accusing rather than self-accepting; "Teachers seem lonely; they fight battles alone and with their consciences, and, it seems, frequently lose" (Lortie, 1975, p. 59). One might come to the conclusion that these teachers are threatened people, that they have little time or spirit or inclination to be cre-ative. Where control, ownership, innovation and relevance are not part of a teacher's roles and responsibilities, the above characteristics are adaptive behavior, effective for survival (which is consistent with Francis Fuller's survival stage of teacher career development, 1969). For such teachers to become creative, confi-dent enquirers, their understanding of themselves and their conditions of practice would have to change.

Mezirow (1981) addresses this dilemma of adult development, growth and change when he writes of perspective transformation. He describes two pathways:

> one is a sudden insight into the very structure of cultural and psychological assumptions which has limited or distorted one's understanding of self and one's relationships. The other is movement in the same direction that occurs by a series of transformations which permit one to revise specific assumptions about oneself and others until the very structure of assumptions becomes transformed. This is perhaps a more common pattern of development. The role transitions themselves are only opportunities for the kind of self-reflection essential for a transformation.
>
> (p. 7)

Writing about experience enables the author to view his/her experiences within broader contexts: social, political, economic and educational. As teachers write about children, for example, they also learn about the lenses through which they are viewing children and teaching. As they determine the focus of their writing they can move from what Lortie describes as "judgemental" per-spectives to what Earle describes as "intuitive" ones; they can move from an external locus of control to an internal one: "Knowing is not necessarily explanatory, but it might be regarded as elucidation: that is, raising to explicit consciousness that which is already implicitly grasped" (Earle, 1976, p. 196). What teachers implicitly grasp is much more than they can say, or know that they know, though this knowledge is used as teachers theorize in practice. Writing taps tacit knowledge; it brings into awareness that which we sensed but could not explain. Ferrucci (1982) writes:

Writing ... can be much more powerful than we may think at first. If we start by freely writing about the issue that concerns us, we will find ourselves expressing things not previously thought of. We have to formulate explicitly that which we feel implicitly, thereby clarifying to ourselves what may have been a confused morass. In this process we may also come to new conclusions and ideas about courses of action to take ... We should not be surprised that unconscious material surfaces so readily in our writing.... Writing stimulates this interchange and allows us to observe, direct, and understand it.

(p. 41)

As teachers write about teaching and return to read what they have written over time, they often find patterns and begin to link experiences:

After becoming familiar with our limiting patterns after looking at them objectively, something will already have changed, for any pattern that is discovered – and fully surfaced, changes. After this first stage of assessment, it is then possible to replace destructive tendencies with more functional ones. [When] We create a new line of force it is like cutting a new pathway in a jungle.

(Ibid., p. 42)

Cutting a pathway through a jungle takes courage and tenacity. There are good reasons why many people are reluctant to plunge into reflective writing. Even as we write biographically (case studies, for example), we find that we learn as much about ourselves and our circumstances as we do about others. When we look at the dynamic nature of teaching and current conditions, we find that it is a balancing act as much as it is anything else. Woods (1977), for one, writes about classroom management and the uses of routine in teaching and maintaining control (and mental health). Note, for example, how disconcerting many teachers find classroom interruptions. While teachers try to maintain a sense of equilibrium in a system where it is constantly threatened, it is not surprising to find that they would resist keeping a journal which is almost guaranteed to present them with new problems. The important difference is that these problems arise from and are set by the teacher: they arise from what the teacher feels it is important to attend to.

Writing is both constructing experience and reconstructing it. "The significance of the event didn't lie where I thought it did at the time." Reality, as Virginia Woolf wrote (and Ferrucci noted above), changes as we look at it. More disconcerting than situations and "reality" changing at different times is the realization of the self, or selves, changing. This is one of the most difficult, and also the most worthwhile, aspects of journal writing. It introduces the writer to the writer; the "multi-minds" (Ornstein, 1987) and the "sub-personalities" (Assagiolo, n.d.). Writing facilitates consciousness of consciousness, what Dewey described as awareness. Describing how the minds work will help to clarify why journal writing works as a means for reflection:

Instead of a single, intellectual entity that can judge many different kinds of events equally, the mind is diverse and complex. It contains a changeable conglomeration of different kinds of "small minds" – fixed reactions, talents, flexible thinking and these different entities are temporarily employed – "wheeled into consciousness" – and then usually discarded, returned to their place, after use.

(Ornstein, 1987, p. 25)

Which of the many small minds gets wheeled in depends on many factors, some within our control, others not.

We are built to respond simply and quickly. Our judgement process operates by a set of fast paths; we build internal categories to simplify our perception and judgements based on a network of invisible structures. We are primed to respond to what's on at the moment and sometimes we over-react. We are primed by emotions to alertness or action to avoid emergencies.... Anything that is given wide publicity in the media ... get fast reactions while constant problems get ignored ... we remain unaware because we do not understand the complexity within ourselves. We are prone to many tragedies because of the over application of the policies of mind. But other tragedies exist within ourselves due to a lack of communication within the separated components of the mind.

(Ibid., p. 32)

The quiet child, the uneventful lesson, the immediate pressure (attendance report, or parent standing at the door), when looked at in context and from an "open" point of view (with permeable constructs; not harried from the moment), might deserve more or less attention; as a lived event in the flow of other lived events, in general, the squeaky wheel gets the grease whether or not it is most in need of it. Systematic, self-critical enquiry, focusing on practice with a personal and professional attitude, enables the writer to ponder curiosities, to hold events for reflection. How the minds work becomes visible through journal writing; educators can use what they find to change their own practice.

The separate mental components have different priorities and are often at cross purposes, with each other and with our life today, but they do exist and, more soberly, "they" are us. It would be a good idea, I think, if we could come to see the primitive bases of many of our judgements and decisions so that we might try to do something about them.

Our problem as individuals is that we often act unconsciously and automatically, thus we do not often know which one of the multiple "small minds" is operating at any time. And often we do not select the appropriate "small minds" at the right time.

We have a simple minded view of other people as well because of the way our mental system operates. It is inevitable – and tragic – that we try to type others.... Each one of us is a crowd of people.

(Ibid., p. 24)

Dewey wrote that "All that the wisest man [person] can do is to observe what is going on more widely and more minutely and then select more carefully from what is noted just those factors which point to something to happen" (1916, p. 146). So simple, yet so difficult, and, if Orstein is correct, so possible. Though he thinks that the observation mind is most likely "a dormant faculty" in most of us (because there has been little reason to notice the "wheeling in" of different minds at different times), he suggests that

> It is a part of the mind which can be developed by first observing the alternations, gradations, and changes that "come over" us; then noting that it is not always necessary to accept the multimind that is "automatically" called up in a situation.
>
> (Ornstein, 1987, p. 85)

By holding the action still in journal writing, the writer can revisit and learn from "automatic" reactions; patterns in the ways a teacher responds to classroom events and situations can be changed once they are recognized to be less effective than other reactions might be. Many teachers find that once they have written a journal for a few months they begin to observe experience as it happens, almost as an outside observer (Holly, 1989) – which, if we think of many small minds (Ornstein, 1987), or the phenomenal self orchestrating sub-personalities (Assagioli, n.d.), could certainly be the case. Virginia Woolf (1978) wrote of the self who writes as different from the self who later reads what is written; Anne Frank (1955) wrote of her ability to observe herself and to read what she had written from alternative perspectives without the slightest bias or need for distortion or judgement.

Summary thoughts

Constructing (and reconstructing) the everyday and unusual events and experiences of classroom life in vignettes and portraits of practice enables the author to direct perspective transformation, usually, in the second of Mezirow's pathways, though often, in recording and revisiting experience, a flash of recognition and insight propels sudden understanding and schematic reorganization. Writing "works" because it enables us to come to know ourselves through the multiple voices our experiences take, to describe our contexts and histories as they shape the many minds and selves who define us and others. Through writing we intentionally focus our attention and in so doing assert and affirm both our ideas, and the mind itself: "assertion is one of the primary acts of mind ... in affirming anything, the mind affirms itself" (Langer, 1982, p. 20). The curiosity and desire to understand that serve as a basis for enquiry (Stenhouse, 1975) are sparked by the spirit and stem from an interest of the self, which, in writing, can hold centre stage long enough to gather meaning. Curiosity has a greater chance to withstand the pull of a myriad of distractions, to be sustained by ethical aims and strategies. This is a continuing challenge, for "meaning is the provisional achievement of a dynamic and somewhat risky process" (Grumet, 1988, p. 459). The process is risky because it is plagued with doubt: "the horror of doubt is natural to consciousness. Doubt is its supreme menace, for it threatens the keystone of the whole mental structure: the affirmation of the self" (Essertier, 1927, pp. 57–58).

Knowing the self means being a self and many current conditions of teaching make this difficult. There is too often cause for doubt as teachers wrestle with what they think and feel is best for the children they teach against much that is mandated and prescribed and at odds with their consciences. The dilemma is noted by John Elliott (1988) who describes teaching as an ethical profession, where efficiency is not the only basis for action. As Philip Jackson (1986) wrote, "teaching is more complicated than most people think, including – strange to say – many teachers". It is so complicated that we need methods of documentation which hold it still long enough to reflect on it and to begin to understand and direct it. But we also need methods which celebrate and respect the complexity of the unique human relationships which are teaching and learning; which keep alive the spirit which moves one to become a teacher, but often gets lost in the motion of "progress" and "development" the longer one stays in teaching.

Note

* Mary Louise Holly is Associate Professor at the College of Education, Kent State University, USA.
† Originally published in: *Cambridge Journal of Education* 19: 1, 71–80.

References

Assagioli, R. (n.d.) *The Act of Will* (London, Penguin Books).

Bussi, A., Amarel, M. and Chittenden, E. (1975) *Beyond Surface Curriculum: an interview study of teachers' understandings* (Boulder, Colo., Westview Press).

Combs, A. and Snygg, D. (1959) *Individual Behavior: a perceptual approach to behavior* (New York, Harper & Row).

Dewey, J. (1916) *Democracy and Education* (New York, Macmillan).

Earle, W. (1976) *Public Sorrows and Private Pleasures* (Bloomington, Ind., Indiana University Press).

Elbaz, F. (1983) *Teacher Thinking: a study of practical knowledge* (London, Croom Helm).

Elbaz, F. (1988) *Knowledge and discourse: the evolution of research on teacher thinking*, paper presented at the Conference of the International Study Association on Teacher Thinking, University of Nottingham, UK, September.

Elliott, J. (1988) Teacher evaluation and teaching as a moral science, in: M.L. Holly and C. McLoughlin (eds) *Perspectives on Teacher Professional Development* (London, Falmer Press).

Essertier, D. (1927) *Les Formes Inférieures de l'Explication* (Paris, Alcan).

Ferrucci, P. (1982) *What We May Be* (New York, St Martin's Press).

Frank, A. (1955) *Anne Frank: the diary of a young girl* (New York, Doubleday).

Grumet, M. (1988) Bodyreading, in: W. Pinar (ed.) *Contemporary Curriculum Discourses* (Scottsdale, Gorsuch Scarisbrick).

Haberman, M. (1988) The influence of competing cultures on teacher development, in: M.L. Holly and C. McLoughlin (eds) *Perspectives on Teacher Professional Development* (London, Falmer Press).

Holly, M.L. (1989) *Teacher Enquiry: keeping a personal-professional journal* (Portsmouth, Heinemann Educational Books).

Holly, M.L. and Walley, C. (1988) Teachers as professionals, in: M.L. Holly and C. McLoughlin (eds) *Perspectives on Teacher Professional Development* (London, Falmer Press).

Jackson, P. (1986) *The Practice of Teaching* (New York, Teachers College Press).

Jersild, A. (1955) *When Teachers Face Themselves* (New York, Teachers College Press).

Kelly, G.A. (1955) *The Psychology of Personal Constructs* (New York, Norton).

Lee, D.D. (1949) Being and value in a primitive culture, *Journal of Philosophy*, 46, pp. 501–515.

Lortie, D.C. (1975) *Teacher: a sociological study* (Chicago, Ill., University of Chicago Press).

Mezirow, J. (1981) A critical theory of adult learning, *Studies in Adult Education*, 32, pp. 3–24.

Nias, J. (1988) Teaching and the self, in: M.L. Holly and C. McLoughlin (eds) *Perspectives on Teacher Professional Development* (London, Falmer Press).

Oja, S.N. (1988) Teachers: ages and stages of adult development, in: M.L. Holly and C. McLoughlin (eds) *Perspectives on Teacher Professional Development* (London, Falmer Press).

Ornstein, R. (1987) *Multimind* (Boston, Mass., Houghton Mifflin).

Schön, D. (1983) *The Reflective Practitioner: how professionals think in action* (New York, Basic Books).

Sprinthall, N. and Sprinthall, L.S. (1980) Adult development and leadership training for mainstream education, in: D. Corrigan and K. Howey (eds) *Concepts to Guide the Education of Experienced Teachers* (Reston, The Council for Exceptional Children).

Stenhouse, L. (1975) *An Introduction to Curriculum Research and Development* (London, Heinemann Educational Books).

Stenhouse, L. (1981) What counts as educational research? in: J. Ruddock and D. Hopkins (eds) *Research as a Basis for Teaching: readings from the work of Lawrence Stenhouse* (1985) (London, Heinemann Educational Books).

Sullivan, E. (1984) *A Critical Psychology* (New York, Plenum Press).

Woods, P. (1977) Teaching for survival, in: P. Woods and M. Hammersly (eds) *School Experience* (London, Croom Helm).

Woods, P. (1988) *Social aspects of teacher creativity*, paper presented at the St Hilda's Conference: Histories and Ethnographies of Teachers at Work, Oxford University, UK, September.

Woolf, V. (1978) *A Writer's Diary* (Bungay, Suffolk, Triad Granada).

26 Narrative, experience and the study of curriculum

D. Jean Clandinin* and F. Michael Connelly[†‡]

The speed with which Schon's (1983, 1987) recent works penetrated the reference lists of teacher education writers has been remarkable. Partly, we can explain the phenomenon as resulting from Schon's work fitting among ongoing lines of inquiry into reflection, practice and their combination. There is another reason, less tangible and more a question of, to borrow a term from Eisner (1979), the educational imagination. We see the practices Schon describes as part of the folklore of teacher education, matters kept alive in staffroom discussion but often referred to negatively outside of schools as the "telling of war stories" and as accounts of mere "learning-by-doing". These accounts are frequently seen by "scientifically" minded teacher-educators as something to be cleansed from student and novice teachers' minds in an attempt to pave the way for more "scholarly" norms of teaching. The remnants of these discredited practices remain in the Canadian (and, perhaps, American) imagination as the kind of education that was acceptable in the less scientific days of teacher education gone by. Schon's books, we like to think, gave modern value to these professional memories.

Schon, of course, does not use temporality, history and memory to make his case. Rather, his logic consists of a reasoned case against "technical rationalism" designed to cleanse the novice professional mind, combined with the presentation of case evidence of good educational practice in the professions. But the explanation of why his rhetorical influence in education is all out of proportion to his argument's substance can be explained narratively. Schon makes it possible for many of us to tell the story of teacher education in a way that runs counter to the technical teacher education we are encouraged to sponsor, and study, and he makes it possible for the story to legitimate our professional memory of reflective practice.

What makes this retelling of the story possible is the sense of reductionism entailed in the idea of technical rationalism. The image of professional practice, held in professional memory and rejected in scholarly discourse, is the thing that has been reduced. A rich whole, for us the professional memory, has been reduced through technical rationalism to a formulated set of rules which "may then be written in a book" (Oakeshott, 1962) (or, we might add, embodied in a master professor or teacher) and taught (or copied through role modeling and education's version of "coaching") to novices. Johnson (1987), in his recent book *The Body in the Mind*, wrote that "without imagination nothing in the world could be meaningful. Without imagination we could never make sense of our experience" (p. ix). The success of Schon's work, we believe, is precisely that it tapped the professional imagination and permitted a reconstruction of the idea of education. It is not only "that none of the theories of meaning and rationality dominant today offer any serious treatment of imagination" (Johnson, 1987, p. ix), it is also the case that imagination is mostly ignored in studies of education. For Johnson, the set of reasons which account for this state of affairs in philosophy is captured by the term "objectivism" which he metaphorically defines as the "god's-eye-view about what the world really is like" (p. x). It is a view that implies that no matter what any particular person happens to believe about it, there is a correct and true view of the world. It is a depersonalized notion of truth and meaning. The god's-eye-view, say Oakeshott and Schon, has become, in studies of the practical, technical rationalism. Technical rationalism is:

> the assertion that what I have called "practical knowledge" is not knowledge at all, the assertion that properly speaking there is no knowledge that is not technical knowledge. The rationalist holds that the only element of knowledge involved in human activity is technical knowledge and what I have called "practical knowledge" is really only a sort of neoscience which would be negligible if it were not positively mischievous. A sovereignty of "reason", for the Rationalist means the sovereignty of technique. The heart of the matter is the preoccupation of the Rationalist with certainty.
>
> (Oakeshott, 1962)

Johnson sees the way of reuniting what the god's-eye-view and technical rationalism have separated and reduced is by "putting the body back into the mind" (Johnson, 1987, p. xxxvi). A disembodied mind permits the certainty needed by technical rationalism. To put the body back into the mind is to wreck havoc with certainty. Emotion, value, felt experience with the world, memory and narrative explanations of one's past do not stand still in a way that allows for certainty.

The suspicion of experience is not the suspicion born of a scientific mind for, as Oakeshott (1962) shows, science, no less than art, is incapable of being reduced to technique and taught out of a book. Those who argue against the study of practice, and the imaginative and narratively generated diversity that goes with it, often define practice as the execution of skills and, ironically, they often argue that to discover and name the skills is to do science. But it is reductionism, and what Dewey (1938) called the "quest for certainty", that marks the technical rationalist and not the doing of science. The doing of science is compatible with narrative and the study of practice in all of its imaginative complexity.

Oakeshott remarks that "the rationalist has taken an ominous interest in education. He has a respect for 'brains', a great belief in training them, and is determined that cleverness shall be encouraged and shall receive its reward of power" (Oakeshott, 1962, p. 32). It is "ominous" because the technical rationalist "has no sense of the accumulation of experience, only of the readiness of experience when it is being converted into a formula: the past is significant to him only as an encumbrance" (Oakeshott, 1962, p. 2). A person with experience is considered, by the technical rationalist, to have "negative capability" (Oakeshott, 1962, p. 2). If the "tabula rasa has been defaced by the irrational scribblings of tradition-ridden ancestors" (Oakeshott, 1962, p. 5) and, one might add, by the experiences of life to date, then, says Oakeshott, the first educational task of the rationalist "must be to rub the slate clean" (Oakeshott, 1962, p. 5). The technical rationalist's interest in education is ominous not because it ignores experience but because experience is seen as a deterrent to the "true" skilled education. In a line that might have been written by Dewey (1938) with respect to his idea of the reconstruction of experience as the foundation of education, Oakeshott writes that "as with every other sort of knowledge, learning a technique does not consist in getting rid of pure ignorance, but in reforming knowledge which is already there" (Oakeshott, 1962, p. 12). Schon picks up this theme in his work on professional education by legitimating our professional memory and making it possible to return to experience, not as a black mark on the mental slate, but as a resource for the education of professionals including teachers.

There is another story at work in the rescuing of a professional image of practice, experience and narrative. Schon and Oakeshott permit us to imagine a Johnson retelling of "the body in the mind", and, metaphorically, to return "upward" to the whole from the technical rationalist's reduced world of skilled practice. There is another retelling of the story "downward" to the whole from a paradigmatic socio-political analysis. Just as reductionism makes the whole into something lesser, sociological and political analysis can also make the whole lesser through the use of abstraction and formalism. The disputes between experientialist wholists and those promulgating formalistic lines of inquiry are no less dramatic, although far less widespread, than those between experiential wholists and technical rationalists. The latter disputes are more widely known throughout the educational literature partly because experiential wholists have imagined technical rationalists as the only, or at least the main, opponent of experience in the study and doing of education. But as the arguments in the curriculum literature between experientialists and formalists make clear, the study of practice, experience and narrative is equally mistrusted in formalism as it is in technical rationalism. Our own work on narrative (Connelly and Clandinin, 1988a, 1988b) has recently come under criticism from both sources, technical rationalism and formalism.

The formalists' argument has been supported from two quite different sources, the study of literature and the philosophy of science. In a discussion of the issues at work, Bernstein (1987) remarks that

> it has become increasingly fashionable to speak of our time as a "postera" – "postmodernity", "poststructuralist", "postempericist", "postwestern", and even "postphilosophic" – but nobody seems to be able to properly characterize this "postera" – and there is an inability and an anxiety in the naming of it.
>
> (Bernstein, 1987, pp. 516–517)

This confusion of the theoretical mind is "a reflection of what's happening in our everyday lives where there is a spread of almost wild pluralism" (Bernstein, 1987, p. 517). "Wild pluralism" is another way of naming the relativism that troubles Booth

(1986) in literary criticism and is an expression of what Popper called the "myth of the framework" (Bernstein, 1987, p. 56). It is a formalistic view; a view that things are never what they are but are, rather, what our framework or point of view or perspective or outlook makes of them. Further, since nothing is as it seems, the only thing worth noticing is the terms, the formal structures, by which things are perceived. One does not teach, one mindlessly reproduces a social structure; one does not have emotionally credited intentions, one has preset expectations; one does not have experiences that are one's own, one merely moves forward by contextual design. Formalists say that the facts of the case, the experience one claims to have, or the data collected by empiricist researchers, have little bearing on their claims. A person, they argue, can never see themselves as they are since they are always something else, specifically, they are whatever social structure, ideology or framework is at work in the inquiry. What we have called the whole (the practical, experience and narrative) is, accordingly, as suspect for the formalist as it is for the technical rationalist. The difference between the two is the place given experience. For the technical rationalist, experience is a black mark on the slate to be wiped clean; for the formalist, experience is something to be ignored. For the formalist, there is, in the end, no agency in experience but only in form. For the formalist, a person merely plays out the hegemonies of politics, culture, gender and framework.

Bernstein's task, it might be argued, is to revivify, in the modern age, Deweyan thought which might, as he says, "through communal critical inquiry" (Bernstein, 1987, p. 511), permit a drawing together of the meanings of both technical rationalism and formalism within a theory of experience. As Bernstein remarks "Dewey had a strong sense of both the historicity and the contextualism of all inquiry and experience" and was opposed to the pluralistic "myth of the framework" which "suggests that 'we are prisoners caught in the framework of our theories; our expectations; our past experience; our language'" (Bernstein, 1987, p. 511). "Inquiry" into teacher education, in the Bernstein–Dewey view, is, at one and the same time, historical and contextual; likewise, the "experience" of teacher education is at once historical (and therefore personal) and contextual. A person being educated is a person with an experiential history which a theory of experience neither wipes away nor ignores as irrelevant. A person being educated is all of these things at one and the same time. This is the task of the narrative study of schooling in which we and others are engaged. And because narrative is a way of talking about Dewey's reconstruction of experience or Oakeshott's "reforming knowledge which is already there" (Oakeshott, 1962, p. 12) it is considered ill-advised for study by the technical rationalist. Likewise, because narrative is a reconstruction of a person's experience in relation to others and to a social milieu, it is under suspicion as not representing the true context and the proper "postera" by formalists. With a wry sense of irony, we observe that technical rationalists and formalists are joined in common cause against the study of experience.

Schon's service to professional memory, therefore, reaches beyond his grasp. The practical imagination needed support not only from the losses of reductionism, that is, a loss of wholistic identity in technical rationalism, but also from the losses of the concrete and material, that is, in the excesses of contextualism and formalism. By writing books which embody a concrete conception of the practical, Schon's reach exceeded his anti-reductionist grasp. Unwittingly, to reverse Johnson's epigram (1987), Schon "put the mind back into the body". The narrative study of experience brings body to mind and mind to body; it connects autobiography to action and an intentional future; it connects these to social history and direction; and it links the pluralistic extremes of formalism to the concreteness of specific actions.

Narrative thought, that is, how one goes about thinking narratively, has several possibilities. Traditional fields of inquiry offer paradigmatic narrative modes as, for example, in history, literature, biography, philosophy, psychotherapy and so forth. Ours is but one possibility within several and is in education (Baker and Greene, 1987; Enns-Connolly, 1985; Britzman, 1989; Bruner, 1986). Our own work, perhaps more prosaically "practical" than most, is to rethink curriculum and teaching in terms of a narrative inquiry which draws on classroom observation and participant observation of the practical, along with the bringing forward of personal experience in the form of stories, interviews, rules, principles, images, and metaphors (Clandinin, 1986; Connelly and Clandinin, 1988a).

The teacher as curriculum topic

In a Dewey (1938) inspired essay on forms of inquiry, Schwab (1962) showed how, in the social and physical sciences, the study of the whole vies for place amid downward (reductionistic) and upward (formalistic) modes of explanation. Our discussion of the study of experience is set forth in order to show where the study of experience fits within what Scwab called the "forms of principles for inquiry" (p. 186) in educational studies. Admittedly, the term "experience" does not make a study wholistic. But "experience" designates the principal phenomenon that marks the relevant whole, an individual person being educated. Narrative, which we have defined as "the making of meaning from personal experience via a process of reflection in which storytelling is the key element and in which metaphors and folk knowledge take their place" (Connelly and Clandinin, 1988b, p. 16), is our conception of the whole. Narrative is temporal, past, present and future, and, as in all storytelling, is a reconstruction of experience. It is a putting of "the mind in the body" and "the body in the mind". The whole, for us, is the narrative that each person tells of herself/himself, or that is told through processes of inquiry. This is not the place to detail the quality of narrative or of *a* narrative except to say that, properly done, it countenances the full implications of what Johnson (1987) intended by putting the body in the mind and its reverse. In narrative inquiry, just as in reading any text, there are multiple possible narratives and/or narrative threads and the judgement of whether or not one is "telling the truth" has to do with criteria such as adequacy, possibility, depth, and sense of integrity. There is no "quest for certainty" in the writing of narrative and so there is a basic opposition in principle between the wholistic ends of narrative inquiry, the reductionistic ends of technical rationalist inquiry and the generalized and abstract ends of formalistic inquiry.

Our particular approach to curriculum requires that a further point be made before we bring forward illustrative case material. The so-called commonplaces are widely acknowledged as specifying the "topics" of curriculum discourse. We know of no argument to deny the forceful legitimacy of subject matter, teacher, learner, and milieu as integral parts of an adequate discussion of curriculum. Some, such as Ben-Peretz (1986), would add to the list but none, to our knowledge, would subtract. Generally speaking, learner, subject matter and milieu are well represented in the literature. But in most of the literature, the teacher as a focus for curriculum discourse tends to be minimized and treated in derivative ways. At the risk of oversimplifying, many milieu curriculum arguments tend to treat the teacher as an unconscious reproducer of inequitable social structures; many subject matter arguments demand rationalistic disciplinary training of teachers; and learner based arguments tend to see the teacher as nurturer. In almost all such curriculum proposals "teacher retraining" is tacked on to the more central topic. Our work puts the teacher in the forefront and constructs a teacher based curriculum argument. It is an argument which conceptually meshes a curriculum for teacher education with a curriculum for those taught.

Our overall argument is constructed on two assumptions, one of which we assert and the other one of which we shall both argue to and from. We assume that studies of school reform, and resistance to it, yield a view of teacher agency such that curriculum plans, whether of milieu, subject matter or learner, founder or prevail on the activities of the teacher. We assume that in the curricular event, it is teachers that reproduce or revolutionize social structures, communicate or reinterpret curriculum context, and cooperate with, or act in opposition to, the nature of their student charges. In short, we propose to entertain the consequences of adopting a teacher topic for curriculum discourse.

The assumption we propose to argue from, and with, might be defined as the assumption of experience and the uses of narrative. We want to rethink the possibilities and potential in Dewey's (1938) idea of experience. As we reflect on experience it is, to us, a remarkable anomaly that general and rhetorical writings on curriculum, textbooks and the like, make experience a key term; likewise, in our everyday discourse about education, the word experience (Deweyian or otherwise) is so common as to be what Schutz and Luckmann (1973) might call the "unexamined ground of the natural world view of a curricularist". Yet, when we turn to curriculum inquiry, especially that branch of curriculum inquiry that refers to teachers, it is as if experience is of little importance to education.

In the remainder of this paper, we bring these two sets of assumptions together. We show how a narratively understood curriculum for teacher education meshes with a curriculum for the teacher's students.[1] In our recent book (Connelly and Clandinin, 1988a), we wrote of this idea as "the teacher's curriculum as a metaphor for the curriculum of the teacher's students".

The internship: laboratory and apprenticeship

Oakeshott (1962) argued against a technical-rationalist view that practical knowledge could be formulated as a set of rules, principles, directions and maxims that could be recorded in a book and taught to novices. On the contrary, he says, "it is a characteristic of practical knowledge that it is not susceptible to a formulation of this kind" (Oakeshott, 1962, p. 10). He argues that "practical knowledge can neither be taught nor learned, but only imparted and acquired. It exists only in practice" (Oakeshott, 1962, p. 11). Practical knowledge is learned through apprenticeship to a master. Undoubtedly, such an education has great advantages over "the book" as an education in practice. But taken to its extreme in teacher education, apprenticeship to a master simply replaces the authority of the technical-rationalist's "book" with the authority of the cooperating teacher.

The principal criticism of this form of apprenticeship in the education of teachers was advanced by Dewey (1938) in his distinction between the laboratory and apprenticeship in teacher education. For Dewey, the laboratory is an occasion for problem-formulation and solution which permits the novice teacher not only to absorb the norms of practice, as in apprenticeship, but also to think for him- or herself, to be reflective and, therefore, to culture the seeds of reform. It is in the laboratory, combined with the best of apprenticeship, that practice is learned as a whole, experientially and with the possibility for reconstruction such that the bonds of biography and culture can be stretched and broken. The potential of the internship for these purposes is seen in the following case study work between Clandinin and an intern teacher, Marie,[2] and her cooperating teacher, Ellen.

The teacher/participant

At the time field records were made, Marie was in her first year of teaching as part of an internship program. She completed a BEd After Degree in Early Childhood Education following a BA and most of an MA in English literature. Marie lived and was educated in different countries as her family was transferred from place to place. She worked in industry for a period of time and then returned to university to pursue teacher education. She was a student in a teacher education class Clandinin taught. She did her primary division student teaching in a class taught by a woman who did a great deal of classroom drama including choral reading, readers' theatre, improvisation and role playing. This is the student teaching experience about which Marie most often talks. She went back to work with this teacher as a volunteer whenever she had time during the two years of her teacher education program.

Marie's internship was in a small school situated in an upper middle class area in a large urban area. She was assigned to a class and a teacher in a new program which combined grade one and kindergarten students. The grade one students attended the program all day and the kindergarten children attended in the afternoon. The cooperating teacher had not taught grade one previously but had considerable teaching experience in kindergarten. Marie was selected for this internship position because she had particular strength in grade one as judged by her student teaching experience. The program was a "model" program and was closely monitored by the school board.

Curriculum of teacher education

Marie was involved in the internship program in a teacher education setting which had some of the features of what we imagine might be contained in a reflective practicum for teacher education. She worked in a classroom with an experienced classroom teacher. As well, she participated in a collaborative way in a research project with Clandinin which contributed, through its methodology, to growth and change. She learned, for the first time on a fulltime basis, how to teach by working in a classroom teaching position. It was an apprenticeship situation with the marks of an internship and a laboratory.

Marie's readiness to depart from the constraints of the apprenticeship is seen in the following set of field notes.

> Marie is in charge of the language arts program in the morning. She recounted one of the stories that she was telling where the students got quite excited. She said that she was glad that Ellen, the cooperating teacher, was not in the room for that. Ellen apparently likes to keep the room quite quiet. Marie likes to let the children get involved in the stories and dramatizations of the stories.... One of Marie's concerns is the non-integrated nature of the day. The subjects are taught as different subject matter and this concerns Marie. She had earlier asked Ellen if they could do a theme on fairy tales. Ellen had said that she did not like themes. Marie sees this as one way of getting some integration into the program.
>
> (Notes to file, 11 September 1985)

Marie, of course, was not acting entirely on her own initiative in her readiness to break with Ellen's practices. Her preferences for stories and dramatizations are connected to her student teaching assignments with yet another teacher; with her experiences at the university in teacher education; and with her education in English literature. While it would be easy to say that, therefore, Marie was not thinking independently, her situation of different practices in an apprenticeship was, after all, the world of practice familiar to us all. Inevitably, we are called upon to thread our own practical way through an environment of competing, sometimes conflicting, actions of others. How Marie does this through the reconstruction of her own, and her students' narratives, is the story to be told in this set of field notes.

Literature, drama and narrative

Even the short excerpt from the field notes quoted above illustrates the wholistic, experiential concern of the novice teacher. Marie's concern for the language arts program, literature, story-telling and dramatization is held together in her thinking by narrative. She wanted the children to "get involved in the stories and dramatizations" not only, we imagine, because of the added meaning involvement brings to interpretation, but because it is a way to create a meaningful narrative thread in the children's daily program. Like many elementary school teachers, she was concerned at the fragmentation of a day organized according to school subjects. This concern is frequently cast as subject matter in opposition to children but, for Marie, the issue was essentially one of continuity and meaning for the children.

A reconstruction of Marie's knowledge

In the first set of field notes, Marie seemed to have little sense of doubt with the possible exception of her concern for the student noise generated by her curriculum. She appeared unworried that her ideas for the language arts program and the use of thematic material were not favored by Ellen. Her confidence was not only connected to her earlier student teaching placement but also to her theoretical training on the use of thematic material. Her success with themes is illustrated in the following field note.

> She said that she is having some trouble choosing themes. She said that she thought it would be easy to choose themes. She talked about one of the assignments last year in a course when they needed to choose themes for a year. She said she had no trouble at all doing that but now she was having trouble choosing themes within which she can provide meaningful learning. She talked about the work she is doing on the Halloween theme. She said she is surprised she is able to do what she is able to do with it. She said for the children in their community, Halloween is a big thing. She said that the children go out trick-or-treating with their parents in the immediate area and then the parents have a party at someone's home for groups of children. She said she has thought about this and sees that Halloween is a significant experience in these children's lives. She talked about being able to link the Halloween theme to ghosts and monsters and how these are the nameless fears of children. She thinks that perhaps that is why it has its power. She said that the children are writing about Halloween in their journals.
>
> (Notes to file, 21 October 1985)

Here, the sense of the problematic characteristic of Dewey's "laboratory" is evident. At first, Marie was simply engaged in the problem of choosing themes but, on reflection, she realized that it was much more difficult for her to choose themes for the class than it was for her to choose themes in the university course. The heart of the issue, again, is narrative. How could she identify thematic material which allowed her curriculum to return children's experience to them in a different way and, hence, for them to tell their own stories in richer and more meaningful ways? A double, or "parallel", narrative was at work, hers and her students'. As Marie began to rethink the idea of "theme" in terms of her students' experience, rather than in terms of her own, she fastened on Halloween because of its importance to her students. On the one hand, she was retelling, for herself, the role of theme in teaching. But deeper than this, it was interesting to see that her reconstruction of the Halloween theme for the children was that Halloween permitted children to think through their "nameless" fears and it was the dealing with these fears, and the power they have in the children's lives, that justified the theme for Marie.

Thus, she was beginning to see things that related to the children's experience, and she was led to different understandings than the one she had in her university class where she chose themes that appealed to her. Now she needed themes that permitted her to build on children's experiences. She found herself working on a Halloween theme which was very much a part of the community and family experience for the children and she was surprised she found something of importance in Halloween. She rethought not only the idea of "theme" but the particular theme of Halloween in terms of fears and powers in children's lives. Halloween became an important part of the school curriculum as she thought about its use and as the children wrote about it in their journals. The second narrative reconstruction was the children's own.

"Transformers" and reconstruction

Marie's concern for reconstruction in the children's lives as the focus of her curriculum was seen by contrasting Halloween with the children's "transformer" toys. Her concern for the transformer toys was evident in the following field records.

> She then went back to talking about the blocks. (Marie here is referring to the building block center where children build with large construction blocks objects large enough within which to play). She asked how much she could impose on the children. She asked if she could tell them what to build. She told me that the children had been playing for several days with their transformers. (These are a particular kind of plaything, parts of which can be moved and the toy is then "transformed" into a totally different play thing. For example, a dinosaur could be "transformed" into the shape of a car by changing some of the parts. There is also a daily cartoon television show about transformers that plays on a local station and that many of the children watch). She said that it was all right dramatic play but it was not as good and not as constructive as when they had played with Goldilocks and the Three Bears. (They had earlier done some work with that story.) She had suggested that they build a cottage for the three bears. She said she supposed even then that she had been interfering in their play. I used the word extend their play. They had talked about what they needed to have a cottage and the children had gone ahead and made the cottage. She had said they had put a roof on it and everything.... Apparently, the children, for the first time, had put on a play. They had started to do it with trick or treating around Halloween and Marie had asked them how they were going to end it. They had gone off to work on it and the way they ended was that they came home and ate the candy and got a stomach ache. They wanted to present it to the parents. Now they wanted to do lots more plays. Several more children were asking to be involved. She wants to take the idea of Little Red Riding Hood and get the parents' help in making tapes and so on.
>
> (Notes to file, 3 October 1985)

In the above field note segment, we saw Marie raising questions about the use of the block center and how it fits with children's experience. Marie's focus on children's literature was apparent but she now wondered about children's experience with dramatization and the way it connected with the experience of building props for the dramatizations which she saw happening at the block center. Through the work with the three bears' cottage, the children understood they could create plays of the stories. They began to use their own experiences of Halloween to write a play. It was their experience that became the subject matter for the play.

Essentially, then, Marie rejected the transformer toys, and their television counterparts, in favor of something more thematically connected with the children's lives, Halloween. But she recognized a dilemma since the children were also interested in the transformers. The dilemma was illustrated in the following field notes.

> She again expressed concern about the block play. She said that she is not sure how different it is for the children to be replaying the television experiences in the block center or whether she imposes it. She sees that the culture, via television, imposes it one way and she imposes it the other. She said that she finds the play doesn't go anywhere for some of the students. She talked about the "transformer" stations and she is not too interested. She helped them build a haunted house. She said that they talked about things like Poltergeist. She said that the children could make the walls shake and they had done a very good job of doing it. She said that the kindergarten children do it with the Grade 1 children and that is why the kindergarten children are able to do as much as they can.
>
> (Notes to file, 21 October 1985)

In the above notes, Marie continued to question her work and connected the Halloween experience to the dramatic block play. Again, she connected Halloween to larger supernatural events such as a poltergeist.

> Marie sent them off to get started in the haunted house. She gave the other children their choice of centers and then they walked over and watched the students at the haunted house. They had built a haunted house with the large blocks. They had made a number of masks that were moved up and down. The walls moved which they said was the Poltergeist. They showed this for two or three minutes and the other students clapped. Then they went off to their centers and the children at the block center continued to work on their haunted house.
>
> (Notes to file, 22 October 1985)

From the field records, it was not at all clear how Marie resolved the dilemma at a conceptual level. But practically, it is clear that she believed there to be more narrative meaning contained in the Halloween dramatization than in the transformer toys and this was the practical route taken. We might well imagine that to the extent that Dewey's sense of the laboratory continued to pervade the internship Marie will come back to questions such as this just as she reconstructed her idea of a theme and of the particular theme, Halloween. But whether or not this eventually occurred, we see how Marie's own narrative of experience drove her partly to reflect upon and think out the curriculum for her students and to act out a curriculum partly in accordance with what she had thought out, and partly in accordance with the underlying narrative beliefs she had about experience, themes, integration and meaning for her children. Thus, Marie has reconstructed her idea of curriculum, and, therefore, in the humble way possible in the ongoing business of schooling, was able to break the bonds of her own university and apprenticeship experience. She had, in effect, broken away from social, theoretical and personal bonds in rethinking her ideas of curriculum. Meanwhile, the students reconstructed their curriculum by deliberately creating a play – a story – in which they were actors. Thus, they not only lived out the story of Halloween, but they saw themselves as participants in the story. It is in storying ourselves that it is possible to remake experience.

Educational entailments

When we think of life as a story, we are given a measure, however modest, of control. We gain a measure of freedom from the prisons of biography and social form. This short vignette of Marie's classroom curriculum and Marie's teacher education curriculum exhibits the sense in which it is possible to imagine reform in the school curriculum through reform in the curriculum for teacher education. We see in microcosm the power of narrative and how it is both lived out unconsciously, and is deliberately imagined, thereby yielding reform and reconstruction in our lives. Neither the hegemonies of form nor the constraints of maxim and rule, nor even the bonds of autobiography, are safe from the reconstructions of narrative.

Acknowledgments

This work was supported by the Alberta Advisory Council on Educational Studies and the Social Sciences and Humanities Research Council of Canada.

Notes

* D. Jean Clandinin is at the University of Alberta.
† F. Michael Connolly is at OISE/University of Toronto.
‡ Originally published in: *Cambridge Journal of Education* 20: 3, 241–253.
1 The illustrations for this paper are drawn from a two year narrative study by Clandinin with a beginning teacher.
2 Marie and Ellen are pseudonyms used to protect the anonymity of the two teachers.

References

Baker, A. and Greene, E. (1987) *Storytelling. Art and Technique* (New York, R.R. Bowker Co.).
Ben-Peretz, M. (1986) Time: the fifth commonplace in curriculum deliberations, paper presented at the Annual Meeting of the American Educational Research Association, San Francisco, April.
Bernstein, R. (1987) The varieties of pluralism, *American Journal of Education*, 95, pp. 509–525.

Booth, W.C. (1986) Pluralism in the classroom, *Critical Inquiry*, 12, pp. 468–479.

Britzman, D. (1989) Who has the floor? Curriculum, teaching and the English student teacher's struggle for voice, *Curriculum Inquiry*, 19, pp. 142–162.

Bruner, J. (1986) *Actual Minds, Possible Worlds* (Cambridge, MA, Harvard University Press).

Clandinin, J. (1986) *Classroom Practice: teacher images in action* (London, Falmer Press).

Connelly, F. Michael and Clandinin, D. Jean (1988a) *Teachers as Curriculum Planners: narratives of experience* (New York, Teachers College Press).

Connelly, F. Michael and Clandinin, D. Jean (1988b) Narrative meaning: focus on teacher education, *Elements*, 19(2), pp. 15–18.

Dewey, J. (1938) *Logic: the theory of inquiry* (New York, Henry Holt and Co.); *Experience and Education* (New York, Collier).

Eisner, E.W. (1979) *The Educational Imagination: on the design and evaluation of school programs* (New York, Macmillan).

Enns-Connolly, E. (1985) *Translation as interpretive act: a narrative study of translation in university-level foreign language teaching*, unpublished doctoral dissertation, University of Toronto.

Johnson, M. (1987) *The Body in the Mind. The Bodily Basis of Meaning, Imagination and Reason* (Chicago, IL, University of Chicago Press).

Oakeshott, M. (1962) *Rationalism in Politics and Other Essays* (London, Methuen).

Schon, D.A. (1983) *The Reflective Practitioner: how professionals think in action* (New York, Basic Books).

Schon, D.A. (1987) *Educating the Reflective Practitioner* (London, Jossey-Bass).

Schwab, J.J. (1962) The teaching of science as inquiry, in: J.J. Schwab and P. Brandwein (Eds) *The Teaching of Science* (Cambridge, MA, Harvard University Press).

Schutz, A. and Luckmann, T. (1973) *The Structures of the Life-world* (Evanston, IL, Northwestern University Press).

27 Alienation within the profession – special needs or watered down teachers?

Insights into the tension between the ideal and the real through action research

Christine O'Hanlon[*][†]

The context

The Education and Library Order 1986 in Northern Ireland has led to the introduction of legislation which is parallel to the 1981 Education Act in England and Wales. The Order was put into effect from 1 January 1986 and teachers are trying to interpret their present position and anticipate their future roles in its wake. There is a general professional anxiety which is related to any great change in the focus of professional roles. The previous categorisation of pupils has led to a proliferation of different special schools and units and different teachers trained or appointed to teach within segregated provision, or in ordinary schools as remedial or class teachers in a more integrated educational environment.

Therefore, the University of Ulster attempted to provide for teachers' further professional development through the special needs option in the BEd (Hons) action research based in-service course. The course is primarily concerned with the professional development of teachers and is designed to help teachers meet current challenges, namely, the major changes occurring in all sectors of education and especially in the field of special needs. The professional development arises from a process of investigation, action and reflection. It begins with a focus on the practical situations that are making demands on teachers, demands that require that they make sense of these situations in their social, historical and political context; and that require an engaging in a systematic process of investigation in order to reveal the personal and social assumptions, values and purposes embedded in their concrete situation.

Often this type of research reveals to teachers the mismatches between the claimed and theoretical values and the actual concrete values of the demands in the situation. However, through the teacher's subsequent explanations for the contradictions and inconsistencies, he/she is enabled to understand the situation better and to construct suggestions and strategies for improvement.

The process of professional development begins with the teacher providing an initial impression of the practical situation and its demands.

The course is unit based and the following account is an analysis of the initial thoughts and discussion of the SEN (special emotional needs) teachers who elected to research special needs through the study of specialised SEN units. In an attempt to relate theory to practice, the SEN unit is designed to begin with an articulation of the teacher's own thinking about the practical situation and its demands; the literature and the tutor's expertise are then used as resources for illuminating professional issues and for extending the teacher's thinking about these issues. As a university tutor I was attempting to improve my own role to a more 'facilitator' role in an effort to better afford teachers the opportunity to contribute their knowledge and expertise, to monitor the outcomes of their activities in order to promote further commitment and to assist with the identification of further training needs. The recording of the teachers' discussions was an attempt to monitor and improve my tutoring role, to engage myself in a process of action research albeit a form of second order action research because I was not working directly with pupils in schools.

The problem

There are many different kinds of teachers in special education. There are the mainstream variety, i.e. remedial teachers, peripatetic teachers, special class and special unit teachers who work primarily within or alongside ordinary schools. There are also the teachers who work separately beyond mainstream placement in special schools and separate units and hospital schools. However, they all share the common focus of teaching pupils with special educational needs. All teachers have a unity, the same professional identity, or have they? They follow similar training patterns, teach the same children and share similar professional problems. Do teachers in the special educational system have a common identity with all teachers? Is there an alienation from the main professional body of teachers through the projected alienation of their pupils? Is there a contagion of rejection experienced by special needs teachers?

Let us begin with this conversation, an excerpt from a discussion among special needs teachers.

A conversation

MARY: How many times have I heard 'Oh she's a typical special needs (remedial) teacher'! then wondered what way one is supposed to react to this obscure comment. This is usually followed by 'she *likes* the kids'. Aren't we all as teachers supposed to like the kids, understand them educationally and emotionally or are we in the job to teach the subject, no matter what factors may influence the situation?

MEG: I would get the same thing. I would get it from the children as well. They say, 'Oh, a special teacher for special kids.' I think that they too soon pick you out, but it doesn't always work to your advantage.

MARY: With the other children it probably doesn't, and with the staff it doesn't either.

MEG: I think it gives you a terrible stigma being a special needs (remedial) teacher.

CHRIS: How did you respond when that was said to you?

MEG: I was quite surprised, but I felt that the children really reflected the teachers' attitudes as well. It comes from the top down, a lot of teachers have exactly the same attitude.

CHRIS: What kind of attitude is that?

MEG: They tend to think you have been chosen because you like them, because you're a soft touch with the youngsters.

MARY: I get that too, you have been chosen because you're very sympathetic towards the youngsters and very understanding of them.

MEG: That it goes with a certain type of teacher. They wouldn't expect you to be as good a disciplinarian or something.

CHRIS: How do you see yourself in relation to that?

MARY: I don't know whether or not you find it in all secondary schools, but in some it's very easy to call the discipline problems remedial. Not correctly so, but it's easy for other members of staff just to use us as a dumping ground; and for other teachers who feel, well, you're the remedial teacher, you're paid for it, we don't want them at all. You get it both ways.

SAM: I find with the staff and often with the parents you're neither fish nor fowl. They don't regard you as a *real* teacher, in their terms it would be a subject teacher. Up to now I have always taught a primary seven class. People think that primary seven is one of the perk jobs in a primary school. Just today, talking to parents they said to me, 'Aw, you're getting a wee break, a wee easy number!' Those were the expressions they used! (Primary seven is the 11+ class where academic aims are paramount, teachers aim to get as many through the 11+ examination into grammar schools as is possible; however the special needs role is an easy option and is seen as not needing the same effort).

MEG: A wee treat, that's right!

MARY: Says you, 'little do they know!'

SAM: I think, too, in the primary school, whenever someone is absent, the boss will come in and say 'look after that class'. In a way, although he doesn't intend to do it, he is belittling your work, because he's saying that it's OK for you to lose your half-hour or hour with those children, but the ordinary class teacher has to be looked after.

MARY: Yes, I've noticed that as well, in our upper school, the senior teachers who are out of the rooms most (doing administration etc.) are thrown in to teach the weakest kids. (Implying administration etc. disrupts low-stream and remedial classes.) They don't mind letting the weak teachers have those kids but they don't let those teachers teach 'O' level kids! (Also it is the weak teachers who are asked to teach the weakest pupils not the GCE 'O' level classes.)

MEG: That's a big problem, the kids that need it more are the kids who aren't getting it.

SAM: I think it's unfortunate that this is the image.

MEG: Your ordinary teacher, your fellow colleagues and that, are not particularly interested in what you teach them. They see it as not that important, because you don't have to do anything in the end as such.

The conversation clearly identifies a feeling of alienation experienced by these teachers. The teachers believe that they are identified through the children they teach: 'A special teacher for special kids.'

Special kids are then, as they clearly indicate, cooled out, streamed out, rejected from the mainstream, school or curriculum in different ways; this is seen in the words 'dumping ground' which is the way one particular teacher saw her school role – which implies that her pupils are the garbage or the refuse of the school.

A primary teacher supports this interpretation and describes teaching primary seven as a perk job, compared to her new role as special needs teacher in the school, and declares, subsequently, that her self-image has been severely dented.

The analogy is used 'I think that they too soon pick you out', i.e. the pupils as well as the staff soon select certain teachers for certain roles. Special needs teachers are 'picked out' from their colleagues as 'special' just like their pupils. In this particular school, pupil selection and banding are practised through referral – are there parallels for the teachers? It is the teachers who pick out the pupils initially in the referral process; is it surprising that the pupils have learned to reverse this process and do it with the teachers?

'Being picked out doesn't always work to your advantage.' Is this an understatement, or an unconscious identification with the pupils? It doesn't always work to the pupils' advantage, so with the process rubbing off on the teachers there are adjustments to be made to a redefined teaching role with its intrinsic disadvantages. The 'other' children pose a problem for the teacher identified within this role as well as the rest of the school staff; the whole school's perception of the teacher changes and brings with it a certain stigma.

In the next statement the notion that the pupils learn from the teachers is overtly confirmed with 'the children reflected the teacher's attitudes'. It comes from the top down, a lot of teachers have exactly the same attitude. This is embodied through the general teacher's view of the special needs teacher, they are sympathetic towards the youngsters and very understanding of them. Special teachers are somehow special like their pupils and show a leaning towards them in sympathetic terms, a suggestion that the special needs teacher is primarily loyal to the pupil rather than to the school ethos.

'You're a soft touch, you're not a good disciplinarian' implies again a certain partiality for the pupils' weaknesses: soft teachers give in easily, disciplinarians are hard and firm and support school rules, teachers without good discipline break ranks with their colleagues.

It is interesting also to note that when the teachers talk they accept the projection of pupil reasons for rejection or referral with 'It's easy to call the discipline problems remedial'. In other words the pupils are undisciplined and remedial, the teachers also are not disciplinarians but soft, types are matched, teachers take on the pupils' identity. The pathology of alienation is begun; through the demotion of pupils, teachers are also subtly degraded. The condition has a contagion or is it contamination?

The special needs teachers not only take on the behavioural aspects of the pupils' role but they also accept the low academic label conferred through the pupils' record of removal from the examination process.

One teacher describes how in her school the weak kids are taught by the weak teachers, but 'they won't let those teachers teach 'O' level kids!'

The reason given for this by another teacher is 'you don't have to do anything in the end as such'. They appear to mean that good or strong teachers take 'O' level pupils, weaker teachers take the non-examination pupils and special needs teachers are not accountable through the examination system, therefore have no main focus or purpose in the school because there is no identifiable product at the end.

This is the beginning of the reflections of teachers in a shared session (which was recorded) on their biographies and roles.

Developing shared understanding through action research

The teachers are required to identify a practical situation upon which they wish to reflect in their first weeks on the course, in subsequent weeks they aim to clarify the initial impression of the practical situation and its problematic demands, through the process of data collection. Group seminars follow this phase to enable teachers to present and to engage in the collaborative analysis of data; the purpose of this is to clarify the practical situation, to generate explanation and to identify possible courses of action. An important aspect of this process is the effective inter-action and communication between teachers during the seminars, and the tutor can enable a more productive collaborative understanding to develop among course members. These discussions took place after the teachers' initial collection of evidence and first attempt to make sense of the school data which involved their own classroom and lesson observations.

The nine teachers used for this analysis varied considerably in terms of their attitude to teaching, their perception of themselves within the school as teachers, and in terms of how they expressed and identified their roles. Their professional contexts included all pupil ages, and different ranges of integrated and segregated SEN provision.

The recordings of the group seminars revealed that teachers, when writing about their own situations, were very individual and different, yet within the group, having articulated their own particular role, the discussion and debate that took place with the other special needs teachers created a communication and shared understanding of common problems.

Some teachers concentrated on what was good about their teaching – others about the restrictions on their role and what made them happy. Some teachers concentrated on their own teaching strategies, while others talked mainly about their pupils.

Nevertheless, a variety of themes emerged from the group's discussions and classroom research. For example, teachers prioritised within their role:

1 their decision-making role for pupils in terms of testing for extra help or for withdrawal or for transfer;
2 their management of time for individual pupils;
3 their approaches to ensure academic or skills development in the three Rs;
4 the ways in which they should create a relaxed classroom climate;

5   the nature and purpose of their particular role in the school context;
6   their specific concerns for the whole child's well-being, personality, and self-esteem;
7   to ensure their knowledge and technical expertise supports the pupils' educational development;
8   to foster good pupil/teacher relationships and inter-pupil relationships;
9   to modify or eradicate pupil difficulties;
10 to find ways in which to motivate pupils and build up their concentration;
11 their concern about overall individual pupils' distinctiveness and uniqueness in group situations.

The teachers' data-gathering methods were discussed and negotiated with the tutor before shared data sessions commenced, during which teachers attempted to support or challenge colleagues on the issues central to the whole debate about special needs. The initial focus was the use of teachers' statements which was based on the assumption that:

1   teachers, through their own classroom experience, can abstract their own individual role;
2   their perceptions of their experiences will be related to their understanding of pupils with special educational needs;
3   teachers aim to improve pupil learning therefore there is likely to be a connection between what teachers do and the context within which it takes place.

In making these assumptions we must be aware of the probability of teachers being influenced by factors other than their classroom experience. Their accounts reflect much more than their professional practice. As action research is designed to investigate and solve problems which have become apparent to the teacher, this depends on the identification of a problem or an issue to be resolved. Teachers need to recognise some deficit in their existing knowledge or practice, combined with self-questioning and careful reflection which leads to conscious decision-making in their role rather than automatic routine classroom action.

In the recorded and observed lessons and discussions there was a substantial amount of data about those aspects of their teaching which teachers valued most. The constructs they used in their accounts form the basis of this analysis. The presentation of their views to their colleagues on the course, their classroom observations and probing questions helped to elucidate and elaborate their conceptions of their own teaching.

The concepts were created after reflections about the essential contradictions within the teachers' own accounts of their role and their observations of school practice. Through the teachers' language it was possible to discern the essential basic ambiguities and to identify the arguments within either a technicist or an intuitionist paradigm. A basic distinction in role focus emerges through the examination of the implicit assumptions embodied within the language used by the teachers to describe their role/situation and the ensuing study of the transcripts and development of the issues which arose within the subsequent group discussions. The transcript was reviewed and assumptions were identified, abbreviated and recorded in lists. These lists were then scanned for similarities of theme and concept.

The ideal and the real

There appeared to be a recurring theme within the special needs teacher's role which was identified in humanitarian, anti-authoritarian, pastoral sense on the one hand; and within a skills based, specialised expert, technical professional sense on the other hand. The basic tension, the basic contradictions emerged in every teacher's account as an apparent ambiguity between their immediate feelings, their concerns, their intuition with their pupils, as against their knowledge of education, and their professional status based on expert skills and training.

These conflicting roles appeared to reflect an opposing professional position which could be explained within a technicist/intuitionist paradigm.

A *technicist* is a teacher who is primarily concerned about the techniques of the profession. He/she is interested in results, in the product of schooling and teaching. Outcomes which are quantifiable will be measured; techniques will be defined in objective terms; and institutional traditional norms will be modelled.

An *intuitionist* is a teacher who is primarily concerned about relationships with pupils. He/she is interested in the process of schooling and teaching/learning situation. Means of achieving this or techniques are defined in subjective, interrelational or interactive terms; and institutional, traditional norms will be modified or altered as part of the improvement/change transformation.

Table 27.1 lays out the main focus and values which lie within each paradigm.

Table 27.1 Contrasting paradigms for SEN teachers

Technicist	Intuitionist
Subject centred	Pupil centred
Academic outcomes/product	Pupil development/process
First loyalty to school aims	First loyalty to pupils
Comradeship with teacher colleagues	Alienation from teacher colleagues
Examination focus	Non-examination focus
Acceptance of school curriculum	Devising alternative curriculum
Return service	Rescue service
Pupil competition	Pupil collaboration
Pupil/pupil interaction	Teacher/pupil interaction
Grading of work	Enjoyment of work
Precision teaching	Intuitive teaching
Mastery of special educational tasks	Personal/holistic development
Intervention	Autonomy
Regular testing	Continuous assessment/self-evaluation
Justification to staff	Justification to pupils
Needs met by school	Needs met beyond school
Assessment and testing important	Self concept and confidence important
Quantitative evaluation	Qualitative evaluation
Instrumental decisions	Moral choices

All teachers believed their role and identity to differ significantly from that of the ordinary teacher, and concepts have been collected into Tables 27.2 and 27.3 which are statements about DIFFERENCES and CONTRASTS within the special needs teachers' roles in relation to the ordinary teacher which further highlights the basic paradigmatic separation.

Ordinary teachers are seen predominantly as subject teachers, their role is to impart knowledge, to get results and support the status quo. On the positive side, they are 'real' teachers, they teach the better able, they follow examination syllabuses and refer difficult pupils. Their shortcomings are that they don't know

Table 27.2 SEN teachers as seen by themselves

Know	more about the whole pupil than ordinary teachers
	how to compromise
Are	different
	relieved from academic pressures
	diagnostic and remedial specialists
	tactful
	a friend and listener
	firm and disciplined
	multi-talented and versatile
Provide	stability and security for pupils
Can	understand the pupil
	improve pupil self-image
	influence the attitude of the peer group
	recognise learning difficulties
	integrate pupils into ordinary classes
	open up and gain real pupil trust
	organise their own curriculum
	counteract school policies
Do	supplement and complement the work of ordinary teachers
	consult with ordinary class teacher re pupil progress
	act as advisors
	prepare additional pupil reports
	test and re-test pupils often
	take time to facilitate pupils
	listen to pupils
	help pupils to feel accepted and important
	help pupils to achieve their potential
	especially like children and young people
	often have a rough time from pupils
	show concern and sympathy which is not soft
	understand kid educationally and emotionally
	have different educational methods and approaches to SEN pupils
	have time to reassure and develop the pupil
	appreciate ANY pupil progress
	emphasise teacher–pupil relationship
	boost pupil's self-confidence
	provide individual pupil programmes (based on pupil strengths and weaknesses)
	have a unique professional position

Table 27.3 Ordinary teacher as seen by SEN teachers

Ordinary teachers:
teach the better able pupils
have an examination syllabus to follow
impart knowledge (predominantly)
expect nothing from remedial pupils
see themselves as real teachers
see the SEN teacher as a watered-down teacher
see pupils differently to the SEN teacher
refer pupils for disturbing classes
see remedial teaching as the soft option
don't know about the whole pupil
don't facilitate the pupils
don't have time to build real relationships with pupils

---

about the whole pupil, don't facilitate the pupils, don't have time to build up pupil relationships, see pupils differently and expect little from pupils who are termed 'remedial' or who have special needs. In the wide range of positive concepts within the special needs teachers' role, they see themselves negatively in only three instances, i.e. the special needs teachers' role dents the self-image, it has a stigma attached, and they have a rough time from pupils. Predominantly the statements are positive and reinforcing and are expressed in words like appreciate, consult, improve, emphasise, boost, act, provide, organise and specialise. The main issues and problems, now, more clearly emerge from the data. Special needs teachers are by nature and role different from ordinary teachers. They differ in focus, practice and clientele. The clientele, or pupils, in some way, because of the problems they bring with them into the teacher's environment, require a special kind of teacher. They require a tolerant person with an individual pupil-centred focus who practices teaching in an idiosyncratic manner. The SEN teacher must be, as a person, tactful, understanding, appreciating, etc., and must employ a range of means to achieve their aims through providing stability and security for pupils, taking time with pupils, organising their own curriculum, etc. The special needs teacher must have certain basic attributes and employ certain techniques in the enactment of the role (see Table 27.4).

These attributes and techniques have been selected from the language used by the teachers in seminars devoted to the description and analysis of the SEN teachers' role, this is, in fact how they describe themselves!

The picture emerges of an individualistic and an original person who doesn't depend on 'outside' direction or policy, but is inner directed through sensitive responses to the pupils' individual needs. As they see the pupils, they also see themselves as special, unique, and non-conformist, flexible to the basic human erratic behaviours of their pupils. As the pupils are marginalised so also are the teachers, the real human characteristics possessed by themselves and their pupils are not always acceptable or recognised within the school and professional context. The product of their efforts with SEN pupils is not measureable in curriculum terms. SEN teachers need a wide range of professional skills which are part of their intuitive craft knowledge, which is not related to academic knowledge.

Table 27.4 SEN teachers as seen by themselves

Personal attributes	Techniques
Tactful	Provide stability and security
Different	Improve self-image
Understanding	Influence peer group
Influential	Counteract school policies
Compromising	Supplement and complement ordinary teachers
Facilitating	Advise other teachers
Stoical	Prepare school reports
Concerned	Test and re-test pupils
Sympathetic	Take time with pupils
Like kids	Help pupils feel accepted
Reassuring	Help pupils feel important
Appreciating	Show concern and sympathy
Aware	Use different educational methods
Friendly	Appreciate pupil progress
Disciplined	Help pupils achieve potential
Multi-talented	Recognise learning difficulties
Firm	Integrate pupils into ordinary classrooms
Versatile	Emphasise teacher/pupil relationship
Supportive	Boost pupils' self-confidence
Open	Organise their own curriculum
Trusting	Devise individual programmes
Individualistic	Diagnose and remediate

A fundamental tension arises within the perception of the special needs teacher of him/herself in just how much of the role is similar to that of the ordinary teacher, and in what way it differs. In the identification of the essential differences, the basis for separation and antipathy emerge and special needs teachers take on the pupils pathology of alienation. They disconnect from the professional ethos of all teachers through their basic different attitudes and pedagogy. This has been demonstrated as the primary focus for the teachers' problems and it is this fundamental dilemma which was the conscious convergence of all the issues raised by the teachers in the discussion and debate which is illustrated through the following excerpt:

Primary dilemma

A watered-down teacher

CLARE: My main role, as I would see it, is that of a diagnostician and remediation specialist, but I see my own limitations in this area – coupled with building relationships.

CHRIS: Do you put a priority on either role?

CLARE: Well, the school would dictate the former possibly, especially now, because of this new Order (new legislation – Education and Library Order 1986). I would like to think that it's the building of relationships. In actual practice, I think I am setting the standards too high. I'm demanding too much of the kids and I'm not getting to know them or build the relationships that I would like to do.

CHRIS: Why do you think the school would emphasise the former because of the new legislation? What do you mean by that?

CLARE: Because the attitude is, if anybody came in, you must be able to say who you've got, why you've got them and justify everything.

OTHER TEACHERS: Yes that's true.

CLARE: Our boss would die if he thought I had a pupil and I wasn't able to list off what's wrong, what help he needed and so on.

MEG: To say why there were absences and so forth.

CLARE: I think he would die if he thought I was sitting most of the period talking to the kids and trying to socialise and that. It's lovely, but I know the science teacher will be coming to me and saying 'What the hell are you doing there? I mean, they can't spell, they can't read, that's your job – get it done!'. So I am being restricted.

MEG: And realistically, you're not going to get anywhere academically until you've got their confidence.

CLARE: I think I've got their confidence, but I still have this problem, that I'm trying to plough ahead and get them to give me such and such work. I am given these spellings by the science teacher and I'm trying to get the kids to learn these spellings because, there, I always get flack from them. You're always feeling you have to justify what you're doing.

PAT: You are being pressurised.

CLARE: Pressurised, yeah; although I can structure my own syllabus, I am still told by the head of maths and the head of English what exam to do, and it has to be academic. I have to get the kids to show they can perform certain academic skills and that.

SAM: You're actually saying that it is still curriculum-centred as opposed to child-centred.

MARY: It is.

CLARE: Yes, even though I would love it to be the other way round, in theory my priorities are the other way, but in actual practice they're not. I am a watered-down teacher. I am a watered-down academic teacher, not a special needs teacher, that's the way I see myself.

Now the essential dilemma emerges – that special needs teachers, because of their non-academic role, have a non-academic value which is unclear. Clare knows how she can gain credit and acceptability again, through becoming a recognised and qualified diagnostician and remedial specialist. She understands that linking with her specialist colleagues involves her development of technical skills, i.e. diagnosis, assessment, testing and remediation, to prove her professional worth and give her a definite 'subject' focus. The subject is diagnostic and remedial expertise. 'Coupled with building relationships' is added as an addendum, important but not essential. On questioning, Clare realises that she would ideally like to develop relationships with pupils more, but feels that the 'school' and the new special needs legislation is putting pressure on her to raise pupils' standards especially in the 3Rs. She finds that demanding more work from pupils doesn't enable her to build the relationships with pupils that she would ideally wish to foster. The technicist role must take precedence over the intuitionist role, if one decides to meet the school's and not the pupils' demands. The pupil is translated through the Principal's views (the boss) into a list of symptoms (what's wrong), and the teacher's skills lie in diagnosing the correct treatment for the presenting symptoms. Even school absence is treated by the school as a symptom of the pupil's learning difficulty. The school clearly expects better standards of reading and spelling, and that's the real job, not pupil understanding.

Meg interjects with the surety that pupils' academic progress depends on the teacher having their confidence (in the sense of trust). Clare responds that she believes that she has their confidence but she is still being pressurised by other teachers to raise literacy standards. She must justify what she does in a manner commensurate with examinations. Clare finally defines the role ideally as a pupil-centred one, but her practice reflects the school-centredness of her efforts within

Table 27.5 Dilemmas

1	Professional membership v. alienation	
	Collegiality with colleagues	Identify with and support of pupils needs
	Subject teacher	paramount
	Loyalty to pupil needs	Loyalty to school aims
2	Focus on subject/pupil	
	Standard and testing for results	Reward for effort and progress
	Transmission teacher role	Facilitator role
3	Furtherance of efforts in home environment/school environment	
	Limited influence for teacher	Increased influence for teacher
	Time consuming	Easier management of curriculum
	More pupil understanding	More inter-professional understanding
4	Pupil disruption negative/positive	
	Teacher must control	Pupil gains attention
	Time from other pupils	Time for pupil
	Teacher is disciplinarian	Teacher is friend
5	Special needs role integrated/separated	
	Professional alienation	Unique position
	Large classes	Individual pupils, small groups
	Low status	Privileged status
	Pupil acceptance/low stigma	Pupil stigma
6	Pupil testing positive/negative	
	Yields pupils for SEN placement	Stigmatises/labels pupils
	Leads to pupil rewards	Leads to low streaming and non-examination classes
		Leads to pupil failure
7	The specialist role negative/positive	
	Reinforces deficit model	Discovers pupil potential
	Concentrates on specific handicap	Integrates and modifies handicap

the mainstream, which causes a great tension for her, if she reverts to the ideal role it removes her from a 'discipline' or 'subject' teacher to be transformed into a wet and watery academic teacher. Implicit in this expression is the opinion that real teachers are academic, i.e. they teach a subject, a specialism, within which pupil progress can be measured, and the teacher's value can be attached to the pupils' achievements; hence low pupil achievement goes with low professional credibility and status.

Through this primary dilemma, later ambient discussion highlights a number of related dilemmas, which emanate from this basic predicament for special needs teachers.

The seven dilemmas centre around the issues of decision-making within the professional environment, the traditions, values and contexts, within which teachers work and their attempts to understand and influence these factors, e.g.:

> How much does the environment beyond the school impinge on or the influence the school situation? Should teachers attempt to change it? How does a specialist role in special needs benefit the pupil, is it more expertise or more professional separation?

Conclusion

School problems experienced by SEN teachers are related to the experience of alienation, the restrictions of the existing examination curriculum, and its effects on both pupils and teachers; the academic rewards for pupils and teachers are obvious, so too are kickbacks from pupils unable to benefit from them which affects their teachers too. Are teachers sceptical of the limitations placed on them by the school and the curriculum? How can the special needs teacher adapt to, and change a role with so many divergences and contradictions? Pupil testing yields fodder for the fringe, supplies pupils to the special educational needs professionals, yet what about the cost in pupil terms?

Special needs teachers define their role in intuitionist terms ideally, they see their role as fundamentally pupil-centred, using qualitative processes and intuitive teaching. Yet the teaching reality doesn't confirm this, the practice is different. When the teachers observe their own practice, describe, record and analyse real classroom situations, they each identify differing degrees of technicist practice, e.g. encouraging pupil competition and quantitative evaluation testing and assessment. Every teacher displayed a variety of pedagogy which could be defined as technicist; however, the teachers who experienced most anxiety and tension in their attempts to understand and interpret their roles were those teachers who were more dependent on technicist practices. The more they engaged in academic practice and assessment to gain status and esteem from within the mainstream profession, the more they experienced a tension in their 'special needs' role. In order to meet the real pupils' needs it was necessary to employ the intuitionist role, yet it was within this paradigm that the experience of alienation within the profession was greatest. Teachers who worked closest to, and within, mainstream experienced the greatest contradictions and tensions in their professional practice. There was a clear connection between the teachers who sought collegiality and professional support from teaching colleagues, and their experience and fear of alienation within the school/educational environment through their use of SEN skills and expertise. However, those teachers who worked in a specialist field in more segregated provision, for example, with mentally handicapped children, articulated the same attitudes, yet didn't experience the same tension through action research because they had a professional autonomy which was not so dependent on the academic ethos of the mainstream, ordinary school.

All the teachers claimed to be pupil-centred, yet they were in fact encouraging pupil competition, grading work, devising individual educational programmes, diagnosing, testing and intervening in and controlling pupils' learning in the classroom. They were practising their role in the manner of a subject with measurable results; it was difficult for them to reconcile the real and the ideal in their teaching when the evidence was collected which revealed their technicist roles.

A final observation is that all the teachers expressed experiences of professional alienation, especially those who worked primarily as remedial teachers in mainstream schools. There was a degree of technicist practice evident in all the teachers' classroom data, yet their professional improvement focused on an emergent intuitionist paradigm. The inherent contradictions in the teaching situation were revealed through the teachers' efforts to improve their pupils' learning, during a reflective process which continues today. My own recordings, reflections and analyses have illuminated my perceptions of the tension and stresses experienced by the teachers, and projected in a tangible manner through discussion in seminars. Once the problems are understood the tension is bearable and capable of resolution.

Note

* Christine O'Hanlon is Lecturer in In-service Training, at the Faculty of Education, University of Ulster at Jordanstown.
† Originally published in: *Cambridge Journal of Education* 18: 3, 297–311.

28 Educational theory and the professional learning of teachers
An overview

*John Elliott**[*][†]

Two visions of professional development

One way of looking at the relationship between educational theory and the professional knowledge of teachers is to see the former as a set of ideas about some aspect of education which has been constructed within a specialised academic discipline by experts who have mastered its particular standards of inquiry. The knowledge and understanding conveyed by such a theory can then be applied by teachers in learning to teach effectively. Professional knowledge, on this view of educational theory, consists of a theoretical understanding of ideas about various aspects of education drawn from disciplines such as philosophy, psychology, sociology and history, plus 'knowing how' to apply them in particular practical situations.

On this *rationalist* view (see Oakeshott, 1962) of the relationship, between educational theory and professional knowledge, the process of theory generation is quite separate from the process of its acquisition and utilisation for practical purposes. The acquisition of professional knowledge is therefore dependent on theory generation within quite specialised disciplines of inquiry into education.

The traditional organisation of both initial and in-service teacher education reflects this *rationalist* view of the relation between educational theory and professional knowledge. Student and in-service teachers acquire theoretical knowledge from the disciplines of education, often taught in separation from each other, and are then expected to apply it in practice.

Over the last decade and a half this pattern of teacher education has been greeted with increasing scepticism by both practitioners in schools and educational administrators who manage resources. They argue there is little connection between the academic theories taught in institutions of higher education and the practical knowledge teachers need to improve their practices in classrooms and schools. Through the operation of the new arrangements in LEAs for in-service education (GRIST), local authority officials and inspectors have had the power to deny teachers access to theory-led teacher education in preference to what is believed to be a more practical competency-based training. The pressure on institutions of higher education to make their teacher education more practical and relevant has also been felt at the level of initial training. Many departments and schools of teacher education within the UK have over the years attempted to respond to these pressures from 'the world of practice', and according to John

Wilson have 'allowed the disciplines of education to wither'. Wilson asks: 'what kind of authority – bearing in mind the nature of education as an enterprise – ought at least some of those staffing such institutions to possess, which is not already possessed in greater quantity elsewhere?'

His answer constitutes an eloquently argued plea for 'the disciplines of education' as a major source of the teacher educator's authority. He regrets that professors of education are increasingly recruited from the ranks of educational administrators or politicians, and that the rank and file of teacher educators largely consists of people whose qualifications stem from their practical experience of either teaching a school subject or working in 'fashionable' fields like multicultural education, gender relations, curriculum development, etc. The problem, as he sees it, is one of demonstrating the relevance and practical value of the educational disciplines. He admits that academics have not made a good job of this in the past, and claims that the specialised topics which the disciplines handle should not be transmitted in abstraction from practical themes and issues which emerge from school experience. Moreover, such themes and issues should constitute areas for interdisciplinary study in which students are able to analyse them from a variety of theoretical perspectives.

What is not clear, in my view, is the extent to which Wilson believes that the development of valid professional knowledge is entirely structured and determined by the differentiated systems of thought embodied in the disciplines, as opposed to the latter simply contributing to such development. Is Wilson offering us a more sophisticated rationalist justification for the disciplines of education or a rather different sort of justification for them? At points it appears to be the former; when, for example, he argues that teachers can only overcome prejudice and bias in their thinking about educational themes and issues by embracing the standards of reasoning embodied in the different disciplines. Such standards of reasoning, according to Wilson, are not relative to particular cultural contexts.

If Wilson is simply proposing a more sophisticated and flexible form of rationalism in teacher education then his position would be consistent with a philosophical perspective on the aims of the academic disciplines, which Maxwell (1984) has called 'the philosophy of knowledge'. Maxwell claims that the basic idea of this philosophical outlook is:

> that inquiry can best help us realise what is of value in life by devoting itself, in the first instance, to achieving the intellectual aim of improving knowledge, in a way which is dissociated from life and its problems, so that knowledge thus obtained may subsequently be applied to helping us solve our problems of living.

Wilson is not, I think, suggesting that the teacher educator's primary role is to help students become experts at knowledge generation within each of the disciplines of education. He implies that the apparent disconnection in the past between theory and practice lies in the tendency of academics to transmit theory solely in the form in which it was generated, i.e. in a way which is dissociated from the practical problems of living. In Wilson's account the primary concern of the teacher educator should be to help the student or teacher utilise specialised know-ledge: helping him or her to apply it to real educational problems and issues. In order to become familiar with such problems and issues teacher educators need to get out into schools and mix with teachers. But there will always be a point, Wilson argues, when some element of dissociation, from the practical topic at hand, is necessary for depth of understanding. In order to utilise a theory students may have to spend a lot of time trying to understand its conceptual basis or the empirical evidence which supports it. I shall now attempt to demonstrate that this view of the teacher educator's role is rather ambiguous. As it stands it can be accommodated within the 'philosophy of knowledge' perspective. But it can also be elaborated in a form which accommodates it within a quite different philosophi-cal outlook.

According to Maxwell there is an alternative philosophical outlook on the aims and purposes of the academic disciplines which he calls "the philosophy of wisdom". Its basic idea is that,

> inquiry, in order to be rational, in order to offer us rational help with realizing what is of value, must give absolute priority to our life and its problems, to the mystery of what is of value, actually and potentially, in existence, and to the problems of how what is of value is to be realized. Far from giving priority to problems of knowledge, inquiry must, quite to the contrary, give absolute pri-ority to articulating our problems of living, proposing and criticizing possible solutions, possible and actual human actions. The central and basic intellec-tual task of rational inquiry, according to the philosophy of wisdom, is to help us imbue our personal and social lives with vividly imagined and criticized possible actions so that we may discover, and perform, where possible, those actions which enable us to realize what is of value in life ... for each one of us the most important and fundamental inquiry is the thinking that we person-ally engage in ... in seeking to discover what is desirable in the circumstances of our lives, and how it is to be realized.

Maxwell cites two basic rules of rational problem-solving within this fundamen-tal form of *practical inquiry*. The first is: articulate, and try to improve the articula-tions of the problems to be solved; and the second is: imaginatively propose and critically assess possible solutions. This is precisely the philosophical perspective which has informed the growth of educational action-research as a form of educa-tional inquiry (see Elliott, 1987). Educational inquiry is not a separate process from the practice of education. It is a form of reflexive practice. Teaching can be con-strued as a form of educational research rather than its object.

The aim of educational action research is not the generation of highly spe-cialised and differentiated theories about education, but the generation of practical wisdom. Wisdom can be defined as a holistic appreciation of a complex practical activity which enables a person to understand or articulate the problems (s)he con-fronts in realising the aims or values of the activity and to propose appropriate solutions. Conceived as an *educational theory*, wisdom constitutes a complex struc-ture of ideas which cannot be broken down into its constitutive elements – as propositions – without loss of meaning. Such an holistic appreciation of educational practice cannot be atomised into psychological, sociological, philosophical theories and retain the status of an educational theory. It may be constituted in part by such theories, but these in isolation do not constitute *educational theories*, although they may be called *theories about education*. It is only the structure as a whole which captures a vision of an educational practice and merits the status of an educational theory. How such structures become publicly accessible is a question we shall address later.

The contribution of the disciplines of education to practitioner-based educational inquiry

If we return to Wilson's 'problem of authority' we can begin to formulate a solution from a 'philosophy of wisdom' perspective. The authority of the teacher educator, from this perspective, must primarily derive from the practical wisdom (s)he has developed through fundamental inquiry into how educational values can be realised in his or her practice (both as a teacher of children and as a teacher of teachers). Such practical wisdom implies that the teacher educator has a working appreciation of the process of practical inquiry through which it is developed.

The holistic theory which structures practical wisdom cannot be transmitted to student teachers in initial or in-service contexts on the basis of assumptions about the dissemination of knowledge which are made by 'the philosophy of knowledge'. The latter assumes that the validity of a theory can be demonstrated quite independently of the thinking of the practitioner who is required to apply it. From a 'philosophy of wisdom' perspective the validity of an *educational theory* cannot be tested independently of a process of practical inquiry in which practitioners discover solutions to problems of realising educational values in their actions. Thus the transmission of an *educational theory* by a teacher educator implies that (s)he must be able to establish conditions of practical educational inquiry, as a context in which his or her 'students' can assess the validity and relevance of the theory in helping them to articulate practical problems and discover appropriate solutions. As a result of such inquiry the students and their teacher educator may reconstruct their prior understandings.

The teacher educator can therefore only transmit educational theory in an educative manner if (s)he also puts him or herself into the role of a learner – who can be educated in turn by his or her students. The authority of the teacher educator does not rest on some 'infallible' *educational theory* but on his or her ability to utilise that theory as a resource for enabling practitioners to construct their own professional knowledge through action research. How this might be done is something we shall again return to later.

It could be argued that all this is no answer to Wilson's problem. It simply legitimates taking teacher education out of the sphere of higher education altogether and locating it entirely within the practitioner system. But the 'philosophy of wisdom' does not negate an important role for 'the disciplines of knowledge' in the development of teachers' professional knowledge. It simply implies the subordination of specialised forms of inquiry aimed at the production of analytic knowledge to a more holistic form of practical inquiry aimed at generating wisdom about how to realise educational values in action.

Maxwell cites two additional rules for this kind of holistic and practically oriented inquiry. The first is that 'in tackling a complex problem it is often helpful to break the given problem up into a number of subordinate, specialised problems'. This moment of analysis is then followed by a moment of synthesis when the solutions to the subordinate problems are 'put together to solve our original, overall problem'. The second rule he cites is that 'in order to develop good ideas for a solution to our given problem it is often helpful to look at solutions to analogous, already solved problems'. This would apply to both the overall practical problem and the subordinate problems of knowledge.

Seen in this light the knowledge produced by the specialised disciplines of education can be seen as intellectual resources for the moment of analysis within the action-research cycle of 'reflection upon action and action upon reflection'. It can be eclectically utilised to deepen the action-researcher's understanding of the particular sub-problems (s)he has analysed a complex practical problem into. But this is only likely to happen if (s)he can apply the second additional rule so that the knowledge generated by the disciplines constitute solutions to problems of knowledge which are analogous to the problems which have emerged from an analysis of his or her practice. The ability of the educational action-researcher to utilise the disciplines of education will therefore depend on the extent to which the specialists within those disciplines subordinate the production of knowledge to the overall aim of helping educational practitioners to improve their articulations of complex practical problems. Maxwell argues that academic work on subordinate problems of knowledge should all be designed 'in one way or another, to help us achieve what is of value in life'.

This view of the relationship between the disciplines of education and practical knowledge has the following implications. First, everyday understandings of educational processes, which are embedded in educational practices and articulations of practical problems and proposed solutions (what Schon has called 'problem-frames'), do not originate, as Wilson appears to suggest, in specialised and differentiated disciplines of inquiry. Rather they originate in the holistic and undifferentiated thinking of educational practitioners as they attempt to realise their educational values in complex practical situations. They are primarily conditioned by the practical aim of realising values.

Second, the theoretical knowledge which disciplines of education produce can only be utilised by practitioners if they are framed and conditioned by an interest in realising common educational values. In this sense the disciplines of education are not value-free and therefore, at least in one sense of the term, not free of ideology.

Third, although specialised inquiries within the disciplines do not determine and structure professional knowledge, they can contribute to its development. The disciplines of education can be viewed as specialised branches of inquiry whose fundamental task is that of facilitating fundamental educational inquiry (action-research). The major task of the philosophy of education is to improve educators' everyday conceptions of the aims of education and the processes in which they can be realised. That of the history of education is to help us to examine and assess the ways complex practical problems of education have been articulated and 'resolved' in the past as a basis for selecting analogies which can improve our articulations of, and proposed solutions to, current educational problems. Psychology and social psychology have the task of improving educational practitioners' articulations of the personal and interpersonal dimensions of educational processes like teaching and learning. The task of sociology is to help the practitioners improve their grasp of the institutional and social contexts in which the practical problems of education arise.

There is an important sense, then, in which we can say that the disciplines of education are a major source of critical standards for analysing aspects of educational practices. But these standards cannot fulfil this function by simply being applied to educational practices which are assumed to exist independently of the thinking and professional knowledge of the persons engaged in them. Structures of knowledge are embedded, often tacitly, in practices and provide the 'problem-frames' (see Schon, 1983) in which practical problems are articulated by practitioners. The disciplines of education provide critical standards for assessing particular components of teachers' knowledge. But they can only carry out this function in a context where teachers themselves are engaged in fundamental educational inquiry in which they articulate practical problems and proposed solutions.

In this context the relationship between the specialist inquirer and scholar as teacher educator and the practitioner is one of partnership and dialogue. The practitioners not only use the knowledge generated by the disciplines to develop their conceptualisation of practical problems but their conceptual schemes can in themselves provide a basis for a critique of the assumptions embedded in the way problems of knowledge have been defined within the specialised and subordinate disciplines. In this sense the teacher educator must always transmit his or her specialised knowledge as intrinsically problematic. Internal standards and methods of validating knowledge within a discipline are always open to a critique from the standpoint of the standards or values which are internal to educational practices and which ultimately define what is to count as professional knowledge. In the final analysis the ultimate validation of specialised knowledge about education is that it enables educational practitioners to discover better solutions to the complex practical problems they confront in realising educational values in action.

We are now in a position to provide a more precise restatement of the source of the teacher educators' authority from a 'philosophy of wisdom' perspective. It lies in his or her knowledge and understanding of the standards and methodological concerns of practical educational inquiry, conceived as a process of action-research. This knowledge and understanding includes an appreciation of the role of the disciplines in educational inquiry, and the ability to facilitate the utilisation of the theoretical knowledge they embody within it.

Academic cultures and practical cultures

Tony Becher's research into the culture of academic disciplines and fields of inquiry suggests that specialists' understandings and interpretations of the forms of reasoning within the disciplines they are engaged in varies considerably both across, and sometimes within, individual disciplines. On the basis of his interview data he identifies two major dimensions in which variation occurs. The first is the general-particular dimension. Conceptions of theorising between and within disciplines can range from the production of deductive general theories through 'hypotheses which embody some measure of generalisation but rest on an appeal to empirical evidence' (what Becher calls 'middle-range theory'), to 'descriptive taxonomies and prescriptive rules of thumb embedded firmly in data yielded by observation and in practical experience'.

The second dimension of variation is between those who attempt to discover 'profound simplicities' underlying complex phenomena and those who, assuming that phenomena are more complicated than they seem (as many historians appear to), see it as their task to describe the idiosyncratic and unique features of phenomena and the ways in which their characteristics vary.

Becher discerned a 'shadowy spectrum' from disciplines which embody some notion of 'inherent order, neatness, and regularity' to those which rest on 'considerations of individual idiosyncrasy and collective variation, and acknowledge the intricacies of interpreting and encapsulating them'. Mathematics and physics tend to fall at the top of the spectrum, economics and chemistry in the middle range, and then biology and sociology before reaching the bottom with history and literary studies. He expresses little surprise with finding that 'the disciplines with highly-developed and coherent general theories ... are by and large those whose subject-matter is simple and orderly'.

Becher not only looked at the cultures of what are traditionally known as 'disciplines'. He also talked to people operating within interdisciplinary fields of inquiry like geography and within fields of inquiry focused on 'professional pursuits' like engineering, law and pharmacy (he didn't look at education but would place it in this category). He characterises the cultures of interdisciplinary fields rather differently from inquiry focused on professional/vocational pursuits. The former tend to reflect the cultures of their contributory disciplines, and they display both 'hard' (general theory/simple) and 'soft' (descriptive/ complex) elements. However, within the culture of the latter he argues 'it is not easy to identify any all-embracing theories ... what replaces them seems to be something as nebulous as Dewey's "problematic" ... or Schon's (1983) "problem frames"'.

It is interesting at this point to note that Wilson claims education is an interdisciplinary field of inquiry, which for Becher would mistakenly imply that its theoretical constructs are largely determined by its constitutive disciplines. His own analysis places educational inquiry as a professional/vocational field of study in which the theories employed are non-specialised everyday conceptions embedded in the relevant forms of practice. However, he also affirms that certain disciplines can make a contribution to refining and developing 'theories' of everyday experience:

> since education ... is a professionally-orientated field of enquiry, it cannot aspire to a set of hard general theories of its own, even to a choice of soft, all-embracing metaphysical perspectives [such as those employed by some schools

of sociology or literary criticism]. It may draw to a limited extent upon the theorising of the disciplines which contribute to it, but much of what passes as education theory is liable to comprise low-level generalisation. In the very nature of its underlying knowledge structure, the common forms which theory takes in this field might be expected to comprise 'models' which describe but do not predict, taxonomies which arrange the data into convenient categories without the scope for extrapolation, and nostrums or procedural propositions whose justification is pragmatically grounded in claims of their practical effectiveness. And on inspection, this would appear to be the case.

Becher argues that there is scope for the disciplines of education to make a contribution to the development of middle-range theories for educational inquiry, i.e. hypothesis inferred from experience rather than deduced from axioms. But disciplines which have some bearing on education will inevitably embody dominantly 'soft' rather than 'hard' cultures.

In general the implications Becher draws from his study of academic cultures for educational inquiry support the account of the relationship between educational theory, the disciplines, and professional knowledge which is implicit in the 'philosophy of wisdom' perspective on intellectual inquiry. If we bring this perspective to bear on Becher's analysis of academic cultures we can argue that disciplines at the 'hard' end of his spectrum tend to be those which are the most specialised and dissociated from the practical problems of everyday experience in the real world. And this perhaps explains the special vulnerability, which Becher remarks on, of the 'hard' disciplines to paradigm shifts.

Although he is able to organise his cultures along a spectrum, Becher notes that the tension between 'hard' and 'soft' cultures tends to be manifested in each discipline. Thus in physics there are those who abandon the high ground in favour of middle-range theories inferred from observational data, while in psychology there are those who have aspired to abandon low-level generalisations and even middle-range theories to develop general theories which provide comprehensive explanations for psychological phenomena.

It might be argued that paradigm shifts in the hard disciplines are activated by those who return to the 'soft' end of the continuum within the discipline to answer questions the general theories ignore. Perhaps a paradigm shift in a 'hard discipline' is a response of that discipline, however invisible, to problems of knowledge which emerge as people in everyday life encounter new sorts of practical problems in realising their values in action. In other words paradigm shifts, even within 'hard' disciplines, constitute attempts to overcome the dissociation of knowledge from life, and reflect renewed efforts to subordinate forms of knowledge production to the realisation of human values in social practices.

Within the 'soft' disciplines there are always people who as part of a quest for order and precision go in search of general theories. After all the academic status of disciplines and other fields of inquiry in universities appears to be organised in a hierarchy from 'hard' to 'soft'. Becher notes the tendency within the 'soft' disciplines for people to embrace rival paradigms of inquiry based on metaphors which are metaphysical in character. These metaphors provide a general orientation to inquiry – for example, 'behaviourism' and 'structuralism' in psychology, and 'functionalism' and 'symbolic interactionism' in sociology – but they cannot be directly connected with evidence. What they appear to do is to symbolically express and legitimate different methodological stances within a discipline on issues surrounding the nature of the subject-matter (simple or complex) and the kinds of theorising appropriate (high-level or low-level).

I would argue that such conflicting paradigms within a discipline at the 'soft' end of the spectrum also reflect a relation between theory and the world of everyday practical experience. In order to analyse the latter in depth it is necessary to generate more specialised branches of inquiry which focus on particular elements within that experience and thereby abstract them from their context. The question for any discipline is: 'how far can it take the process of abstraction and simplification in search of order and precision before it ceases to have any relevance to people's practical interests and concerns?'

Paradigm conflicts within the disciplines of education are essentially issues about the nature and form of the standards of reasoning which ought to prevail in them. I personally cannot see, as Wilson appears to, how such issues can be internally resolved without reference to the practical cultures which prevail in society. Peters (1974) once argued that he could not understand why American psychologists so enthusiastically embraced 'behaviourism' as a theoretical orientation to understanding persons. He then lived in America for a period and 'realised', he claimed, that 'behaviourism' constituted a basic assumption which underpinned people's interpersonal relations with each other. The whole point of his paper was that psychological theories are framed by assumptions embodied in particular practical cultures. This, for me, implies that the 'standards of reasoning' which prevail in a discipline necessarily reflect the cultures embedded in everyday social practices, even through their precise application in the context of a discipline can in turn modify the content of such cultures.

Altrichter and Posch, in a paper on 'grounded theorising' and 'action research', attempt to show how the processes of theory-generation within specialised disciplines might become more continuous with the reflective features of professional action, and therefore make their theoretical products more utilisable in elaborating practical problems and solutions. They argue that the theory-generating process itself is necessarily structured, not only by the researchers' prior theoretical endeavours within a discipline, but also by their everyday experience of living. Theory-generation, they claim, is founded upon 'a "theoretical nucleus" which will contribute to the more elaborate "theory" in some way or another'. If specialist researchers, they suggest, saw their own inquiries as reflexive practices, and made explicit the practical concerns which tacitly guide them, they would enable others to utilise the products of their inquiries in mutual practical discourse about problems of living.

Standards of reasoning in educational inquiry

There are good reasons from a 'philosophy of wisdom' perspective for locating teacher education within institutions of higher education. One of the unfortunate consequences of the dominance of the 'philosophy of knowledge' perspective in these institutions is that the generation of knowledge within the disciplines, and its transmission, has become detached from the problems and issues of everyday living. This is not only harmful for the disciplines, it also harms the growth of reflective practice in the wider society. The situation can only be rectified if academics place their commitment to their discipline or interdisciplinary field of inquiry in the broader context of a primary commitment to a form of inquiry which attempts to resolve the practical problems of everyday living. This implies a commitment to collaborative inquiry with practitioners operating in various institutional contexts and social enterprises. In this context it is the role of the academic not only to bring his or her discipline's standards of reasoning to bear in the analysis of practical problems and issues, but also those which are internal to the relevant social practice which in themselves are contestable because such standards derive from different practical traditions.

The academic in the field of education should be the guardian of standards of educational inquiry which are implicit in the practical traditions that inform educational practices, not just the guardian of the standards of reasoning employed in his/her specialism. This not only means representing those standards in collaborative forms of inquiry with educational practitioners and policy-makers, it also means helping educationalists to clarify these standards and the forms of practical reasoning they imply.

Since educational practices can be informed by a plurality of traditions the academic should not seek to avoid commitment to a particular outlook. His/her job is to help practitioners committed to a particular tradition to articulate, clarify and discuss the form of reasoning. But in doing so (s)he will welcome dialogue with the advocates of alternative educational outlooks and encourage the practitioners (s)he is working with to view such dialogue as a methodological necessity for deepening their understanding of educational practice. The academic in education should be making important contributions to mapping out the methodological principles which the process of practical educational inquiry entails. Efforts in this direction are illustrated by Altrichter and Posch, Sockett, House, Kroath, Whitehead and Mary Louise Holly.

Altrichter and Posch give us a timely warning of the dangers in borrowing strategies employed in some of the 'soft' disciplines as a methodological basis for action research. They focus on the currently fashionable 'grounded theory' approach of Glasser and Strauss. It is a superficially attractive one because of its apparent openness to the complexity of social action and building theory inductively from data. But Altrichter and Posch point out that its strategies, for deriving theory inductively from data, embody assumptions which can alienate teachers from the task of reflectively developing the practical theories or 'problem-frames' tacitly embedded in their practices.

First, they argue, it operates with a restricted notion of theory as a set of well-codified propositions which constitute the end products of inquiry. This tends to rule out giving the professional knowledge embodied in practitioners' practices (knowledge-in-action) the status of theory. Second, and related to this, the emphasis on entering the field of inquiry in an unprejudiced state of mind restricts the practitioner's capacity to utilise his or her biases (tacit professional knowledge) in articulating practical problems and devising solutions to them. Third, the approach in general conveys a rationalist view of the relationship between theory and practice which renders the latter a form of technical-rational action in which theory guides the selection of technical means for achieving pre-defined ends, but throws no light on the nature of the ends in themselves. This view implies a division of labour between the researcher as theory-generator and practitioner as theory-applier. Even when it is the practitioner doing the research (s)he operates in a dual role, with the practitioner role subordinated to the requirement to apply the theory developed in the researcher role when selecting technical means to pre-defined ends. 'Grounded theorising' becomes a method for getting practitioners to view their practices as technical-rational activities.

Altrichter and Posch claim that education is essentially a moral practice aimed at the realisation of values, not so much as an extrinsic outcome of an activity, but within the form of the activity itself. This view is very consistent with Stenhouse's 'process model' of curriculum development as an alternative to an 'objectives model'. The importation of a 'grounded theory' methodology developed by a certain school of sociologists, as a basis for educational action-research can only, according to Altrichter and Posch, serve to distort the nature of educational practice. Methodologists of teacher-based educational inquiry should, Altrichter and Posch argue, 'concentrate on further developing reflective features of professional action which in the context of practice itself are responsible for enhancing the quality of action'. In this respect they make reference to the contributions of Schon (1983) and Argyris *et al.* (1985) in identifying what these features are.

However, Sockett argues that any comprehensive account of educational inquiry must not simply attend to the reflective dimensions of this process, but also to the nature of the practice itself. Professional knowledge is knowledge of a particular practice. Sockett claims that what counts as knowledge will be governed by the professional standards implicit in an educational practice itself. He argues that 'it is *within* the profession of teaching that we locate the standards of research practice'. Sockett sees a special role for philosophers of education in helping to articulate what these standards are. There is a need, he argues, to develop an epistemology of educational practice as a context for developing a methodology of inquiry. The form of reasoning which governs such inquiry will fundamentally depend on how the standards implicit in an educational practice are viewed.

Sockett argues that if a practice like teaching is to count as an educational enterprise then its standards must refer to certain moral values. His paper is largely an initial attempt to map out some of those values; namely, those of *care*, *courage* and *truth*. His account is highly consistent with a 'philosophy of wisdom' perspective on the aims of practical inquiry, i.e. to realise values in social practices. But it illuminates the difference between a social practice and forms of technical-rational action.

On Sockett's account values are not only extrinsic outcomes of social practices. They are also qualities inherent in the practices themselves. What makes teaching an educational practice is not so much its instrumental effectiveness in producing extrinsically related learning outcomes, as the realisation of certain moral values.

Such values characterise a desirable relationship between teachers and learners, *within* the activity of teaching itself. Sockett believes that we are losing our vision of teaching as an educational practice framed by moral values, and instead interpreting it as a purely technical-rational activity governed by standards of instrumental reasoning. It is the task of an epistemology of educational practice to keep that vision alive as a context for developing a methodology of *educational* inquiry.

If the standards of practical educational inquiry are moral standards, then what form does theorising take in educational inquiry. This is a question which Whitehead addresses. He argues that any *educational theory* must provide an answer to the question: 'how can I improve my educational practice?' This question is only a particular form of the basic question of all practical inquiry; namely, 'how can I realise my values in practice?' Whitehead claims, rightly in my view, that the specific form of the question arises from a teacher's personal experience of his/her 'self' as 'a living contradiction', as a negation of the values by which (s)he would like to define him or her 'self' as an educator.

If educational values are qualities of the 'self' manifested in activities like teaching, as both Whitehead and Sockett claim, then in realising such values the teacher also realises him/herself. But this is not necessarily a reflexive process, in which a teacher's 'self' objectifies itself as a 'me' and thereby constitutes an object of inquiry for 'I'. The 'self' can be realised in action in the absence of reflexive consciousness. This only emerges for a teacher experiencing his/her practice as the negation of the educational values (s)he wants to realise within his/her teaching. This is what Whitehead means by the experience of the 'self' as a 'living contradiction'. He claims it is the necessary foundation for the fundamental question of educational inquiry and the starting point for all educational theorising. Such theorising is the reflexive or 'dialogical' (to use Whitehead's terminology) activity of the teacher who is consciously striving to realise him/herself as an educator in practice by overcoming the experience of negation. Educational theorising for Whitehead, is a form of reflexive inquiry aimed at realising the 'self-in-action'. This is why Whitehead argues that an educational theory is the basis of a teacher's claim to know his or her own professional development.

Whitehead concludes that an educational theory, as an answer to the fundamental reflexive (or dialogical) question, cannot be fully stated in the form of propositional logic, because it does not refer to things which are posited as existing independently of the theoriser. An educational theory can only be constructed in concrete forms of educational practice. Hence, Whitehead talks about a 'living educational theory' which is 'part of the living form of the practice itself'. (A point which echoes the Stenhousian idea of a curriculum as a practical embodiment of educational theory.) Such a theory-in-action, argues Whitehead, constitutes both a description and explanation of an educational practice. The form of the practice itself offers an holistic account of the practical wisdom that cannot be fully articulated in propositional terms, i.e. an account of the values which define education and at the same time explain how they are realised.

Whitehead's point that the reflective practices of teachers embody descriptions and explanations of how to realise educational values is highly consistent with Aristotle's account of moral inquiry in his *Ethics*. He argued that moral values cannot be understood by simply examining the meaning of the terms we use to express them in language. This is because moral values are fundamentally defined in and through the actions we undertake to realise them. The implication of this is that our social practices embody 'descriptions' of our values. And we only develop such 'descriptions' by reflecting upon our actions and ways of improving them.

Aristotle's account also illuminates the inseparability of ends and means in moral practices. Ends as values are realised *in* the courses of action we engage in as means. This is why such courses of action can offer not only descriptions of values, but also explanations of how they are realised.

Whitehead's account of educational theory explains Altrichter and Posch's claim that the inductive bias of 'grounded theory' methodologies is inconsistent with the idea of teaching as a moral practice. Since educational theory, according to Whitehead, cannot be formulated in the form of propositions it can only be communicated through 'records' of concrete events.

Whitehead's view of educational theory is rather different from the view that such theories cover all 'tacit knowledge', 'knowledge-in-action', 'problem-frames', etc. As answers to a reflexive or 'dialogical' question they are consciously developed. From this standpoint we might distinguish between tacitly acquired professional knowledge about how to realise educational values in activities like teaching, and the reflexively acquired professional knowledge which is developed through action-research in response to an experienced problem of realising the 'self', and the values which define it, in practice. The latter kind of professional knowledge necessarily constitutes a critique of tacitly acquired or held professional knowledge, and a development of it. This explains Whitehead's view that in giving others access to records of his or her reflective attempts to realise educational values a teacher invites them to examine the validity of a claim to know his or her own professional development. But Whitehead's view of educational theory leads him to point out that these records must not only provide evidence of the theory (concrete forms of action) but also of the process by which it was theorised (dialogic reflection with self and others).

Whitehead refers to the trouble he gets into when he attempts to transfer these methodological principles as a basis for teacher education in his own university. The fact that teacher education programmes still largely assess teachers' capacities to theorise about education in terms of their ability to formulate theory in prepositional form is a major indicator of the persistent power of the 'philosophy of knowledge' perspective in universities. If teacher educators are to realise their own educational values in their work with teachers within institutions of higher education they will, like Whitehead, have to undertake their own second order action research into ways of transforming the practical culture of academe.

Whitehead's account of the nature of educational theorising is supported by House *et al.*'s case study of the processes of reflection engaged in by a young university teacher of educational psychology as she attempts to improve her teaching. It is interesting that 'the record' of her actions and reflections is constructed by the teacher's peers (the authors) and not herself. I will return to the question of who constructs 'the record', and why it is necessary later. House *et al.* point out that although the university teacher is teaching formal psychological theories to student schoolteachers, she appears to make little use of such theories in learning to teach herself. Rather, she initially draws on her past experiences as a student and imagines what worked with her and what didn't. It is on the basis of such examples that she infers courses of action as 'hypotheses' about what could or could not work in her situation. But many of the cause–effect inferences she makes are not technical in their fundamental structure. As the authors demonstrate, her interests and concerns go well beyond technical considerations like getting the students to pass tests. She is concerned that they have opportunities to discover personal meaning and significance in the subject-matter, and experiments with a succession of strategies to this 'effect'. Following Sockett one might argue that what she was attempting to do was to realise the value of 'care for students as persons' in her teaching methods. Her inferences are therefore imagined solutions to the problem of realising her educational values in her teaching.

All this is highly consistent with Whitehead's account of educational theorising, and it is interesting that this young teacher, through such a process, comes out top in a rating of teaching quality in her faculty. However, House *et al.* illuminate the evidential basis of the teacher's reflection-on-action. It lies in her own personal and professional life history. The teacher does not imagine possible problem solutions simply on the basis of reflection-on-actions undertaken in the immediate past. The repertoire of cases within her stored experience, and which she draws on in reflection, extends far back in time. The fact that teacher education generally pays so little attention to helping student and in-service teachers to recover their 'life histories', particularly with respect to their experiences of schooling as pupils, is perhaps the highest indicator of its present incapacity to foster practical educational inquiry as the foundation of teachers' professional development.

House *et al.*'s case study of educational theorising is very consistent with those Schon used to illustrate the ways in which professionals draw on a stored repertoire of past experiences as the basis for their reflections *in* and *on* their actions. Like Schon's accounts, that of House *et al.* demonstrates that the form of practical theorising is primarily structured by stored practical examples of personal experience rather than stored sets of theoretical propositions. But House *et al's* case study also shows how formal theory can be incorporated into personal experience. The teacher's students were eventually able to utilise Kohlberg's theory of moral development (her subject-matter) by personally reconstructing its meaning as they reflected upon their actual responses in a simulated 'moral' situation. Their experience in this situation can subsequently be drawn on as they confront similar moral dilemmas in real life. But in doing so they will also draw on Kohlberg's moral theory since it has been incorporated into their personal understanding of the experience.

The repertoire of concrete and personal experiences which constitute an individual's professional knowledge is not necessarily uninfluenced by formal theories expressed in prepositional form; as indeed Whitehead acknowledges. Such experiences can incorporate them when they are mediated by reflexive practice.

There is a great deal of 'educational research' currently being undertaking within the 'psychology of education' into the nature of teachers' tacit practical theories, and within 'the sociology of education' into the professional cultures which shape them. The growth of such research within the disciplines of education reflects an increasing awareness of the role of tacit knowledge and the professional cultures/traditions it draws on in shaping and determining the practices of teachers. (In the second volume we shall have contributions from researchers working in these areas.) Such research cannot be dissociated from certain practical concerns abroad in society with how to improve teaching quality.

Kroath's paper, which draws on both German psychological research into teachers' practical theories and the action research perspective on them developed within the UK, reminds us that research into teachers' thinking can be utilised to terminate teachers' practical theories and cultures, in contrast to the aim of making them explicit in a form which enables teachers to improve them through their own reflective inquiry.

Kroath describes how research into 'subjective theories' by some German educational psychologists is being applied to in-service education programmes in the form of an 'exchange approach' to changing teachers' practices. The approach involves making 'deficient' elements in a teacher's subjective theory explicit and then getting him or her to replace it with a formal psychological theory as a basis for changing the practice. As Kroath points out, the assumption which underpins this approach is that the subjective theories of teachers are less valid than the psychological theories which replace them. The whole approach represents a renewed attempt to make a rationalist form of teacher education more effective by controlling not simply the acquisition of formal theory, but also the conditions under which formal theory is applied in practice.

If effective, the 'exchange approach' would not only change elements in teachers' practices, it would also change the way they viewed their practices more generally. The approach encourages teachers to see teaching as the technical-rational activity of applying instrumental rules derived from theory, rather than as the moral activity of realising values *in* the activity as a whole.

Kroath expresses considerable scepticism towards the 'exchange approach' as a theory of teacher change. This scepticism is based on two case studies he carried out to test the usefulness of alternative change theories. The other change theory he tested was that of educational action research. A teacher was asked to articulate a problem in her practice and then to reflect upon it in the light of questions posed by her peers.

The 'exchange theory' test involved asking the teacher to comment on a video-taped extract of his lesson, and then carrying out an in-depth interview to reconstruct and validate the elements in the tacit theory which underpinned the teacher's commentary. This reconstructed subjective theory then served as the basis for a discussion in which Kroath (a psychologist) challenged elements in the teacher's theory which appeared to be deficient in the light of psychological theory. Kroath reports that the experiment made no impact on the teacher's subjective theory: 'The teacher did not intend to change any aspect of his theory' although he found the exercise a 'stimulating experience'.

The 'action research' test involved a group of teachers in a problem identification process called 'analytic discourse'. The aim was to help teachers analyse their practical problems by looking at them from a variety of points of view, in response to questions from peers, and thereby develop new ways of articulating them. One teacher was extremely defensive in this process, but retired from the group to listen to a tape-transcript of her session at home. Detached from the situation, she gradually developed the confidence to face the questions of her peers in private. As she did so she experienced a profound change in her subjective theory of teaching. She realised that her 'jokes' in the classroom, which had created a problem of control, did not, as she believed, realise the value of making the subject more interesting. They were simply part of her attempt to please the children and win popularity with them. This insight evidently produced 'immediate changes in her teaching style and self-concept as a teacher'.

Kroath's account of how the action research approach changed a particular teacher's practice provides a concrete illustration again of Sockett's and Whitehead's point; that educational theory is a form of practitioner-based moral inquiry in which the practitioners attempt to discover the conditions under which they can realise their educational values, and therefore themselves, in action. The teacher in Kroath's second case study discovers why her jokes constitute an obstacle to, rather than a means of making her subject-matter interesting. But she would never have learned these things if she had not initially experienced herself as 'a living contradiction' in the classroom. The problem she brought to the group was defined by the values she wanted to realise in her classroom. She wanted to make her subject interesting to the children. She thought her jokes expressed this intention. The problem she experienced was that they distracted the children from the subject-matter. The teacher experienced herself as the source of these inconsistencies, which was why she became defensive under questioning from her peers. But it was the starting point for her theorising. She wanted to understand why her jokes did not convey the interest of her subject. And it is in this context that she makes a discovery about herself: her teaching was permeated by the desire to please. This insight changed her 'problem-frame' and enabled her to imagine new problem-solutions.

The methodological principle so graphically illustrated in Kroath's paper is that problems for practical educational inquiry are not simply problems about practitioners' theories-in-action but problems about the 'selves' they manifest in their practices. If teacher educators ignore this principle they are likely to fall into the danger of attempting to shape teachers' practices as a form of technical-rational action rather than moral endeavour.

Constructing 'mirrors' of the self-in-action: the role of teacher-educators

In facilitating practical educational inquiry or action research it is the task of teacher education to establish conditions which enable teachers to develop their *reflexive powers*, i.e. their capacities to monitor the self-in-action and to direct its future development in the professional context. Central in this task is the construction of records which 'mirror' the self-in-action and enable teachers to reflect about their educational values and the extent to which they are being realised. Such records are important vehicles by which teachers communicate their experience as a basis for dialogue with others.

Dialogue is an important context for developing, as well as validating, educational theory of the kind Whitehead describes. In dialogue teachers are able to utilise reflectively not only the repertoires of personal experience which originate in their own 'life histories', but also the experiences of each other.

This sharing of experience, in practical discourse about each other's problems and issues, enables teachers to incorporate significant cases within the professional experience of other practitioners into their own 'stock of professional knowledge'. In this way a common 'stock of professional knowledge' is constructed and continuously reconstructed as a basis for educational theorising. Practical discourse is therefore the process by which the generalisability of educational theories, encapsulated in cases of professional practice, are established and tested. In dialogue with others, teachers naturalistically generalise (see Stake, 1985) insights and wisdom embodied in case records and descriptions of other practitioners' experiences to their own.

It is this idea of educational inquiry as a form of practical discourse about particular problems and issues which has guided the development of case study approaches to the evaluation of educational programmes by such researchers as Stake (1976), MacDonald (1973) and Simons (1986). Within this approach cases of the programme-in-action are constructed in collaboration with participants, validated in dialogue with them, and then circulated more widely as a basis for discussion about the merits of the programme amongst the interested parties. Much case study evaluation and research in education can be seen as a broad educational strategy for promoting informed practical discourse amongst teachers and other educational practitioners, e.g. administrators and policy-makers.

There are no precise methodological rules for constructing records to enable educational practitioners to reflect on their practices in dialogue with others. Whether practitioners construct the records themselves with support from teacher educators, or construct them collaboratively with the latter, or whether the teacher educators construct the records but validate them with practitioners, will all depend on the context, e.g. how experienced and confident the practitioners are in reflecting on their practices, the boundaries of the cases to be constructed, the numbers of people involved, and institutional constraints on time etc. It is a matter for *second order* action research by the teacher educators involved, in the light of the values they want to realise as facilitators of *first-order* action research.

There is also little room for dogma about methods for constructing and handling records, e.g. about the relative emphasis to be placed on observational records, such as video and tape recordings, compared with written accounts and subjective records, such as self-commentaries and interview transcripts. There is no such thing as a single valid method, set of procedures, or battery of techniques for facilitating practical educational inquiry. This should be borne in mind when reading a growing number of handbooks and manuals on 'how to do action research'. They can be useful guides for teachers and teacher-educators, but when readers lack much understanding and appreciation of the methodological principles and standards which underpin action research they run into the danger of helping to technologise the thinking of both teachers and their educators. The purpose of applying techniques of data collection, recording, and analysis is to enable teachers to mirror and reflect upon the self-in-action and not to objectify the situation in a form which dissociates the self from its actions.

Methods, procedures, and techniques for constructing 'mirrors' which enable practitioners to reflect about their practices in public discourse with others can, in a certain context, have the unintended side effect of preventing people from developing their reflexive powers. This is a context in which practitioners have received no help to reflect in some private space about their practices. At best they conceal themselves from public and private scrutiny by producing sophisticated rationalisations for the practices 'on record'. At worst they experience, as illustrated in one of Kroath's case studies, so much anxiety that they erect strong self-defence mechanisms which may subsequently persist. In either case the capacity for a reflexive dialogue with 'self is diminished.

Mary Louise Holly's work on helping teachers to reflectively reconstruct their personal and professional experiences over time through writing, in diary or journal form, has been a welcome corrective to a tendency to emphasise the construction of public records. One could indeed argue that developing a capacity to reflect about one's practice in private is a necessary psychological condition, at least within our culture, for being able to participate reflectively in practical public discourse. It protects individuals, as Holly argues in 'Reflective writing and the spirit of inquiry', against the hierarchical power structures which constrain free and open discourse in public settings and thereby restricts the thinking of at least some participants. This is again neatly illustrated in one of Kroath's case studies. The teacher's capacity to self-reflect in the 'analytic discourse' process is inhibited by the presence of an authority figure. Holly suggests that private reflection may well be a necessary precondition for the development of a strong professional teacher culture, which is both built on reflective practice and able to resist the hierarchical imposition of ideological frameworks which are anti-educational.

She is not making out a case for private rather than public reflection or even for a sequence of reflection from 'private' to 'public'. Her views are perfectly compatible with the principle that a process of private reflection should operate concurrently and interactively with a process of public dialogue. But they do imply that the capacity for private self-reflection is ontologically prior to the capacity to self-reflect in public. This is consistent with Whitehead's view of educational theorising as being grounded in the emergence of a dialogical relation between 'I' and 'me'. It is necessary to establish the internal discourse as the context for discourse with others. Of course the public discourse can feedback into the private discourse, but the fundamental process is the latter. Again, this is illustrated by the teacher in Kroath's second case study, who found it necessary to retreat from public to private space in order to begin to reflect about her practice.

The same methods and techniques for constructing public records of practice can be employed for constructing private records. But the advantage of reflective writing techniques, as described by Holly, is that it is far easier for practitioners to carve out private spaces for reflective writing than for constructing records which require hardware like video and tape recorders.

It could well be the case that teacher educators have revealed very limited methodological understanding in foisting upon teachers forms of data collection and analysis which have been borrowed from 'research on education' within the behavioural science disciplines. Such techniques may well inhibit a fruitful inter-action between self-reflection in private and public spaces, because teachers will find it difficult to utilise them in reconstructing their experiences in private. They will then either 'fall away' at the hands of an over-demanding technology, or in trying to master it, come to see themselves as academic researchers. When they take the latter option they will tend to screen the 'self out of the construction of their practices by objectifying the data.

One advantage of Holly's approach, compared to other methods of recording is that it is more comprehensive in its scope. It doesn't simply reconstruct current experience but also past personal and professional experiences which can be linked to it. In this way teachers can recover and reconstruct their 'life histories' and thereby reflectively improve the repertoire of cases they utilise in analysing prob-lems and proposing solutions.

Holly's paper implies that since reflective writing appears to be the most access-ible and comprehensive method of privately 'mirroring' the self-in-action, there should be some continuity between this method and those employed for construct-ing public records. A teacher educator or researcher, for example, who constructs a record of a teacher's practices without allowing a self-account produced in private to become part of the record, thereby infringes important *criteria* of validity; namely, those of comprehensiveness and relevance. Underpinning such criteria is a *principle of continuity* between private and public self-reflection which rests on the ontological primacy of the reflexive self in educational inquiry.

In conclusion, the papers I have referred to, taken together, imply a coherent set of methodological criteria which specify the kind of inquiry process it is the responsibility of teacher educators and specialist researchers in education to foster as a context for their own activities. These may be summarised as follows:

1   Since educational inquiry originates in practitioners' experiences of the prac-tical problems they face in realising their educational values, it should not be confused with disciplines of knowledge which address specialised problems within the field of education.
2   Since educational inquiry is a self-reflective (reflexive) form of educational practice, which aims to improve practitioners' articulations of their practical problems and their ability to propose and test practical solutions, it should not be treated as a separate activity to the practice of education itself.
3   Since the standards of reasoning which govern educational inquiry are consti-tuted by the values which are internal to an educational practice, they should not be confused with the standards of reasoning which shape theorising within the specialised disciplines of knowledge.
4   Since the aim of educational inquiry is to develop the practical wisdom of practitioners its outcome should not be regarded as a form of propositional knowledge.
5   Since educational theories are structures of practical wisdom reflectively developed in forms of educational practice, they can only be holistically por-trayed in records of reflective practice.

6   Since educational inquiry is a process whereby practitioners articulate problems and propose solutions on the basis of inferences drawn from analogous cases, in their own and each other's past experience, then such inquiry must give practitioners' opportunities to reflectively reconstruct, in both private 'biographical' reflection and public discourse, their case repertoires.
7   Public records of reflective practice should incorporate records of private autobiographical reflection under conditions of access controlled by the individuals concerned.
8   Since in educational inquiry the acquisition of propositional knowledge is subordinate to the acquisition of practical wisdom, then such knowledge can only be utilised, and thereby practically validated, if the specialised problems it addresses are analogous to questions which emerge from practitioners' own analyses of their practices.

Notes

* John Elliott is Professor of Education, at the University of East Anglia.
† Originally published in: *Cambridge Journal of Education* 19: 1, 81–101.

References

Argyris, C., Putnam, R. and McLain Smith, D. (1985) *Action Science. Concepts, Methods and Skills for Research and Intervention* (San Francisco, Calif., Jossey-Bass).
Elliott, J. (1987) Educational theory, practical philosophy and action research, *British Journal of Educational Studies*, 35(2).
MacDonald, B. (1973) Briefing decision-makers, in: E.R. House (ed.) *School Evaluation: the politics and process*, pp. 174–187 (Berkeley, Calif., McCutcheon).
Maxwell, N. (1984) *From Knowledge to Wisdom: a revolution in the aims and methods of science* (Oxford, Basil Blackwell).
Oakeshott, M. (1962) Rational conduct, in: *Rationalism and Politics and other Essays* (London, Routledge & Kegan Paul).
Peters, R.S. (1974) Personal understanding and personal relationships, in: T. Mischel (ed.) *Understanding Other Persons* (Oxford, Basil Blackwell).
Schön, D. (1983) *The Reflective Practitioner: how professionals think in action* (London, Temple Smith).
Simons, H. (1986) *Getting to know Schools in a Democracy: the politics and process of evaluation* (Lewes, Falmer Press).
Stake, R.E. (1976) The countenance of educational evaluation, *Teachers' College Record*, 68, pp. 523–540.
Stake, R.E. (1985) An evolutionary view of program improvement, in: E.R. House (ed.) *New Directions for Educational Evaluation* (Lewes, Falmer Press).

29 Still no pedagogy?

Principle, pragmatism and compliance in primary education

Robin Alexander*†

Introduction

In 1981, Brian Simon published 'Why no pedagogy in England?' (Simon, 1981). On 20 May 2003 the UK government unveiled *Excellence and enjoyment: a strategy for primary schools* (DfES, 2003a).

'Why no pedagogy?' is an academic critique which commands attention by force of argument and evidence. *Excellence and enjoyment* relies on large print, homely language, images of smiling children, and populist appeals to teachers' common sense. Substantively, it seeks to secure professional goodwill, and possibly to disarm criticism, by relaxing the pressure of government prescription and targets. But beyond this surface appeal are important statements on learning, teaching, curriculum and assessment, which are arguably the core of that pedagogy whose absence Simon deplored. On these and other matters, *Excellence and enjoyment* designates itself not just a National Primary Strategy but also a 'blueprint for the future' (DfES, 2003a, para 8.14). It therefore provides an appropriate test of how far, a quarter of a century on, Simon's criticisms remain valid.

Simon believed that pedagogy – the act and discourse of teaching – was in England neither coherent nor systematic, and that English educators had developed nothing comparable to the continental European 'science of teaching'. Consequently, teachers here tended to conceptualise, plan and justify their teaching by combining pragmatism with ideology but not much else. This approach, he believed, was reinforced in their training, where trainees encountered an educational theory which they could not readily connect with what they saw and did in schools.

Simon traced this condition back, in part, to the Victorian public school view that education should be concerned with 'character' rather than the intellect, and partly to the heavily utilitarian mission of the elementary schools which existed at the opposite end of the Victorian educational spectrum – delivering the 3Rs, social conformity, and cheapness with or without efficiency – and from which today's primary schools directly descend. Though Simon readily acknowledged the growing influence of psychology on educational thinking during the later twentieth century, he did not concede, even when he re-visited his 'Why no pedagogy?' article in the 1990s, that it or its cognate disciplines yet offered anything approaching the coherent pedagogy which he could point to elsewhere in Europe (Simon, 1994).

Of course, all education is grounded in social and indeed political values of some kind, and necessarily so; and Simon himself was nothing if not ideological in his sustained pursuit of causes such as non-selective secondary education. So his critique is less a rejection of ideology as such than a complaint that the enacting of social and political values through the specific and complex activity we call teaching cannot be undertaken on the basis of ideology alone, or even ideology leavened with pragmatism. Ideology may define the ends in teaching and hint at aspects of its conduct, but it cannot specify the precise means. Professional knowledge grounded in different kinds of evidence, together with principles which have been distilled from collective understanding and experience, are also called for, in order that – as Paul Hirst put it some years ago – teachers are able to make 'rationally defensible professional judgements' both while they teach and in their planning and evaluation (Hirst, 1979, p. 16).

But Simon's was nevertheless an uncompromising assessment, and it was open to challenge even in 1981. Research on professional thinking published at about the same time as 'Why no pedagogy?' showed how the decision-making of individual teachers, especially those who had advanced beyond mere 'coping' into the reflective judgement of mature expertise, was much more principled, informed and subtle than the Simon characterisation seemed to allow (Berlak and Berlak, 1981; Schön, 1982; Elbaz, 1983; Calderhead, 1984; Clark and Peterson, 1986). But Simon was concerned less with the many private theories of teaching and learning than with the theory and discourse which were collective, generalisable and open to public scrutiny.

Simon's claim provoked interest in all sorts of places and 'Why no pedagogy?' has become one of the more frequently cited academic titles of recent years. Interestingly it has gained this distinction mainly since government and its agencies started issuing pedagogical pronouncements at a level of prescriptive detail which was unthinkable when the first and even the second of Simon's two articles on this theme appeared. For the second 'Why no pedagogy?' article was published in 1993, just a year after an initiative in which I myself was involved, the so-called 'three wise men' enquiry on behalf of the UK government into the evidential basis of primary education at Key Stage 2. The document which came out of that initiative began by quoting the then Secretary of State, also named Clarke, who roundly insisted that 'questions about how to teach are not for Government to determine' (Alexander et al., 1992, para 1).

In the 2003 Primary Strategy, Secretary of State Charles Clarke echoes Kenneth Clarke's assurance: 'A central message of this document is that teachers have the power to decide how they teach, and ... the Government supports that' (DfES, 2003a, para 2.7). If some people were cynical about the intentions of Clarke, K. in 1991 – given that he launched the so-called 'three wise men' enquiry with a pre-emptive strike in the form of a letter to every primary school in England, telling their heads exactly what he expected the enquiry to conclude before a word of its report had been written – then the contrary evidence about the present government's approach to pedagogy should make them even more wary about the protestations of Clarke, C. in 2003; decisively so since the introduction of the National Literacy and Numeracy Strategies in 1998 and 1999, which are nothing if not pedagogical prescriptions, but also in view of other evidence which this paper considers.

I have explained the title 'Still no pedagogy?' and trust that the significance of the subtitle's themes of *principle, pragmatism* and *compliance* is also apparent. Since the launch of New Labour's *Education, Education, Education* project in 1997, ministers and DfES have elevated the quintessentially pragmatic mantra 'what works' to the status of ultimate criterion for judging whether a practice is educationally sound; and the word 'compliance' – not to mention sanctions such as 'special measures' or withdrawal of that accreditation by which compliance is enforced – feature prominently in the procedural vocabulary of DfES, Ofsted and the Teacher Training Agency (TTA). We shall need to establish whether the Primary Strategy's new criteria for defining pedagogical quality still stop there or whether educational principle is now discernible.

Conceptualising pedagogy

Part of the 'Why no pedagogy?' problem is the word 'pedagogy' itself. It is used more frequently than in 1981, but still does not enjoy widespread currency in England. The spectrum of available definitions ranges from the societally broad to the procedurally narrow. Basil Bernstein (1990) saw pedagogy as a 'cultural relay' and located it within his grand theory of social structure and reproduction. However, in England pedagogy is commonly used in a more restricted sense, to equate with the practice of teaching. Symptomatic of this narrower definition is the complaint by Anthea Millett, the previous head of TTA: 'I am always struck by how difficult teachers find it to talk about *teaching*. … They prefer to talk about *learning*. By contrast, they can talk with great clarity about … curriculum, assessment … [and] classroom organisation … almost anything except teaching itself', an agenda which she said should cover 'competence, excellence and failure in teaching methods' (Millett, 1999).

To be fair, I think many of us who have been in this business for a while recognise the condition to which Anthea Millett was referring. There certainly was a time when it was common to hear people in primary education say things like 'let's talk about learning, not teaching' or 'child, not curriculum', or 'learner-centred not teacher-centred', and this kind of oppositional pedagogical discourse has been tracked on both sides of the Atlantic (Entwistle, 1970; Alexander, 1984, 2000, 2002). It illustrates Simon's concern about the dominance of ideology over principle, and of course sets up dichotomies which are unnecessary and unhelpful, not just when they become part of that 'discourse of derision' which passes for educational debate in some newspapers and among some politicians (Wallace, 1993, p. 324), but also within the teaching profession itself. However, Millett's definition compounds rather than resolves the problem, for it simply weights the dichotomy at the other end and excludes matters such as learning, curriculum, assessment and classroom organisation, which are arguably essential not just to a comprehensible pedagogy but also, as it happens, to a meaningful discussion of Millett's own preferred pedagogical agenda of 'competence, excellence and failure in teaching methods' (Millett, 1999). Tellingly in this era of centralisation and tight political control, her definition also excludes any sense of how pedagogy connects with culture, social structure and human agency, and thus acquires educational *meaning*. Such matters, the definition dangerously implies, are either unimportant or not for teachers to worry about.

In contrast to all this, the continental view of pedagogy, especially in northern, central and eastern Europe, brings together within the one concept the act of teaching and the body of knowledge, argument and evidence in which it is embedded and by which particular classroom practices are justified. Thus, at a typical Russian pedagogical university, pedagogy encompasses: 'general culture' comprising philosophy, ethics, history, economics, literature, art and politics; together with elements relating to children and their learning – psychology, physiology, child development, child law; and as a third group, aspects relating to the subjects to be taught, or *didaktika* and – linking all the elements – *metodika*, or ways of teaching them. The subject element, *didaktika* in Russia, *la didactique* in France, *die Didaktik* in Germany, subdivides variously into, for example, *allgemeine Didaktik* and *Fachdidaktik* (general and specialist or subject didactics) in Germany, *didactiques des disciplines* and *transpositions didactiques*, or *savoir savant* and *savoir enseigné* (scholarly and taught knowledge) in France (Moon, 1998; Alexander, 2000, pp. 540–563). These are equivalent to what Lee Shulman (1987) calls 'content' and 'pedagogical content' and TTA's precursor body, CATE, called 'subject' and 'subject applications' (DES, 1989).

Of course, English etymology doesn't help us here. Respectable though on the continent both 'pedagogy' and 'didactics' may be, here we can never completely escape the way 'pedagogy' suggests the pedantry of the pedagogue (and indeed through their shared Greek root the words are related) and 'didactics' elides with the chalk-and-talk intimations of 'didactic'. Thus pedagogy and didactics, to many, suggest just one kind of teaching, traditional direct instruction.

The problem of terminology and discourse is not completely one-sided. What is frequently missing in continental debate about education is the rich discourse surrounding the idea of *curriculum*, which in Britain and the United States is more fully developed. That, I submit, is partly because both of those countries inherited traditions of curriculum decentralisation which meant that curriculum matters were always bound to be contested, even more so when their governments sought to curtail that autonomy by introducing a national curriculum in England from 1988 and state curriculum standards in the USA from about the same time. In contrast, in many continental countries the scope and balance of the school curriculum had long been centrally determined and the remaining questions concerned the character of the subjects of which it was constituted and how they should be taught. There are of course oppositional curriculum discourses there too: that of Pierre Bourdieu in France is a prime example (Bourdieu and Passeron, 1970).

The prominence of curriculum in English educational discourse has meant that we have tended to make pedagogy subsidiary to curriculum. My own preferred definition has it the other way round. Pedagogy is the act of teaching together with its attendant discourse. It is what one needs to know, and the skills one needs to command, in order to make and justify the many different kinds of decisions of which teaching is constituted. Curriculum is just one of its domains, albeit a central one.

With this ground-clearing in mind, let us return briefly to Millett's belief that pedagogy should concern itself with competence, excellence and failure in teaching methods rather than learning, curriculum and assessment. The demarcation is precise and absolutist. It is replicated by DfES and its agencies. In tenor and purpose this preferred pedagogy deals with judgement rather than substance and justification; and with teaching rather than the wider sphere of morally purposeful activity, of which teaching is a part, which we call education. Teachers, in this characterisation, are technicians who implement the educational ideas and procedures of others, rather than professionals who think about these matters for themselves.

That is one kind of definition. Here is an alternative: if pedagogy is the discourse which informs and justifies the act of teaching and the learning to which that teaching is directed, then substance must *precede* judgement, or at the very least the two should go hand in hand. Otherwise it is hard to know by what criteria judgements of competence, success and failure in teaching can be devised and defended.

In the alternative pedagogy, the teacher engages, as a matter of necessity, with a number of distinct but related domains of ideas and values. First, and most immediately, these are concerned with:

- *children*: their characteristics, development and upbringing;
- *learning*: how it can best be motivated, achieved, identified, assessed and built upon;
- *teaching*: its planning, execution and evaluation; and
- *curriculum*: the various ways of knowing, understanding, doing, creating, investigating and making sense which it is desirable for children to encounter, and how these are most appropriately translated and structured for teaching.

With, that is to say, what is to be taught, to whom, and how. But teaching takes place in a context and responds to requirements and expectations. At its most immediate this context, and its requirements and expectations, comprise:

- *school*, as a formal institution, a microculture and a conveyor of pedagogical messages over and above those of the classroom;
- *policy*, national and local, which prescribes or proscribes, enables or inhibits what is taught and how.

There's a third group, for schools and policies in turn have their larger contexts, and both they and teaching are informed by purposes and values. It may be argued – it is certainly assumed – that in a centralised system of public schooling government policy is purpose enough. But even the pedagogy of compliance is not immune from:

- *culture*: the web of values, ideas, institutions and processes which inform, shape and explain a society's views of education, teaching and learning, and which throw up a complex burden of choices and dilemmas for those whose job it is to translate these into a practical pedagogy;

- *self*: what it is to be a person, an individual relating to others and to the wider society, and how through education and other early experiences selfhood is acquired;
- *history*: the indispensable tool for making sense of both education's present state and its future possibilities and potential.

Where the first four domains *enable* teaching and the next two *formalise* and *legitimate* it, the last three *locate* it – and children themselves – in time, place and the social world, and anchor it firmly to the questions of human identity and social purpose without which teaching makes little sense. They mark the transition from teaching to education.

Such a list is a start, but obviously not the whole story. So, for example, if we take the domain *teaching* from the first group, it can be conceptually elaborated in several different ways. In my own comparative analysis of international classroom data, for which I needed a framework which was comprehensive yet culturally-neutral, I started with the irreducible proposition that 'teaching, in any setting, is the act of using method x to enable pupils to learn y'. From this I constructed a generic model comprising the immediate context or *frame* within which the act of teaching is set, the *act* itself, and its *form*, and then a set of elements within each such category. The core acts of teaching (*task, activity, interaction* and *assessment*) are framed by *space, pupil organisation, time* and *curriculum*, and by *routines, rules* and *rituals*. They are given form, and are bounded temporally and conceptually, by the *lesson* or teaching session (Alexander, 2000, pp. 323–325).

A framework of this kind can serve both descriptive and prescriptive purposes, and its elements can in turn be elaborated further, as was necessary both within the comparative project in question (Alexander, 2000, pp. 297–528) and in a linked series of applied projects on classroom talk which the comparative research has prompted since then, with the Qualifications and Curriculum Authority, the National Numeracy and Literacy Strategies, and the local authorities of North Yorkshire and Barking and Dagenham. In the latter, the action nexus of *task, activity, assessment* and (especially) *interaction* are transformed into a set of principles and indicators of 'dialogic teaching' by way of research on the relationship between spoken language, cognition and learning, and with reference to explicit social values about the kinds of interactive relationship which are implied by the concept of citizenship. This transformation in turn affects the five framing elements and the overall form of lessons. (Alexander, 2003a, 2003b, 2004).

This example underscores a second imperative. It is not enough to delineate the themes of pedagogical discourse: we must also recognise how they inform each other. In the example here, the particular approach signalled by the term 'dialogic teaching' seeks simultaneously to attend to a viable concept of teaching, to evidence about the nature and advancement of human learning, and to the conditions for education in a democracy, in which the values of individualism, community and collectivism stand in a complex and sometimes tense contrapuntal relationship (Alexander, 2001).

No less important, if an intelligent pedagogy dictates attention to domains of ideas and values such as these, and to ways of organising and relating them, it also

requires that we are aware that such ideas can be, and are, engaged w'
ent ways. Simon, as we have seen, commends the continental view of
teaching grounded in explicit principles relating to what children iₙ
common. Eisner prefers the idea of teaching as an *art* in the sense that it is parti,
improvisatory, is 'influenced by qualities and contingencies that are unpredicted ...
[and] the ends it achieves are often created in process' (Eisner, 1979, p. 153).
Argyris and Schön (1974, pp. 3–12) show how in understanding professional practice it is essential to distinguish the 'espoused theory ... to which one gives allegiance' (as in the science of teaching) from the 'theory-in-use' which actually,
regardless of what one claims to others, informs one's practice. Taking this further,
Sally Brown and Donald McIntyre reveal how the work of experienced teachers is,
as a matter of day-to-day reality, grounded to a considerable extent in a *craft* knowledge of ideas, routines and conditions, which they map empirically in respect of
pupils, time, content, the material environment and teachers themselves (Brown
and McIntyre, 1993). Combining paradigms, Nate Gage (1978) and Maurice
Galton commend the *science of the art* of teaching in which scientific pedagogic
principles are applied 'in a flexible manner, according to the characteristics of a
particular group of pupils, taking into account the context in which they are
working' (Galton *et al.*, 1999, p. 184).

Clearly, pedagogy is a somewhat more complex enterprise than may be recognised by those who reduce effective teaching to 'what works', or 'best practice'
lessons downloaded from government websites.

The 2003 Primary Strategy

In the light of all this, what can we say about the pedagogy of the Government's
2003 Primary Strategy? Time or space do not allow me to comment comprehen-
sively, so I'd like to pick out three aspects – learning, teaching and curriculum –
which relate especially to what I have identified as the necessary core of pedagogical
discourse, and in as far as it expatiates on these themes the Primary Strategy qualifies
as a pedagogical statement. Before that, however, we need to consider, in light of the
paragraphs above, the tone, character and purposes of the document as a whole.

Tone and intention

First there's the soft sell of that title: *Excellence and enjoyment*. The default vocabulary for education policy since 1997 highlights 'standards', 'driving up standards'
'underperforming', 'failing', 'intervention', 'hard-hitting', 'the challenge ahead',
'step change', 'tough', 'new', 'tough new', 'world class', 'best practice', 'delivery' and
so on (DfEE, 2001). 'Enjoyment' sits unconvincingly with the more familiar ministerial machismo, and in the wake of the unrelenting tide of initiatives, targets and
public criticism of schools' performance since 1997, a certain amount of professional scepticism towards the geniality or even hedonism of 'enjoyment' might be
understandable.

On the question of the character of the new discourse, apart from the fact that
it is frequently ungrammatical and offers bizarre constructions like 'Every LEA will

have a Primary Strategy Manager to provide a one-stop shop support service for primary schools' (DfES, 2003a, p. 6) and 'One common complaint about … extra funding was that a lot of it came in ring-fenced pots' (DfES, 2003a, para 8.8), the more serious point is that it privileges some kinds of discourse – specifically the pragmatic and political – at the expense of others. Value-positions are pervasive throughout, but few are argued or justified. The report is positively messianic in its confident prefacing of problematic assertions by 'we believe', 'we want', 'we need', and 'we will'. 'What works' and 'best practice' are, by the same token, presented as givens. And though the report defines an 'excellent primary school leader' as someone who is 'systematic and rigorous in using evidence to inform the development of teaching' (DfES, 2003a, para 6.2), very little evidence is actually cited in the report itself. Instead, the reiterated appeal to experience and common-sense – 'Every teacher knows' (for example, DfES, 2003a, para 4.1) – and the wilful amnesia in respect of the accumulated findings of published research on learning and teaching, not to mention the ignoring of findings from the government's own inspections, make it clear that the Strategy is about something other than argument and justification.

So what *is* it about? The Strategy's intentions are more opaque and contradictory than at first sight they seem, especially when the document is set alongside other statements of current education policy. Central to the Strategy's message is the avowed commitment to increasing the autonomy of schools and teachers:

> Teachers have the freedom to decide how to teach – the programmes of study state *what* is to be taught but not *how* it is to be taught … the National Literacy and Numeracy Strategies, though they are supported strongly, are not statutory … Ofsted will recognise and welcome good practice … teachers and schools can decide which aspects of a subject pupils will study in depth … how long to spend on each subject … QCA guidance suggesting how much time should be allocated to each subject is not statutory…. Our aim is to encourage all schools to … take control of their curriculum, and to be innovative.
>
> (DfES, 2003a, paras 2.4 and 2.8)

And so on. Legally, the claims about what is and is not statutory are correct, but how many teachers will take this as an invitation to reduce the time spent on literacy and numeracy in order to free time for the rest of the curriculum, knowing as they do how much hangs on the next round of literacy and numeracy targets?

In any event, the messages on this matter are decidedly mixed. The Strategy's DfES press release emphasises that 'testing, targets and performance tables are here to stay' (Downing Street, 2003). The 'key aim' agreed by the Ministerial Primary Education Programme Board which oversaw the development of the Strategy was 'to produce a common approach to teaching and learning across the curriculum … identifying the key teaching and learning approaches that the [Literacy and Numeracy] strategies have promoted and provide materials and training to help teachers transfer them more widely' (DfES, 2002a, p. 1). Against the ostensible offer of autonomy, we have the continuing pressure of testing, targets and performance tables and the creeping hegemonisation of the curriculum by the Literacy and

Numeracy Strategies, with three-part lessons, interactive whole class teaching and plenaries soon to become a template for the teaching of everything.

The summation of the Strategy's doublespeak on professional autonomy comes in Chapter 8, 'Realising the vision'. Here, quite apart from the hubris of that word 'vision', there is the problem of its juxtaposition with words redolent of a rather different purpose (my italics below):

> We have set out our *vision*, but we want it to be a shared *vision*.... We intend to spread the *dialogue* more widely.... This document is just the starting point for that vital *dialogue* which will shape the future of primary education.... This document begins to offer a *blueprint* for the future...
>
> (DfES, 2003a, paras 8.14–8.17)

Vision? Dialogue? Blueprint? Elsewhere in the report there is less ambiguous talk of 'the project' (DfES, 2003a, para 8.17). How can it be all of these?

Political culture and the rewriting of educational history

Behind this ambiguity of intent – a desire to be seen to be offering freedom while in reality maintaining control – lies a by no means ambiguous view of recent education history and the condition of the teaching profession. Its exponents and guardians are not so much the Primary Education Programme Board which oversaw the writing of the Primary Strategy, or even the Secretary of State, but the Downing Street Policy Unit.

Some months ago I found myself sharing a platform with Michael Barber, formerly director of the DfES Standards and Effectiveness Unit and now head of the Prime Minister's Delivery Unit. The occasion was a conference in Moscow attended by Russian Ministry of Education officials and academics at which I spoke about my international comparative research on pedagogy and primary education, in which Russia features prominently, and Michael Barber gave a glowing account of New Labour's education project/vision/blueprint. He added:

> Until the mid-1980s what happened in schools and classrooms was left almost entirely to teachers to decide.... Almost all teachers had goodwill and many sought to develop themselves professionally, but, through no fault of their own, the profession itself was uninformed.... Under Thatcher, the system moved from *uninformed professional judgement* to *uninformed prescription*.
>
> (Barber, 2001, pp. 13–14, his italics)

Note how heavily professional ignorance features in this historical pathology, and how it is presented as an inevitable concomitant of professional autonomy. To be free to decide how to teach is to be uninformed. If you were teaching before 1988, you might care to ponder what those sweeping phrases 'the profession itself was uninformed ... uninformed professional judgement' say about your competence. Members of the Thatcher/Major governments of 1988–1997 might even wish to contest the charge of 'uninformed prescription'; certainly their advisers on QCA's precursor bodies (NCC, SEAC and SCAA) and Ofsted's HMI predecessors could do so. It sets things up nicely, of course, for the transformation achieved by New Labour and the Utopia which is now in sight:

> The 1997–2001 Blair government inherited a system of *uninformed prescription* and replaced it with one of *informed prescription*.... The White Paper signals the next shift: from *informed prescription* to *informed professional judgement*.... The era of informed professional judgement is only just beginning.... The era of informed professional judgement could be the most successful so far in our educational history.... It could be the era in which our education system becomes not just good but great.
>
> (Barber, 2001, pp. 13–14. The final sentence was added to the 2002/2003 versions of Barber's paper)

Note the abrupt tonal gear-change, half way through this extract, from narrative to incipient political rant. In similar vein, Barber's Downing Street colleague Andrew Adonis, the Prime Minister's principal Education Adviser, in a paper to the international Policy Network (studying government material prepared for international rather than home consumption can be very illuminating) writes of 'the dire situation in England' as New Labour found it in 1997, and with particular reference to places like Cambridge's Faculty of Education: 'For most teachers, professional development has traditionally been haphazard, off-site, barely relevant, poorly provided, and a chore at best' (Adonis, 2001, p. 14). I don't need to labour the point: the Barber–Adonis line is as distorted and partisan an account of recent educational history as one is likely to find, yet *realpolitik* dictates that it's the one that counts. Quite apart from its disparaging view of the competence of teachers and the quality of teacher training before 1997, its sweeping dismissal of that period as one of 'uninformed professional judgement' or at best 'uninformed prescription' simply ignores the vast body of information of which many in the education world were acutely aware: HMI reports on individual schools; HMI national surveys on primary and secondary education; Central Advisory Council and other major independent reports on primary, secondary, further, higher and teacher education, and on English, mathematics, the arts and special needs (Plowden, Newsom, Crowther, Robbins, James, CNAA, UCET, Bullock, Cockcroft, Gulbenkian, Warnock); HMI and DfES/DfE/DfEE documents on the curriculum; local evidence on standards of attainment from LEA annual tests administered in all primary schools; the results of public examinations in secondary schools; further national evidence on pupil attainment in English, maths and science at the ages of 7, 11 and 15 from the sampled assessment programmes of the Assessment and Performance Unit begun in 1975; reports from Commons Select Committees, the accumulated body of curriculum guidance and materials from the Schools Council and its successors the SCDC, NCC, SEAC and SCAA; generous in-service provision in LEAs, colleges and universities; and of course research.

Even on the more limited matter of information about *standards* in primary education with which Barber and Adonis are particularly concerned, the 1991–1992 so-called 'three wise men' enquiry on primary education was able to interrogate six major domains of published data dealing with standards, most of them annual and cumulative: APU tests, LEA tests, NFER tests and surveys, HMI inspections, National Curriculum assessment, and the programme of IEA international achievement studies of which the PIRLS report on reading literacy marks just the latest example (Alexander *et al.*, 1992, paras 24–50; IEA/ISC, 2003). The 'three wise men' report as a whole cited nearly 100 separate sources of published evidence as well as the extensive pre-Ofsted HMI database and research material in the pipeline (Alexander *et al.*, paras 55–62). Uninformed professional judgement? There was, then as now, a positive glut of information.

This being so, it is clear that in the post-2001 era of 'informed professional judgement' to be 'informed' is to know and acquiesce in what is provided, expected and/or required by government and its agencies – DfES, NLNS, Ofsted, QCA, TTA – no less and, especially, no more. You may be steeped in educational research and/or the accumulated wisdom of 40 years in the classroom, but unless you defer to all this official material your professional judgements will be 'uninformed'. As Adonis says in his Policy Network paper, writing of university faculties and departments of education: 'We have *imposed* a new national curriculum for initial teacher training, setting out the standards and content of training courses, which all providers *must* follow' (Adonis, 2001, p. 14, my italics, his verbs). Not much room for alternative professional judgement there; and little evidence of government relaxing the iron grip of educational centralisation. If you teach, or train teachers, on the basis of other kinds of knowledge you are uninformed. For 'informed professional judgement', then, read 'political compliance'.

The Primary Strategy holds to this view. It shows little awareness of evidence from outside the charmed circle of government and its agencies; and no awareness of what even previous governments and government agencies did before 1997, the year in which, apparently, history and real education began. Political analysts might suggest that rewriting history has become a habitual device of government, especially within highly adversarial systems such as ours, and we should therefore not be surprised at its use in a high-stakes policy field like education (Alexander, 1998a). New Labour can also claim, rightly, that their Conservative predecessors were no slouches when it came to mythologising the past, scapegoating professionals and demonising doubters (Alexander, 1997a, pp. 183–287; Galton *et al.*, 1999, pp. 10–38); and Berliner and Biddle (1995) have documented, tellingly and in detail, the same process at work in the United States from the Reagan era onward. Interestingly, the terms commentators use to connote this process – 'myth', 'mythologise', and now 'spin' – somehow manage to render it benign and even acceptable. Few are prepared to call claims like those cited above what they really are: lies.

The failure of *Excellence in schools* in this regard is one of omission. It does not so much rewrite history as ignore it. But in so doing, it tacitly performs its own act of compliance to the Downing Street line: the same line, in fact, that produced the prime ministerial assault on comprehensive education in September 2000 whose mendacity was so scathingly exposed in one of Simon's last articles (Simon, 2000).

Learning

The striking feature of the Strategy's account of learning is its insistence on *individualisation*:

> Learning must be focused on individual pupils' needs and abilities.... Every teacher knows that truly effective learning focuses on individual children.... The new Primary Strategy will actively support more tailoring of teaching to individuals....Workforce reform will ... be critical to helping teachers focus on individual children's needs.... Increasing the focus on individual children will serve every child.
>
> (DfES, 2003a, p. 39 and paras 4.1–4.5)

In fact, the chapter is not about learning at all, but *social inclusion*, which in itself is a proper and urgent concern, and having trumpeted the importance of individualisation the report then goes on to talk about the needs of specific *groups*: children with special needs; children from minority ethnic backgrounds; the gifted and talented – for which, apparently, in that inimitable Ofsted prose, provision is 'now good or better in almost half of primary schools and satisfactory or better in some 90 per cent of primary schools' (DfES, 2003a, para 4.8).

Interestingly, though, gender is not included in this list, even though David Hopkins, DfES Standards Director, blamed boys for the nation's failure to meet the 80 per cent literacy target in the 2002 KS2 tests, and Schools Minister David Miliband said that schools and society should tackle the 'laddish culture' in order to motivate boys to do well in school (DfES, 2002b).

Yet that heavy emphasis on individualisation, and the promise of support for individualised teaching, throws up problematic messages. That children are individuals is self-evident, but how far can this truism be applied in the context of other than one-to-one and small group teaching? The Strategy's authors chose to ignore the classroom research of the 1980s, including major projects from Leicester, London, Exeter and Leeds universities, which showed the limits to fully individualised teaching in classes of 20, 25 and 30 or more children (Galton and Simon, 1980; Bennett *et al.*, 1984; Mortimore *et al.*, 1988; Alexander, 1997a). They ignored the subsequent international research, including that reviewed for Ofsted by Reynolds and Farrell (1996), which drew attention to the way teaching in many continental and Asian countries respects individuality yet structures learning tasks on the basis of what children have in common and tries as far as possible to bring all the children in a class along together, thus reducing the wide range of attainment and the long attainment 'tail' which has for long been such a prominent feature of English primary classrooms. Most surprisingly, they ignored one of the central contentions of the government's own flagship Literacy and Numeracy Strategies, that treating learning as a *collective* process, notably through interactive whole class teaching, actually benefits individuals.

More fundamentally, the Strategy's account of learning – such as it is, for the document specifies *conditions* for learning but not its character or process – bypasses the shift in learning theory from what Bruner (1996) calls an 'intrapsychic' view which conceives of the child as a 'lone scientist' to a psycho-cultural account which emphasises the necessarily social and interactive character of early learning, and argues the case for intersubjectivity as essential to cultural socialisation. And, hardly surprisingly, there's no mention either of the implications for school learning of recent advances in neuroscience. Had any of this been within the strategists' consciousness they would not have confined their consideration of the importance of talk in learning to one brief and passing mention of National Curriculum English Attainment Target 1, speaking and listening (DfES, 2003a, p. 28).

The section of the report which purportedly deals with learning is also notable for the way it removes any remaining ambiguities about whether the Strategy offers freedom or constraint: 'Learning *must* be focused on individual pupils' needs and abilities.' (DfES, 2003a, p. 39). Further:

> We have developed a model of intervention for children experiencing difficulties in literacy or mathematics, based on three waves:
>
> Wave One: the effective inclusion of all pupils in a high quality, daily literacy hour and mathematics lesson (Quality First Teaching). Wave Two: small group, low-cost intervention – for example, booster classes, springboard programmes, or other programmes linked to the National Strategies. Wave Three: specific targeted intervention for pupils identified as requiring special educational needs support.
>
> (DfES, 2003a, para 4.6)

So prescription it is then, after all: obligatory individualisation, a 'three wave' model of intervention, and – though they are supposed to be non-statutory – the National Literacy Hour and Numeracy Lesson for every child in the land. Almost submerged in the mire of contradiction and confusion here, or overwhelmed by the tsunami, is one of the biggest contradictions of all: if the 'model of intervention' is for just one group of children – those experiencing learning difficulties – why is it imposed upon all the others?

Insidiously, the report seeks to legitimate or disguise its impoverished reasoning on learning by peppering this section with populist phrases like 'Every teacher knows that truly effective learning and teaching focuses [*sic*] on individual children' and 'Most schools already use assessment for learning.' (DfES, 2003a, paras 4.1, 4.2). Do they really? Not according to the Kings' assessment for learning research (Black and Wiliam, 1998).

Teaching

Though the Primary Strategy's view of learning unnervingly contradicts the Literacy and Numeracy Strategies while yet endorsing them, in the chapter on *teaching* the two Strategies are more securely in the saddle:

> The Literacy and Numeracy Strategies have, according to all those who have evaluated them, been strikingly successful at improving the quality of teaching

and raising standards in primary schools. But we need to embed the lessons of the Literacy and Numeracy Strategies more deeply.... In the best schools, teachers are using their understanding of the principles behind the literacy and numeracy strategies.... We want a new approach that will help more schools and teachers to ... apply the principles of good learning and teaching across the whole curriculum.

(DfES, 2003a, paras 3.2–3.5)

So at last we come to some *principles*. But would Simon be happy with those which are listed in the report's box headed 'The principles of learning and teaching'? It instructs us that:

Good learning and teaching should

- *Ensure that every child succeeds:* provide an inclusive education within a culture of high expectations.
- *Build on what learners already know:* structure and pace teaching so that students know what is to be learnt, how and why.
- *Make learning vivid and real:* develop understanding through enquiry, creativity, e-learning and group problem-solving.
- *Make learning an enjoyable experience:* stimulate learning through matching teaching techniques and strategies to a range of learning styles.
- *Enrich the learning experience:* build learning skills across the curriculum.
- *Promote assessment for learning:* make children partners in their learning.

(DfES, 2003a, p. 29)

Does this mean anything? Precious little, I submit. We would do better to go back to Comenius in 1657, whose ideas on pedagogical structure and pace are far in advance of those in the Primary Strategy (Keatinge, 1896). If that seems obscurantist we could certainly with profit revisit more recent classic pedagogic specifications such as Lawrence Stenhouse's curricular 'principles of procedure' or Jerome Bruner's 'theory of instruction' (Stenhouse, 1975; Bruner, 1966). In contrast, most of the items above are aspirations obvious to the point of banality: of course we want every child to succeed, to build on what learners know, to make learning vivid, real and enjoyable. How many teachers, though, will read this list, experience a Eureka flash of recognition and thank DfES for a profound and novel insight of lasting practical value? The only item here which has a recognisable empirical basis is the final one, which hints at the important ideas about assessment for learning and its implications for classroom talk which have come from Paul Black and his colleagues in the London King's group (Black and Wiliam, 1999; Black *et al.*, 2002). Values are central to pedagogy but, as I argued earlier, on their own they cannot define its operational procedures.

Apart from being of dubious provenance, the Strategy's 'principles' also contain more than their fair share of non-sequiturs. What is the connection between building on what learners know, structuring and pacing teaching, and ensuring that students know what is to be learned; or between enjoyment and matching teaching techniques to learning styles? Apart from that, what *is* a 'learning style', and what indeed is a 'learning skill'? Better to define them, for 'learning skills' in particular are liberally scattered across the entire document.

It could be argued that the virtue of so bland a specification is that it makes positive and encouraging noises about the general spirit of pedagogy while leaving teachers free to devise their own more meaningful principles of pedagogic procedure. But if principles have so little purchase on practice, what, really, is their point?

The more contentious the Strategy's claims, the more authoritatively they are expressed. The Strategy's prescription for the future character of primary teaching, quoted above, is predicated on the assertion that (my italics) 'The Literacy and Numeracy Strategies have, *according to all who have evaluated them*, been strikingly successful at improving the quality of teaching and raising standards in primary schools' (DfES, 2003a, para 3.2). That claim, I am afraid, is also open to question. If the OISE (University of Toronto) evaluation commissioned by DfES delivers qualified approval for the Literacy and Numeracy Strategies – 'There is considerable evidence … that teaching has improved substantially since the Strategies were first introduced' (Earl *et al.*, 2003, p. 3) – it also warns that 'the intended changes in teaching and learning have not yet been fully realised' (p. 8) and, more critical still for those who would use the Strategies as the template for teaching across the entire primary curriculum, it admits that 'it is difficult to draw conclusions about the effect of the Strategies on pupil learning' (p. 3).

Perhaps, in claiming a ringing research endorsement for the Literacy and Numeracy Strategies DfES wasn't referring to the official NLNS evaluation at all, but to other studies, though it did say 'according to *all* who have evaluated' the strategies, not 'some'. But I'm afraid that this 'all' looks more and more shaky. Quite apart from the ambivalence of the OISE evaluation itself and the methodological questions about that evaluation which Harvey Goldstein (2000) has raised, Margaret Brown's five-year longitudinal study of numeracy teaching and attainment has concluded pretty devastatingly that the Numeracy Strategy 'has had at most a small effect on attainment in most areas of numeracy' (Brown *et al.*, 2003a). A similar point is made by Sig Prais, whose no less devastating (though contested) critique of the methodology of the PISA survey of the educational attainment of 15 year olds shows how that study produced upward bias in English students' mathematical test scores to the extent of compromising their high ranking relative to other countries and, hence, government claims that this ranking shows the beneficial effects of government policy (Prais, 2003; Adams, 2003).

Other studies – by Janet Moyles, Linda Hargreaves, Frank Hardman, David Skidmore and indeed myself – have looked closely at the pupil–teacher interaction on which a large part of the success of the strategies is intended and claimed to rest, and have found that while teaching methods, patterns of classroom organisation and the handling of time, space and resources have changed considerably in literacy and numeracy lessons, practice below the structural surface has changed rather less. Pupil–teacher interaction is still dominated by closed questions, brief answers which teachers do not build upon, phatic praise rather than diagnostic feedback, and an emphasis on recalling information rather than on speculating and problem-solving. (Alexander, 2000, pp. 474–490; English *et al.*, 2002; Skidmore, 2002; Hardman *et al.*, 2003; Moyles *et al.*, 2003).

These findings confirm those from earlier research, including my own CICADA study, which compared pupil–teacher discourse before and after the arrival of the National Curriculum, and Maurice Galton's ORACLE follow-up project (Alexander *et al.*, 1996; Galton *et al.*, 1999). Moreover, the Literacy and Numeracy Strategy directors themselves have acknowledged this: the absence of change at those deeper levels of classroom discourse which can impact so powerfully on children's learning is the main reason why they and QCA have commissioned materials from myself and colleagues in Barking and Dagenham LEA to support 'teaching through dialogue' (QCA/DfES, 2003a). It is why QCA has at last turned its attention to that neglected attainment target En1, Speaking and Listening (QCA, 2003; QCA/DfES, 2003b). And it is why LEAs such as Barking and Dagenham and North Yorkshire have launched major programmes to transform classroom talk and hence, they hope, lift tested literacy standards off the 'plateau' on which, in 2001, they stalled (Alexander, 2003b). No mention of any of this, of course, in the Primary Strategy: there, speaking and listening rate just one brief mention, as I have noted.

In fact, against the Strategy's confident claim that every evaluation of NLNS has endorsed its success in transforming teaching and raising standards, it's hard to find even *one* study that actually provides such an endorsement. Perhaps the Primary Strategy's authors had in mind the annual Ofsted Literacy and Numeracy Strategy evaluations. These are certainly very positive, though they are not so much evaluations as checks on compliance with the teaching changes – whole class teaching, three-part lessons, plenaries, the use of big books, writing frames and approved assessment materials, and so on – which the strategies require. (Ofsted, 2002a, 2002b). Consider, for example, Ofsted's finger-wagging 'not all teachers are using the strategy's assessment materials … some do not know about them' (Ofsted, 2002b, para 93). However, such renegades apart, schools are indeed toeing the line:

> The Literacy and Numeracy Strategies were centrally conceived and directed, and our data suggest that schools have generally been inclined to acquiesce to, and approve of, such direction. Such compliance bodes well for implementing the Strategies.
>
> (Earl *et al.*, 2001, p. xii)

But compliance with something believed to be admirable does not guarantee that it is. And a culture of compliance reinforces policies and practices, good or bad, but cannot *test* them. As if to underline this fatal flaw, the Ofsted evaluation of the first four years of the Literacy Strategy heads its list of 'improvements' produced by the NLS with 'widespread use of the NLS framework for teaching.' (Ofsted, 2002a, para 149). Compliance is ultimately tautologous.

In similar vein, though it is claimed that the Literacy Strategy is firmly based on national and international evidence, DfES took the extraordinary step, *after* the Strategy had been implemented, of commissioning an academic, Roger Beard of Leeds University, to discover what that evidence might be (Beard, 1998).

Curriculum

And so to the Strategy's pronouncements on the primary curriculum. Twenty years ago I suggested that one of the abiding legacies of the elementary education system was that we had not one primary curriculum but two, the 'basics' and the rest. That is to say, a high status, protected and heavily assessed 3Rs 'Curriculum I' which was justified by reference to utilitarian values, and a low priority, unassessed, vulnerable and even dispensable 'Curriculum II' of the arts and humanities which was justified by high-sounding but ultimately empty notions of a 'rounded' or 'balanced' education (Alexander, 1984). The National Curriculum simply translated the Curriculum I/II divide into the vocabulary and attendant values of 'core' and 'other foundation' subjects, and over the ensuing years successive governments ensured that the whole became more and more difficult to handle by avoiding the radical re-assessment of the Victorian formula of 'basics plus trimmings' which a twenty-first century curriculum required and simply bolting on more and more – science, ICT, design and technology, citizenship, PSHE, a modern foreign language – all the time insisting that the time for Curriculum I – at least 50 per cent of the week – was sacrosanct so the ever-expanding range of other subjects were forced to compete, and settle, for less and less.

The depressing logic of this situation is now all too clear. At the start of the last National Curriculum review, in 1997, I argued that we had a chance to tackle this problem and subject the primary curriculum to a principled review based on fundamental questions about the kind of world we now inhabit, the much-changed character of this country's economic and social life, and the consequent needs and rights of children, now and as adults (Alexander, 1997b). Instead, the Government insisted that there should be minimal change to the curriculum because nothing must deflect teachers' attention from the 2002 literacy and numeracy targets. In January 1998, the Government underlined that message by removing primary schools' obligation to teach the specified content of the non-core subjects. Since then, as Ofsted reports and indeed the OISE NLNS evaluation have shown, many schools have all but given up on the original 1988 National Curriculum notion of children's absolute entitlement to a genuinely broad curriculum in which the arts and humanities are treated with no less seriousness – even if with rather less time – than literacy and numeracy (Ofsted, 2002a, 2002c, 2003a; Earl *et al.*, 2003).

The Primary Strategy does nothing to alleviate the problem. True, it talks of 'children's entitlement to a rich, broad and balanced set of learning experiences' (DfES 2003a, para 3.1), but by ring-fencing the Literacy and Numeracy Strategies it ensures that the listed Curriculum II initiatives – creativity, the languages strategy, the PE and sport strategy, music – though separately admirable, will in conjunction have a hard time of it. Especially so, since the Primary Strategy proposes at one and the same time to 'widen the scope and range of the curriculum', and to 'reduce the curriculum to make it more manageable' (DfES, 2002a, pp. 1–3). From so elementary a logistical contradiction there can be scant grounds for hope.

The problem manifests itself in logistical terms certainly, but fundamentally it's one of *values*. In a Primary Strategy called 'Excellence and enjoyment' it is made very clear that the 3Rs provide the excellence and the rest delivers the enjoyment: Curriculum I and II yet again. Elsewhere 'standards' are opposed to 'enrichment', even to curriculum itself.

The division is firmly institutionalised, too. In 1997, as a founding Board member of QCA, I asked the then Minister of State Estelle Morris why the Literacy and Numeracy Strategies were run by the Department and the rest of the curriculum by QCA, when the new body had been set up expressly to bring coherence to the hitherto fragmented worlds of curriculum, assessment and qualifications. 'Ah but Minister' one of her aides smoothly interjected, 'literacy and numeracy aren't curriculum, they're *standards*, and standards are the Department's responsibility, not QCA's.' Literacy is standards, not curriculum: ponder, for a moment, this brutal dismissal of the civilizing ideals of universal literacy and of the efforts of the many who have fought for them.

In his Policy Network Paper, Andrew Adonis confirms this revealing perception: 'the raising of literacy and numeracy standards … is now a *self-contained* mission in its own right' (Adonis, 2001, p. 9) – and elsewhere in the system the continuing Curriculum I/II gulf, and the sense that all that really matters at the primary stage is literacy and numeracy 'standards', plus perhaps the 'modernising' subjects of science and ICT, is strongly reinforced. Thus TTA requires newly qualified teachers to 'know and understand the curriculum for each of the National Curriculum core subjects, and the frameworks, methods and expectations set out in the National Literacy and Numeracy Strategies', but merely to 'have sufficient understanding of a range of work' (whatever that means) in the rest, including history *or* geography but – bizarrely – not both (DfES/TTA, 2002, p. 7). Ofsted full primary teacher training inspections concentrate on 'English, mathematics and, when at all possible, science' but sample the rest on the basis of what happens to be available, while the short inspections don't even require that (Ofsted, 2002d, pp. 23, 84). The new Ofsted school inspection framework, which takes effect from September 2003, is no less casual in its approach to Curriculum II: English, mathematics, science and ICT *must* be inspected, and in depth, but for the rest the requirement is simply, in Ofsted's words 'work seen in other subjects.' (Ofsted, 2003b, p. 8).

There's little evidence, then, that the newfound commitment to breadth and balance in the primary curriculum is serious. Were it so, teacher training and inspection requirements would reinforce rather than undermine it, and the entire curriculum enterprise would be co-ordinated by a single agency, rather than be split between QCA and DfES. (If, that is, it is really necessary for the curriculum to be centrally controlled as well as prescribed – but that's another story.)

But all is not lost, for in 2002 Ofsted discovered a link between breadth, balance and standards, and it is chiefly this that has fuelled the change in the government's curriculum rhetoric: this, and the need to be seen to respond positively to the increasing pressure from the arts and sports lobbies. Ofsted found that of the 3,508 primary schools inspected in 2000–2001, just 206, or under 6 per cent, achieved both high test scores in English and mathematics *and* consistently excellent teaching and learning across the full range of the National Curriculum. They argued, commendably, that contrary to popular opinion the National Curriculum *is* manageable, and, crucially, that it was the breadth and richness of the curriculum which helped secure the quality of teaching and learning in literacy and numeracy in these schools, and – conversely – that the wider curriculum gave children and teachers a meaningful context in which to apply, reinforce and extend 'the basics' (Ofsted, 2002c).

But of course we knew this already. The famous 1978 HMI survey of primary schools, of which – as of so many other key pieces of historical evidence – the Primary Strategists seem unaware, reported that the schools which performed best in the basics invariably did so in the context of a broad curriculum encompassing work in the arts and humanities which was well planned and taught (DES, 1978). Then, in 1996, the Conservative government asked Ofsted to examine the relationship between the 1996 KS2 SAT results and curriculum breadth, posing the particular question 'Had schools which did well in the 1996 tests done so at the expense of curriculum breadth and diversity?'

The answer was a resounding 'No', and this time Ofsted showed that the earlier basics-breadth correlation held across *all* primary schools:

> Schools which did well in the tests also provided a broad and balanced curriculum.... Schools awarded a high grade for curriculum balance and breadth score well in the tests and those awarded lower grades score less well. This trend persists across all schools analysed, regardless of their context.
>
> (Ofsted/DfEE, 1997, paras 2 and 7)

The report's publication coincided with the arrival of New Labour, the Literacy and Numeracy Strategies and the attendant targets for 2002: 75 per cent of 11 year olds to reach Level 4 in mathematics, 80 per cent in English. Like the 1978 HMI primary survey the 1997 Ofsted report confirmed what commonsense dictated: you cannot successfully teach literacy and numeracy in a curriculum vacuum. But New Labour were convinced that the rest of the curriculum was a distraction from the targets (and, possibly, a threat to the position of the Secretary of State, who had said that he would resign if the targets were not met). The government ignored the Ofsted report and pushed ahead with its decision to free schools from the obligation to teach the programmes of study of the non-core subjects. Ofsted did not press the point. The report was not publicised. It was an example of burying bad news of which Jo Moore would have been proud. Except that the news was good – or, to be precise, good educationally but bad politically. (For a detailed account of this episode, see my evidence to the 1998 Commons Education Committee enquiry into the work of Ofsted: House of Commons, 1999, pp. 144–154.) With that recent history in mind, with the Literacy and Numeracy Strategies firmly in place, and with a continuing commitment to targets, albeit managed differently, who can possibly believe the Primary Strategy's avowed commitment to 'a rich, broad and balanced set of learning experiences?' (DfES, 2003a, para 3.1).

Do we still need to argue that education is meaningless without the arts and humanities, and without a more generous concept of the teaching of English than basic reading and writing competence alone, or – as persuasively argued by Rowan Williams (2000) – a more coherent approach to moral education? The demeaning reduction of these to 'enjoyment' and 'enrichment', and the readiness of the Government to sacrifice them on the altar of 'standards' (as opposed to standards) signals that they remain insecure.

There are two further failures on the Primary Strategy's curriculum front. The first and most obvious is the total absence of real vision about the future of the primary curriculum, a deficiency for which the report's heavy reiteration of the word 'vision' provides no more than a tattered figleaf. Nor does the current version of the National Curriculum offer very much more. Its published goals (DfEE/QCA, 1999, pp. 11–12) are an extraordinary ragbag of values which if they were deliverable would secure a nation of men and women at once dynamic, entrepreneurial, athletic, ruthless, successful, rich, multi-skilled, possessed of encyclopaedic knowledge, humane, compassionate, modest, religious, tolerant, cultured, ascetic – and thoroughly confused about their identity. They are what you get if you handle the demands of large numbers of interest groups by adding each one to a lengthening list without attempting to establish whether they are compatible. (For a comparative critique of the 1999 National Curriculum aims in an international context, see Alexander, 2000, pp. 125–126, 155–158.)

The second failure is to come to terms with the managerial implications of a broad and complex curriculum. The Primary Strategy has a chapter entitled 'Workforce reform' which essentially seeks to sell the Government's policy on classroom assistants (DfES, 2003a, chapter 7). The more necessary workforce reform was argued in the 1986 Select Committee report on primary education which said that the demands of a modern curriculum could not reasonably be met by schools staffed on the basis of one generalist class teacher per class. The Committee secured the agreement of the then Secretary of State, Keith Joseph, for 15,000 extra teachers to inject curriculum flexibility into England's 20,000 primary schools (House of Commons, 1986). The agreement was not implemented. The so-called 'three wise men' report of 1992 took this argument forward, commending a broader repertoire of teaching roles in primary schools ranging from generalists through consultants and semi-specialists to specialists, to enable the full curriculum to be adequately managed and taught, and insisted that to allow schools the necessary staffing flexibility the long-established primary–secondary funding differential must be challenged (Alexander et al., 1992, paras 139–150). That idea didn't get far, partly because it had resource implications which the Commons Education Committee investigated but which the then government passed smartly to the LEAs (House of Commons, 1994a, 1994b); partly because many primary teachers – wrongly – saw it as a threat to the class teacher system; and partly because secondary heads, in turn, thought that the money would be taken from them. Then during the 1980s and 1990s there were numerous attempts to find ways of maximising the impact of teachers' specialist subject strengths, within a framework of roles variously called 'curriculum co-ordinator', 'consultant', 'adviser', 'subject leader' and 'curriculum manager'.

The Primary Strategy's chapter 'Leadership in primary schools' talks about leadership in highly generalised terms, focusing on heads and the novelties of 'consultant leaders' and a 'leading practice' programme, but in a way which is utterly divorced from the day-to-day demands of the curriculum. Again, of all the debates

about curriculum management of the past 20 years, including maj
enquiries, it seems utterly unaware. (For an account of these, see
1998b, pp. 6–13.)

Meanwhile, it is hard to escape the conclusion that the erosion of c
breadth over the past few years has been a consequence of a persistent ..usai by
successive governments to grasp the managerial and resource implications of a curriculum which has outgrown the elementary model of 'basics plus trimmings' for
which the Victorian class teacher system was just about adequate. The government's 1998 decision to make the non-core subjects effectively optional, and the
sad fate of these subjects in many schools since the Literacy and Numeracy Strategies began to bite, suggest that the curriculum has been used as the safety-valve,
as a way of side-stepping the true 'workforce reform' which primary schools needed.
Judged in strictly educational terms, the 1998 decision looks at best ill-informed
and at worst – since government was warned of its likely consequences – cynical.
The doctrine of 'cheap but efficient', one century on, has resolved the growing mis-
match between educational task and professional resources by trimming the education rather than re-assessing the resources. This nettle the Primary Strategy has, in
its turn, failed to grasp. Teaching assistants may be useful, but in the context of
children's statutory curriculum entitlement they are no substitute for a staffing
policy which provides each primary school with a team of professionals who
between them have the range and depth of subject knowledge to do full justice to
every aspect of the curriculum for every child, and the flexibility to deploy such
knowledge as required.

Conclusion

In as far as it offers perspectives on learning, teaching, curriculum, assessment and
school management – all of them major themes from my first two domains of pedagogical discourse – and links these to the pursuit of national educational goals, the
2003 Primary Strategy certainly qualifies as a pedagogical statement. Given its belief
that it can harness enjoyable means to achieve excellent ends, it is properly ambitious. Because it comes from Government it must be taken seriously.

Between May and November 2003, and again from January 2004, DfES organised conferences for primary heads, teachers and 'consultant leaders' at which ministers and officials, ostensibly in consultative mode, will discuss how the Primary
Strategy and its 'vision' are to be taken forward. In rather different mode, the published job specification of the man charged with overseeing this process, the newly-
appointed Primary Strategy Director, pins him not to the Strategy's hope of a
curriculum enshrining excellence, enjoyment, breadth and balance, but to the narrower objective of embedding the Literacy and Numeracy Strategies, meeting the
national targets for English and Mathematics and ensuring continuity with the
KS3 Strategy (DfES, 2002c). This task has been subcontracted as a commercial
operation to CfBT whose job it is, in DfEE's words, to 'deliver the Strategy'.

This more instrumental remit rather undermines the rhetoric of consultation
and freedom which is being used to sell the Strategy to teachers, especially when
what is to be 'delivered' is so fundamentally deficient. About all but the narrowest

range of evidence concerning the impact of recent policies on primary education the Primary Strategy displays amiable ignorance, and such evidence as it does cite – for example that relating to the impact of the National Literacy and Numeracy Strategies – it is not above bending to suit its larger political purposes. As for the wider evidence and debate about children, learning, teaching, curriculum and culture – in which, I have suggested, even a minimal pedagogy should be grounded – a few insouciant platitudes masquerading as 'principles' are as close as we get. These, secondary school colleagues may care to note, have been replicated in a policy for the entire school system, not just primary schools (DfES, 2003b).

The Primary Strategy manifests a lamentable detachment from questions of identity, culture and history (my vital third domain of pedagogical discourse), a studied ignorance about the state of education before 1997, and a crude instrumentalism of purpose which is in no way disguised by the rhetoric of 'enjoyment' and 'enrichment'. The Strategy is ambiguous to the point of dishonesty about the Government's true intentions towards primary education. It fails to observe that most essential condition for the growth of knowledge and understanding and the improvement of the human condition, by which researchers in all disciplines are bound absolutely – *cumulation*, knowing what has gone before, learning from it, evaluating it, building on it. By ignoring this condition, the Strategy not only ensures that much of what it offers is open to challenge; it also perpetuates rather than resolves some of the most deeply-seated problems of English primary education, notably in the areas of curriculum and curriculum management. It also subverts its own avowed intentions, for such a stance is deeply at odds with what education should be about.

In all these matters, as in the wider spectrum of public policy in recent years, that 'destruction of the past', which so concerned Eric Hobsbawm in his assessment of contemporary British consciousness (Hobsbawm, 1995, p. 3), seems to be a conscious political act rather than an unfortunate casualty of laudable political ambition. For, as I have illustrated, this 'Strategy' is caught in the Downing Street web of instinctive spin – not just of the policy of the moment but of history itself.

More obviously, the Primary Strategy is badly written, poorly argued and deeply patronising in its assumption that teachers will be seduced by Ladybird language, pretty pictures, offers of freedom and enjoyment, and populist appeals to their common sense. There is no case, no argument, some fragments of a strategy, but certainly no vision. Meanwhile, 150 local authorities have dutifully appointed their primary strategy directors. If they value their Ofsted inspection ratings they cannot do otherwise.

And what, a quarter of a century on, of Simon's 'Why no pedagogy?' Pedagogical research has progressed considerably since then, and in the cumulative body of scholarship and evidence about children, learning, teaching and culture which the Primary Strategy has chosen to ignore, not to mention the collective experience of the teachers it claims to respect, I would submit that we have had for some time both an ample basis for a coherent and principled pedagogy and a viable alternative to the pseudo-pedagogy of the Primary Strategy.

Government though, listening only to those who are on its payroll or who speak its language, believes it knows better. Under our now highly centralised and interventive education system those who have the greatest power to prescribe p⁄ seem to display the poorest understanding of it, and the discourse becomes n₁. in the habitual bombast, mendacity and spin of policyspeak. The pedagogy of principle has yet to be rescued from the pedagogy of pragmatism and compliance.

Postscript: what price evidence-based policy and practice?

This article started as an open lecture in the Cambridge University Faculty of Education 2002–2003 Research Lecture series and in that form, especially following somewhat sensationalising press coverage (for example, Ward, 2003) it was widely disseminated. Among the resulting responses, three are particularly relevant to the case I have tried to make.

First, my charges about the Strategy's cavalier approach to evidence have provoked from the DfES Standards and Effectiveness Unit a counter-claim that *Excellence and enjoyment* is 'based on the latest evaluation and research evidence', and that the national literacy and numeracy strategies 'were based firmly on research evidence … which is one of the main reasons why … they have been successful in raising standards and improving the quality of teaching and learning' (Hopkins, 2003). Yet, second, Margaret Brown's most recent analysis of the evidential basis of the national numeracy strategy casts further doubt on the sustainability of such claims (Brown *et al.*, 2003b). Third, DfES has hastily sought to plug some of the more obvious gaps in the Strategy's prospectus of pedagogical reform, notably in respect of the role and quality of classroom talk. As we have seen, the Strategy mentions talk but once, and very briefly (DfES, 2003a, para 3.3). However – perhaps stung by criticism on this score – DfES now claims that the improvement of talk is central to the Strategy. It has not only written 'speaking and listening' prominently into its Strategy training materials for the autumn and spring terms of 2003–2004 (for example, DfES, 2003c, DfES/QCA, 2003) but in so doing has made unattributed use of material published elsewhere, notably on dialogic teaching.

This kind of reactive or opportunistic appropriation not only smacks of control freakery but also calls further into question the government's much-vaunted principle of 'evidence-based' policy and practice, which surely implies a process which is much more considered and critical. In truth, if DfES seems ambivalent about where it stands on this matter, Downing Street is not. David Hopkins' endorsement of the research connection, cited above, contrasts with the dismissive claim of Tony Wright, Blairite Chair of the Commons Public Administration Committee that 'the National Literacy Strategy and the National Numeracy Strategy were both undisputed successes which produced extraordinary results without the involvement of academics, and if they had waited for academics to produce this policy it would have taken four years' (Quoted in Brown *et al.*, 2003b, p. 655). In the same way that the Barber/Adonis Downing Street line on professional development invalidates the teacher-friendly rhetoric emanating from DfES, so the outright rejection of academic research by prime-ministerial appointee Wright undermines the department's avowed respect for evidence. Such developments confirm the continuing hegemony of the culture of pragmatism and compliance.

Notes

* Robin Alexander is at the University of Cambridge, UK.
† Originally published in: *Cambridge Journal of Education* 34: 1, 7–33.

References

Adams, R. J. (2003) Response to 'Cautions on OECD's recent educational survey (PISA)', *Oxford Review of Education*, 29(3), 377–389.

Adonis, A. (2001) *High challenge, high support* (London, Policy Network). Alexander, R. J. (1984) *Primary teaching* (London, Cassell).

Alexander, R. J. (1997a) *Policy and practice in primary education: local initiative, national agenda* (London, Routledge).

Alexander, R. J. (1997b) Basics, cores and choices: towards a new primary curriculum, paper presented at the *SCAA Conference on Developing the School Curriculum*, June.

Alexander, R. J. (1998a) Reinventing pedagogy, rewriting history, *Parliamentary Brief*, November.

Alexander, R. J. (ed.) (1998b) *Time for change? Primary curriculum managers at work* (Warwick, University of Warwick Centre for Research in Elementary and Primary Education).

Alexander, R. J. (2000) *Culture and pedagogy: international comparisons in primary education* (Oxford, Blackwell).

Alexander, R. J. (2001) Border crossings: towards a comparative pedagogy, *Comparative Education*, 37(4), 507–523.

Alexander, R. J. (2002) Dichotomous pedagogies and the promise of comparative research, paper presented at the *American Educational Research Association Annual Conference*, New Orleans, 3 April.

Alexander, R. J. (2003a) Talk in teaching and learning: international perspectives, in: *New perspectives on spoken English* (London, QCA), 26–37.

Alexander, R. J. (2003b) *Talk for learning: the first year* (interim evaluation of North Yorkshire County Council's Talk for Learning project) (Northallerton, North Yorkshire County Council).

Alexander, R. J. (2004) *Towards dialogic teaching: rethinking classroom talk* (York, Dialogos).

Alexander, R. J., Rose, A. J. and Woodhead, C. (1992) *Curriculum organisation and classroom practice in primary schools: a discussion paper* (London, DES).

Alexander, R. J., Wilcocks, J. and Nelson, N. (1996) Discourse, pedagogy and the National Curriculum: change and continuity in primary schools, *Research Papers in Education*, 11(1), 81–120.

Argyris, C. and Schön, D. (1974) *Theory in practice: increasing professional effectiveness* (San Francisco, Jossey-Bass).

Barber, M. (2001) *Large-scale education reform in England: a work in progress*. A paper for the *Managing Education Reform Conference*, Moscow, 29–30 October. The paper was also presented, with small modifications, to the *Federal Reserve Bank of Boston 47th Economic Conference*, 19–21 June 2002, and the Technology Colleges Trust *Vision 2020 Second International Conference*, October/November/December (in which form it is available on the Internet).

Beard, R. (1998) *National Literacy Strategy: review of research and other related evidence* (London, DfES).

Bennett, N., Desforges, C., Cockburn, A. and Wilkinson, A. (1984) *The quality of pupil learning experiences* (London, Lawrence Erlbaum).

Berlak, A. and Berlak, H. (1981) *Dilemmas of schooling: teaching and social change* (London, Methuen).

Berliner, D. C. and Biddle, B. J. (1995) *The manufactured crisis: myths, fraud and the attack on America's public schools* (Cambridge MA, Perseus Books).

Bernstein, B. (1990) *The structuring of pedagogical discourse. Class, codes and control, Vol 4* (London, Routledge).

Black, P. and Wiliam, D. (1998) Assessment and classroom learning, *Assessment in Education*, 5(1), 7–71.

Black, P. and Wiliam, D. (1999) *Inside the black box: raising standards through assessment* (London, School of Education, King's College).

Black, P., Harrison, C., Lee, C., Marshall, B. and Wiliam, D. (2002) *Working inside the black box: assessment for learning in the classroom* (London, School of Education, King's College).

Bourdieu, P. and Passeron, J.-C. (1970) *Reproduction in education, society and culture* (London, Sage).

Brown, M., Askew, M., Rhodes, V., Denvir, H., Ranson, E. and Wiliam, D. (2003a) Characterising individual and cohort progression in learning literacy: results from the Leverhulme 5-year longitudinal study, *American Educational Research Association Annual Conference*, Chicago, April.

Brown, M., Askew, M., Millett, A. and Rhodes, M. (2003b) The key role of educational research in the development and evaluation of the National Numeracy Strategy, *British Journal of Educational Research*, 29(5), 655–672.

Brown, S. and McIntyre, D. (1993) *Making sense of teaching* (Buckingham, Open University Press).

Bruner, J. S. (1966) *Toward a theory of instruction* (New York, W.W. Norton).

Bruner, J. S. (1996) *The culture of education* (Cambridge, MA, Harvard University Press).

Calderhead, J. (1984) *Teachers' classroom decision-making* (London, Holt, Rinehart and Winston).

Clark, C. M. and Peterson, P. L. (1986) Teachers' thought processes, in: M. C. Whitrock (ed.) *Handbook of research on teaching* (New York, Macmillan).

DES (1978) *Primary education in England: a survey by HM Inspectors of schools* (London, HMSO).

DES (1989) *Initial teacher training: approval of courses.* Circular 24189 (London, Department of Education and Science).

DfEE (2001) *Schools: building on success* (London, The Stationery Office).

DfEE/QCA (1999) *The National Curriculum: handbook for primary teachers in England and Wales* (London, DfEE/QCA).

DfES (2002a) *A Primary Strategy 2002–2007* (London, DfES Primary Education Programme Board, 27 May).

DfES (2002b) Press release, 26 May.

DfES (2002c) published job specification for the Primary Strategy National Director.

DfES (2003a) *Excellence and enjoyment: a strategy for primary schools* (London, Department for Education and Skills).

DfES (2003b) *The core principles: teaching and learning; school improvement; system wide reform* (consultation paper) (London, Department for Education and Skills).

DfES (2003c) *Primary leadership programme presenter's file, Part 1: focusing on expectations* (DfES 0475/2003) (London, Department for Education and Skills).

DfES/QCA (2003) *Speaking, listening, learning: working with children in Key Stages 1 and 2* (Primary Strategy training handbook for primary teachers and headteachers, DfES 0626/2003) (London, Department for Education and Skills).

DfES/TTA (2002) *Qualifying to teach: professional standards for qualified teacher status and requirements for initial teacher training* (London, TTA).

Downing Street (2003) *Primary schools strategy launched* (press release), 20 May.

Earl, L., Levin, B., Leithwood, K., Fullan, M. and Watson, N. (2001) *Watching and learning 2: OISE/UT evaluation of the implementation of the National Literacy and Numeracy Strategies* (Toronto, Ontario Institute for Studies in Education).

Earl, L., Watson, N., Levin, B., Leithwood, K. and Fullan, M. (2003) *Watching and learning 3: final report of the external evaluation of England's National Literacy and Numeracy Strategies* (Toronto, Ontario Institute for Studies in Education).

Eisner, E. W. (1979) *The educational imagination* (London, Macmillan).

Elbaz, F. (1983) *Teacher thinking: a study of practical knowledge* (New York, Nichols).

English, E., Hargreaves, L. and Hislam, J. (2002) Pedagogical dilemmas in the National Literacy Strategy: primary teachers' perceptions, reflections and classroom behaviour, *Cambridge Journal of Education*, (32)1, 9–26.

Entwistle, H. (1970) *Child-centred education* (London, Methuen).

Gage, N. (1978) *The scientific basis of the art of teaching* (New York, Teachers College Press).

Galton, M. and Simon, B. (1980) *Progress and performance in the primary classroom* (London, Routledge).

Galton, M., Hargreaves, L., Comber, C., Wall, D. and Pell, A. (1999) *Inside the primary classroom: 20 years on* (London, Routledge).

Goldstein, H. (2000) The National Literacy and Numeracy Strategies: some comments on an evaluation report from the University of Toronto. Published communication from Professor Goldstein to the OISE evaluation report's principal author, Lorna Earl, July.

Hardman, F., Smith, F. and Wall, K. (2003) 'Interactive whole class teaching' in the National Literacy Strategy, *Cambridge Journal of Education*, 33(2), 197–215.

Hirst, P. (1979) Professional studies in initial teacher education: some conceptual issues, in R. J. Alexander and E. Wormald (eds) *Professional studies for teaching* (Guildford, SRHE), 15–29.

Hobsbawm, E. (1995) *Age of extremes: the short twentieth century 1914–91* (London, Abacus).

Hopkins, D. (2003) Strategies based on real research (letter), *Times Educational Supplement*, 3 October.

House of Commons (1986) *Achievement in primary schools: third report from the Education, Science and Arts Committee* (London, HMSO).

House of Commons (1994a) *The disparity in funding between primary and secondary schools: Education Committee second report* (London, HMSO).

House of Commons (1994b) *Government response to the second report from the committee (the disparity in funding between primary and secondary schools)* (London, HMSO).

House of Commons (1999) *The work of OFSTED: fourth report of the Education and Employment Committee. Session 1998–9, Volume 3* (London, The Stationery Office).

IEA/ISC (2003) *PIRLS 2001 international report: IEA's study of reading literacy achievement in primary school in 35 countries* (Chester Hill, MA, Boston College).

Keatinge, M. W. (1896) *The great didactic of John Amos Comenius* (London, A. and C. Black).

Millett, A. (1999) Why we need to raise our game, *Independent*, 11 February.

Moon, B. (1998) *The English exception: international perspectives on the initial education and training of teachers* (London, UCET).

Mortimore, P., Sammons, P., Stoll, L., Lewis, D. and Ecob, R. (1988) *School matters: the junior years* (London, Open Books).

Moyles, J., Hargreaves, L., Merry, R., Paterson, F. and Esarte-Sarries, V. (2003) *Interactive teaching in the primary school: digging deeper into meanings* (Maidenhead, Open University Press).

Ofsted (2002a) *The National Literacy Strategy: the first four years 1998–2002* (London, Ofsted).

Ofsted (2002b) *The National Numeracy Strategy: the first three years 1999–2002* (London, Ofsted).

Ofsted (2002c) *The curriculum in successful primary schools* (London, Ofsted).

Ofsted (2002d), *Handbook for the inspection of initial teacher training (2002–2008)* (London, Ofsted).

Ofsted (2003a) *The education of six year olds in England, Denmark and Finland: an international comparative study* (London, Ofsted).

Ofsted (2003b) *Inspecting schools: framework for inspecting schools, effective from September 2003* (London, Ofsted).

Ofsted/DfEE (1997) *National Curriculum assessment results and the wider curriculum at Key Stage 2: some evidence from the Ofsted database* (London, Ofsted).

Prais, S. J. (2003) Cautions on OECD's recent educational survey (PISA), *Oxford Review of Education*, 29(2), 139–163.

QCA (ed.) (2003) *New perspectives on spoken English in the classroom* (London, QCA).

QCA/DFES (2003a) *Teaching through dialogue* (London, QCA and DfES).

QCA/DFES (2003b) *Speaking, listening, learning: working with children in KS1 and 2* (London, QCA and DfES).

Reynolds, D. and Farrell, S. (1996) *Worlds apart? A review of international surveys of educational achievement involving England* (London, HMSO).

Schön, D. A. (1982) *The reflective practitioner: how professionals think in action* (London, Temple Smith).

Shulman, L. S. (1987) Knowledge and teaching: foundations of the new reform, *Harvard Educational Review*, 57(1), 1–22.

Simon, B. (1981) Why no pedagogy in England? in: B. Simon and W. Taylor (eds) *Education in the eighties: the central issues* (London, Batsford), 124–145.

Simon, B. (1994) *The state and educational change: essays in the history of education and pedagogy* (London, Lawrence and Wishart).

Simon, B. (2000) Blair on education, *Forum*, 42(3), 91–93.

Skidmore, D. (2002) Teacher–pupil dialogue and the comprehension of literary texts. Unpublished paper, Reading, University of Reading.

Stenhouse, L. (1975) *An introduction to curriculum research and development* (London, Heinemann).

Wallace, M. (1993) Discourse of derision: the role of the mass media in the educational policy process, *Journal of Educational Policy*, 8(4), 321–337.

Ward, H. (2003) Guru attacks 'deeply patronising' strategy, *Times Educational Supplement*, 19 September.

Williams, R. (2000) *Lost icons: reflections on cultural bereavement* (London, Continuum).

Wragg, E. C. (1993) *Primary teaching skills* (London, Routledge).

Index

Tables are indicated by italic page numbers and figures by bold.